Economic Thought and U.S. Climate Change Policy

American and Comparative Environmental Policy
Sheldon Kamieniecki and Michael E. Kraft, series editors

Economic Thought and U.S. Climate Change Policy

edited by David M. Driesen

The MIT Press
Cambridge, Massachusetts
London, England

For information about special quantity discounts, please email special_sales@ mitpress.mit.edu

This book was set in Sabon by Westchester Book Group, and was printed and bound in the United States of America. Printed on recycled paper.

Library of Congress Cataloging-in-Publication Data

Economic thought and U.S. climate change policy / edited by David M. Driesen.
  p.   cm.—(American and comparative environmental policy)
Includes bibliographical references and index.
ISBN 978-0-262-04252-9 (hardcover : alk. paper)—ISBN 978-0-262-54198-5
(pbk. : alk. paper)
1. Climatic changes—United States.   2. Climatic changes—Government
policy—United States.   3. Climatic changes—Economic aspects—United
States.   4. Climatic changes—Environmental aspects—United States.   I. Driesen,
David M.
QC981.8.C5E2146   2010
363.738'745610973—dc22

                                                                    2009028707

10   9   8   7   6   5   4   3   2   1

To my wife, Jeanne Otten

Contents

Series Foreword

As the unprecedented economic crisis of 2008–2009 demonstrated well, ideas about the way markets and government behave can be exceptionally important. Public policy tends to reflect prevailing ideas, particularly when they are widely shared, and a good example is the commitment to deregulation in the financial sector in the 1990s and 2000s that was a major underlying cause of the nation's economic collapse. The same argument applies to environmental policy, which has relied heavily on command-and-control regulation, evident in policies that were either first enacted or significantly changed in the 1970s such as the Clean Air Act, the Clean Water Act, and the Resource Conservation and Recovery Act. Yet the role of government in these policies is constrained in ways that are not always well understood, for example, by a fundamental belief in private property rights and a relatively unfettered market economy. Such beliefs necessarily limit how far policymakers are prepared to go to protect public health and the environment as they try to balance the costs and benefits of new regulations. Belief in the virtues of a market economy also are evident in many proposals for reforming environmental policy, such as making greater use of market-based incentives and offering flexible regulation that promotes efficiency in the use of resources. A positive view of the potential of markets is evident as well in proposals to address global climate change, where various forms of cap-and-trade systems lie at the center of public debate.

To better understand the opportunities and constraints related to use of market-based environmental policies, we need to know more about neoliberal theoretical perspectives and concepts, their strengths and weaknesses, and their appeal to policymakers. There are varied meanings to the term neoliberalism, but at heart it refers to a political philosophy rooted in the concepts of neoclassical economic efficiency that strongly supports the operation of free markets and is skeptical about the legitimacy and effectiveness of governmental intervention to allocate society's resources. In this book eleven contributors from the fields of law, public policy, and philosophy offer unabashedly critical analyses of neoliberal ideas in climate change policy, and they suggest more appropriate ways to design policy for the years ahead. The authors review and critique U.S. climate change and energy policies, note the inherent limitations of using conventional methods of cost-benefit analysis in this policy area, describe industry's framing of the issues and its long resistance to serious action on climate change, and consider a range of philosophical, economic, and political ideas related to social justice, ethics, the precautionary principle, and sustainability.

The book comes at an opportune time. Following a presidential administration that often denied the reality of climate change and limited the U.S. government's role largely to funding scientific research and promoting voluntary initiatives, the Obama administration clearly is setting a different course. Policy debate in Congress also reveals an increasing willingness to confront climate change and to redirect U.S. energy policy away from reliance on fossil fuels to renewable sources, energy conservation, and efficiency through a variety of new initiatives. In this context, the arguments presented here are particularly important. If the United States is now at a "tipping point" in terms of scientific evidence and public and policymaker support for action, which kinds of policies are most promising and which are not?

The book illustrates well the goals of the MIT Press series in American and Comparative Environmental Policy. We encourage work that examines a broad range of environmental policy issues. We are particularly interested in volumes that incorporate interdisciplinary research and focus on the linkages between public policy and environmental problems and issues both within the United States and in cross-national settings. We welcome contributions that analyze the policy dimensions of relationships between humans and the environment from either a theoretical or empirical perspective. At a time when environmental policies are increasingly seen as controversial and new approaches are being implemented widely, we especially encourage studies that assess policy successes and failures, evaluate new institutional arrangements and policy tools, and clarify new directions for environmental politics and policy. The books in this series are written for a wide audience that includes academics, policymakers, environmental scientists and professionals, business and labor leaders, environmental activists, and students concerned with environmental issues.

We hope they contribute to public understanding of environmental problems, issues, and policies of concern today and also suggest promising actions for the future.

Sheldon Kamieniecki, University California, Santa Cruz
Michael Kraft, University of Wisconsin–Green Bay
American and Comparative Environmental Policy Series Editors

Preface

This book grew from the work of the Center for Progressive Reform (CPR), a virtual think tank at the forefront of developing ideas to further environmental safety. CPR's leadership asked me to formulate a plan for the organization's climate change work. It seemed that an organization of scholars should address the role of ideas in climate change. And ideas, particularly the idea that government should regulate markets either not at all or very reluctantly, have played a large and often underappreciated role in U.S. climate change policy. But we wanted to do more than pinpoint the role of neoliberalism, the cultural veneration of free markets, in climate change policy's failure; we wanted to develop ideas that would provide a better, more appropriate framework for addressing climate change and other environmental ills.

This book, then, stemmed from my proposal to address economic thought's role in climate change policy in a critical, yet constructive, way, and it came to fruition thanks to the willingness of CPR Member Scholars to contribute to and shape these pages. They worked diligently at developing and expanding the ideas at the heart of this project.

Robert Glicksman, a CPR scholar from George Washington University and a contributor to two chapters in this book, deserves special mention in this regard. He not only wrote key pieces, but also helped me pull the whole book together. He generously hosted a workshop for authors at the University of Kansas, which served as a focal point for our efforts to integrate the disparate chapters into as coherent a whole as possible. And he provided valuable editorial suggestions to me and other contributors along the way.

I also need to thank my research assistants, Myriah Jaworksi and Janet Moon, who helped take some of the burden off my shoulders and those of contributing authors struggling to fulfill their commitments to this project while meeting other competing obligations. Chris Ramsdell,

Syracuse University's Center Coordinator, helped edit the chapters and organize the entire project. I'm fortunate to have somebody so attentive to detail and so attuned to the nuances of writing working with me. I'd also like to thank, at the MIT Press, Clay Morgan and the series editors for their faith in this project and their valuable suggestions about how to improve it.

As I write this, the end of the United States' failure to address climate change appears to be in sight. It is quite possible that not long after this book is published (or if we're slow or Congress is fast, before then), the United States Congress under a new president will begin, at long last, to seriously address climate change. But we have a long way to go. And the ideas that this book examines will remain important in shaping the ongoing and belated effort to address climate change that we hope will ensue. The scholars creating this work hope that this book will provide useful lessons for a long and serious effort to address one of the most serious environmental problems the United States, and the rest of the world, has ever faced.

Contributors

Frank Ackerman   Senior Economist, Stockholm Environment Institute–U.S. Center, Tufts University

John S. Applegate   Walter W. Foskett Professor of Law, Indiana University School of Law–Bloomington

Carl Cranor   Distinguished Professor of Philosophy, University of California, Riverside

David M. Driesen   University Professor, Syracuse University

Robert L. Glicksman   J. B. and Maurice C. Shapiro Professor of Environmental Law, The George Washington University Law School

Lisa Heinzerling   Professor of Law, Georgetown University Law Center (on leave of absence)

Thomas O. McGarity   Joe R. and Teresa Lozano Long Endowed Chair in Administrative Law, University of Texas School of Law

Christopher Schroeder   Charles S. Murphy Professor of Law and Public Policy Studies, Director of the Program in Public Law, Duke University School of Law

Amy Sinden   Associate Professor of Law, Temple University Beasley School of Law

Joseph P. Tomain   Dean and Nippert Professor of Law, The University of Cincinnati College of Law

Robert R. M. Verchick   Gauthier–St. Martin, Eminent Scholar Chair in Environmental Law, Loyola University, New Orleans

Introduction

David M. Driesen

Until recently, U.S. climate change policy has appalled the world. The United States, formerly a world leader in addressing international environmental challenges, became the most important developed country opponent of vigorous action on climate change in the 1990s. It successfully opposed a European effort to place a firm target for greenhouse gas reduction in the United Nations Framework Convention on Climate Change near the beginning of that decade, and insisted on weakening the Kyoto Protocol toward its end. In 2001, President Bush drove the United States from its place as laggard cooperator into a position of outright opposition to effectively addressing climate change, repudiating the Kyoto Protocol and steadfastly insisting on allowing only ineffectual voluntary actions to address this growing global threat.

Since the United States emitted more greenhouse gases than any other country in the world during this period, this failure to cooperate in global efforts to address climate change has produced drastic consequences. It has contributed to a rise in global emissions, which has increased temperatures and raised sea levels. Scientists link the warming to which we have wantonly contributed to droughts in countries already suffering from malnutrition (and in the United States), inundation of coastal areas, massive extinction of species, a likely increase in the violence of hurricanes (like Katrina), and a spread of infectious diseases.[1] Because the gases the United States and other countries pumped into the atmosphere during this period will remain there for a very long time, the United States has helped commit the world to increased global warming and many associated harms for years to come. Furthermore, its posture has made it impossible to secure commitments from developing countries, some of whom, like China and India, have greatly increased emissions. These relatively poor countries, understandably and with considerable international precedent, have taken the view that those who created the global warming problem must take serious steps to address it before it is fair to ask them to invest scarce resources in addressing climate change.[2]

Although the United States' posture toward international negotiations has changed radically since the 2008 election, we continue to struggle with this legacy. We are now playing catch-up and remain less eager or able to take on ambitious goals to support allies who committed themselves to addressing climate disruption seriously more than a decade ago.

Why did the United States fail so utterly to address the most pressing environmental issue of this age? This book shows that economic thought has played an important role in this failure and critically examines the economic ideas influencing U.S. climate change policy.

In particular, the United States' failure arose from an ideological climate that embraced free markets as the solution to all economic and social issues and regarded vigorous government action as anathema. This ideological climate famously led to a failure to adequately regulate the financial industry that produced an economic collapse in 2008. But it influenced government's approach in a variety of areas, leading to deregulation of formerly regulated industries, privatization of government services, and a lack of vigor in ongoing efforts to protect public health, safety, and the environment. While institutional inertia allowed already existing environmental programs to remain in place—at least nominally—during this period, neoliberalism—the belief in free markets—made it very difficult to take on the challenging new problem of global warming.

Neoliberalism continues to influence global climate change policy, even though much has changed with the election of Barack Obama as president of the United States and the 111th Congress. Market-based mechanisms, one of neoliberalism's main policy prescriptions, remain central to new federal efforts to address global climate change and the ongoing academic debate about how best to address global climate disruption. This policy prescription reflects a continued faith in free markets, even if the firmness of the faith has eroded somewhat with the stock market crash that began in 2008.

The Neoliberal Model

Belief in markets and reluctance to have government solve pressing problems stem from the neoliberal perspective that dominated U.S. policy throughout the 1990s and the early twenty-first-century Bush presidency and remains influential today. The term *neoliberalism* describes a "revived form of traditional liberalism" that champions free markets in an economy gone global.³ As geographer David Harvey puts it, "neoliberalism is ... a theory ... that proposes that human well-being can best be advanced by liberating entrepreneurial freedoms and skills within an institutional framework characterized by strong private property rights, free markets and free trade."⁴

Several corollaries follow. First, neoliberalism generally presumes that free markets are much better at allocating resources and labor than are governments. This implies that government should avoid regulation whenever possible. Second, when governments regulate, they should usually choose regulation that is justified in cost-benefit terms. This implies a rejection of the idea of acting in the face of serious harms, unless a cost-benefit analysis shows that a certain action is economically efficient. Third, when governments must intervene, they should do so by creating new kinds of markets in new kinds of goods, such as newly available radio frequencies, "electricity futures," or pollution credits. The goal should be to maximize the near-term cost-effectiveness of regulation.

Neoliberalism draws intellectual support from neoclassical economic efficiency concepts. The first efficiency concept is *allocative efficiency*— the maximization of the welfare of all individuals in a society in the aggregate. This welfare maximization is the goal of neoclassical economics, which traces its roots to utilitarianism. Unlike nineteenth-century utilitarians, however, who viewed the goal of social policy as the maximization of aggregate levels of pleasure or happiness, neoclassical economists reject the notion that levels of welfare or happiness can be compared across individuals.⁵ They avoid that problem by adopting "preference satisfaction" or "willingness to pay" as the currency of individual well-being.⁶ Thus, by simply measuring people's willingness to pay for things as expressed in markets, economics avoids the philosophical conundrums of having to make interpersonal welfare comparisons.⁷

Although models of actual markets posit that market transactions are efficient because they benefit all parties involved, economists recognize that this definition of efficiency has no use in the context of government policymaking. Accordingly, economists turn to a slightly different definition of efficiency with "somewhat less conceptual appeal but much greater feasibility":⁸ *potential Pareto* or *Kaldor–Hicks* efficiency. Under this definition, a government action (such as a regulation) is efficient if it produces sufficient benefits to allow those who gain from the regulation to fully compensate those who stand to lose from it, even if nobody in fact compensates the losers.⁹ Kaldor–Hicks efficiency, then, is the maximization of overall social welfare, where overall social welfare is a measure of the preference satisfaction of all individuals in society in the aggregate.[10] Cost-benefit analysis attempts to determine, at least in an approximate way, whether government regulations or programs meet the test of Kaldor–Hicks efficiency.[11]

The second efficiency concept, that of cost-effectiveness, posits that governments should choose regulatory techniques that minimize the short-term costs of meeting any regulatory goal. This idea has led to great reliance on global emissions trading as the instrument of choice for addressing global warming.

This book employs the idea of "framing" to guide its analysis of the relationship between economic thinking and U.S. climate change policy. Ideas almost always influence government policy, as Deborah Stone has argued.[12] Government policy reflects human beings' decisions about what problems to address and how to address them. People in government usually join government in order to accomplish something worthwhile, and their sense of what is worthwhile depends on their notions of the good. As government officials work together in an institutional context, prevailing ideas influence the culture of the institutions of which they are a part. Even when venal motives influence people in government, ideas frequently play a role. Politicians, for example, must take their constituents' views into account in deciding what to do. Most citizens' views about what to do reflect the ideas that they accept.

The political science literature maintains that political actors "frame" issues to make their preferred policies attractive to voters and policymakers.[13] In describing policies, they choose phrases and make arguments that appeal to ideas that voters may find congenial. Framing affects the symbols invoked in political discourse and the selection and portrayal of facts. The literature on framing explains that politicians and lobbyists employ frames to highlight "some elements of reality while obscuring" others. The goal is to choose frames likely to appeal to a significant segment of a society, employing frames that have influence within a culture.[14] The literature recognizes that framing has been important in influencing climate change policy and environmental policy more generally.[15]

Neoliberal ideals influenced the framing of climate change policies over the past several decades. When President George H. W. Bush defended his failure to address climate change by stating that "The American Way of Life is not open to negotiation," he framed the issue in neoliberal terms.[16] The statement suggests that gas-guzzling SUVs and free markets define America, and that paying the costs of climate change mitigation would interfere with aspects of the American lifestyle, something conceivable only if the costs of mitigation forced people to reduce energy use in ways that seriously changed their way of life. By suggesting that curtailment of energy use would compromise the American lifestyle, Bush suggests an interference with free markets that forces people out of their SUVs, or even out of their cars. The choice of a frame linking climate mitigation to lifestyle change suggests that sophisticated political operators believed that even during an era when the American people knew that global warming was a problem, they had sufficient allegiance to free markets to make this framing effective.

We do not claim that ideas constitute the only force that contributed to the U.S. failure. Raw political pressure from those opposed to regulation from a purely self-interested perspective also played a role. Obviously, powerful fossil fuel interests lobbied to prevent action on climate change, something we analyze in chapter 4. But, as Michael Kraft and Sheldon Kamieniecki have pointed out, business interests also employ framing to secure adoption of their ideas.[17] The analysis in this book highlights the connection between business's choice of frames and economic thought. Raw power cannot explain business's success in derailing climate change policy without some understanding of ideas; for powerful interests have opposed almost every environmental policy the United States has ever adopted, and still the United States has usually addressed important environmental issues in a reasonably serious way. Furthermore, powerful lobbies with interests in resisting progress on climate change exist in other countries too, but many of those other countries have begun to address climate change more seriously than we have.

Perceptions of scientific uncertainty played some role in the United States' failure. Yet, even in the early 1990s, the science of global warming exhibited less uncertainty than the science relied upon to vigorously address many other environmental issues.[18] The United States government responded to the science and the lobbying with much less willingness to take firm action than it exhibited in confronting serious new threats in the past. We suggest that the climate of ideas prevailing in the 1990s and the first half of this decade played a significant role in this deviation from past practice, that is, that this failure to regulate greenhouse gas emissions is but one symptom of a larger shift toward a neoliberal ideology—an ideology that often eschews government interference with markets entirely and relies heavily on market models to craft policy on those occasions when the government does act.

Attitudes toward the science changed as extreme neoliberalism receded. Although a surprisingly large minority of the public remains skeptical of the basics of global warming science, most now accept the scientific community's conclusion that our greenhouse gas emissions have disrupted the global climate and will continue to do so in the future. Even businesses have abandoned the more extreme scientific claims they championed during the 1990s and the early twenty-first century. Public recognition of the science's validity has provided increasing support for a meaningful federal effort to address global warming, such that both major presidential candidates and most successful congressional candidates supported action on global warming in the 2008 election. Neoliberalism continues to play a role in how policy actors react to the science, however. Its emphasis on quantifying costs and benefits makes it difficult to respond appropriately to some of the nonquantifiable aspects of the science even in an age that appreciates the need to address climate disruption. These nonquantifiable aspects include the longevity of greenhouse gases' life in the atmosphere and the potential of feedback loops to make climate change even more disruptive than the models' quantitative projections would indicate. Neoliberalism's continued influence on our perception of climate disruption science shows the importance of understanding neoliberalism's influence on climate change.

This book not only describes how economic thought has influenced politics, with the help of the framing concept; it also critiques the most important economic ideas. In analyzing the economic thought that influenced the U.S. government's failure to act during this period we borrow an analytical framework set forth in *The Economic Dynamics of Environmental Law*.[19] This framework assumes that government should design policy to confront major problems like global warming with an eye toward producing a desirable direction of change over time.[20] Although the costs and benefits of actions designed to affect the future are rarely clear, the overall direction of desirable change can be.[21]

Economic dynamic theory employs institutional economic ideas to evaluate policies' ability to induce desirable changes. In particular, it adopts Douglass North's idea of adaptive efficiency, that when we cannot calculate the costs and benefits of our actions, we should try to maximize future choices under conditions of uncertainty.[22] If we use up fossil fuel now, the choice of using it in the future will not be available. Furthermore, if we permit greenhouse gases to accumulate in the atmosphere, we probably cannot later choose whether or not to prevent climate-related disasters. All of this points toward a policy stance favoring a rapid movement away from fossil fuels, the heart of the global warming problem.

Economic dynamic theory's concern with change over time leads to an emphasis on the importance of stimulating desirable innovation. It therefore is much more concerned about a system's capacity to induce desirable changes, than about whether each move forward (or backward) is efficient in an economic sense. Economic notions of efficiency emphasize that all decisions, even policy decisions, should generally create marginal costs equaling marginal benefits. Economic dynamic theory views such equilibriums as temporary phenomena carrying much less significance than the overall direction of change over time.[23]

In evaluating policies and the laws that carry them out, economic dynamic theory relies heavily on the analysis of economic incentives. But it makes this analysis far more systematic and comprehensive than the approach prevailing in the academy or among government policymakers. It employs institutional economic tools along with insights from public choice theory. It evaluates economic incentives' capacity to induce various kinds of changes not just by noting the direction in which the incentives push, but also by evaluating how various incentives will likely influence real economic and political actors.[24]

Economic dynamic analysis also pays close attention to the idea of path dependence, an important idea in the climate change context. Institutional behavior, including information processing and response to incentives, depends critically on past decisions and investments. Thus, the owner of a coal-fired power plant faced with increased demand for electricity is likely to modify the existing plant, rather than construct a new gas-fired power plant, because the previous decision to build the original plant makes that decision easier. By contrast, a new entrant today seeking to meet a similar demand might well construct a natural gas power plant. This path dependence identifies a crucial issue in climate change, that of technological lock-in. It is widely recognized that institutions with substantial investments in dirty coal-fired power or oil exploration and production will find it cost-effective to either not address global warming at all or to do so in an incremental fashion, with minor modifications that do not substantially threaten the value of previous investments. The technologies that they helped create or refine become locked in, in the sense that the actors making the key technological choices find it costly to change course, even if the present course moves us toward disasters of unprecedented scale. This effect can become very great, because vast networks of technologies and institutions are built around fundamental technologies, such as gasoline-burning car engines.[25] Efficiency-based thinking tends to support the status quo, the continuation of "business as usual." In the climate change context, this means continuing to use technologies that produce large emissions of greenhouse gases, because such thinking emphasizes the known costs of moving away from an established path, and has little capacity to address the unknown benefits and cost savings stemming from starting down a new path.

Finally, economic dynamic analysis shares the concern of public choice theory with power, which is important with respect to the justice dimensions of climate change. Public choice theory assumes that powerful interest groups exercise disproportionate power in political processes.[26] Economic dynamic analysis adds to this account by looking at various kinds of institutional arrangements' capacity to empower various groups. In the climate change context, for example, one might ask whether some institutional arrangements might turn renewable energy providers into a powerful interest group. Thus, economic dynamic analysis considers the allocation of resources among groups and whether such allocation is likely to spur or inhibit sought-after change over time, whether or not the allocations are efficient.

This book explores the relationship between neoliberal ideas and the U.S. failure to act in part I. In part II, the book advocates new thinking to guide future responses to global warming and other key environmental problems. In short, this book critically evaluates the ideas that led to this embarrassing failure in hopes of learning from our mistakes, redressing past failures, and avoiding future debacles on climate change and other important environmental issues.

The first part of this book begins with a chapter presenting basic background on the failure of the United States to address global warming, including an introduction to the relevant facts and ideology. Chris Schroeder and Robert Glicksman discuss the history of the United States' failure to specifically address greenhouse gas emissions. They also review the science to provide a sense of the peril we face, largely because of this failure to adequately address climate change. They explain the roots of this failure to adequately address climate disruption in the antigovernmental neoliberal ideology that prevailed during this period.

Because energy production is the primary cause of global warming, we devote a chapter to that specific topic. Joe Tomain explores the failure of energy policy to move forcefully toward a model embracing energy efficiency and renewables.

The remaining chapters in part I discuss the role of particular ideas in the failure to address climate change. Frank Ackerman discusses the role of cost-benefit analysis in climate change policy. During this period, key actors embraced a particular economic model for policymaking. Under this model, the government should not address an environmental harm, no matter how devastating, unless a quantitative analysis shows that the benefits of a particular environmental measure outweigh its costs. This model converts avoided environmental harms into benefits and demands that economists reduce these environmental benefits into dollar amounts. Policymakers and academics often treat estimates of the projected dollar-denominated costs and benefits of proposed policies as facts. But Frank Ackerman shows that the models used to estimate the costs and benefits of global warming depend heavily on the modelers' assumptions. Moreover, these models suffer from hubris; their efficacy depends on a belief that the only important matters are whatever the modeler is able to quantify. Ackerman suggests a new approach that can employ quantitative analysis more modestly, so as not to fall into the trap of treating unquantifiable environmental harms as unimportant.

Robert Glicksman dissects the industry approach to opposing environmental policies, which it used successfully in attacking proposals to seriously address climate change. The antiregulatory environment fostered by neoliberalism allowed this approach to succeed to a greater extent than it had when more environmentally friendly ideas prevailed.

Amy Sinden discusses another matter closely linked to the embrace of cost-benefit analysis, the abandonment of justice. She describes the inequities at the heart of the climate change problem. The developed countries have caused the problem of climate change, yet it harms people in developing countries much more severely than those in the countries providing most of the greenhouse gas emissions. Furthermore, climate change will probably impact unborn generations more severely than the generations that produced most of the warming. She explains how embrace of cost-benefit analysis led us to ignore our responsibilities to avoid harming others.

Rounding out part I, David Driesen shows how neoliberal ideology caused the United States to successfully advocate exceptionally broad global environmental benefit trading as the centerpiece of the Kyoto Protocol. Under this approach countries need not meet their targets for reducing greenhouse gas emissions under the Kyoto Protocol if they pay somebody else in another country to take equivalent actions in their stead. This advocacy of environmental benefit trading opened up a rift between developing and developed countries that complicates future cooperation on climate change policy in a number of ways. Having insisted on this money-saving approach in order to make climate change action more palatable in the United States, the United States still declined to ratify the Kyoto Protocol. This chapter shows that broad environmental-benefit trading poses risks to both long-term cooperation and to realizing planned emission reductions. It also shows that so far, this approach has not produced the sorts of innovation needed for long-term efforts to address climate change. The neoliberal political climate led the United States to risk poor performance in order to maximize cost savings through trading. This problem continues to haunt U.S. climate change policy, in spite of the election of politicians more amenable to addressing the climate change issue seriously.

Part II of the book takes up the question of what ideas might productively supersede the neoliberal model's reliance on cost-benefit analysis, knee-jerk support for market-based mechanisms, and a rejection of justice claims. Although Obama repudiated neoliberal tenets to some degree in the 2008 election, a new framework has not yet emerged to supplant it. So the need for guidance is acute.

This part begins with Carl Cranor establishing a moral framework for action on global warming. While each of us contributes to global warming (driving and using electricity leads to greenhouse gas emissions), we do not individually harm anybody. Global warming arises because of the aggregate effect of many people's activities on atmospheric concentrations of greenhouse gases. Cranor argues that we have a *collective duty* to act to avoid undesirable outcomes outside our borders. This collective duty requires binding commitments to address global warming—precisely what the United States failed to deliver in the past. He explores in some detail the role of individuals and institutions in carrying out this duty, arguing that each individual citizen has both a duty to take political action to assure that government addresses global warming and an individual duty to take some steps to reduce her own carbon footprint.

John Applegate next advocates a precautionary approach to environmental policy, which basically means that the existence of uncertainty does not justify inaction. He explores four elements of the precautionary principle, showing how it helps establish *triggers* for action, influences the *timing* of responses to emerging problems, guides the proportionality of *response*, and requires *iteration*—continued learning about emerging problems. This chapter offers an important response to criticisms of the precautionary principle rooted in allegiance to neoliberal cost-benefit analysis.

Lisa Heinzerling, however, challenges the notion that uncertainty pervades the climate change science. She argues that we should think of climate change as a "post-precautionary" problem, because the science, at least with respect to the basic causes and nature of the phenomenon, is not characterized by significant uncertainties. The solidity of the science makes a case for meaningful action strong, even without invoking the precautionary principle.

Thomas McGarity provides a much needed treatment of the problem of estimating costs in the context of global climate change. The U.S. rejection of the Kyoto Protocol relied heavily on the argument that meeting our Kyoto reduction target would be too costly. McGarity provides an overview of the techniques economists have used to estimate the costs of addressing global climate change. He then explains why these techniques have tended in the past to overestimate the cost of abating pollution. Cost estimates represent guesses about what future costs will be once a regulatory program is enacted, and depend heavily on the analysts' assumptions. McGarity suggests that analysts should make their premises transparent and avoid unrealistically optimistic assumptions. Finally, he argues against "safety-valve" measures that would authorize an agency to sell additional permits if a predicted carbon price is exceeded, because such a mechanism could produce excess emissions and uncertainty undermining needed investment in abatement technology. He concludes that the wide variance in cost estimates and the possibility of unconscious bias in selection of assumptions suggest that policymakers should exercise caution in relying on individual cost estimates.

Amy Sinden and Carl Cranor survey theories of ethics and justice in order to delineate more precisely the moral duties of the United States toward the global community. They argue for a prospective equal shares approach to distributing the burden of reducing greenhouse gases globally. This approach comports with basic justice concepts, namely corrective justice, avoiding unjust enrichment, and equalizing burdens. It requires vigorous action by the United States because of the United States' historical contribution to the problem and high current per capita emissions. They also discuss how intergenerational equity should influence the United States' climate change policy.

David Driesen then discusses policy options for reducing greenhouse gas emissions. He argues that we should make adoption of sustainable technology the major goal governing the choice of environmental instruments, rather than the goal of minimizing compliance costs for this generation. In particular, the goal should be to displace fossil fuels with more suitable technologies. He explains how new types of economic incentive programs and better design of emissions trading can help us achieve this goal.

Robert Verchick focuses on the problem of adaptation to the adverse consequences of global warming that are already inevitable because of past greenhouse gas emissions. He describes the principles of justice that support our contribution to developing country efforts to save as many people as possible from the climate disasters we have set in motion. He also shows how to implement the duty to aid developing countries' adaptation efforts. He explains the options developing countries face in trying to adapt and evaluates how we could best contribute to their efforts to ameliorate the harms that U.S. neoliberal policy has helped set in motion. A concluding chapter then sums up the book's lessons and raises some questions for future research.

Too often we attribute our collective actions to impersonal forces beyond anybody's control. Thus, many will be tempted to ascribe the U.S. failure to act to the fecklessness of George W. Bush or the vise-grip of special interests on policy. But this is too simplistic. President Bush's predecessors also did nothing to address global warming with considerable backing from Congress. And special interest pressures do not wholly explain the widespread support for inaction. Of course, individuals in government choose policies, and special interests influence them. But in a democracy people come to power in part and maintain it in part by offering a worldview that either governing elites or people in general accept to some degree. And special interests do not always carry the day; if they did environmental law would not exist.[27] The ideas of any age influence how people respond to new circumstances. Ideas matter, and ideas hostile to protective government can cripple our ability to deal with global environmental problems.

While this book contains diverse ideas and proposals, the authors share a generally skeptical view of neoliberalism. This general commonality helps the book, we hope, reach a greater level of coherence than many edited volumes achieve. Because the literature contains few books that discuss neoliberalism's weaknesses and fewer still that recommend alternative approaches,[28] a need exists to collect and present viable alternatives to standard neoliberal environmental policy recommendations. As the neoliberal case has been ably advanced elsewhere, there is no need for another book defending its prescriptions. Numerous edited volumes advance economic solutions to climate change and other problems, where every contributor shares a neoliberal outlook.[29] Furthermore, as we show, in the policy arena, corporations have generously funded think tanks to advance the neoliberal perspective. Those interested in more detailed defenses of neoliberalism can refer to works cited in the notes. This book helps balance a decidedly unbalanced literature.

The ideas offered in this book offer guidance on how to think better about climate change and about environmental policy more generally. We hope these ideas gain acceptance and help the United States move from its position as the most notorious climate change laggard to a position of honor as a climate change leader.

Notes

1. See Cynthia Rosenzweig et al., "Assessment of Observed Changes and Responses in Natural and Managed Systems," in Intergovernmental Panel on Climate Change (IPCC), *Climate Change 2007: Impacts, Adaptation, and Vulnerability*, Contribution of Working Group II to the Fourth Assessment Report of the Intergovernmental Panel on Climate Change, ed. Martin Parry and Osvaldo Canziani (Cambridge: Cambridge University Press, 2007), pp. 79–131.

2. See Joyeeta Gupta, *The Climate Change Convention and Developing Countries: From Conflict to Consensus?* (Dordrecht: Kluwer Academic Publishers, 1997).

3. *Oxford English Dictionary*, 3rd ed., s.v. "Neo-liberal"; see generally Dag Einar Thorson and Amund Lie, "What Is Neoliberalism?" (Department of Political Science, University of Oslo, 2006), http://folk.uio.no/daget/What%20 is%20Neo-Liberalism%20FINAL.pdf; David Harvey, *A Brief History of Neoliberalism* (Oxford: Oxford University Press, 2005).

4. Harvey, *A Brief History of Neoliberalism*, p. 2.

5. See Amartya Sen, "The Possibility of Social Choice," *American Economic Review* 89 (1999): 349–378, 352; Oscar Lange, "The Foundations of Welfare Economics," *Econometrica* 10 (1942): 215–228, 215; cf. Sen, "The Possibility of Social Choice," pp. 356–360 (arguing that interpersonal welfare comparisons are possible).

6. Nicholas Kaldor, "Welfare Propositions of Economics and Interpersonal Comparisons of Utility," *Economics Journal* 49 (1939): 549–550, 549.

7. See Richard A. Posner, "Utilitarianism, Economics, and Legal Theory," *Journal of Legal Studies* 8 (1979): 103–140, 129–130.

8. See David M. Driesen, "The Societal Cost of Environmental Regulation: Beyond Administrative Cost-Benefit Analysis," *Ecology Law Quarterly* 24 (1997): 545–617. "[D]ecisions producing Kaldor-Hicks efficiency do not have the virtues associated with free market exchange" because they do not involve consensual transactions. Driesen, "Societal Cost," p. 579.

9. See Edward J. Mishan, *Cost-Benefit Analysis: An Introduction* (New York: Praeger, 1971), p. 390.

10. Measuring and comparing social costs and benefits in order to evaluate the Kaldor-Hicks efficiency of actual policy initiatives raises considerable theoretical and practical difficulties. See Amy Sinden, "In Defense of Absolutes: Combating the Politics of Power in Environmental Law," *Iowa Law Review* 90 (2005): 1405–1511, 1423–1430.

11. See Matthew D. Adler and Eric A. Posner, "Rethinking Cost-Benefit Analysis," *Yale Law Journal* 109: 165–247 (demonstrating that CBA achieves, at best, an approximation of the Kaldor-Hicks efficiency criterion).

12. Deborah A. Stone, *Policy Paradox: The Art of Political Decision Making* (New York: Norton, 1997), p. 11.

13. Ibid.

14. Sheldon Kamieniecki, *Corporate America and Environmental Policy: How Often Does Business Get Its Way?* (Stanford: Stanford University Press, 2006), p. 59.

15. See, e.g., Judith Layzer, "Deep Freeze: How Business Has Shaped the Global Warming Debate in Congress," in *Business and Environmental Policy: Corporate Interests in the American Political System*, ed. Michael Kraft and Sheldon Kamieniecki (Cambridge, MA: MIT Press, 2007); Kamieniecki, *Corporate America*; Robert M. Entman, "Reporting Environmental Policy Debate: The Real Media Biases," *Harvard International Journal of Press/Politics* 1, no. 3 (1996): 77–92.

16. J. Timmons Roberts and Bradley C. Parks, *A Climate of Injustice: Global Inequality, North-South Politics, and Climate Policy* (Cambridge, MA: MIT Press, 2007), p. 3.

17. Kamieniecki, *Corporate America*, p. 60; see also Ronald Libby, *Eco-Wars: Political Campaigns and Social Movements* (New York: Columbia University Press, 1998).

18. U.S. General Accounting Office, *Global Warming: Emission Reductions Are Possible as Scientific Uncertainties Are Resolved*, GAO/RCED 90-58 (Washington, D.C.: General Accounting Office, 1990), p. 19; Keith Schneider, "New View Calls Environmental Policy Misguided," *New York Times*, March 21, 1993.

19. David M. Driesen, *The Economic Dynamics of Environmental Law* (Cambridge, MA: MIT Press, 2003).

20. David Driesen and Charles Hall, "Efficiency, Economic Dynamics, and Climate Change: A Critical Look at the Neoclassical Paradigm for Environmental Law," *Digest: National Italian American Bar Association Law Journal* 13 (2005): 1–33.

21. Driesen, *Economic Dynamics*, p. 215.

22. Douglass C. North, *Institutions, Institutional Change, and Economic Performance* (Cambridge: Cambridge University Press, 1990), p. 81; see also Robert N. Stavins, *A U.S. Cap-and-Trade System to Address Global Climate Change* (Brookings Institution, 2007), p. 16, http://www.brookings.edu/projects/hamiltonproject/Research-Commentary.aspx (pointing out that basing pollution abatement targets on cost-benefit analysis is not feasible in the climate change context, because the benefits cannot be quantified); Martin Weitzman, "Structural Uncertainty and the Value of Statistical Life in the Economics of Catastrophic Climate Change" (Working Paper 07-11, AEI Brookings Joint Center, 2007), http://aei-brookings.org/admin/authorpdfs/redirect-safely.php?fname=../pdffiles/WP07-11_topost110607.pdf.

23. Driesen, *Economic Dynamics*, p. 4; Robin Paul Malloy, *Law and Market Economy: Reinterpreting the Values of Law and Economics* (Cambridge: Cambridge University Press, 2000), pp. 32–33.

24. Driesen, *Economic Dynamics*, p. 8.

25. Robin Cowan and Staffan Hulten, "Escaping Lock-in: The Case of the Electric Vehicle," *Technological Forecasting and Social Change* 53, no. 1 (1996): 61–79.

26. See Morris P. Fiorna, *Congress: Keystone of the Washington Establishment* (New Haven, CT: Yale University Press, 1989); William H. Riker, *Liberalism against Populism: A Confrontation between the Theory of Democracy and the Theory of Social Choice* (San Francisco: Freeman, 1982); Dennis G. Mueller, *Public Choice against Populism: A Confrontation between the Theory of Democracy and the Theory of Social Choice* (San Francisco: Freeman, 1982); David R. Mayhew, *Congress: The Electoral Connection* (New Haven, CT: Yale University Press, 1974); Amartya K. Sen, *Collective Choice and Social Welfare* (San Francisco: Holden-Day, 1970); Kenneth J. Arrow, *Social Choice and Individual Values* (New Haven, CT: Yale University Press, 1963); James M. Buchanan and Gordon Tullock, *The Calculus of Consent: Logical Foundations of Constitutional Democracy* (Ann Arbor: University of Michigan Press, 1962); Mark Kelman, "On Democracy-Bashing: A Skeptical Look at the Theoretical and 'Empirical' Practice of the Public Choice Movement," *Virginia Law Review* 74 (1988): 199–273; Daniel Farber and Philip Frickey, "The Jurisprudence of Public Choice," *Texas Law Review* 65 (1987): 873–927.

27. Richard L. Revesz, "Federalism and Environmental Regulation: A Public Choice Analysis," *Harvard Law Review* 115 (2001): 553–641, 572.

28. Cf. Ekko C. van Ireland, Joyeeta Gupta, and Marcel Kok, eds., *Issues in Climate Change Policy: Theory and Policy* (Cheltenham: Elgar, 2003); James C. Whites, William Wagner, and Carole N. Beal, eds., *Global Climate Change: The Economic Costs of Mitigation and Adaptation* (New York: Elsevier, 1991); William D. Nordhaus, ed., *Economics and Policy Issues in Climate Change* (Washington, D.C.: Resources for the Future, 1998); Howard Coward and Thomas Hurka, eds., *Ethics and Climate Change: The Greenhouse Effect* (Waterloo, Ontario: Wilfrid Laurier University Press, 1993); Jan Corfee Morlot and Shardul

Agrawala, eds., *The Benefits of Climate Change Policies: Analytical and Framework Issues* (Paris: Organisation for Economic Co-operation and Development, 2004).

29. See, e.g., Andrew J. Hoffman, ed., *Global Climate Change: A Senior-Level Debate at the Intersection of Economics, Strategy, Technology, Science, Politics, and International Negotiation* (San Francisco: New Lexington Press, 1998); Brian P. Flannery and Charlotte A. B. Grezo, eds., *IPIECA Symposium on Critical Issues in the Economics of Climate Change* (London: IPIECA, 1997); Carlos De Miguel, Xavier Labandeira, and Baltasar Manzano, eds., *Economic Modeling of Climate Change and Energy Policies* (Cheltenham: Elgar, 2006); Darwin C. Hall and Richard B. Howarth, eds., *The Long-Term Economics of Climate Change: Beyond a Doubling of Greenhouse Gas Concentrations*, vol. 3 of *Advances in the Economics of Environmental Resources* (Amsterdam: Elsevier, 2001); F. L. Toth, ed., *Cost-Benefit Analyses of Climate Change: The Broader Perspectives* (Basel: Birkhäuser, 1997); Ferenc L. Tóth, ed., *Fair Weather? Equity Concerns in Climate Change* (London: Earthscan, 1999); Irving M. Mintzer et al., eds., *Confronting Climate Change: Risks, Implications, and Responses* (Cambridge: Cambridge University Press, 1993); James M. Griffin, ed., *Global Climate Change: The Science, Economics, and Politics* (Cheltenham, UK: Elgar, 2003); James P. Bruce, Hoesung Lee, and Erik F. Haites, eds., *Climate Change 1995: Economic and Social Dimensions of Climate Change* (Cambridge: Cambridge University Press, 1996); Jan Corfee Morlot, ed., *Climate Change: Mobilising Global Effort* (Paris: Organisation for Economic Co-operation and Development, 1997); Kendra Okonski, ed., *Adapt or Die: The Science, Politics, and Economics of Climate Change* (London: Profile Books, 2003); Michael A. Toman, ed., *Climate Change Economics and Policy: An RFF Anthology* (Washington, D.C.: Resources for the Future, 2001); Michael Faure, Joyeeta Gupta, and Andries Nentjes, eds., *Climate Change and the Kyoto Protocol: The Role of Institutions and Instruments to Control Global Change* (Cheltenham: Elgar, 2003); Norman J. Rosenberg et al., *Greenhouse Warming: Abatement and Adaptation* (Washington, D.C.: Resources for the Future, 1989); Onno Kuik, Paul Peters, and Nico Schrijver, eds., *Joint Implementation to Curb Climate Change: Legal and Economic Aspects*, vol. 2 of *Environment and Policy* (Dordrecht: Kluwer Academic Publishers, 1994); Organisation for Economic Co-operation and Development, *Climate Change: Evaluating the Socio-economic Impacts* (Paris: Organisation for Economic Co-operation and Development, 1991); Organisation for Economic Co-operation and Development, *Responding to Climate Change: Selected Economic Issues* (Paris: Organisation for Economic Co-operation and Development, 1991); Peter Hayes and Kirk Smith, eds., *The Global Greenhouse Regime: Who Pays? Science, Economics, and North–South Politics in the Climate Change Convention* (Tokyo: United Nations University Press, 1994); Robert Mendelsohn and James E. Neumann, eds., *The Impact of Climate Change on the United States Economy* (Cambridge: Cambridge University Press, 1999); Rudiger Dornbusch and James M. Poterba, eds., *Global Warming: Economic Policy Responses* (Cambridge, MA: MIT Press, 1991); Stephen H. Schneider, Armin Rosencranz, and John O. Niles, eds., *Climate Change Policy: A Survey* (Washing-

ton, D.C.: Island Press, 2002); Thomas E. Downing, Alexander A. Olsthoorn, and Richard S. J. Tol, eds., *Climate, Change, and Risk* (London: Routledge, 1999); Tim Jackson, Katie Begg, and Stuart Parkinson, eds., *Flexibility in Climate Policy: Making the Kyoto Mechanisms Work* (London: Earthscan, 2001); and Walter Sinnott-Armstrong and Richard B. Howarth, eds., *Perspectives on Climate Change: Science, Economics, Politics, Ethics*, vol. 5 of *Advances in the Economics of Environmental Resources* (Amsterdam: Elsevier, 2005).

I

The Neoliberal Model's Contribution to U.S. Failure to Address Climate Change

1

The United States' Failure to Act

Christopher Schroeder and Robert L. Glicksman

This chapter canvasses the role of economic ideas in causing the United States' failure to act and the consequences of that inaction. We begin with an account of the role of ideas.

I. The Role of Ideas in Slowing the United States Response to Global Climate Change

A. A Matter of Timing: When the Climate of Ideas Was Receptive to Bold Action, the Idea of Climate Change Was Not Ready

In the relatively brief period between 1970 and 1980, the United States took great strides forward in addressing substantial environmental problems, enacting many of the laws that laid the foundation for the country's current approach to a broad range of environmental problems. Progress came as environmental concerns fueled a genuine social movement that was capable for a time of pushing back against the strong resistance that laws often face when they benefit diffuse interests and impose costs on concentrated interests. Citizens rallied, organized, and raised their collective voices in a call for action. Elected officials responded to those calls to shape the backbone of the nation's environmental policy in relatively short order and with an amazing degree of bipartisan support. Though not sufficient to "solve" the major problems they addressed, these statutes and the regulatory policies they launched have measurably improved conditions compared to what would have been the case had they not been enacted.

Although the sweep of environmental policies legislated into existence in this period is both impressive and vast, none of the new laws explicitly addressed global climate change.[1] The very real potential for human activity to alter the climate was not unknown at the time, and research into the problem was ongoing, but the metes and bounds of the problem had not been well described. The public focused instead on an array of more immediate and visible environmental problems—everything from rivers on fire, to deadly smog trapped by temperature inversions, to pesticides threatening entire species. So when the environmental movement opened a window of opportunity for policymakers to act decisively, climate change had not matured enough to take its place alongside endangered species, urban air pollution, wastewater treatment, and hazardous pesticides on the policy agenda.

By the time a scientific consensus on the subject of climate change began to form in the 1980s, the political dynamics had shifted to one that has made progress on this issue enormously more difficult. While explicating the full dimensions of that shift[2] would require much more space than is available here, any telling of the story would have to include a prominent role for two influential neoliberal ideas. These are, first, a belief in the superiority of private markets over government management of collective problems, and second, a heavy reliance on the disciplines of science to guide social progress by defining problems and solutions.

In different ways, appeals to markets and to science each tap into a deep-seated American skepticism toward government by promising to cope with problems in ways that avoid partisan bickering, influence peddling, and wasteful bureaucracies.[3] Markets promise a solution that relies heavily on the private behavior and the discipline of the market. Science promises a solution that is above politics. "Science stands for the possibility of unanimity, of an end to bickering and strife. Quantification is raised up as a neutral, objective language, a basis for minimizing arbitrariness, and hence for overcoming suspicion and winning allies."[4]

During the boom in environmental policy, confidence in government initiatives temporarily overcame such native skepticism toward such efforts. On the one hand, faith in the market was at a low ebb in the 1960s and 1970s, while faith in science actually reinforced rather than undermined support for government initiatives.

As for markets, instead of being a redoubt to fend off appeals for government action, market theory actually traced some of the root causes of environmental problems back to markets themselves. Neoclassical market theory teaches that markets malfunction in the presence of environmental externalities. In theory, markets can generate wealth and allocate resources in socially attractive ways, but only if market prices reflect all significant costs associated with transactions. Whenever the costs of using up environmental amenities like clean air and water do not get reflected in market prices, actors in the marketplace will overuse the environment as a waste disposal site for air, water, and solid wastes because the market causes them to perceive the environment to be a free resource by failing to recognize the real costs associated with its use. This critique of markets as a source of modern society's failure to cope adequately with environmental damage was prominent prior to and during the environmental decade of the 1970s.[5]

As a further stimulus for government intervention into markets, during the 1960s and '70s people redirected some of the skepticism normally reserved for their government toward big institutions in general, and big business in particular. John Kenneth Galbraith advanced a soon-to-be widely known argument that the effective and constructive operation of capitalism required strong countervailing institutions to balance the market power of large concentrations of wealth and thus prevent the abuse of this power.[6] Galbraith's institutional critique resonated with a perception of large corporations as authoritarian institutions, answerable to no one, imposing conformity, stifling creativity, supporting segregation, and profiting from a disastrous war. In this time period, then, mistrust of industry was running high,[7] making business leaders reluctant to oppose popular legislation as aggressively as they had even in the very recent past.[8] Attention-grabbing incidents, like General Motors' surveillance of Ralph Nader, seemed to reinforce a general distrust toward big private enterprises. It was a time when business was on the defensive, and so was the market.

At the same time, the most notable scientific success of the era had come about when government acted boldly to stimulate its achievements. In his famous "Man on the Moon" speech in 1961, President Kennedy had judiciously mixed elements of urgency and competence. Invoking the challenge posed by the earlier launch of Sputnik by the Soviet Union, Kennedy told the country that we were rich in the resources needed to answer that challenge—all we lacked was a sense of urgency and a national commitment:

I believe we possess all the resources and talents necessary. But the facts of the matter are that we have never made the national decisions or marshaled the national resources required for such leadership. We have never specified long-range goals on an urgent time schedule, or managed our resources and our time so as to insure their fulfillment.[9]

When Neil Armstrong stepped off the lunar module on July 20, 1969, Kennedy's promise to put a man on the moon before the end of the decade was dramatically fulfilled.

The environmental initiatives of the 1970s took advantage of the wave of technological optimism generated by the lunar success.[10] At the same time as the country was coming to believe that we faced serious and urgent environmental problems, it also was convinced that as a nation we possessed the knowledge, resources, and innovative capacities to solve those problems, if only we would make "the national decisions [and] marshal the national resources required." Just as in the case of the lunar landing, all that was holding us back from solving our environmental problems was that "[w]e have never specified long-range goals on an urgent time schedule, or managed our resources and our time so as to insure their fulfillment."

B.   The Belief in Market Superiority Favors Voluntary Approaches

The confluence of market skepticism and optimism about harnessing science and technology through bold government programs did not last long. By the mid-1970s, the economy was not doing well. Sentiment shifted away from criticizing the major engines of the American economy toward wanting to restore them to good health. The Business Roundtable, a group formed in direct response to the failure of business to exert greater influence over the Clean Air Act Amendments of 1970, began stressing and publicizing the burden that regulation placed on those engines of commerce. Murray Weidenbaum, an academic who would go on to become Chairman of President Reagan's Council of Economic Advisors, received wide attention for a coauthored paper entitled "The Cost of Federal Regulation of the American Economy," which in 1978 placed a $100 billion price annual price tag on all federal regulations.[11]

Attacking the drag put on the economy by the new environmental regulations was part and parcel of a larger resurgence of the idea of market superiority. Friedrich von Hayek and Milton Friedman, the two most prominent intellectuals who extolled the ability of capitalism to produce wealth and prosperity as well as to advance freedom, each won the Nobel Prize in Economics, in 1974 and 1976, respectively. As we began to enter the high-tech age, market proponents increasingly asserted that the enormous superiority that markets have over government as engines of growth gives them an advantage that far outweighs any perceived cost of market failure. They argued further that national policy must be increasingly concerned about American competitiveness vis-à-vis rising economies around the world. It was during this period, for instance, that the Japanese auto manufacturers began to make serious inroads into the American automobile markets, at the same time as Detroit automakers were complaining that the new environmental regulations were driving up their costs and damaging their ability to compete. At the same time as globalization constituted a threat, moreover, it also served as the basis for an argument that market failures would be modulated best by the market itself, because the global marketplace would discipline firm behavior and would not permit inefficient operations to stay in business long.

A considerable amount of financial support from business interests helped sustain and advance the intellectual resurgence of the marketplace. Robert Kuttner writes that "tens of millions of dollars [were] pumped into right-wing foundations to bolster unregulated, free-market capitalism."[12] Beyond its financial support for building up the stock of ideas that supported free-market capitalism, business and industry also greatly improved their ability to press those ideas on policymakers. Compared to the early 1970s, by the end of the decade business and industry were much better organized to mount sophisticated lobbying campaigns that pressed these refurbished intellectual defenses of the marketplace and the critique of the damage caused by excessive regulation.[13] Individual firms and trade associations committed more staff and resources to lobbying. Some, such as the National Automobile Dealers Association and the International Council of Shopping Centers, were well established and effective organizations that had stayed on the sidelines early in the decade but subsequently mobilized vigorously for the battles in the later '70s, such as those around the 1977 amendment to the Clean Air Act.[14]

With the election of Ronald Reagan in 1980, the political and intellectual environment changed even more dramatically. President Reagan stressed lowering taxes and reducing the size of the federal government. In his first inaugural address, he famously declared that "Government is not the solution to our problem. Government *is* the problem." With that pronouncement the executive branch pivoted away from the prior decade and into a new one in which a belief in the superiority of the market became its official policy.

In a political environment not hospitable to any new government initiatives, and even less so to *major* new initiatives, proposals for any further interventions in the name of environmental quality became presumptively suspect, as perceptions of markets and business as part of the problem were replaced by perceptions of them as efficient producers of economic well being. Accordingly, when the international community began to mobilize around the climate change issue in the 1980s, many Americans were well primed to react with considerable skepticism about the need for a regulatory response to the problem.

The United States did participate in the early international negotiations concerning climate change and was one of the 180 nations that by 1992 had signed the Framework Convention on Climate Change (UNFCCC) during the Rio Conference on Environment and Development.[15] Later that year the United States became the first industrialized nation to ratify the Convention.[16] The United States, however, opposed binding targets. As a result, the Convention created no binding commitments, in spite of support for them by the European Union. Instead, the Framework Convention inaugurated both information-gathering measures and regular meetings of the participants in the convention (the conference of the parties, or COP) to negotiate such commitments for the future. COP-3, held in Kyoto, Japan, produced the Kyoto Protocol, an agreement among the industrialized countries for binding obligations, individualized nation by nation. Had the United States ratified Kyoto, it would have obligated itself to reduce its total emissions of greenhouse gases (GHGs) to 7 percent below 1990 levels.

Of course, the United States never did ratify Kyoto. Prior to the Kyoto meeting, the Senate signaled its opposition, adopting the Byrd–Hagel resolution by a vote of 95 to 0. The presumption against regulation based on market superiority and the excessive costs of regulation suffused the debate on the resolution. During the 1980s, opponents of climate change legislation repeatedly attacked adoption of any significant government policy as much too costly. The cost estimates differed greatly, but press attention invariably focused on those estimates projecting substantial costs for the U.S.[17] A Department of Energy study during the Clinton administration projected gasoline prices increasing from $1.39 to $1.91 and 20 percent to 86 percent increases in the price of electricity.[18] An industry-funded study from the Wharton School found even higher costs. It projected losses of 2.4 million jobs and $300 billion in national GDP, for an average annual per household cost of $2,700, with a near doubling of electricity prices and $.65 per gallon increases in gasoline prices.[19]

A better approach, the Kyoto critics claimed, could come through trusting markets and supporting voluntary measures undertaken by private industry and driven by market dynamics. The Clinton administration's initial 1993 Climate Change Action Plan had proposed voluntary measures to achieve the UNFCCC goals.[20] Although Clinton later moved toward mandatory regulations,[21] these were not put into effect before George W. Bush assumed office, and in June, 2001, President Bush issued a statement repudiating such mandatory measures, "rejecting the Kyoto

Protocol and favoring voluntary actions, increased scientific research and market mechanisms."[22]

C.   Trust in Science Fosters Wait-and-See Attitude

Faith in science has played two roles in slowing down effective action on global climate change. First, the need for scientific innovation in order to solve the climate change problem was invoked alongside the faith in markets as a reason to refrain from centralized regulation and to favor voluntary action. Climate change, the argument goes, demands a massive technological shift that can come only through technological innovation. One of the basic reasons to subscribe to market superiority in the first place, the skeptics believe, is the demonstrated capacity of markets to foster innovation. "Any government-enforced solution," warned the executive director of the Global Climate Coalition (a coalition of energy companies), "would raise the specter of an antigrowth bureaucracy."[23] The Coalition favors voluntary free-trade partnerships with developing countries through which existing energy companies would sell energy-efficient technologies to the emerging economies.[24]

Second, arguments based on a supposedly inadequate understanding of climate change turn calls for more science into a reason to delay government responses until better science is available. Critics well understand that if they can maintain an atmosphere of uncertainty and controversy surrounding the science, they can draw on U.S. reluctance to embrace large-scale government programs in order to support instead a counsel of caution and more study, rather than action. So long as the science of climate change is perceived to be inconclusive or debatable, it will be that much more difficult to commit to government programs to address the problem.

By the early 1980s, more and more scientists were becoming exercised about the lack of attention being given to climate change. Even when scientists spoke out more aggressively, however, they tended to emphasize the slow pace of research. Thus, when Wallace Broecker wrote to a senator saying that "the CO_2 problem is the single most important and the single most complex environmental issue facing the world," with the "clock ticking away," he joined his concern with a call for a better research program.

Congress did begin to listen somewhat more attentively later in the decade of the 1980s. Led by a young congressman named Al Gore, who had been a student of climate scientist Roger Revelle at Harvard, congressional hearings on the global warming problem begun in the early

'80s were able to prevent the Reagan administration's proposed deep cuts into federal research on climate change.[25] Research continued during the 1980s, as did congressional hearings in which Representative and then Senator Gore showed a real commitment to the issue. For most of the 1980s, to the extent the public was paying attention to atmospheric modification, it was still because of the ozone-depletion problem, which had quickly become a leading item on the international environmental agenda. In 1987, negotiations opened in Montreal on what would become the Montreal Protocol, signed by President Bush the next year. The success of the Montreal process on the international scene created a sense of optimism that the time might be right to engage in a similar process to address global climate change. Many had concluded that the key to the Montreal success was the broad international scientific consensus that had emerged prior to the substantive negotiations. Seeking to replicate that formula, the international community agreed to form the Intergovernmental Panel on Climate Change (IPCC).

At this stage, the IPCC became for a time an unwitting foot soldier in the larger effort to maintain the attractiveness of a wait-and-see policy. The best way to stall action on the subject, in the words of one White House memorandum, is "to raise the many uncertainties."[26] That would have the effect "of justifying increased research funding while delaying policy decisions—a win for both the scientists and the politicians!"[27] The formation of the IPCC could thus both be touted as progress in better understanding the problem and simultaneously used as an excuse for delaying policy initiatives while awaiting IPCC findings. Over time, of course, the IPCC would go over to the other side, as it were, as each iteration of the IPCC process has produced a larger and larger sphere of conclusions about which the scientific consensus has become strong. Accordingly, each iteration of the carefully negotiated summaries for policymakers contains ever more specific conclusions about the dynamics of the climate transformation that increased GHGs will likely produce as well as about the global consequences of that transformation if the world community fails to respond.

Even as the IPCC reports were being strengthened, the climate change skeptics did not retreat from an insistence that the science just was not yet convincing enough to warrant action. In a memorandum to Republican candidates about how to package their message, one noted Republican strategist highlighted the importance of trumpeting the uncertain state of science: "Voters believe that there is no consensus about global warming in the scientific community. Should the public come to believe that the scientific issues are settled, their views about global warming will change accordingly. Therefore, *you need to continue to make the lack of scientific certainty a primary issue in the debate*, and to defer to scientists and other experts in the field."[28]

With consensus growing stronger within the scientific community itself, maintaining the appearance of scientific dissensus as the 1990s unfolded required ever increasing effort. Ross Gelbspan's 1997 book, *The Heat Is On*, documents energy industry organizations' nurturing, funding, and publicizing of the views of a handful of scientists who were climate skeptics;[29] Congress' own dwindling but influential group of skeptics made these same "experts" the central focus of periodic hearings held on Capitol Hill.[30]

The efforts of the climate change skeptics to maintain the appearance of dissensus has been aided by the norms of U.S. journalism. Overwhelmingly, the media understands its obligation to produce fair and objective reporting as an obligation to report both sides of a dispute, without commenting on whether one view is more legitimate than the other.[31] This may well be the correct norm in reporting on social or political issues,[32] and in reporting on a scientific dispute it does of course have the distinct benefit of not demanding that generalist journalists attempt to sort out which side of a scientific debate has the better point of view. Notwithstanding this, the norm has functioned in the context of climate change to promote within the public a sense that the scientific community is still uncertain and divided about the most basic climate change questions— whether the man-made greenhouse gas effect, fueled overwhelmingly by the carbon energy economy, is really occurring, and whether we face global temperature rise as a result. On these basic questions, however, there is an overwhelming scientific consensus.

Nonetheless, as a result of the amplification of the voices of a very few climate skeptics, assisted by the media's understanding of its own role, a good percentage of the U.S. public believes that there is far more disagreement among scientists than there really is. In a poll taken in August, 2007, for instance, 42 percent of those asked thought there was a "lot of disagreement among climate scientists about whether human activities are a major cause of global warming."[33]

II.   The Consequences of That Failure (The Peril We Face)

In fact, the recognized causal links between human activities (such as fossil-fuel combustion and deforestation) and climate change provide a basis for pursuing policies to curtail those activities. Some questions remain steeped in genuine uncertainty, such as the extent, timing, and geographical distribution of many of the changes yet to occur. The answers depend, of course, on what steps governments, including our own, take to address climate change. As the chapter in this volume on the precautionary principle indicates, however, the uncertainty itself has significant implications for the design of climate change policies.

A. What We Know about the Existence and Causes of Climate Change
The processes of climate change clearly have begun. The most obvious change has been a warming of the earth's atmosphere. Eleven of the twelve warmest years since 1850 occurred between 1995 and 2006. Over the last fifty years, the linear warming trend (0.13° C per decade) is nearly twice what it was over the last 100 years. Warming rates for the lower and mid-tropospheric regions of the atmosphere are similar to those for surface air temperatures over this period. Warming surface air temperatures have caused rising sea surface temperatures. Further, scientists have confirmed an increase in the average atmospheric water vapor content over both land and water and in the upper troposphere, as warmer air holds more water vapor.[34] These changes have been more extreme in some places than in others. Average Arctic temperatures increased at almost twice the global average rate over the past century. Precipitation has increased significantly since 1900 in the eastern portions of North and South America, northern Europe, and northern and central Asia. In the Mediterranean and southern Africa, the climate has been dryer.

The causes of climate change are also beyond reasonable debate. The IPCC concluded in 2007 that "it is *extremely unlikely* that global climate change of the past 50 years can be explained without external forcing, and *very likely* that it is not due to known natural causes alone."[35] The IPCC defined "very likely" as a 90 to 99 percent likelihood. It found that "most of the observed increase in global average temperatures since the mid-20th century is *very likely* due to the observed increase in anthropogenic greenhouse gas concentrations."[36] The most important anthropogenic GHG is carbon dioxide (CO_2), which humans generate primarily by burning fossil fuels. Land use changes, especially deforestation, also have contributed to rising CO_2 concentrations. Global atmospheric concentrations of CO_2 have increased from a preindustrial value of about 280 parts per million (ppm) to 379 ppm in 2005, an amount far in excess of the natural range over the last 650,000 years. Moreover, the problem is accelerating. The annual growth rate in CO_2 concentration was larger between 1995 and 2005 than during any other period since 1960. Atmospheric concentrations of methane, another, more potent GHG, have increased from a preindustrial value of about 715 parts per billion (ppb) to 1,774 ppb in 2005.

B. Uncertainties about Future Projections

The global climate is undoubtedly changing in significant and unprecedented ways due to human activities. The extent of the resulting future warming and associated changes is less certain. IPCC computer simulations have projected that even if radiative forcing agents such as CO_2 were held constant at 2000 levels, warming at a rate of about 0.1° C per decade would still occur. This change is referred to as *committed climate change*, or the further change in global mean temperature if atmospheric composition, and hence radiative forcing, is held constant.[37] The IPCC has explained that if GHG concentrations were held fixed, climate change would continue to occur because of the thermal inertia of the oceans and ice sheets and their long time scales for adjustment.[38] The troposphere adjusts quickly to changing conditions, but the upper oceans may take decades, and the deep oceans and ice sheets centuries or millennia, to adjust, so that "it takes a very long time for the atmospheric variables to come to an equilibrium."[39] The staying power of GHGs in the atmosphere requires reductions in future GHG emissions to stabilize atmospheric concentrations. A failure to *reduce* emissions will yield higher atmospheric concentrations.

The IPCC has also projected the impact of various higher levels of GHG emissions. Although currently available computer models can provide best estimates and an assessed likelihood range for each scenario, they do not allow further precision. Assuming the highest level of GHG emissions, the IPCC's best estimate is an increase of 4.0° C by the end of this century and a likely range of between 2.4 and 6.4° C.[40] Obviously, no one knows what the level of GHG emissions will be for this period. Further, data deficiencies prevent the IPCC's models from building in uncertainties in the climate-carbon cycle feedback to reflect the possibility that the changes that have already occurred may themselves generate additional warming. Higher temperatures, for example, cause plants and soils to absorb less carbon from the atmosphere and permafrost to thaw and release methane gas.[41] Even ignoring these additional uncertainties, the world is likely to look very different if average temperatures increase by 6.4° C instead of 2.4° C by century's end. Moreover, different regions will experience different rates and extents of warming regardless of the mean increase. The IPCC concluded that all of North America is very likely to warm this century and that the annual mean warming is likely to exceed the global mean in most areas. The *Stern Review* concludes that "the scientific evidence points to increasing risks of serious, irreversible impacts from climate change associated with business-as-usual (BAU) paths for emissions."[42]

C.   The Consequences of a Warming Climate

The cause-and-effect linkage between rising surface air and sea surface temperatures is intuitive. But these increases can result in additional, less obvious consequences. These include dramatic changes in extreme weather events and weather patterns, rising sea levels, adverse human health effects, disruptions in social stability, and changes in wildlife habitat and species. Some of these changes have already begun. No one can predict the precise magnitude or geographical distribution of further changes, for many of the reasons that make predictions of the level of future warming difficult. Consequently, policy decisions on whether and how to address climate change must be made despite considerable uncertainty.

D.   Seasonal Changes and Extreme Weather Events

The IPCC attributes changes in the large-scale atmospheric circulation to rising GHG concentrations. Extreme heat waves, heavy precipitation, and more intense and longer droughts have become more common due to human-induced climate change. Increases in tropical sea surface temperatures also appear to be correlated with an increase in the intensity of tropical hurricanes. The IPCC finds it likely that future tropical cyclones, including hurricanes that affect the south Atlantic and Gulf Coasts of the United States, will become more intense as global warming continues, with stronger peak wind speeds and more precipitation.

The IPCC also expects that extratropical storm tracks will move toward the poles, causing wind, precipitation, and temperature patterns to change. Increased precipitation is very likely in high latitudes. Decreases are likely in subtropical land regions. Daily heavy rainfall events may increase, even in regions experiencing mean rain decreases. Annual mean precipitation is very likely to increase in Canada and the northeastern United States, but decrease in the southwestern United States.[43] As rainfall decreases and earlier snowmelts cause late-summer droughts to increase, wildfire risks in the western United States will rise, especially at high elevations.[44]

Warming air temperatures have already caused snow cover to decrease in most regions. These changes can affect the availability of fresh water as spring runoff patterns change. Permafrost and seasonally frozen ground have shrunk in areas of the northern hemisphere. The IPCC projects contracting snow cover and widespread increases in thaw depth over most permafrost regions.[45] The degree of these changes depends on the level of GHG emissions over the next century.

E.   Rising Sea Levels and Changing Ocean Chemistry

Melting ice and warming sea surface temperatures, which cause water to expand, have contributed to sea level changes. Glaciers and ice caps have experienced widespread mass loss. Between 1963 and 2003, the average rate of global mean sea level rise was 1.8 ± 0.5 mm per year. According to the IPCC, melting of the Greenland and Antarctic ice sheets very likely has contributed to sea level rises over the past decade.

The situation is very likely to get worse, but how much worse is unclear. The IPCC expects sea levels to continue to rise for the next several decades by 1.3 ± 0.7 mm per year.[46] Its projections for sea level rise by the end of the twenty-first century range from 0.18–0.38 to 0.26–0.59 meters, depending on the level of GHG emissions and the amount of water contributed by further melting of the Greenland and Antarctic ice sheets.[47] If the rate of ice flow from Greenland and Antarctica between 1993 and 2003 were to grow linearly with global average temperature change, the upper ranges of sea level rise would increase by 0.1 to 0.2 meters.[48]

Coastal flooding may make some areas of the United States uninhabitable. Areas vulnerable to flooding include portions of Florida with 10 percent of its population.[49] Boston and Atlantic City are expected to experience what used to be once-a-century coastal flooding once every year or two by the end of the century if summer temperatures rise in the range of 3 to 7° C.[50] In areas such as the Everglades and the Gulf Coast, flooding and increased storm surges could destroy or degrade wetlands. This damage could adversely affect the costs of real estate and insurance, the commercial fishing and recreation industries, and the value of the ecosystem services provided by wetlands.[51] Because wetlands serve as a break on hurricanes, their destruction is likely to increase the ferocity of future storms.

Ocean chemistry also has changed, as an increase in dissolved CO_2 has resulted in more acidic water. Oxygen concentrations and salinity have increased in most ocean basins. The IPCC expects these trends to continue, as rising atmospheric concentrations of CO_2 further acidify the oceans. Average global surface ocean pH is projected to fall between 0.14 and 0.35 units by the end of the century, on top of the 0.1 unit decrease that has occurred since preindustrial times.[52] Ocean acidification can make the water inhospitable to aquatic wildlife and adversely affect the food chain.

F. Adverse Public Health Effects

Rising surface air temperatures may have significant adverse human health consequences, some of which have already begun. The IPCC has attributed heat-related mortality in Europe, infectious disease vectors in some areas, and allergenic pollen at Northern Hemisphere northern latitudes to climate change.[53] Physicians at the World Health Organization attributed to climate change a 2007 outbreak in Castiglione di Cervia, Italy, of a disease similar to dengue fever. The disease is spread by tiger mosquitoes, which previously had been unable to live outside of the tropics. As temperatures warmed, portions of Italy became hospitable to the mosquitoes, causing the appearance and spread of a disease that had never occurred there.[54]

Looking forward, climate change is likely to cause many adverse health effects. Warming may cause more heat-related deaths from cardiovascular, cerebrovascular, and respiratory disease. Heat waves in North American cities are likely to increase in frequency, intensity, and duration this century.[55] Among those most vulnerable to heat cramps, heat exhaustion, heatstroke, and death are the elderly, babies and infants, people taking prescription medications such as beta-blockers, physically unfit or overweight individuals, those engaged in vigorous exercise outdoors, urban populations, those of lower socioeconomic status, and people living alone.[56]

A buildup of atmospheric GHGs is also expected to cause an increase in ground-level ozone pollution, which has been linked to impaired lung function, asthma, and cardiovascular disease. The frequency of unhealthy air quality in the summer could increase significantly by mid-century in large U.S. cities.[57] Rising temperatures may facilitate the growth of allergens that cause respiratory problems; rising CO_2 increases the timing and release of bioallergens such as ragweed.[58]

The incidence of infectious diseases may worsen due to the proliferation of mosquitoes, ticks, and fleas, which are sensitive to subtle changes in temperature and humidity.[59] Climate change will allow these disease-carrying insects to spread to places where humans lack immunities, causing more widespread incidence of diseases such as malaria. In the United States, rainfall increases could outstrip the capacity of wastewater treatment systems. The resulting water pollution could contaminate drinking water supplies by bacterial infections from giardia, cryptosporidium, and fecal coliform.[60]

If agricultural output falls due to temperature increases and accompanying drought, malnutrition is likely to rise, particularly in developing countries.[61] If so, increases in child mortality can be expected.[62] Environmental changes such as threats of coastal flooding also may lead to increases in psychiatric disorders such as anxiety, depression, and suicide.[63]

The IPCC has projected that climate change will produce some health benefits in temperate areas, such as fewer deaths from cold exposure. But it concluded that rising temperatures' negative health effects will outweigh these benefits, especially in developing countries. Although the balance of positive and negative impacts, generally and to health in particular, will vary by location, the balance will shift more heavily to the negative side as temperatures continue to rise.[64]

G. Economic and Social Disruption

Climate change has the potential to generate worldwide economic and social dislocation. The IPCC concluded that the costs and benefits of climate change for society will vary widely by location, but that net effects will tend to be more negative the larger the change in climate.[65] The poorest nations are likely to suffer the most from climate change because they tend to be warmer already than developed regions, their economies depend heavily on climate-sensitive economic sectors such as agriculture, and they will find it difficult or impossible to afford adaptive measures.

The chaos following Hurricane Katrina in 2005 is indicative of the kinds of social shocks that even one-time dramatic climate events can cause. Severe flooding destroyed New Orleans and wrecked the lives of many of its inhabitants. If melting polar ice caps cause sea levels to rise significantly, coastal areas may be flooded, necessitating massive migrations.[66] The areas to which refugees migrate may be unable or unwilling to accommodate them, especially if the ethnicities of relocating and resident peoples differ. The potential for serious social strife is obvious.

Coastal flooding and storms may damage infrastructure such as roads, bridges, and utility lines. Some of these problems are already occurring. Rising sea levels, deteriorating permafrost, and unusually violent storms have made some of the Alaskan barrier islands with indigenous Inuit populations uninhabitable. The 34 First Nations reservations located in the boreal forest of northern Ontario have become increasingly isolated as temperature increases melt routes to the outside world and impede access to supplies.

The IPCC has projected that water supplies stored in glaciers and snow cover will decline due to climate change and that water availability will decline in regions supplied by meltwater. It is not difficult to imagine violent conflicts developing over access to scarce water supplies. More than one-sixth of the world's population will be at risk from either flooding or reduced water supplies if temperatures increase by another 2–3° C in the next fifty years.[67]

If increases in temperature, drought, and desertification reduce crop yields, food shortages and widespread civil unrest may result. Climate change has already adversely affected crop production. Warming since 1981 has resulted in annual combined losses of maize, wheat, and barley of about $5 billion per year, as of 2002.[68] The IPCC believes that productivity for some crops will increase slightly at mid- to high latitudes for local mean temperature increases of up to 1–3° C, but that productivity will decrease with larger temperature increases. At lower latitudes, especially in seasonally dry and tropical regions, crop productivity will fall even if temperatures increase by only 1–2° C, exacerbating the risk of hunger.[69] For North America, the IPCC has projected that moderate climate change early this century will increase aggregate yields of rain-fed agriculture, but that crops near the warm end of their suitable range or dependent on highly utilized water resources are at risk.[70] Similarly, fisheries are likely to suffer as sea surface temperatures increase.

Climate change may exacerbate international conflicts and threaten national security. According to a group of retired U.S. military leaders, climate change acts as a "threat multiplier" in fragile regions because it may contribute to massive exiles from hard-hit areas such as low-elevation coastal areas, insurgencies, genocide, guerrilla attacks, and global terrorism.[71] Climate-related events have contributed to past violent conflicts. West Africa, the Nile Basin, and Central Asia are candidates for similar problems if climate change is not effectively addressed.[72] These kinds of social disruptions will likely extend beyond the areas in which they begin. They are likely to have ripple effects, so that even countries not directly affected by a particular aspect of climate change will have to address problems such as mass migrations, increases in terrorism, or disruptions in economic markets that originate elsewhere.

H.   Wildlife Effects

Wildlife, as well as people, is at risk from climate change, and the effects on wildlife could impact humans. Some animal species are already suffering the adverse effects of climate change. As the natural sea ice habitat of polar bears shrinks, more pregnant bears are giving birth on land. If ice continues to melt, pregnant bears foraging offshore will no longer be able to reach the coast in advance of denning. In the United States, Yellowstone grizzlies are at risk. Whitebark pines, an essential source of food for these bears, have been infested by mountain pine beetles that thrive in warmer temperatures. Loss of the trees would threaten the bears' survival. Myriad changes of this sort are likely to occur as landscapes change in ways that make it difficult or impossible for dependent wildlife to adapt.

Adverse effects of climate change on wildlife may affect human food supplies. Scientists report that climate change has already negatively affected freshwater salmon habitat, and the habitat deterioration associated with climate change will hamper salmon recovery efforts, especially in relatively pristine, high-elevation streams.[73]

The effects of climate change on wildlife and their ecosystems may be more subtle but no less important. Oceanic absorption of CO_2 is causing water chemistry changes that could adversely affect corals, mollusks, and plankton and disrupt marine food webs. Warmer water killed about one-third of coral reefs at monitoring sites in the Caribbean in 2005, a death rate faster than would be attributable to natural fluctuations.[74] Some scientists attribute the extinction of harlequin frogs and golden toads in Costa Rica to global warming, though others disagree.[75] The proponents of this theory claim that rising sea surface and air temperatures caused by human-induced global warming facilitated the growth and spread of a pathogenic chytrid fungus, which killed the amphibians.[76] Scientists fear the first loss of an entire taxonomic class (amphibians) since the dinosaurs became extinct.[77]

The consequences of the loss of a single species, no less an entire taxonomic class, are impossible to predict. The elimination of even one species can cascade throughout an ecosystem. Predators of that species may find food to be scarcer, while the prey of the eliminated species may thrive. As much as one quarter of all of the species on earth could be at risk of extinction by 2050 due to climate change.[78] Species threats and losses are the proverbial canaries in the coal mine, warning us about the risks to other species, including humans, dependent on the altered ecosystems.

Conclusion

The science of climate change was not mature when the climate of ideas favored government intervention to protect the environment. As the science grew more certain, economic ideas favoring unrestrained markets and disfavoring government intervention made it impossible to make progress on the issue. Those fighting government intervention actively sought to exaggerate the uncertainties associated with climate change science. Unfortunately, climate change attributable to human activity has already begun. To a certain extent, further change is inevitable. But the degree to which climate change wreaks havoc in the long term on natural systems and peoples will largely depend on what society decides to do from this point on. As the *Stern Review* indicates, "there is still time to avoid the worst impacts of climate change, if we take strong action now."[79] But "our actions now and over the coming decades could create risks of major disruption to economic and social activity, on a scale similar to those associated with the great wars and the economic depression of the first half of the 20th century. And it will be difficult or impossible to reverse those changes."[80]

Notes

1. The 1970 Clean Air Act (CAA) Amendments' definition of an "air pollutant" has always been written broadly enough to encompass carbon dioxide and other greenhouse gases, as *Massachusetts v. EPA*, 127 S. Ct. 1438 (2007) has recently confirmed. But the Environmental Protection Agency in its early days was preoccupied with addressing the more visible and seemingly more pressing issues of ground-level pollution. In those days, it never seriously entertained the notion of deploying its CAA authority to tackle climate change, and by the time a consensus had formed around the seriousness of the problem, it had become a larger policy and political footnote than the agency was inclined to confront voluntarily.

2. See Lazarus, *The Making of Environmental Law* (Chicago: University of Chicago Press, 2004), for an excellent treatment of the shifting landscape in Washington on environmental issues. For a treatment of the broader shifts in politics and ideas that influenced the environmental legislative agenda but much more as well, see Thomas Edsall, *Building Red America* (New York: Basic Books, 2006), pp. 154–210.

3. See John Hibbing and Elizabeth Theiss-Morse, *Congress as Public Enemy* (New York: Cambridge University Press, 1998) (attributing much of the public's skepticism toward and disapproval of Congress to the fact that the fractious, argumentative, partisan squabbling that typifies much political debate are routinely on open display there).

4. Theodore Porter, *Trust in Numbers: The Pursuit of Objectivity in Science and Public Life* (Princeton: Princeton University Press, 1995), p. 210.

5. For some early influential expressions, see J. H. Dales, *Pollution, Property, and Prices* (Toronto: University of Toronto Press, 1968); William F. Baxter, *People or Penguins: The Case for Optimal Pollution* (New York: Columbia University Press, 1974); Charles Schultze, *The Public Use of the Private Interest* (Washington, D.C.: Brookings Institution, 1977).

6. John Kenneth Galbraith, *American Capitalism: The Concept of Countervailing Power* (Boston: Houghton Mifflin, 1952); John Kenneth Galbraith, *The New Industrial State* (Boston: Houghton Mifflin, 1967).

7. See, e.g., Robert L. Rabin, "Federal Regulation in Historical Perspective," *Stanford Law Review* 38 (1986), p. 1293: ("In the 1970s, big business was truly on the defensive as the public seemed responsive to a wide variety of concerns about the quality of life. An entire series of initiatives resulted—on auto safety, product design, air and water pollution control, scenic conservation, and occupational health and safety, to mention only the most significant—which manifested a distinct bias against economic growth. The political climate made it virtually impossible to oppose such programs in principle").

8. In the debate leading up to the Air Quality Control Act of 1967, for example, the coal coalition had been able to secure important concessions, and did not draw back from imposing government regulations aimed at improving environmental quality. See David Vogel, "A Case Study of Clean Air Legislation 1967–1981," in *The Impact of the Modern Corporation*, ed. Betty Bock et al. (New York: Columbia University Press, 1980), p. 326.

9. Special Message to the Congress on Urgent National Needs, May 25, 1961, http://www.jfklibrary.org/Historical+Resources/Archives/Reference+Desk/Speeches/.

10. The environmental movement benefited from the specific scientific achievements of space travel in a second way. The "blue marble" pictures of the earth taken from the early space flights provided dramatic visual confirmation of the earth as simultaneously a gorgeous and yet fragile place, reinforcing the call to action of the environmental movement.

11. Murray L. Weidenbaum and Robert DeFina, *The Cost of Federal Regulation of Economic Activity* (Washington, D.C.: American Enterprise Institute, May 1978), Reprint 88. At the time, Weidenbaum and DeFina were colleagues on the economics faculty of Washington University. The AEI pamphlet was actually preceded by a paper by DeFina, "Public and Private Expenditures for Federal Regulation of Business," St. Louis, November 1977, mimeo, Working Paper No. 27, Center for the Study of American Business, which first reported the $100 billion/year figure.

12. Robert Kuttner, *Everything for Sale: The Virtues and Limits of Markets* (1996), quoted in Edsall, *Building Red America*, pp. 195–196.

13. See, e.g., Vogel, "A Case Study of Clean Air Legislation," p. 339 ("[The 1977 clean air legislation was] the most aggressively lobbied and probably the most complex pieces [*sic*] of legislation approved by Congress in at least a quarter of a century.... By the mid-1970s, the enormous stakes involved in federal regulation of air pollution had become much more apparent than they were at the beginning of the decade.... For the companies regulated under the provisions of 1970 legislation, the 1977 amendments represented their first important opportunity to modify those particular aspects of the 1970 law, and its interpretation by EPA and the courts, that they regarded as unreasonable").

14. Ibid., pp. 348–350.

15. See Scott Barrett, *Environment and Statecraft* (Oxford: Oxford University Press, 2005), pp. 368–369.

16. George Pring, "The United States Perspective," in *Kyoto: From Principles to Practice*, ed. Peter Cameron and Donald Zillman (London: Kluwer Law International, 2001), p. 185.

17. See, e.g., Cass R. Sunstein, "Of Montreal and Kyoto: A Tale of Two Protocols," *Harvard Environmental Law Review* 1, no. 30 (2007): 31.

18. Pring, "The United States Perspective," p. 196.

19. WEFA, *Global Warming: The High Cost of the Kyoto Protocol* (1998), http://www.heartland.org/custom/semod_policybot/pdf/11399.pdf.

20. See http://gcrio.org/USCCAP/toc.html.

21. See John R. Justus and Susan R. Fletcher, *Global Climate Change: Major Scientific and Policy Issues* (CRS Report RL33602, August 11, 2006), p. 9:

On November 11, 2000, President Clinton issued a statement on "Meeting the Challenge of Global Warming" in response to the results of the report *Climate Change Impacts on the United States: The Potential Consequences of Climate Variability and Change*. In his statement, Clinton said his administration would promulgate new regulations for U.S. electric power plants, imposing emissions caps on sulphur, nitrogen oxides, mercury, and CO_2. He also called for establishment of a domestic emissions trading program and promised a continued U.S. leadership role in climate change to set an example for other industrialized countries. Clinton announced he would take such steps as necessary to keep the United States on target for meeting Kyoto Protocol goals, if certain concessions were made regarding international adoption of flexible mechanisms such as emissions trading, the clean development mechanism (CDM), credit for carbon sinks, and accountable, legally-binding, compliance mechanisms.

22. Ibid., p. 10.

23. Ross Gelbspan, *The Heat Is On: The High Stakes Battle Over Earth's Threatened Climate* (Reading, MA: Addison-Wesley, 1997), p. 100.

24. Ibid.

25. Ibid., p. 20.

26. *New York Times*, April 21, 1990, p. B4.

27. Reported in Ryan Meyer, "Intractable Debate: Why Congressional Hearings on Climate Fail to Advance Policy," *Perspectives in Public Affairs* 3 (2006): 85.

28. Frank Luntz, Luntz Research Corporation, *Straight Talk* (2002), p. 137, http://www.ewg.org/files/LuntzResearch_environment.pdf.

29. Gelbspan, *The Heat Is On* (1997), pp. 33–61. See also esp. p. 33 ("Over the last six years, the coal and oil industries have spent millions of dollars to wage a propaganda campaign to downplay the threat of climate change. Much of that money has gone to amplifying the views of about a half-dozen dissenting researchers, giving them a platform and a level of credibility in the public arena that is grossly out of proportion to their influence in the scientific community").

30. Ibid., pp. 63–83.

31. Ibid., pp. 57–58 ("The professional canon of journalistic fairness requires reporters who write about a controversy to present competing points of view. When the issue is of a political or social nature, fairness—presenting the most compelling arguments on both sides with equal weight—is a fundamental check on biased reporting. But this canon causes problems when it is applied to issues of science. It seems to demand that journalists present competing points of view on a scientific question as though they had equal scientific weight, when actually they do not").

32. See the preceding note.

33. Newsweek Poll conducted by Princeton Survey Research, August 1–2, 2007 ($N = 1002$, MoE ± 4), http://www.pollingreport.com/enviro.htm. Only 47 percent thought scientists mostly agreed.

34. Intergovernmental Panel on Climate Change (IPCC), *Climate Change 2007: The Physical Science Basis*, Contribution of Working Group I to the Fourth Assessment Report of the Intergovernmental Panel on Climate Change, ed. Susan Solomon et al., pp. 2–3, 5, 7, http://ipcc-wg1.ucar.edu/wg1/wg1-report.html (cited hereafter as IPCC 2007: Physical Science).

35. Ibid., p. 10. The British Government–sponsored report, *The Stern Review*, stated that "[a]n overwhelming body of scientific evidence indicates that the Earth's climate is rapidly changing, predominantly as a result of increases in greenhouse gases caused by human activity." Nicholas Stern, *The Economics of Climate Change: The Stern Review* (Cambridge: Cambridge University Press, 2007), p. 3 (cited hereafter as *Stern Review*).

36. IPCC 2007: Physical Science, p. 10.

37. IPCC, *Climate Change 2007: The Physical Science Basis*, Technical Summary, p. 68 (Feb. 2007), http://ipcc-wg1.ucar.edu/wg1/Report/AR4WG1_Print_TS.pdf (cited hereafter as IPCC 2007: Working Group I Technical Summary).

38. IPCC 2007: Physical Science, p. 68. See also United Nations Foundation, Sigma Chi, The Scientific Research Society, *Confronting Climate Change: Avoiding the Unmanageable and Managing the Avoidable* (Feb. 2007), p. 3, http://www.unfoundation.org/files/pdf/2007/SEG_ExecSumm.pdf (stating that "significant

harm from climate change is already occurring, and further damages are a certainty. The challenge now is to keep climate change from becoming a catastrophe"); *Stern Review*, p. 11 ("Additional warming is already in the pipeline due to past and present emissions").

39. IPCC 2007: Physical Science, p. 68.

40. IPCC, *Climate Change 2007: The Physical Science Basis*, Summary for Policymakers, p. 13 (Feb. 2007), http://ipcc-wg1.ucar.edu/wg1/Report/AR4WG1_Print_SPM.pdf (cited hereafter as IPCC 2007: Working Group I Policymakers Summary).

41. *Stern Review*, p. 2.

42. Ibid., p. iii.

43. IPCC 2007: Physical Science, p. 887.

44. Kristine L. Ebi et al., *Regional Impacts of Climate Change: Four Case Studies in the United States* (Dec. 2007), pp. 22–38, http://www.pewclimate.org/regional_impacts.

45. IPCC 2007: Working Group I Policymakers Summary, p. 13.

46. IPCC 2007: Physical Science, p. 68.

47. Ibid., p. 70.

48. IPCC 2007: Working Group I Policymakers Summary, p. 14.

49. Elizabeth A. Stanton and Frank Ackerman, *Florida and Climate Change: The Costs of Inaction* (Nov. 2007), p. v, http://www.ase.tufts.edu/gdae/Pubs/rp/FloridaClimate.html.

50. Peter C. Frumhoff et al., *Confronting Climate Change in the U.S. Northeast: Science, Impacts, and Solutions* (July 2007), p. xi, http://www.climatechoices.org/assets/documents/climatechoices/confronting-climate-change-in-the-u-s-northeast.pdf.

51. See Ebi et al., *Regional Impacts of Climate Change*, pp. 42–52; Stanton and Ackerman, *Florida and Climate Change*.

52. IPCC 2007: Working Group I Policymakers Summary, p. 14.

53. Intergovernmental Panel on Climate Change (IPCC), *Climate Change 2007: Impacts, Adaptation, and Vulnerability*, Contribution of Working Group II to the Fourth Assessment Report of the Intergovernmental Panel on Climate Change, edited by Martin L. Parry and Osvaldo Canziani, Summary for Policymakers (New York: Cambridge University Press, 2007), p. 3, http://www.ipcc-wg2.org (cited hereafter as IPCC 2007: Working Group II Policymakers Summary).

54. See Elisabeth Rosenthal, "As Earth Warms Up, Virus from Tropics Moves to Italy," *New York Times*, Dec. 23, 2007, p. 21 (nat'l. ed.).

55. Intergovernmental Panel on Climate Change (IPCC), *Climate Change 2007: Synthesis Report*, Contribution of Working Groups I, II, and III to the Fourth Assessment Report of the Intergovernmental Panel on Climate Change (Geneva: IPCC, 2007), http://www.ipcc.ch/pdf/assessment-report/ar4/syr/ar4_syr_spm.pdf (cited hereafter as IPCC 2007: Summary Synthesis Report).

56. Ebi et al., *Regional Impacts of Climate Change*, pp. 16–17.

57. See Union of Concerned Scientists, *How to Avoid Dangerous Climate Change: A Target for U.S. Emission Reductions* (Sept. 2007), p. 7, http://www.ucsusa.org/global_warming/science/emissionstarget.html (projecting a 70 percent increase in hazardous ozone days in North America if mean air temperatures increase by 2.5° C to 3.5° C).

58. See U.S. Environmental Protection Agency, *A Review of the Impact of Climate Variability and Change on Aeroallergens and Their Associated Effects*, 71 Fed. Reg. 78,432 (Dec. 29, 2006).

59. For discussion of the impact of climate change on infectious and respiratory diseases, see Center for Health and the Global Environment, Harvard Medical School, *Climate Change Futures: Health, Ecological, and Economic Dimensions* (ed. P. Epstein and E. Mills, Nov. 2005), pp. 32–52, http://www.climatechangefutures.org/report/index.html.

60. Association of Metropolitan Water Agencies, *Implications of Climate Change for Urban Water Utilities* (Dec. 2007), p. 9, http://www.docuticker.com/?p=18394.

61. The World Health Organization reported in 2005 that global warming during the previous 30 years directly contributed to 150,000 deaths annually worldwide. The culprits included heat waves that can cause heart failure or trigger crop failures that cause malnutrition, and climate fluctuations that alter the transmission of infectious diseases. See *Impact of Regional Climate Change on Human Health*, http://www.nature.com/nature/journal/v438/n7066/abs/nature04188.html.

62. *Stern Review*, p. 108.

63. See Andy Haines and Jonathan A. Patz, "Health Effects of Climate Change," *Journal of the American Medical Association* 291, no. 1 (2004): 99–103.

64. IPCC 2007: Working Group II Policymakers Summary, pp. 7–8.

65. Ibid., p. 7.

66. If global temperatures rise by 2 to 5° C over the next fifty years, cities such as New York, London, and Tokyo will be at high risk. *Stern Review*, Executive Summary, p. vi.

67. Ibid. About 200 million people live in coastal flood zones that are at risk. Ibid., p. 111.

68. David B. Lobell and Christopher B. Field, "Global Scale Climate-Crop Yield Relationships and the Impacts of Recent Warming," *Environmental. Research Letters* 2, no. 1 (March 2007): 1–7.

69. IPCC 2007: Working Group II Policymakers Summary, p. 6.

70. Ibid., p. 10.

71. See C. N. A. Corporation, *National Security and the Threat of Climate Change*, http://securityandclimate.cna.org/.

72. *Stern Review*, Executive Summary, p. viii.

73. See James Battin et al., "Projected Impacts of Climate Change on Salmon Habitat Restoration," *Proceedings of the. National Academy of Science* 104, no. 16 (Apr. 17, 2007): 6720–6725.

74. See R. A. Feely, Christopher L. Sabine, and Victoria J. Fabry, *The Pew Charitable Trust Science Brief: Carbon Dioxide and Our Ocean Legacy* (April 2006), http://www.pewtrusts.org/uploadedFiles/wwwpewtrustsorg/Reports/Global_warming/carbon_dioxide_ocean_legacy.pdf; J. A. Kleypas et al., *Impacts of Ocean Acidification on Coral Reefs and Other Marine Calcifiers: A Guide for Future Research* (June 2006), http://www.ucar.edu/news/releases/2006/report.shtml.

75. See, e.g., Andrew C. Revkin, "Link to Global Warming in Frogs' Disappearance Is Challenged," *New York Times*, Mar. 25, 2008; Karen R. Lips et al., "Riding the Wave: Reconciling the Roles of Disease and Climate Change in Amphibian Declines," *PLoS Biology* 6, no. 3 (March 2008), http://biology.plosjournals.org/perlserv?request=get-document&doi=10.1371%2Fjournal.pbio.0060072#special.

76. See J. Alan Pounds et al., "Widespread Amphibian Extinctions from Epidemic Disease Driven by Global Warming," *Nature* 439, no. 7073 (Jan. 12, 2006): 161–167.

77. See Joseph R. Mendelson, III, et al., "Confronting Amphibian Declines and Extinctions," *Science* 313, no. 5783 (July 7, 2006): 48 (stating that climate change may be encouraging conditions ideal for spread of fungus that kills amphibians).

78. Patrick O'Driscoll, "Animals Scramble as Climate Warms," *USA Today*, June 5, 2006. See also Jay R. Malcolm et al., "Global Warming and Extinctions of Endemic Species from Biodiversity Hotspots," *Conservation Biology* 20, no. 2 (April 2006): 538–548 (projecting the loss of as many as tens of thousands of hot-spot endemic plant and vertebrate species if CO_2 concentrations double).

79. *Stern Review*, p. vi.

80. Ibid.

2

Dirty Energy Policy

Joseph P. Tomain

Fossil fuel energy policy is a paradigmatic example of how an idea, a peculiar free market ideology, has captured U.S. politics and markets to the benefit of industry interests and to the detriment of environmentally sensitive and economically valuable alternatives. Neoliberal free market rhetoric has framed the debate about energy, and, consequently, about ensuing government institutions and policies, in terms of sustaining a healthy economy and protecting national security.[1] Government should support, and lightly regulate, fossil fuels, the argument goes, as good (and necessary) for our country to have and enjoy a healthy economy. More importantly, in a dangerous and troubled world, a sound fossil fuel policy is also necessary (and good) for our country's domestic and global security. In short, free market ideology, especially as employed by the fossil fuel industry, is insensitive to the economic dynamics that can stimulate innovation, open new markets, and bring new technologies online, which can respond to the challenges of climate change.

Fossil fuel favoritism has been the core concept in U.S. energy policy for over a century. Protection of oil, natural gas, and coal interests has resulted in increased greenhouse gas emissions while limiting the role of energy efficiency and renewable resources. Our nation's energy ideology focuses on solving energy problems by increasing the supply of fossil fuels and keeping the price of fossil fuels low through subsidies and other measures. Traditional energy policy is, thus, dependent on a well-worn path that produces dirty energy, discourages cleaner alternatives, and disadvantages the emergence of new markets and new technologies by tilting the economic playing field toward itself.

This chapter opens with a snapshot of our energy mix and its relationship to climate change. The chapter then demonstrates three propositions. First, free market rhetoric has been used to frame energy policy helpful to the fossil fuel industry and harmful to the environment. Second, the regulatory history of energy policy demonstrates how that rhetoric has been incorporated in laws, regulations, and political institutions such that energy policy has been dependent on a fossil fuel policy path for over a century. Third, framing rhetoric and path-dependency coalesce in a broad set of economic benefits flowing directly to the fossil fuel industry. Fossil fuel favoritism comes with two price tags—a dirty environment and a refusal to aggressively pursue a more economically dynamic, alternative energy policy that is responsive to the challenges of global warming.

I.   U.S. Energy Profile and Carbon Footprint

In the middle of the nineteenth century, the U.S. energy economy underwent a transition from whale oil and wood to fossil fuels, predominantly oil and coal. The dominant use of fossil fuels continues today. Consumption of energy in the United Sates is 100 quadrillion BTUs of energy per year, and fossil fuels account for 85 percent of that consumption comprising oil (40 percent), coal (23 percent), and natural gas (22 percent).[2]

The U.S. energy profile can be roughly divided between transportation and electricity, with coal and natural gas responsible for generating nearly three-quarters of the electricity. Oil dominates the transportation sector, while coal-fired electricity dominates residential, commercial, and industrial heating and cooling.

The figures about U.S. energy consumption and pollution are familiar. The United States has less than 5 percent of the world's population and consumes roughly 20 million barrels of oil per day. Our pollution profile is consistent with our consumption pattern. The United States consumes 25 percent[3] of the world's energy and generates 25 percent of its CO_2 emissions. The electricity industry accounts for 39 percent of those emissions and the transportation sector accounts for 33 percent.[4] Consequently, any program for reducing carbon emissions must address the amount of oil consumed by vehicles and the amount of coal burned to generate electricity.

II.   Protectionist Assumptions

Traditional energy policy has been framed by three assumptions, each of which purports to adhere to free market ideology, and all of which favor and protect fossil fuel interests. Policymakers have assumed that energy consumption correlates directly with economic growth, that big energy is better energy, and that private markets are efficient and hence preferable. Instead of sustaining truly free, competitive markets, these three assumptions led to an energy policy protective of the fossil fuel industry at the expense of the environment.

The most attractive assumption behind traditional energy policy is that there is a direct and positive correlation between energy consumption and economic growth—the more energy we use, the stronger our economy will be. This assumption has worked in the past as a national energy infrastructure was constructed and as the economy expanded. However, there is no invariable, direct, positive correlation between energy and the economy. Instead of resembling a straight-line graph that rises continually to the right so that economic growth accompanies energy production and consumption, the more realistic energy–economic relationship resembles a flattening S-curve, as shown in figure 2.1.[5] The curve flattens because no society can continue to consume its natural resources, produce harmful waste, and expect the economy to expand indefinitely. If energy production is left unregulated, the pollution that is generated will dampen the economy. The more realistic long-run curve will either flatten or, more likely, dip down revealing an eroding economy.

The second assumption is that bigger is better (and cheaper). This second assumption is based on the idea that economies of scale can reduce costs and, through increasing sales, profits will soar. It is cheaper, and

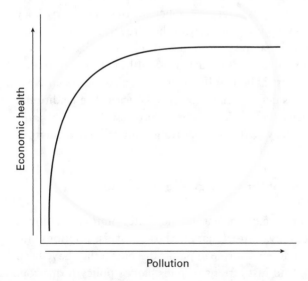

Figure 2.1

more profitable, to produce 10,000 barrels of oil than one barrel because exploration and drilling costs are spread more widely. It is cheaper to generate 1,000 megawatts of electricity for 1,000 homes than to have 1,000 homes each generate their own. Large-scale power plants, oil companies, coal mines, and natural gas pipelines and LNG ports can produce conventional fossil fuels at scale at a lower per unit cost than if the scales were reduced.

Like the first assumption, economies of scale have their limits. Power plants have an optimal size; electricity generation can be greatly reduced in scale and distributed more closely to its customers; cars can realize improving fuel economies; and, selling energy efficiency as a product is continually becoming more profitable.[6]

The final assumption is that private markets and private investments are efficient and, therefore, are the preferred method for social ordering and for determining which goods and services are bought and sold in markets. This masks the historic role that governmental largesse has played in creating and sustaining the fossil fuel industry. What is egregiously wrong with such free market rhetoric is that it was almost never true for fossil fuels. Oil and natural gas companies, as well as electric utilities and coal companies, have greatly benefited from government-established energy policies in a variety of ways that will be demonstrated below.

Combined, the assumptions have been extremely powerful. They have framed the debate and analysis of energy policy for over a century. They have led to the creation of energy industries that are large-scale, capital-intensive, national and global in scope, and centralized. And, the government is a full partner in supporting a fossil-fuel-heavy energy policy. The framing assumptions make it difficult to recognize the social costs of pollution and to consider alternative energy policies. The traditional assumptions with their free market rhetoric have established a path-dependent energy economy with its supporting political and regulatory structure.

III.   Regulatory History of Dirty Energy—1859 to 1980

Throughout most of the twentieth century, the United States has enjoyed a healthy energy economy. Unfortunately, those past assumptions not only continue to play a dominant role in public discourse; they have been embedded in the laws and institutions responsible for policy formation.

Traditional or hard path[7] energy policy makes path-dependency easy and puts new policy formation at a disadvantage.

Federal administrative regulations in the first half of the twentieth century favored fossil fuels. The U.S. Fuel Administration was created to promote oil for use in World War I; the Federal Oil Conservation Board was created to stabilize prices in the 1920s; and, the Petroleum Administration for War and the Solid Fuels Administration for War promoted the use of oil and coal respectively in World War II.[8]

In the early decades, state oil regulations affected the industry most directly and were designed to keep the industry healthy by not allowing too much oil into the market at any one time. In the 1930s, as flush fields were discovered in Louisiana, Texas, and Oklahoma, oil prices fell to less than 10 cents per barrel. Through conservation and market demand regulations, states were able to control the supply of oil by limiting the amount of oil that could be produced and placed on the market, thus maintaining prices. Additionally, state regulations attempted to preserve property rights through proration and unitization rules intended to reduce the incentive of any one owner to drain fields of oil lying under the lands of other surface owners. These state regulations protected oil interests by keeping prices propped up and protected states' interests by keeping oil revenues and taxes flowing. During this period, the federal government complemented state regulations with the passage of the Interstate Oil Compact in 1935, which was an agreement among seven oil-producing states to conserve the resource and avoid waste.

In 1948, oil imports exceeded oil exports for the first time and the alarm was sounded on energy independence. To protect domestic oil producers against cheap foreign oil, in 1959, the Eisenhower administration enacted the Mandatory Oil Import Program, which limited the amount of oil imported into the United States and thus subsidized domestic producers by keeping prices artificially high in the name of national security. The MOIP is just the first in a series of oil independence strategies, none of which have had any impact in reducing oil imports or oil consumption.

As domestic oil reserves decrease and as world prices rise, there is pressure on the industry to search for oil in new places, including public lands. The U.S. government owns approximately one-third of all lands in the country and over one-half of the lands west of the Mississippi River, including the outer continental shelf. The development of public lands for oil is governed through a series of statues that regulate the leasing, exploration, and extraction of resources on those lands.[9]

Recent debates about drilling in the Arctic National Wildlife Refuge (ANWR) highlight the central problem. These federally owned lands, together with the natural resources on them, are held in the public trust. The difficulty is that there is no single public interest in those lands. Some lands are preserved as wilderness, others are held for recreation, and others are leased for the minerals, timber, grazing grasses, fossil fuels, and the other minerals they contain. Consequently, as our need for energy resources continues and grows, federal lands look more and more attractive to energy producers. Although conservation interests have thwarted drilling in the ANWR so far, government has frequently allowed drilling on public lands with less visibility.

IV.   Regulatory History of Dirty Energy—1980 to the Present

In the last third of the twentieth century, energy industries, including fossil fuel industries, confronted a series of challenges. Energy prices were no longer reliably low; energy supplies were no longer so easy to locate; and environmental costs were painfully apparent. Nevertheless, our fossil-fuel-dominant energy policy remained resistant to change even as a new, more responsive, twenty-first-century energy policy was being discussed.[10]

Twenty-first-century energy policy has its roots in the closing decades of the previous century. In 1977, the Department of Energy (DOE) was established[11] as an umbrella office for multiple federal energy agencies and programs. The DOE, particularly through its Energy Information Administration, coordinates energy research and reporting but leaves policy largely unaffected. The DOE drafts energy messages to Congress, reports annually on the state of our energy economy, and makes projections about future energy needs and resources, yet has no authority to coordinate planning across energy industries.

During the Carter administration, two major pieces of energy legislation were passed, the National Energy Act (NEA) and the Energy Security Act (ESA).[12] The ESA was aimed at moving energy policy away from the conventional energy resources of oil, coal, natural gas, and nuclear power to alternative and renewable resources. The act never achieved its goals. The major provision in that legislation was the creation of the U.S. Synfuels Corporation for the development of synthetic fuels that would extract oil and gas from coal, oil shale, and tar sands. These "alternatives" were simply exotic fossil fuel substitutes for conventional fossil fuels and did nothing to move the country away from a fossil-fuel-dominated energy policy. More spectacularly, the Synfuels Corporation was an $88 billion failure, as Congress finally recognized when it abolished this corporation after six years of operation. Synfuels were simply too expensive to make, so we reverted to using conventional fossil fuels. Today, as oil prices escalate, synfuels development is back in the news. The ESA was also intended to stimulate greater use of renewable alternative resources such as solar, wind, biomass, and geothermal while making conservation an active part of our energy planning. Although the Act created an awareness of these resources, vigorous markets did not develop and renewable resources made little contribution to the energy mix.

The Carter energy legislation did not achieve long-term oil independence, did not coordinate energy policies, did not open alternative markets, and did not stimulate an energy transition from conventional to alternative fuels. Carter's ambition faltered because his innovative approach to energy went contrary to the country's already path-dependent model of energy policy and contrary to the market. The market, with regulatory assistance, controlled and supported the production and consumption of fossil fuels. The hoped-for transition failed because our reliance on government-supported fossil fuel markets did not send proper long-term price signals to consumers.

The next significant legislation, the Energy Policy Act of 1992 (EPAct 1992), smoothed out some rough bumps in the previous legislation and was intended to be a response to the 1970s energy crisis by reducing our country's growing dependence on foreign oil. The act removed some of the impediments to investment in electric power and furthered the development of new sources of electricity generation that began under the National Energy Act. The 1992 act also continued natural gas deregulation, provided tax relief to independent oil and gas producers and to synfuels producers, streamlined nuclear power regulation, authorized research into clean coal technologies, and initiated production tax credits for wind and biomass while extending production tax credits for solar and geothermal power. Yet, even with provisions for alternative and renewable resources, EPAct 1992 was heavily protective of fossil fuels.

The NEA, ESA, and EPAct 1992 were the precursors of the first energy legislation of the new century—the Energy Policy Act of 2005 and the Energy Independence and Security Act of 2007. Both acts largely continue traditional energy policies. Vice President Cheney's *National Energy Policy* (NEP), published in 2001, formed the basis for EPAct 2005. The NEP addressed the urgent need for more energy production, arguing that we are facing the most significant energy shortage since the mid-1970s and that we will need a 32 percent increase in energy production by 2020.[13] The NEP also emphasized the preference for private sector energy production, the need for more oil refineries, the possibility of drilling in the ANWR, and the need for an improved electricity infrastructure. The NEP also spoke about the need for more nuclear power while giving a nod to conservation and to alternative and renewable energy resources.

Upon signing EPAct 2005 into law, President Bush explicitly emphasized the key economic assumption behind traditional energy policy—the more energy we consume, the healthier our economy will be "so people can realize their dreams."[14] The traditional economic assumption about a direct energy–economy link contained in EPAct 2005 shows no awareness of the need for a more dynamic energy policy in the face of climate change.

EPAct 2005 stayed true to traditional energy policies, and although it does not authorize drilling in the ANWR, it streamlines nuclear power plant licensing and construction, allows for the fast tracking of liquid natural gas (LNG) facilities, promotes clean coal projects, and mandates a survey for the outer continental shelf for further oil and gas exploration and production. EPAct 2005 significantly loosened restrictions on electric utilities, which has enabled greater industry concentration.[15] While industry restructuring has been stalled,[16] electricity prices remain high[17] and greater coal consumption is anticipated with the expansion of production.

President Bush had a post-Katrina opportunity to address energy once again and he did so in his 2006 State of the Union message. The message seemingly paid significant attention to the new energy thinking by recommending investment in zero emission coal technologies as well as investments in solar and wind power. The message also recommended increased R&D funding for hybrid cars, batteries, and ethanol so that we can begin to wean ourselves from oil imports. This message was not followed up with hard investments. If we go inside the numbers of the State of the Union, we find that its total estimated investment would be about $236 million or 1/40th of the $10.8 billion *quarterly* profit that Exxon enjoyed in 2007. The energy message also recommended research and development of new batteries and earmarked the miserly sum of $6.7 million for such investment.[18]

In his 2007 State of the Union Address, President Bush continued the new energy rhetoric saying we must reduce gasoline use 20 percent, thus cutting Middle East oil imports by 75 percent.[19] Yet, since that speech, we have done nothing to implement a transition to less dirty fuels. Not only do we continue to depend on Middle East oil, our wealth transfer to that part of the globe is staggering. With oil selling at over $90 a barrel, there is a wealth transfer from the United States to the Middle East of about $90 million per day or over a quarter of a trillion dollars per year.

On December 19, 2007, President Bush signed the Energy Independence and Security Act at the instigation of the Democrat-controlled Congress. The act does move the needle toward an alternative policy. The act requires fuel producers to use at least 36 billion gallons of biofuels in 2022. Oil demand is intended to be reduced by setting national fuel economy standards at 35 miles per gallon by 2020. This is the first fuel economy increase since 1975. The act also includes provisions to improve energy efficiency in lighting standards in federal buildings and setting new, higher efficiency appliance standards.

V. Fossil Fuel Favors

There are a variety of financial benefits flowing to the fossil fuel industry. From direct subsidies[20] to lax enforcement, fossil fuel interests enjoy notable financial advantages over new energy entrants that are attempting to respond to climate change challenges. Quantifying the dollar value of subsidies is extremely difficult, if not impossible.[21] There are direct and indirect subsidies, which do not lend themselves to a common metric. Further, there is no single source, government or private, to find accurate and reliable data. Consequently, this section presents a rough catalog of those incumbent benefits.

A. EPAct 2005
The energy funding in EPAct 2005 is tilted heavily in favor of fossil fuels despite the calls for new initiatives favoring new energy sources. The text of EPAct 2005 itself stated that it would provide $14.5 billion for energy industries.[22] A House Minority Report indicated that 85 percent of the $14.5 billion would go to oil, coal, and nuclear power.[23] Other commentators confirm the House Report.[24] Production tax credits for wind, geothermal, and some types of biomass fuel, established in the EPAct 1992, apply only to projects that are online before January 1, 2008, and were not extended in EPAct 2005,[25] although they have been renewed in the past.

Going inside the numbers also reveals the Washington game of "authorization versus appropriation." A statute can "authorize" any amount of funding, but those monies never reach the hands of intended recipients unless Congress later "appropriates" the funds for the targeted purposes. By way of example, EPAct 2005 "authorized" about $300 million for photovoltaic programs, but as of February 2007 no funds had been appropriated. By contrast, EPAct 2005 provided for over $1.5 billion in tax credits for coal gasification projects and received requests for over $2.7 billion that are being processed.[26]

EPAct 2005 also contains hidden subsidies, such as authorization for the Secretary of the Department of Interior to forgive royalty payments to oil and gas exploration companies, which have notoriously avoided paying royalties in the past.[27] This point will be developed below. EPAct authorizes the Department of the Interior to map outer continental shelf lands for leasing, exploration, and production, thereby aiding private oil companies' efforts to explore for oil. The Federal Energy Regulatory Commission is given siting jurisdiction over LNG plants, thereby taking away regulatory review from state and local governments. Coal technologies are subsidized at over $2 billion for the Clean Coal Power Initiative and $2.5 billion for the Clean Air Coal Program while expanding coal leasing opportunities on federal lands.[28]

B. Coal

Coal is the country's second largest fossil fuel in the energy sector: it dominates electricity production, and it is responsible for about 10 percent of global CO_2 emissions. The coal industry is different from and is differently regulated than the oil industry. Where the oil industry is dominated by a handful of integrated, international firms, the coal industry comprises hundreds of coal producers operating about 2,000 mines. Where oil regulations were driven by economic concerns about quantity and price, coal regulations are concerned with health, safety, and the environment.

The Clean Air Act aims at managing and reducing air emissions from the coal burned in electric power plants. The Surface Mining and Reclamation Control Act, as its name indicates, aims at protecting the land from damaging surface mining through returning the land to its original contour and conditions before the mining began. The Clean Water Act is intended to protect streams and valleys from harmful discharge in coal mining processes. And health laws, such as the Black Lung Act, are intended to protect miners from or compensate them for the damages that they suffer.

The coal industry has been the beneficiary of a great amount of at best benign, but nevertheless profitable, neglect. All of the above cited regulations have been underenforced. Lands are not fully reclaimed, reclamation standards were relaxed during the Bush II administration, streams and valleys continue to receive the detritus from nearby coal mines, the industry continues to fight the imposition of the clean air standards,[29] and miners continue to work in unsafe conditions, as the recent tragedies in the Crandall Canyon and Sago mines attest.

C. Oil Taxes and Accounting[30]

Energy tax policy follows energy politics. For most of the twentieth century, tax policy favored the exploration, production, and distribution of oil and natural gas resources and did nothing to encourage conservation or renewable resources. The most notable tax incentive for the oil industry has been the oil depletion allowance, which allows an oil company to deduct all or part of its mineral investment. The depletion allowance was based on the idea that since oil is a wasting resource, then a tax break can be used to compensate for, and encourage, that investment. The counterargument is that other businesses treat such investment as an understandable business risk that is built into their price structure and investment policy. Depletion rules operated in such a way that under the proper circumstances, depletion deductions could exceed the original cost of investment. The depletion allowance reduced tax liability for oil companies in a greater measure than allowed in other business firms.

Another financial incentive was to allow oil and gas producers to treat drilling costs, such as labor, materials, supplies, and repairs as expenses. Expenses could be deducted in the year in which they are incurred instead of capitalizing them and writing them down over a period of years as other businesses do. In this way these "intangible drilling costs" were recouped in the first year, leaving more capital available for other investments. Both devices reduced the tax liability of oil companies to such an extent that, combined, these tax subsidies have resulted in little or no income tax for much of the petroleum industry.

D. The Oil Royalty Treatment

There are tens of thousands of oil and gas leases on public lands both onshore and offshore, which account for about 35 percent of the oil and 26 percent of the natural gas produced in the United States. In exchange for the opportunity to develop public lands and produce oil and natural gas, the lease holder is obligated to pay royalties, sometimes as much as 18 percent, into the U.S. Treasury. Royalty payments, however, have been less than reliable.

In the mid-1990s, by way of example, petroleum engineers discovered a conspiracy by several oil companies to depress the value of oil and then understate the total amount of royalties owed to the United States. A *qui tam* whistleblower lawsuit was filed under the False Claims Act against a dozen oil companies in Texas alleging that the oil companies underpaid royalties from 1980 through 1998. The prosecution of the suit resulted in payments in excess of $450 million.[31] It has been estimated that oil companies underpaid the Treasury approximately $500 million annually.[32]

In response to those estimates, Congress passed legislation that established the Minerals Management Service (MMS) within the Department of Interior to oversee royalty payments. The MMS, however, has come under Congressional and public criticism, which resulted in an internal investigation revealing lax royalty enforcement to the benefit of the oil industry. Recently, the Office of the Inspector General of the Minerals Management Service released a report on False Claims Act allegations that were filed by employees and former employees of MMS against their own department.[33] The report chronicles the allegations by the employees, as well as the claims of retaliation against them for their whistleblowing. The Inspector General wrote that the Mineral Management Program within MMS is "fraught with difficulties," including "the bureau's conflicting roles and relationships with the energy industry" which contributed to a "profound failure" to hold "together one of the Federal Government's largest revenue producing operations."[34] By way of one example, the MMS did not automatically calculate interest owed on the royalty payments but relied instead on the oil companies' own calculations.

In their *qui tam* suits, MMS employees, frequently auditors in the field, alleged that oil companies underreported royalties owed and underpaid interest payments. One employee's lawsuit claimed that the oil company would sell oil to a marketing company at a reduced price in exchange for marketing services. The oil company, in turn, would use the reduced price without including the value of the marketing services to calculate the royalties owed to the United States. A week after the lawsuit became public, the employee lost his job because of a "departmental reorganization."

In another case, the employees charged that the oil companies routinely underreported interest payments and that when the MMS employees reported the underpayments to their supervisors, the supervisors refused to take action. These complaining employees were removed from their jobs at MMS and were given below-entry-level positions at the Bureau of Land Management, another Interior Department agency.

The Inspector General's report does not calculate the amount of royalties possibly lost as much as it reveals the agency's failure to clearly define and fulfill its mission. An earlier report suggested that the government might lose about $10 billion over a decade just because of a legal mistake in oil and gas leases that had been ignored.[35] Consistent with the Inspector General's report was a 2006 IG audit that revealed that MMS did not have an effective compliance system, which prevented it from fully determining the costs and benefits of compliance reviews.[36] Given both reports, it is clear that MMS is dysfunctional and that the dysfunction benefits fossil fuel interests.

Conclusion

Oddly, neoliberalism has supported fossil fuel favoritism, with fossil fuel's dominance being viewed as somehow natural, in spite of the strong tradition of active government support for it. The assumptions that increased energy consumption is key to economic growth, that bigger is better, and that private markets should dominate social ordering have provided powerful neoliberal framing that supports unsustainable reliance on fossil fuels. This neoliberal framing has prevented dynamic economic change aimed at replacing fossil fuels with energy efficiency and renewables from gaining much traction.

Notes

1. See, e.g., *"Set America Free": A Blueprint for U.S. Energy Security* (policy position statement, Set America Free, coalition of national security interest groups), http://www.setamericafree.org/blueprint.pdf.

2. Energy Information Administration and U.S. Department of Energy, *Annual Energy Review 2006* (Washington, DC: GPO, June 2007), p. 8, http://www.eia .doe.gov/aer/pdf/aer.pdf.

3. Energy Information Agency, U.S. Department of Energy, International Energy Annual 2004, "World Primary Energy Production, 1980–2004" (July 2006), http://www.eia.doe.gov/pub/international/iealf/tablef1.xls.

4. Michael B. Gerrard, ed., *Global Climate Change and U. S. Law* (Chicago: ABA Publishing, 2007), pp. 8–9.

5. See e.g., Herman E. Daly, "Economics in a Full World," *Scientific American* 293, no. 3 (2005): 100–107, 100; Amory B. Lovins, *Soft Energy Paths: Toward a Durable Peace* (Cambridge, MA: Ballinger Publishing, 1977), chaps. 1–2.

6. See Daniel C. Esty and Andrew S. Winston, *Green to Gold: How Smart Companies Use Environmental Strategy to Innovate, Create Value, and Build Competitive*

Advantage (New Haven, CT: Yale University Press, 2006); Worldwatch Institute, *2008 State of the World: Innovations for a Sustainable Economy* (New York: W. W. Norton, 2008).

7. Lovins, *Soft Energy Paths*, chap. 2.

8. See John G. Clark, *Energy and the Federal Government: Fossil Fuel Policies, 1900–1946* (Urbana: University of Illinois Press, 1987).

9. See Mineral Lands Leasing Act of 1920, 30 U.S.C. §1331 *et seq.*; Mineral Leasing Act of Acquired Lands, 30 U.S.C. §351 *et seq.*; Outer Continental Shelf Lands Act, 43 U.S.C. §1331 *et seq.*

10. See, e.g., National Commission on Energy Policy, *Ending the Energy Stalemate: A Bipartisan Strategy to Meet America's Energy Challenges* (Washington, D.C.: National Commission on Energy Policy, 2004), http://www.energycommission.org/ht/a/GetDocumentAction/i/1088; William J. Clinton Presidential Foundation, Energy Forum, *New Thinking on Energy Policy*, http://www.clintonfoundation.org/120604-nr-cf-gn-env-usa-fe-new-thinking-on-energy-policy.htm; Energy Future Coalition, *Challenge and Opportunity: Charting a New Energy Future* (Washington, D.C.: Energy Future Coalition), http://www.energyfuturecoalition.org/pubs/EFCReport.pdf; Center for American Progress, *Progressive Priorities: An Action Agenda for America* (Washington, D.C.: Center for American Progress, 2005), http://www.americanprogress.org/projects/progressivepriorities/prog_priorities.pdf.

11. Department of Energy Organization Act, 42 U.S.C. § 7101 *et seq.*

12. National Energy Act, P.L. 95-618 (1978); Energy Security Act, P.L. 96-294 (1980).

13. National Energy Policy Development Group, *National Energy Policy* (Washington, D.C.: The White House, May 2001), p. 1-1.

14. See White House Press Release, "President Signs Energy Policy Act," Oct. 8, 2005, http://www.whitehouse.gov/news/releases/2005/08/20050808-6.html.

15. See, e.g., Richard D. Cudahy, "Deregulation and Mergers: Is Consolidation Inevitable?" *Public Utilities Fortnightly* (Oct. 15, 1996): 46, http://www.pur.com/pubs/1921.cfm; Richard Stavros, "Merger Frenzy," *Public Utilities Fortnightly* (Apr. 2007): 22.

16. The main culprits in frustrating the deregulation of the electric industry are the Enron scandal, the California energy crisis of the summer of 2000, and the Northeast blackout in August 2003. See, e.g., Sidney A. Shapiro and Joseph P. Tomain, "Rethinking Reform of Electricity Markets," *Wake Forest Law Review* 40 (2005): 497–543.

17. David Cay Johnston, "Competitive Era Fails to Shrink Electric Bills," *New York Times*, Oct. 15, 2006.

18. See David B. Sandalow, "President Bush and Oil Addiction," Feb. 3, 2006, http://brookings.edu/views/op-ed/fellows/sandalow_20060203.htm.

19. White House, "State of the Union 2006," Jan. 31, 2006, http://www.whitehouse.gov/stateoftheunion/2006; White House, "State of the Union 2007," Jan. 23, 2007, http://www.whitehouse.gov/stateoftheunion/2007.

20. See generally, Norman Myers and Jennifer Kent, *Perverse Subsidies: How Tax Dollars Can Undercut the Environment and the Economy* (Washington, D.C.: Island Press, 2001), pp. 5–9.

21. Compare Douglas Koplow and Aaron Martin, *Fueling Global Warming: Federal Subsidies to Oil in the United States* (Cambridge, MA: Greenpeace, 1998), http://archive.greenpeace.org/climate/oil/fdsuboil.pdf (oil subsidies in 1995 amount to between $15.7 and $35.2 billion); and Ronald J. Sutherland, *"Big Oil" at the Public Trough?: An Examination of Petroleum Subsidies* (Cato Institute: February 1, 2001), http://www.cato.org/pubs/pas/pa-390es.html (oil industry not a beneficiary of subsidies).

22. Energy Policy Act of 2005, 42 U.S.C. §§101–237.

23. House Committee on Government Reform, Minority Staff Special Investigations Division, *Flash Report: Key Impacts of the Energy Bill—H.R. 6* (Washington, D.C.: GPO, July 2005), http://oversight.house.gov/documents/20050726164801-76366.pdf; see also Robert L. Bamberger and Carl E. Behrens, *Energy Policy: Comprehensive Energy Legislation (H.R. 6, S. 10) in the 109th Congress* (Washington, D.C.: Library of Congress, Congressional Research Service, July 29, 2005).

24. Jonathan D. Salant, "U.S. Energy Industry's Lobbying Pays Off with $11.6 Bln in Aid," *Bloomberg News,* July 27, 2005, http://www.bloomberg.com/apps/news?pid=10000103&sid=agbeVimf04Ec&refer=us; U.S. PIRG and Friends of the Earth, *Final Energy Tax Package Overwhelmingly Favors Polluting Industries* (Washington, D.C., July 27, 2005).

25. Energy Information Administration, U.S. Department of Energy, *Annual Energy Outlook 2007: With Projections to 2030* (Washington, D.C.: GPO, February 2007), p. 16.

26. Ibid., pp. 18–19.

27. See Edmund L. Andrews, "U.S. Drops Bid Over Royalties from Chevron," *New York Times,* Oct. 31, 2006; Edmund L. Andrews, "U.S. Agency To Review Oil Royalties," *New York Times,* Nov. 2, 2006; Edmund L. Andrews, "House Votes to Rescind Oil Drillers' Tax Breaks," *New York Times,* Jan. 19, 2007.

28. See Kevin J. McIntyre, Martin V. Kirkwood, and Jason F. Leif, eds., *Energy Policy Act of 2005: Summary and Analysis of the Act's Major Provisions,* §1.4 (Newark, N.J.: Matthew Bender, 2006).

29. See *Environmental Defense Fund v. Duke Energy Corp.,* 127 S.Ct. 1423 (2007); see also Consent Decree, *United States v. Am. Elec. Power Serv. Corp.,* No. C2-99-1250 (S. D. Ohio Oct. 9, 2007) ($4.6 billion settlement of Clean Air Act "new source review" standards litigation between the U.S. Environmental Protection Agency, nine states, and seven utilities).

30. See Mona Hymel, "The United States' Experience with Energy-Based Tax Incentives: The Evidence Supporting Tax Incentives for Renewable Energy," *Loyola University Chicago Law Journal* 38 (2006): 43–80; Salvatore Lazzari, *Issue Brief for Congress: Energy Tax Policy,* Congressional Research Service Report, No. IB10054 (April 22, 2005), http://kuhl.house.gov/UploadedFiles/

energy%20tax.pdf; Salvatore Lazzari, *Issue Brief for Congress: Energy Tax Policy: An Economic Analysis*, Congressional Research Service, No. RL30406 (June 28, 2005), http://cnie.org/NLE/CRSreports/05jun/RL30406.pdf.

31. See, e.g., *United States ex rel. Johnson v. Shell Oil Co.*, 33 F.Supp.2d 528 (E.D. Tex. 1999); see also a brief description of the case by one of the law firms involved in the suit at Helmer, Martins, Rice & Popham, "Several Major Oil Companies Repay Royalties Owed to United States of Nearly One Half Billion Dollars," http://www.fcalawfirm.com/cases/case003.html (last visited Apr. 14, 2008).

32. See, e.g., Jan Laitos et al., *Natural Resources Law* (St. Paul, MN: Thompson West, 2006), pp. 991–992.

33. Office of the Inspector General, Department of the Interior, *Investigative Report, Minerals Management Service: False Claims Allegations* (September 7, 2007), http://www.doioig.gov/upload/Qui%20tam.pdf.

34. See transmittal letter filed with the Investigative Report, Memorandum from Inspector General Earl E. Devaney to Secretary Dirk Kempthorne, Sept. 19, 2007, Washington, D.C., http://www.doioig.gov/upload/Qui%20tam.pdf.

35. See Edmund L. Andrews, "Inspector Finds Broad Failures in Oil Program," *New York Times*, Sept. 26, 2007.

36. Department of the Interior, Office of Inspector General, *Audit Report: Mineral Management Service's Compliance Review Process*, Report No. C-IN-MMS-0006-2006 (December 6, 2006).

3

Cost-Benefit Analysis of Climate Change: Where It Goes Wrong

Frank Ackerman

While the climate science debate is approaching closure on the big questions, the climate *economics* debate is just beginning. Doubt or uncertainty about the science is no longer important in shaping public policy; the influence of the climate skeptics is rapidly diminishing. Instead, the divisive issue now is the fear that vigorous climate initiatives could hurt the economy—a fear that is implicitly endorsed by many mainstream economists.

The alleged danger is that we might do "too much" to reduce emissions, resulting in costs that would outweigh some economists' estimates of the benefits. As President George W. Bush said in 2005, "Kyoto would have wrecked our economy. I couldn't in good faith have signed Kyoto."[1] This fear has had bipartisan support: Bush was echoing the conclusion of a 1998 study by the Department of Energy's Energy Information Administration (EIA), which projected that the moderate emission reductions called for by the Kyoto Protocol could result in losses of up to 4 percent of U.S. gross domestic product (GDP).[2] The EIA analysis was based on conventional cost-benefit analyses of climate policy, and was reviewed by some of the most prominent economists in the field.

The Kyoto analyses were not an aberration. Many economists have achieved a breathtaking timidity in the face of the climate crisis. For example, Yale economist William Nordhaus, the best-known economist writing about climate change today, pays lip service to scientists' calls for decisive action. He finds, however, that the "optimal" policy is a very small carbon tax that would reduce emissions only 25 percent below "business as usual" levels by 2050—in other words, allowing emissions to rise to almost double the 1990 level by mid-century.[3] (In contrast, several European governments and U.S. states have called for reductions of 50 percent to 80 percent below 1990 levels by 2050.) Yale economist Sheila Olmstead and Harvard economist Robert Stavins deem the Kyoto Protocol "deeply flawed" and recommend instead that we allow emissions to rise for a few decades before requiring any reductions.[4] AEI-Brookings economist Robert Hahn, MIT economists Paul Joskow and Richard Schmalensee, and others, filed a legal brief before the Supreme Court—funded by automobile dealers associations across the country—opposing EPA regulation of carbon emissions from automobiles, claiming that such regulation would be expensive and inefficient.[5] Antienvironmental gadfly Bjørn Lomborg endorses the guess by Richard Tol, a widely published European climate economist, that the optimal tax on carbon dioxide emissions is a mere $2 per ton.[6]

These recommendations, and similar ones from other economists, rest on a series of errors. High discount rates, standard in economics, trivialize harms occurring in the future: at a 6 percent discount rate, it is not even "worth" spending $3 today to prevent $1000 of damages 100 years from now. Dubious hypotheses about the advantages of global warming have crept into the models; Nordhaus assumes, for example, that rich Northern countries will experience warmer weather as a valuable subjective benefit, offsetting some of the real damages from climate change.[7] An abstract, unrealistic theory of efficiency is still widely used to attack commonsense regulation of auto emissions and much more.[8] The inescapable uncertainty about the tipping point for catastrophic changes is replaced by "best guess" estimates about future growth and how to increase it. Put enough of these assumptions together, and the problem threatens to disappear: the combination of high discount rates and hypothesized near-term benefits would, indeed, make the optimal carbon tax appear to be close to zero. Tol's $2 per ton of carbon dioxide would raise gasoline prices by all of $0.02 per gallon, an increase that would not make the oil industry lose any sleep—or make the world lose any noticeable quantity of emissions.

New debate over climate economics erupted in late 2006 with the *Stern Review*, a report to the British government prepared by former World Bank economist Nicholas Stern. In his review, Stern found that the damages expected from business as usual would be many times more expensive than the costs of a dramatic reduction in carbon emissions. Although it is a ponderous and imperfect document, the *Stern Review* clearly demonstrates that economic judgments of climate change are strongly dependent on a handful of key assumptions, such as the choice of a discount rate and the treatment of uncertainty. Many economists, deeply committed to their own questionable assumptions on these issues, were quick to criticize and reject Stern's findings.

Lost in the debate was the need for a new approach that goes forward, not backward, from Stern's efforts. A credible climate economics, one that is in tune with the increasingly ominous scientific understanding of the problem, requires an understandable, comprehensive alternative to the narrow cost-benefit techniques and passive conclusions of "economics as usual."

This chapter has three sections:

• a discussion of William Nordhaus's DICE model, the best-known of the conventional cost-benefit analyses of climate change;
• a comparison with the economic analysis of the *Stern Review*, focusing on the reasons for Stern's different findings; and
• suggestions for construction of a better approach to climate economics.

I. DICE Games[9]

DICE presents a good example of the conventional approach to climate economics. To perform a cost-benefit analysis, it is necessary to project costs and benefits over a century or more. Thus a linked economic–environmental model is needed. DICE combines a simplified climate model with a standard economic growth model (see diagram in figure 3.1). Neither of these models, on its own, produces unusual or exceptional results. Rather, the questionable assumptions enter in the features that link and govern these submodels: the damage function (feedback of environment onto economy); the abatement cost function (feedback of economy onto environment); and the discount rate (a key to the optimization process, indirectly setting priorities for the model and for public policy).[10] These features cannot be confirmed by empirical data; instead, theorizing and guesswork inevitably shape the crucial features of the model. Damages are subject to considerable uncertainty, and frequently cannot be given meaningful monetary values. Costs of abatement depend on hypotheses about the dynamics of technological change, which can have perverse effects on the model's recommendations. Overall, the results are extremely sensitive to untestable input assumptions; equally plausible alternative assumptions yield results very different from Nordhaus's "optimal" outcomes.

This section examines the problems hidden in the damage function and the abatement cost function of DICE 2007. The Nordhaus perspective on discount rates is discussed in the next section, where it is contrasted with the very different treatment in the *Stern Review*.

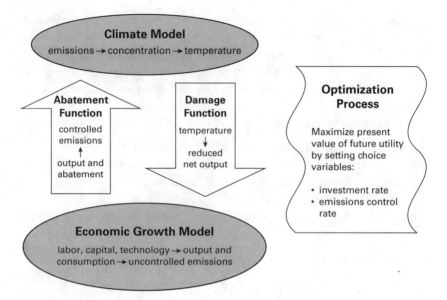

Figure 3.1
Structure of DICE

A.   Quadratic Damages

How much does climate change harm economic performance? Economic models such as DICE frequently employ a simplified damage function, summarizing the expected damages as a function of temperature increases. It is a common intuition that damages should grow faster than temperature; that is, 4° of temperature increase would be more than twice as bad as 2°. DICE adopts one of the simplest mathematical forms that ensures a more than proportional response to global warming: damages are a quadratic function of temperature increases.

Specifically, DICE 2007 assumes that damages are described by the equation

$$\text{Output net of climate damages / Gross output} = 1/(1 + AT^2) \qquad (1)$$

Here T is the temperature increase, and A is a constant. As long as the ratio of net to gross output is close to 1.0, equation (1) is approximately equivalent[11] to

$$\text{Damages / Gross output} = AT^2 \qquad (2)$$

The constant A is derived from somewhat detailed calculations, presenting Nordhaus's best guesses at the damages from 2.5° and from 6° of warming. In the words of the Nordhaus "lab notes" explaining the derivation of the DICE 2007 equations, "We have parameterized by assuming that the damage function is to the 2th power [*sic*]. It is then calibrated to 2.5 degrees C."[12]

The lab notes also show that the estimate of damages from warming is an astonishingly low 1.77 percent of world output at 2.5°; this value is used to set the constant A in equations (1) and (2). The data on damages at 2.5° are largely taken from earlier work by Nordhaus; they include six categories of ordinary, noncatastrophic damages, plus an estimate of potential catastrophic damages, weighted by the assumed probability of a catastrophic event. A long march through the details of the damage estimate at 2.5° would be required to understand exactly what has gone wrong here. One of the categories is the subjective value of warming; as in the previous version of DICE, most of the world is assumed to place a substantial positive value on 2.5° of temperature increase.[13]

The bottom line is that the Nordhaus damage function trivializes the climate problem. At 2.5° of warming, the world is at or perhaps just beyond the threshold where truly dangerous, irreversible changes become likely, in the opinion of many observers (see, e.g., the *Stern Review*, discussed in the next section). For Nordhaus, that ominous temperature causes losses of less than 2 percent—less than one year's economic growth for most countries. The combination of that low estimate with the quadratic form of the equation means that the increase in damages is relatively leisurely: at 5°, well into the zone where irreversible, disastrous change becomes a major risk, the Nordhaus damage function projects losses of 7 percent of output. (The Nordhaus lab notes also present the incredible estimate of a mere 8.2 percent loss of output at 6 °, which would have implied an even lower value for A in equations (1) and (2), if it had been used.)

There is almost no evidence about the exact shape of the damage function; if, instead of being quadratic, it is proportional to temperature cubed, then even with the Nordhaus estimate at 2.5°, damages are 14 percent of output at 5 degrees. If damages are proportional to the fifth power of temperature—and neither Nordhaus nor anyone else has proved that they are not—then at 5° the world loses more than 56 percent of output to climate damages.[14] In other words, there is no information here about how fast damages will grow, unless the shape of the damage curve can be known with certainty. But the shape cannot be known, at least until it is much too late to do anything about it.

B. The Ever-Shrinking Cost of Abatement

While climate damages are trivialized in DICE, the cost of abatement is assumed to undergo inexorable shrinkage over time. A review of other studies and models, described in abbreviated and opaque terms, yields estimates of the cost of a carbon-free "backstop technology" that could replace all fossil fuels.[15] The backstop technology is projected to cost around $1200 per ton of carbon emissions today, declining to about half that amount by 2100. Nordhaus then pegs the cost of abatement to the backstop technology: as the fraction of emissions being abated approaches 100 percent, the marginal cost of abatement approaches the backstop technology cost. Abatement costs start out cheap and rise rapidly as more and more abatement occurs; when 50 percent of emissions are abated, the cost is only 14 percent of the backstop cost.[16]

Thus the automatic, or at least policy-independent, decline in the assumed cost of the backstop drives down the cost of abatement as well. This creates a bias in favor of inaction: in the world of DICE, if you don't like the cost of abatement, just wait for it to come down. The rising value of damages, combined with the declining cost of abatement, will eventually make it attractive to reduce emissions. This may help to explain one of Nordhaus's principal policy conclusions:

> One of the major findings in the economics of climate change has been that efficient or "optimal" economic policies to slow climate change involve modest rates of emissions reductions in the near term, followed by sharp reductions in the medium and long term. We might call this the *climate-policy ramp*, in which policies to slow global warming increasingly tighten or ramp up over time.[17]

The ramp, however, has been built into the abatement cost function, by (arbitrary) design. Consider how different the situation would be with a more realistic picture of technology costs. Assume that the cost of abatement declines more rapidly when more money is spent on researching, developing, and deploying new technologies. Then waiting to stroll up the climate policy ramp is no longer the obviously optimal strategy. One could, instead, set out to create a steeper ramp (perhaps it looks more like a ladder out of the pit, or a bridge across the abyss), and solve the problem more quickly. The option of spending money to accelerate the development of technology occurs naturally to many people; it takes a sophisticated model to make it disappear.

Not only does DICE exclude the opportunity to invest in abatement technology; ordinary investment in emissions abatement is assumed to be unproductive. It neither adds to next year's output nor enters into the utility function that measures consumer well-being.[18] There is no possibility here that jobs will be created by abatement spending, or that energy-efficiency investments will increase useful output while reducing emissions. Rather than potentially opening a promising new path toward development centered on clean technology, abatement spending in DICE is like a medically necessary but foul-tasting medicine, of which everyone hopes to have as little as possible, as late as possible.

The damage function and the abatement cost function are not the only problems in DICE; its results also depend, for example, on the relatively high discount rate, discussed in the next section. But since neither the damage function nor the abatement cost function is known with any precision, the results of the modeling exercise are driven by the built-in assumptions about these relationships. Assume that climate damages grow relatively slowly, while abatement costs come down automatically (and abatement spending is a pure loss to the economy), and you will naturally find that going slow is the winning strategy. With different assumptions, another model is possible—and another model could, with equal or greater plausibility, reach a qualitatively different conclusion.

II. Much Less Wrong: The Economics of the *Stern Review*[19]

The scientific evidence is now overwhelming: climate change presents very serious global risks, and it demands an urgent global response. . . . The benefits of strong, early action considerably outweigh the costs.[20]

This central conclusion from the *Stern Review* will not come as a surprise to scientists who study climate change. Nor will it startle those who are troubled by the early signs of global warming, including the intensification of extreme and variable weather conditions. But in the world of academic economics, it is so unusual that it requires detailed justification.

Stern found that under business as usual (i.e., assuming no new policies to reduce carbon emissions), the concentration of greenhouse gases in the atmosphere could reach double the preindustrial level as early as 2035. This would essentially commit the world to more than 2°C of warming. By the end of the century, business as usual would lead to more than a 50 percent chance of exceeding 5°C of warming, implying disastrous changes in natural ecosystems and human living conditions around the world.

Stern describes the impacts of unchecked warming in both qualitative and quantitative terms; the qualitative images are perhaps more sweeping and powerful. For example, human actions create "risks of major disruption to economic and social activity, on a scale similar to those associated with the great wars and the economic depression of the first half of the 20th century."[21] American readers should remember that this was written in a country where the memory of World Wars I and II loomed considerably larger than in the United States.[22] An average global warming of 5° (all temperatures cited here are in degrees Celsius) would cause "a radical change in the physical geography of the world [that] must lead to major changes in the human geography—where people live and how they live their lives."[23] The qualitative descriptions of climate impacts are discussed in the final section of this chapter. Most of the economic debate, however, concerns Stern's quantitative estimates.

The economic model used in the *Stern Review* finds that the damages from business as usual would be expected to reduce GDP by 5 percent based on market impacts alone, or 11 percent including a rough estimate for the value of health and environmental effects that do not have market prices ("externalities," in the jargon of economics). If the sensitivity of climate to CO_2 levels turns out to be higher than the baseline estimates, these losses could rise to 7 percent and more than 14 percent, respectively. A disaggregated description of impacts by sector and region is generally in agreement with these numbers, according to the *Stern Review*. Stern speculates that an adjustment for equity weighting, reflecting the fact that the impacts will fall most heavily on poor countries, could lead to losses valued at 20 percent of global GDP. These figures are substantially greater than the comparable estimates from most economists.

Stern maintains that these damages can be largely avoided, at much lower cost, through emissions reduction. Stabilization at 500 to 550 parts per million (ppm) of CO_2-equivalent[24] in the atmosphere would avoid most, though not all, of the "business as usual" damages. Both direct estimates of mitigation costs and a review of results from many different models suggest that stabilization at this level would cost about 1 percent of GDP. Stabilization below 450 ppm, according to Stern, is no longer feasible in view of the high concentration of greenhouse gases already present in the atmosphere; he suggests the relevant range of targets is now 450–550 ppm of CO_2-equivalent.[25]

The extensive criticisms of the *Stern Review*'s economics raise two key points: the discount rate is said to be too low; and the treatment of risk and uncertainty is said to be inappropriate.[26] In the opinion of a number of economists who have discussed the *Stern Review*, these criticisms invalidate Stern's conclusion that the costs of climate mitigation are much smaller than the benefits.

A.   Choosing a Discount Rate

Because the climate impacts of today's decisions span such long periods of time, the choice of a discount rate is one of the most important factors in the economic analysis of climate change. Stern's preferred discount rate, 1.4 percent (explained below), is much lower than the rates used in traditional climate economic models. For William Nordhaus, "the *Review's* radical view of policy stems from an extreme assumption about discounting. . . . this magnifies impacts in the distant future and rationalizes deep cuts in emissions, and indeed in all consumption, today."[27]

In selecting the appropriate discount rate for long-term public policy decisions, economic theory often distinguishes between two components. The *rate of pure time preference* is the discount rate that would apply if all present and future generations had equal resources and opportunities. In addition, there is a *wealth-based component* of the discount rate, reflecting the assumption that if future generations will be richer than we are, then there is less need for us to invest today in order to help them protect themselves. In the notation of the *Stern Review*, the discount rate, r, is the sum of these two parts:

$$r = \delta + \eta g \tag{3}$$

Here δ is the rate of pure time preference, and g is the growth rate of per capita consumption. If per capita consumption is constant, implying that $g = 0$, then the discount rate $r = \delta$. The second parameter, η, determines how strongly economic growth affects the discount rate. A larger value of η implies a larger discount rate, and hence less need to provide today for future generations (as long as per capita consumption is growing).

Nordhaus's critique centers on Stern's value for δ, the discount rate that would apply if all generations were equally well off. Stern reviews and endorses the philosophical arguments for viewing all generations as people of equal worth, deserving equal rights and living conditions.[28] These arguments are often taken to imply that pure time preference should be zero. However, many economists believe that people reveal their time preferences through choices about savings and other actions affecting the future, and deduce from this that the rate of pure time preference must be greater than zero. (If every generation were equally important to people today, the economists object, wouldn't we all be saving a lot more—perhaps most of our incomes—for the future?) In addition, pure time preference precisely equal to zero causes technical problems in some economic theories.[29]

Stern just barely avoids setting pure time preference equal to zero. While generally accepting the philosophical arguments for treating all generations equally, he also observes that there is a small, but nonzero, probability that future generations will not exist—for example, if a natural or man-made disaster destroys most or all of the human race. The probability of the destruction of humanity is, arbitrarily, assumed to be 0.1 percent per year; pure time preference is therefore set equal to 0.1 percent. That is, Stern suggests that we are only 99.9 percent sure that humanity will still be here next year, so we should consider the well-being of people next year to be, on average, 99.9 percent as important as people today.

To calculate the discount rate using equation (3), Stern estimates that the growth of per capita income will average 1.3 percent per year, and sets $\eta = 1$. Thus his discount rate is

$$r = \delta + \eta g = 0.1\% + (1 * 1.3\%) = 1.4\% \tag{4}$$

Nordhaus interjects another idea from economic theory: in an abstractly perfect market economy, the discount rate should match market interest rates, or rates of return on capital. This is simply the neoliberal perspective on valuing the future. In general, neoliberalism assumes that unregulated markets make the ideal allocation of resources to competing uses; the observed balance between the production of apples and oranges, or between buses and limousines, must be optimal by definition. The same applies to the allocation of resources between present and future generations; the market rate of interest is the price that conveys that trade-off. In a textbook world of perfect markets and perfect rationality, where everyone is well informed and has access to capital markets, and everyone thinks about short-term investments and long-term policies in a consistent manner, the discount rate would be equal to the interest rate, since both would express individuals' preferred trade-off between current and future incomes. Ignoring the many reasons why this bit of theory might not apply in the real world, Nordhaus maintains that the discount rate should initially match an interest rate of about 5 to 6 percent above inflation. (This discussion uses "real," or inflation-adjusted, quantities throughout.) To achieve this goal he argues that pure time preference, δ, should be 1.5 percent, and η should be 2. The result is that the current "social cost of carbon," or optimal carbon tax, is one-tenth as high for Nordhaus as for Stern.[30]

Partha Dasgupta presents a complementary critique of Stern, addressing a different aspect of the discount rate.[31] Focusing on the ethical implications of discounting, he interprets δ as the measure of the trade-off between present and future, independent of wealth differences, and η as the measure of the trade-off between rich and poor, independent of time differences. In this framework,

η = 0 implies that *every dollar is of equal value* regardless of who receives it; η = 1 implies that *every 1 percent increase in a person's income is of equal value* regardless of the wealth of the person who receives it; and η > 1 implies that a 1 percent increase in income is of greater value to a poorer person.

Dasgupta endorses Stern's argument that δ is close to zero, but maintains that equity requires much more concern for the poor, reflected in a larger η; Dasgupta suggests a range of 2 to 4. If per capita incomes are expected to continue growing in spite of climate change, as most economists (including Stern) assume, then using a larger η in equation (1) leads to a higher discount rate, and indirectly, to less investment in the future.

How can a concern for equity lead to doing less for future generations? The source of the paradox is the economists' assumption that future generations will be better off than we are; in this story, it is assumed that we are the poor, and those who come after us are the rich. If that were true, then as modern Robin Hoods, we could strike a blow for equality by taking money from our children's inheritance and spending it on ourselves today. On the other hand, if climate change or other problems will make future generations worse off, the argument reverses itself: in that case, the present generation should do much more for its poorer descendants. If the lives of future generations will be sufficiently worse than ours, the discount rate could even become negative, implying that $100 of benefits in the future would be worth more than $100 today. Dasgupta has raised this possibility in other writings on the subject.

Of course, not everyone is equally wealthy within any generation; Dasgupta's strong views on equity would also call for substantial redistribution within the present generation. Indeed, Dasgupta hints that Stern's η = 1 (as opposed to η = 2 or more) reflects an insufficient concern for the problems of poverty today—as well as an excessive concern for the well-being of the allegedly more affluent generations to come.

Stern's responses to criticisms on the discount rate[32] reiterate the ethical arguments for pure time preference being close to zero. At $\delta = 1.5\%$, he suggests, you are telling your grandchildren that their lives and incomes are only half as important as your own, simply because they live 50 years after you. Stern is more willing to consider changes in η, though not to the extent that Dasgupta proposes. (If Dasgupta's proposed values for η were appropriate, Stern observes, very radical redistribution within the present generation, from rich to poor, should be high on the political agenda.)

Sensitivity analyses by the Stern team show that with either $\delta = 1.5\%$ or $\eta = 2$, much though not all of the present value of climate damages would be eliminated; however, the remaining damages would still exceed the costs of mitigation.

B.   Understanding Uncertainty

The second major innovation in the Stern analysis is the treatment of risk and uncertainty connected to climate change.[33] Although the broad outlines and major findings of climate science are increasingly definite, many crucial details remain uncertain and may not be known until it is too late to do anything about the problem. Both the expected severity of climate impacts and the probability of an abrupt catastrophe are strongly connected to temperature increases, which in turn are strongly connected to atmospheric concentrations of greenhouse gases. However, the precise strength and timing of these relationships remain uncertain. Some of the uncertainty can be addressed by further research, but some may reflect the inherent unpredictability of nonlinear systems such as the earth's atmosphere—the problem that motivates the fields of chaos theory and complexity theory.

Stern introduces issues of uncertainty into the economic calculations in three ways.[34] The first involves the sensitivity of climate to greenhouse gas concentrations. The baseline scenario follows the IPCC's Third Assessment Report (2001) in assuming that a doubling of preindustrial CO_2 concentrations would lead to warming of 1.5–4.5°. Some newer research suggests that climate feedback mechanisms may increase sensitivity beyond that level.[35] Accordingly, Stern's high climate sensitivity scenario assumes that the same doubling of atmospheric CO_2 would lead to 2.4–5.4°.

Second, the PAGE model, used in the *Stern Review*, includes an estimate for the risk of an abrupt climate catastrophe. The model assumes that once a threshold temperature is reached (the threshold itself is uncertain, but averages 5° above preindustrial temperatures) the probability of catastrophe increases by 10 percent for every additional degree C of warming; the catastrophe has a value of 5 to 20 percent of output.[36] As Stern notes, this is based on the treatment of catastrophe in Nordhaus's DICE model.

Finally, PAGE is designed to reflect risks throughout its calculations, through a statistical technique known as Monte Carlo analysis. For 31 key parameters, PAGE assumes that there is a range of possible values. For each of these parameters, the model randomly selects a value from the range of possibilities, each time it is run. The model is run repeatedly—1,000 times, in this case—and the weighted average of the results is used as the model's estimate.[37] Sensitivity analyses show that Stern's treatment of uncertainty is comparable in importance to the discount rate in determining the outcome of the model.[38]

Stern's treatment of uncertainty has attracted relatively little attention from economists who think he has gone too far. On the other hand, there have been responses from others arguing that Stern may have understated the problem of climate risk and uncertainty. In a brief comment specifically on Stern's treatment of catastrophic damages, Paul Baer argues that much greater catastrophic impacts should have been included, starting at lower temperatures.[39] Stern's target for climate stabilization, according to Baer, would entail significant risks of the complete melting of the Greenland ice sheet, an important, much-discussed example of a climate catastrophe. Based on the nonzero risk of catastrophic damages at lower temperatures, Baer speculates that the optimal target for CO_2 levels and temperature stabilization should be lower than Stern's proposals.

Martin Weitzman argues at length that uncertainty is the key to the climate problem.[40] He describes Stern as being "right for the wrong reason," because Stern places too much emphasis on a debatable cost-benefit analysis, but too little on the need for social insurance against low-probability, catastrophic events. Weitzman applies a framework developed in the analysis of financial markets, where standard theories fail to explain puzzling patterns of behavior. Those standard theories assume that investors can learn, through repeated experience, the probability distribution of the full range of possible market outcomes. But when (as usual) market structures are changing over time, there is never enough experience that is relevant to the current structure. In particular, it is intrinsically impossible to learn much from experience about the probability and magnitude of the extreme tails of a changing distribution—such as the worst-case outcomes that could lead to very large losses. Investors appear to worry a great deal about those unpredictable worst-case outcomes, a fact that explains a number of otherwise puzzling financial market results.

The analogy to climate change, according to Weitzman, is that we should worry less about calibrating the most likely outcomes and more about insurance against worst-case catastrophes. Thus the IPCC's Fourth Assessment Report (2007) offers six "equally sound" scenarios, with a mean temperature increase over the next century of 2.8°C—well within the range of the ongoing debate over the impacts of predictable and expected damages. (Stern follows one of the IPCC scenarios, namely A2, in projecting somewhat greater damages from a century of business as usual.) Much more important than the mean prediction is the fact that, according to Weitzman, the same IPCC report can be read as implying a 3 percent probability of a temperature increase greater than 6°C: a point at which we

are located in the terra incognita of what any honest economic modeler would have to admit is a planet Earth reconfigured as science fiction . . . [where] mass species extinctions, radical alterations of natural environments, and other extreme outdoor consequences will have been triggered by a geologically-instantaneous temperature change that is significantly larger than what separates us now from past ice ages.[41]

Even in the absence of a monetary valuation of these disastrous events, there is no doubt that the benefits of avoiding 6° warming would be enormous. Risk aversion, in the face of truly catastrophic risks, outweighs the details of any ordinary cost-benefit calculation.

Although still confined within a cost-benefit framework, the Stern analysis introduces several useful innovations, broadening and advancing the discussion of climate economics. The *Stern Review* is far from being a perfect analysis, but it is much less wrong than its predecessors. It lays to rest the peculiar notion that standard economics necessarily counsels inaction in the face of global crisis. At the same time, it is part of an unfinished story, leading toward a more adequate economic understanding of climate change and climate policy options. The final section of this chapter presents the outlines of a better approach to climate economics.

III. Economics as if Climate Mattered

What is needed to create an economic analysis that takes the climate crisis seriously?[42] There are three essential elements of a new climate economics: discount rates that reflect our responsibility to the future; a central focus on the role of uncertainty; and a reinterpretation of the costs of climate policy. The *Stern Review* deserves credit for its treatment of the first one and a half of these three points—a much better grade than can be given to Nordhaus's DICE model and other conventional analyses, but still not enough to guide further analysis and develop appropriate policies for climate protection.

A. Discounting the Future
The costs and benefits of climate change, and of climate policies, are spread out across decades and centuries. Thus numerical estimates of total costs and benefits are inevitably present values, and are completely dependent on the choice of discount rate. Any comparison of the total costs and benefits of climate scenarios is a statement about present values, and is valid only for one discount rate. With the same underlying data, a different discount rate would yield different totals, and in most cases, a different balance between costs and benefits.

Much has been written about the economic and philosophical issues involved in choosing discount rates, but there is nothing approaching a resolution to the debate. It is indeed a choice; the appropriate discount rate for public policy decisions spanning many generations cannot be deduced from private market decisions today, or from economic theory. A lower discount rate places a greater importance on future lives and conditions of life. To many, it seems ethically necessary to have a discount rate at or close to zero, in order to respect our descendants and create a sustainable future. Chapter 2 of the *Stern Review* provides a thorough discussion and persuasive argument for very low discount rates.

In practice, the discount rate is decisive for economic evaluation of climate change, regardless of the analytical framework. In a model such as DICE, switching from a high to a low discount rate can change the social cost of carbon from a very low to a very high value, thereby supporting much more extensive mitigation policy.[43]

B. Facing the Worst-Case Scenario
Climate outcomes are uncertain in several respects, ranging from short-term variations in weather to the long-term sensitivity of the climate to greenhouse gas concentrations, to the probability of irreversible catastrophes. Since people are risk-averse, climate uncertainty makes climate change look more threatening, and justifies more immediate action: the

worst scenarios loom much larger than the best ones, in averaging or evaluating the range of possible outcomes.

In his recent work, discussed in the previous section, Martin Weitzman argues that the problem of uncertainty is even deeper than this.[44] Calculations of expected values, even when done with Monte Carlo analyses, assume a known probability distribution for each uncertain outcome or parameter—often a normal distribution, with thin tails. But Weitzman points out that we are inevitably inferring the probability distribution from a limited amount of empirical information, resulting in an estimated distribution that itself is uncertain and thus has fat tails. Such a distribution defeats the calculation of expected values; in the tail of the distribution, climate damages can grow faster than the probability of those damages declines. In a technical sense, this implies that the expected value of damages is infinite, or unbounded.

If a crucial parameter such as climate sensitivity is in effect being estimated from N observations, we know very little about the tails of the distribution describing events that occur with probability $1/N$ or less. Yet with no firm upper bound on the damages that could result, it is these low-probability, high-cost outcomes that people inevitably worry most about. (A survey of expert opinion about the expected severity of climate damages, carried out and relied on by Nordhaus, itself turns out to have a fat-tailed distribution, with a noticeable minority of truly ominous estimates.[45])

As Weitzman's densely mathematical argument emphasizes, the most crucial uncertainties cannot be resolved until it is much too late to do anything about climate change. This provides a strong argument for a precautionary, rather than cost-benefit, approach to climate policy. The science of catastrophic climate risks should lead to an absolute cap on allowable increases in temperature and/or CO_2 concentrations; the proper role for economic analysis is then a cost-effectiveness analysis of the least-cost method for remaining under the cap.

Cost-effectiveness analysis of climate and energy policy is by no means a trivial enterprise; it involves important uncertainties, choices about emerging new technologies, and time spans of many decades. Yet cost-effectiveness analysis escapes from the paradoxes of monetization, and it greatly reduces the problems of uncertainty and the impacts of discounting. Such an approach abandons the attempt to define a "damage function" relating temperatures to total monetary damages; instead, it assumes, consistent with nontechnical common sense, that exceeding the cap would risk causing damages too great to calculate or tolerate.

C. Interpreting the Costs of Climate Policy

The implicit assumption of cost-benefit analysis is that the costs of new initiatives are bad, and must be outweighed by the benefits in order to justify changes in the status quo. This assumption is a direct consequence of the neoliberal faith in unregulated markets. Since consumers are assumed to have chosen whatever purchases bring them the greatest welfare, market outcomes are thought to be optimal; any new costs can be interpreted as decreasing welfare. This presumes that consumers are well informed about the implications of their choices, which may be quite inaccurate in the case of carbon emissions and climate change. And in terms of equity, the market makes decisions on the basis of "one dollar, one vote." Therefore, unconstrained market outcomes are only optimal if one accepts the existing distribution of resources; a redistributive policy that imposes costs on the wealthy could increase welfare for the majority. Since the poorest parts of the world will generally suffer more, and sooner, than the rest of us from climate change, the question of equity should be central to climate policy.

Another implicit assumption is that the costs under consideration are painfully large, perhaps prohibitive, making it of utmost importance to guard against expensive new undertakings. But in climate models estimating impacts over a century or more, the costs must be interpreted in the context of expected economic growth. Costs as great as 5 to 6 percent of GDP by 2100—much higher than the Nordhaus estimates for Kyoto, or even the *Stern Review* estimates for global mitigation costs—would amount to only a trivial delay in the ongoing growth of income assumed by most models. In an economy where per capita incomes were growing at 2 percent per year, people would on average be 6.3 times as rich in 2100 as they were in 2007. If climate mitigation costs amount to 6 percent of output, the result would be a three-year delay in the century of growth: income net of climate costs would not reach 6.3 times the 2007 level until 2103.[46]

There is yet another sense in which the costs of climate policy need to be reinterpreted. An effective climate policy is not a simple subtraction of resources from the existing market economy (as it would be if current market outcomes were truly optimal); rather, climate policy involves choosing a different path for future economic and technological development. The costs of such a policy do not disappear; they get spent on creating a new set of industries. Technological change is imperfectly understood in economics; the neoliberal framework has little to contribute to this fundamental question. In reality, technological change appears to be a path-dependent process characterized by economies of scale in the emerging industries. Public initiatives can lead to the creation of successful new development paths: the "costs" of decades of government, particularly military, investment in microelectronics after World War II led to the more recent successes of private enterprise in extending those technologies and applying them in computers, cell phones, and countless other products. In hindsight, it would seem odd to describe the early public expenditures on miniaturizing electronics as costs that reduced welfare; rather, they shaped the development path of late-twentieth- and early-twenty-first-century technologies and industries. As that process advanced, new jobs, incomes, profits, and products were created, and our way of life was transformed.

The massive effort that is needed to address the climate crisis today could do the same for the decades to come. Suppose that we spend money today to launch a new set of technologies and industries based on maximizing energy efficiency, renewable energy production, and sequestration, thereby creating the jobs, incomes, and products that shape the life of the next generation. Our descendants will not blame us for having reduced the level of short-term shopping opportunities at the mall. They will be especially happy to get a more tolerable climate as part of the package.

Notes

1. Associated Press, "Bush: Kyoto Treaty Would Have Hurt Economy," June 30, 2005, http://www.msnbc.msn.com/id/8422343/.

2. Energy Information Administration, "Impacts of the Kyoto Protocol on U.S. Energy Markets and Economic Activity," 1998, http://www.eia.doe.gov/oiaf/kyoto/kyotorpt.html.

3. William Nordhaus, *The Challenge of Global Warming: Economic Models and Environmental Policy*, September 2007 version (http://nordhaus.econ.yale.edu/dice_mss_091107_public.pdf, accessed February 2008), 16. His contrast between reductions measured relative to business as usual and relative to 1990, pp. 16–17, implies that global emissions in 2050 under business as usual would be 2.5 times the 1990 level—which amounts to roughly 1.5 percent annual growth over those 60 years. Thus 25 percent below business as usual in 2050 is 75 percent of 250 percent, or 188 percent of 1990 emissions.

4. Sheila Olmstead and Robert Stavins, "An International Policy Architecture for the Post-Kyoto Era," *American Economic Review* 96, no. 2 (May 2006): 35–38.

5. William J. Baumol et al., "Regulating Emissions of Greenhouse Gases Under Section 202(a) of the Clean Air Act," October 2006, http://www.aei-brookings

.org/admin/authorpdfs/page.php?id=1336. Footnote 1 on page 1 lists the 42 automobile dealers associations that provided financial support.

6. Bjorn Lømborg, *Cool It: The Skeptical Environmentalist's Guide to Global Warming* (New York: Alfred A. Knopf, 2007), 31. See also Frank Ackerman, "Hot, It's Not: Reflections on *Cool It,* by Bjørn Lomborg *Climatic Change* 89, no. 3–4 (2008): 435–446.

7. Frank Ackerman and Ian Finlayson, "The Economics of Inaction on Climate Change: A Sensitivity Analysis," *Climate Policy* 6, no. 5 (2006): 509–526. This article critiques the earlier (2000) version of Nordhaus's DICE model; the 2007 version (Nordhaus, *Challenge of Global Warming*) still incorporates the assumed benefit of warming, but constrains the aggregate damage function to be strictly positive (i.e., it rules out net global benefits from warming, an anomalous result in the earlier DICE that is criticized in Ackerman and Finlayson).

8. For a critique of this approach to regulation, see Frank Ackerman and Lisa Heinzerling, *Priceless: On Knowing the Price of Everything and the Value of Nothing* (New York: The New Press, 2004).

9. This section draws heavily on work in progress, done jointly with my colleague Elizabeth A. Stanton.

10. This account is based on DICE 2007, as described in Nordhaus, *Challenge of Global Warming*. The model's equations are in that document's Appendix A, p. 142.

11. This is just algebra: for small x, $1 / (1 + x)$ is approximately equal to $1 - x$.

12. William Nordhaus, "Accompanying Notes and Documentation of DICE-2007 Model: Notes on DICE-2007.delta.v8 as of September 21, 2007," p. 24, October 2007, http://nordhaus.econ.yale.edu/Accom_Notes_100507.pdf, accessed February 2008.

13. Ackerman and Finlayson, "Economics of Inaction."

14. These estimates are derived from equation (2) with a varying exponent, calibrated to 1.77 percent of output at 2.5°.

15. Nordhaus, *Challenge of Global Warming*, p. 41.

16. The cost of abating a fraction, x, of emissions is modeled as 2.8 times the backstop cost, ensuring that costs rise rapidly as x approaches 1.

17. Nordhaus, *Challenge of Global Warming*, p. 101.

18. This is not explicitly stated, but it is implied by the DICE equations in Nordhaus, *Challenge of Global Warming*, p. 142: Utility depends on consumption (equation A.1); consumption plus investment equals net output (A.7, A.8); net output is calculated from gross output by subtracting abatement costs as well as climate damages (A.4); only the investment included in net output, not abatement costs, contributes to the productive capital stock that increases next year's gross output (A.9).

19. This section is based on Frank Ackerman, *Debating Climate Economics: The Stern Review vs. Its Critics*, July 2007, http://www.ase.tufts.edu/gdae/Pubs/rp/SternDebateReport.pdf.

20. *Stern Review: The Economics of Climate Change*, Executive Summary (long), pp. 1–2, http://www.hm-treasury.gov.uk/media/4/3/Executive_Summary.pdf.

21. *Stern Review: The Economics of Climate Change*, Executive Summary (short), p. 1, http://www.hm-treasury.gov.uk/media/9/9/CLOSED_SHORT_executive_summary.pdf.

22. Unlike the United States, the UK experienced heavy bombing during World War II. UK deaths, as a percent of population, were 3 times the U.S. level in World War II, and 20 times the U.S. level in World War I. (See, e.g., the Wikipedia entries on "World War I casualties" and "World War II casualties.")

23. *Stern Review*, short executive summary, p. 1.

24. These Stern calculations of CO_2-equivalent emissions include about 50 ppm contribution from non-CO_2 greenhouse gases; thus this range is comparable to 450–500 ppm of CO_2 alone.

25. This is comparable to 400–500 ppm of CO_2 alone (see previous note). The rationale for this target range is spelled out in chapter 13 of the *Stern Review* and is discussed below.

26. Other critiques, regarding the details of cost and benefit calculations, are also discussed in Ackerman, "Debating Climate Economics." The other critiques have generally received less attention than the controversies over discounting and uncertainty.

27. William Nordhaus, "The *Stern Review* on the Economics of Climate Change," May 3, 2007, p. 9, http://nordhaus.econ.yale.edu/stern_050307.pdf, accessed February 12, 2008.

28. *Stern Review*, chapter 2 and its appendix.

29. With zero pure time preference, models of economic growth behave illogically when extended to an infinite time horizon. It is not clear whether this is a fatal flaw in an analysis limited to a few centuries.

30. Nordhaus, "The *Stern Review*," pp. 29–32. Nordhaus uses different notation and terms; for clarity of exposition, the Stern notation and terminology are used throughout this chapter.

31. Partha Dasgupta, "Comments on the *Stern Review*'s Economics of Climate Change," revised December 12, 2006, http://www.econ.cam.ac.uk/faculty/dasgupta/STERN.pdf.

32. See the *Stern Review*'s postscript, appendix to the postscript, and other recent writings on the *Stern Review* Web site.

33. Formally, risk is often taken to mean events where different outcomes have known probabilities, in contrast to uncertainty, where the probabilities are unknown. However, this distinction is often blurred in informal discussion, such as the text of this section.

34. See the summary in one of the Stern team's responses to critics: Simon Dietz et al., "Reflections on the *Stern Review* (1): A Robust Case for Strong Action to Reduce the Risks of Climate Change," *World Economics* 8, no. 1 (January–March 2007): 121–168.

35. See James Hansen, Makiko Sato, Pushker Kharecha, David Beerling, Robert Berner, Valerie Masson-Delmotte, Mark Pagani, Maureen Raymo, Dana L. Royer and James C. Zachos, "Target Atmospheric CO_2: Where Should Humanity Aim?," *Open Atmospheric Science Journal* 2 (2008): 217–231, and earlier research cited there.

36. *Stern Review*, p. 153.

37. The results are weighted by "utility," or consumer satisfaction, which Stern assumes is equal the logarithm of consumption. (This is a common, but far from universal, assumption in economic analyses.) Compared to an unweighted average, this procedure gives greater weight to model runs where climate damages are greater and incomes are lower.

38. Dietz et al., "Reflections."

39. Paul Baer, "The Worth of an Ice-Sheet: A Critique of the Treatment of Catastrophic Impacts in the *Stern Review*," http://www.postnormaltimes.net/blog/archives/2006/12/the_worth_of_an_1.html, December 23, 2006.

40. Martin Weitzman, "The *Stern Review* of the Economics of Climate Change," February 2007, http://www.economics.harvard.edu/faculty/weitzman/files/JELSternReport.pdf; see also the more in-depth treatment in Weitzman, "On Modeling and Interpreting the Economics of Catastrophic Climate Change," January 2008, http://www.economics.harvard.edu/faculty/weitzman/files/modeling.pdf. Both accessed February 12, 2008.

41. Weitzman, "The *Stern Review*," pp. 18–19.

42. This section draws heavily on Ackerman, "Hot, It's Not."

43. Ackerman and Finlayson, "Economics of Inaction."

44. Weitzman, "The *Stern Review*"; "Modeling and Interpreting."

45. Tim Roughgarden and Stephen H. Schneider, "Climate Change Policy: Quantifying Uncertainties for Damages and Optimal Carbon Taxes," *Energy Policy* 27 (1999): 415–429.

46. Christian Azar and Stephen H. Schneider, "Are the Economic Costs of Stabilizing the Atmosphere Prohibitive?," *Ecological Economics* 42 (2002): 73–80.

4

Anatomy of Industry Resistance to Climate Change: A Familiar Litany

Robert L. Glicksman

American industries have long been hostile to environmental regulations that increase operating costs and reduce profits. Although industry may have been unprepared for, and thus poorly organized to resist, early federal environmental legislation,[1] it quickly marshaled its forces. Regulated or potentially regulated entities, their trade associations, and their lobbyists began a concerted effort to defeat, delay, and weaken environmental regulation.

In the early 1970s, politicians presented themselves as more committed to environmental protection than their opponents to try to ride the crest of public support for strong environmental legislation.[2] In that atmosphere, it was relatively easy for Congress to adopt significant new legislation, and the initial versions of the modern Clean Air and Water Acts passed Congress with virtually no dissent.[3]

By the beginning of the 1980s, however, a significant shift had occurred in the American political environment. That shift, and the neoliberal ideology that fueled it, produced a federal government that was far more receptive to industry's efforts to obstruct and weaken environmental law. Industry's antiregulatory arguments, which to that point had fallen largely on deaf ears in Washington, D.C., now found a receptive audience among environmental policymakers. The pivotal turning point was the election of Ronald Reagan as president in 1980, followed by Republican capture of the U.S. Senate. The free market ideology to which the Reagan administration was strongly committed became even more deeply entrenched when Republicans captured control of both houses of Congress in 1994 and of both the executive and legislative branches of the federal government in 2000. The ascendance of this ideology allowed regulatory opponents to frame their arguments, which previously had relatively little impact, in terms that struck a responsive chord with politicians and provided the arguments with new traction.

This chapter describes the process by which regulatory opponents successfully relied on free market ideology to couch their opposition to health, safety, and environmental regulation in terms that resonated with the American public in ways it never had before. They portrayed regulation as the product of overreaching, meddlesome, and power-hungry bureaucrats that would detract from rather than enhance social welfare. In doing so, regulatory opponents enabled politicians to justify their efforts to derail and weaken protective regulation in terms consistent with pursuit of the public interest, rather than as a quid pro quo for the support of narrow special interests. The chapter also analyzes how industry and its political supporters have relied on a familiar litany of anti-regulatory arguments generated by conservative ideologues to throttle efforts to tackle climate change.

I. Laissez-Faire Liberalism Redux

The market-based ideology that increasingly shaped federal regulatory policy beginning in 1981 has been described as "the contemporary reincarnation of the nineteenth century 'laissez-faire' liberalism that advanced the primacy of 'the market' over 'government regulation.'"[4] Proponents of this ideology view "state abstention from economic protection [as] the foundation of a good society."[5] They contend that an efficient market represents the path to public well-being because undisturbed market competition produces incentives to maximize productivity and individual responsibility. They regard the market as a reflection of neutral, value-free laws and view government as the problem, to which a commitment to the protection of private property rights, "privatization, decentralization, and deregulation are the answers."[6] This "cultural exaltation of the market"[7] conceives of regulation as a means of diverting resources from efficiency-maximizing citizens to special interests and bloated government bureaucracies, with the inevitable consequence of shrinking the overall economic pie.[8]

Worse yet, according to regulatory foes, the government tends to be incompetent and regulatory programs often produce unintended consequences, harming the very interests they are designed to protect. According to free market proponents, progressive regulatory programs (like environmental protection regimes) are often poorly designed, creating government failures that are worse than the market failures they purport to correct.[9] Regulation often diverts resources away from productive endeavors into compliance efforts whose costs exceed their benefits.

Indeed, compliance costs reduce profitability, reduce wages, and make it harder for employees to afford a healthy lifestyle. Further, regulation makes American businesses less competitive in international markets and creates incentives to relocate overseas where the absence of regulation yields lower operating costs.

As a fallback argument, when regulation cannot be completely derailed, free market proponents argued that regulation to redress market failures (such as the imposition of unwarranted externalities) should mimic the operation of a well-functioning free market to the extent possible. They urged regulators to rely on cost-benefit analysis to determine the appropriate level of regulation. Cost-benefit analysis would send in a regulatory context the same kinds of price signals that the free market would provide, absent market failure, to achieve efficient resource allocation. It would prevent government from engaging in excessive and counterproductive regulation.

II. The Growing Ascendancy of Free Market Ideology

These ideas began to influence federal environmental policy around 1980. The Republican Party's platform in 1980 committed it to alleviating "the crushing burden of excessive regulation," singling out the EPA's "excessive" efforts to achieve zero risk. The platform also promised a "war on overregulation."[10] Once President Reagan took office, he declared that government is the problem, not the solution to society's ills.[11] Reagan administration officials and the president himself, who voiced "a longstanding ideological commitment to shrinking the role of the federal government,"[12] railed against "big government," bureaucratic red tape, and the social policies of "tax and spend liberals." Even when government had a legitimate role to play, state and local governments were presented as better situated to protect the public than the federal government. By casting aspersions on the federal government's efforts to protect the public from industry, Reagan encouraged the belief that his administration's opposition to social regulation coincided with the interests of the average American.

The new antiregulatory rhetoric also sought business as its audience. The government's increased hostility to social and economic regulation developed at the same time that conservative thinkers such as William Simon, Irving Kristol, and Richard Scaife attacked such regulation. They preached to the business community that "ideas were important" and that they should promote those "sympathetic to the interests of business."[13]

They encouraged business to frame opposition to regulation in terms of the detrimental impact it would have on the general public, and to argue that the free market was better suited to protecting private property and enriching the lives of ordinary Americans. By 1994, the essence of the antiregulatory credo was captured in Phillip Howard's book, *The Death of Common Sense*, which portrayed government regulators as incompetent bunglers whose irrational decrees were suffocating America.[14]

Together, conservative academics, business interests, and their political allies successfully painted a portrait of health, safety, and environmental regulation as worse than the ills it was designed to ameliorate. As one environmental scholar has put it, "the actions taken by the business community effectively established the political and intellectual foundation for a series of subsequent reform efforts that have challenged the basic tenets of the environmental protection laws that Congress enacted in the 1970s."[15] More specifically, the free market ideology that opposed regulation, and the federal government's receptivity to it, resulted in a cosmic shift in the burden of proof. Industry no longer had to justify pursuing activities that create health, safety, and environmental risks. Instead, government had to justify intervening in the market by demonstrating that, against all odds, regulation would enhance, not diminish social welfare.[16] In this way, the federal policymaking process became less responsive to those urging protection for health, safety, and the environment. By framing opposition to regulation in the rhetoric of free market liberalism, conservative ideologues helped policymakers to wrap their own unwillingness to support regulation in the American flag, rather than appearing to be the lapdogs of big business.

III.   The Antiregulatory Litany

The entrenchment of free market ideology made policymakers more receptive to a litany of claims by industry that sought to prevent or weaken regulation. These antiregulatory arguments surfaced repeatedly. Facing undesirable regulatory initiatives in Congress or federal agencies, industry and its political allies typically began by asserting that there was no problem that warranted regulation or that, even if there was, they did not create it. If those arguments did not defeat regulation, industry tended to claim that no technologically practical solution existed to resolve the problem. If that argument failed, industry usually argued that regulation would have unacceptable adverse economic consequences (either for the regulated industry or for the nation), and that, even if regulation was affordable, its costs would outweigh anticipated regulatory benefits. The final antiregulatory salvo sometimes sought effort to portray regulation as an unwarranted intrusion on personal liberty and individual rights (including private property rights). The rise of free market liberalism after 1980 afforded these claims a legitimacy they previously lacked, and provided cover for politicians sympathetic to the opponents of regulation. Particular elements of the litany have been more or less successful in defeating regulation in different circumstances. The strategy of relying on it has remained remarkably stable, however, and it typically delays regulation even when it does not prevent it.

The remainder of this chapter provides examples of industry's invocation of these themes to throttle environmental regulation. It then describes how antiregulatory crusaders have used the same arguments to convince policymakers and the public that climate change regulation is premature, inadvisable, and not worth the heavy costs it will impose on the U.S. economy.

IV. The Litany in Action

A. "Prove It!"

The most obvious strategy for defeating regulation is to deny the existence of a problem worthy of government attention. One example of this strategy relates to the health risks posed by environmental tobacco smoke (ETS), or second-hand smoke. When the EPA issued a report in the 1990s finding that ETS causes lung cancer in humans, the Occupational Safety and Health Administration (OSHA) considered restricting workplace exposure to ETS. Internal tobacco industry memoranda describe the industry's efforts to deny that ETS creates health risks by, among other things, attacking the scientific validity of the EPA's report. As part of its "decade-long efforts to cast doubt upon EPA's risk assessment initiative,"[17] the industry sought out scientists who would "belittle the risks posed by ETS."[18] These scientists sent letters to prominent medical journals contesting any findings that ETS posed cancer risk. They published their own studies refuting the EPA's report. Tobacco industry advertising ridiculed the EPA's position, and the industry even sued the EPA (unsuccessfully) to force the EPA to disavow its ETS report.[19]

Another prominent example of the denial strategy relates to the debate during the 1980s over acid rain. Two prominent supporters of free market environmentalism claimed that "there is little evidence that acid rain is causing widespread problems."[20] Politicians supportive of the coal mining industry questioned both the need for and the legitimacy of a regulatory program to control sulfur dioxide, which is emitted by coal-burning facilities. Senator Robert Byrd of West Virginia expressed concern that "reality may very well diverge from [the] theory" used to support the 1990 Clean Air Act's "bold new regulatory approach" for abating acid rain. Dissenting from a Senate Report proposing regulation, Senator Steve Symms asserted that Congress should have deferred regulation in light of the speculative nature of the scientific evidence concerning the existence, causes, and effects of acid rain.[21] Similarly, the Reagan administration refused to back measures to combat acid rain due to continuing questions about the extent of the problem.[22] When EPA Administrator William Ruckelshaus proposed a modest regulatory program, Office of Management and Budget (OMB) Director David Stockman ridiculed it, and action was deferred until the first Bush administration.[23] The opponents of regulation cited claims by some scientists that acid rain would be beneficial, for example, by increasing soybean productivity and pine needle growth.[24]

B.   "It's Not My Fault"

When the evidence of an environmental problem becomes sufficiently overwhelming that credible denials are no longer possible, regulatory opponents must resort to fallback arguments. They frequently claim that even if a problem exists, it is not being caused by the targets of regulation. An oft-ridiculed political example was President Reagan's suggestion that trees are responsible for more air pollution than industry.[25]

A more serious example is the tobacco industry's notoriously persistent effort to deny a connection between tobacco smoke and lung cancer, heart disease, and other adverse health consequences. The tobacco industry's campaign of denial included congressional testimony by tobacco company executives who denied any knowledge that their products were addictive. But the industry's entire antiregulatory campaign was based largely on denial of proof of a causal link between tobacco use and adverse health effects. The campaign entailed a multifaceted, "concerted public relations effort to create and perpetuate controversy over the question whether cigarettes are harmful to health," including "careful orchestration and eventual suppression of internal research into the health issues raised by cigarettes." These efforts occurred "despite the industry's extensive knowledge of the actual health risks of smoking. Tobacco manufacturers have long known that cigarettes cause cancer, emphysema, and lung disease."[26] The tobacco industry's strategy was to "fram[e] consensus as controversy."[27] It sought to generate and perpetuate confusion and uncertainty about any possible link between smoking and illness by "smearing and belittling" studies purporting to establish a link between cigarettes and disease, overwhelming those studies with mass publication of studies with opposing results, and challenging the validity of studies finding such a link in public debate.[28] According to one court, the tobacco industry knew for decades about the health risks of smoking. "Despite that knowledge, they have consistently, repeatedly, and with enormous skill and sophistication, denied these facts to the public, to the Government, and to the public health community."[29] Industry sought to avoid regulation, liability in tort actions brought by smokers and their families, and threats to the industry's economic viability.

The tobacco industry's fight to create and sustain doubt about the health risks posed by smoking is the most egregious example of efforts to avoid regulation by denying responsibility for a health, safety, or environmental problem. But other examples abound. Businesses that manufacture and use chemicals suspected of being carcinogenic or creating other health risks have often denied that their products could possibly be responsible for those effects. The Lead Industries Association attacked the EPA's efforts to limit lead pollution by denying both that lead concentrations in human blood at the levels deemed unacceptable by the EPA were dangerous and that the use of lead as a fuel additive was responsible for unhealthy blood lead levels.[30] In the late 1970s, industry sought to defeat OSHA's efforts to adopt regulations limiting workplace exposure to carcinogenic substances by, among other things, contesting the validity of animal bioassay data as predictors of human cancer risk. They also blamed lifestyle choices such as diet and alcohol consumption, rather than chemical exposure, as being primarily responsible for any rise in cancer incidence. In addition, they postulated the existence of safe threshold levels of exposure below which disease would not develop.[31] The Reagan administration relied on uncertainty over the effects of exposure to formaldehyde to justify refusing to regulate it as a carcinogen.[32]

C.   "I Can't Help It!"

The next logical step in the parade of arguments by those seeking to forestall regulation is that there is no technologically feasible way to avoid a health, safety, or environmental problem that has been linked to a particular industry or activity. The automobile industry has long been the poster child for this strategy. When Congress authorized the EPA in 1970 to restrict tailpipe emissions of carbon monoxide, hydrocarbons, and nitrogen oxides, industry responded by claiming that compliance by the regulatory deadlines would be impossible.[33] EPA Administrator Ruckelshaus refused to extend the deadline, but a court overturned that decision at industry's behest, ruling that the EPA's denial was arbitrary because the risks of an erroneous denial exceeded the risks of an erroneous grant.[34] Industry used the same impossibility argument to convince Congress to grant further extensions in 1977. These delays made it impossible for many areas, particularly urban areas with extensive automobile traffic, to achieve timely compliance with the EPA's health-based air quality standards.[35]

The remarkable part of this story is that, at least according to the Justice Department in an antitrust suit filed in 1969, the major U.S. automakers had conspired "not to compete in research, development, manufacture, and installation of [automotive pollution] control devices, and did all in their power to delay such [activities]." The department concluded that the industry "ignored promising inventions, refused to purchase pollution-control technologies developed by others, delayed installing smog controls already available and known to them, and at times disciplined members of the cartel whose adherence to the collective suppression effort might temporarily waver."[36] Shortly before Congress passed the Clean Air Act of 1970, the industry signed a consent decree with the Justice Department that "at least implied that the big three manufacturers had in fact illegally worked together to thwart air pollution control."[37]

D.   "It's Not Worth It!"

Sometimes, the targets of regulation cannot plausibly argue that there is no problem worthy of regulation, that any problem is someone else's fault, or that proposed solutions are beyond current technological capacity. Regulatory opponents rarely give up simply because these arguments are unavailing. Instead, they often move on to the next component of the litany by contending that regulation is too expensive or that the costs of regulation exceed the anticipated regulatory benefits, making regulation counterproductive.[38] Sometimes, they claim that the total cost of social regulation is exorbitantly high,[39] or that the costs of all regulation of a particular kind (such as regulation of air polluting activities) exceed regulatory benefits.[40] These arguments are more commonly made, often with greater impact on policymakers, in the context of efforts to prevent, delay, or weaken particular instances of social regulation.

Industry and its political allies routinely claim that regulation will result in dramatic adverse economic consequences. The auto industry, in addition to relying on the alleged unavailability of control technology to delay tailpipe emission standards, asserted that emission controls would result in "business catastrophe."[41] Industry also asserted that the stratospheric ozone depletion and acid rain control provisions adopted in 1990 would cause the prices of consumer goods made with chlorofluorocarbons and the cost of electricity to increase precipitously. In retrospect, these cost estimates often turn out to have been wildly inflated. One study of the economic impact of a dozen major environmental regulatory programs found that in each case, both industry and the federal government overestimated compliance costs. In all but one instance, preregulatory estimates exceeded actual compliance costs by more than 100 percent.[42] The oil industry, for example, claimed that the cost of phasing out lead as a fuel additive would cost billions of dollars more than it did. The coal and electric utility industries greatly overstated the costs of controlling acid rain.[43]

Another version of this strategy is to assert that, even if regulation will enhance health or safety, its costs will exceed the benefits achieved. A recent example involves the EPA's efforts to control ground-level ozone, which can cause respiratory tract problems. When the EPA announced in 2007 that it was considering lowering allowable ambient ozone concentrations, Senator James Inhofe of Oklahoma, a frequent and vocal opponent of air pollution regulations, charged that the EPA's plan would "impose significant costs on counties and states across the country with too little environmental benefit."[44]

Clearly, regulatory opponents believe they are more likely to strike a responsive chord with the public by asserting that environmental regulation will create hardships for the American public than by complaining about the impact of regulation on corporate profits, shareholder dividends, and executive compensation. Even though the doomsday scenarios painted by regulatory skeptics should not be taken at face value, they present pro–free market regulators with a plausible reason for weakening regulation.

E. "That's Not Fair!"

One final strategy for avoiding regulation is to assert that it will interfere with desirable lifestyle choices for average Americans, infringe on cherished freedoms, or impair private property rights. Conservative commentators such as Irving Kristol have claimed that regulatory interference with the market will ultimately cause "the destruction of freedom"[45]

One good example involves the government's efforts to reduce automobile air pollution and encourage the production of energy-efficient vehicles. The auto and highway construction industries have engaged in public relations campaigns to convince consumers that pollution and fuel efficiency standards will cause sharp price increases for new cars and reduce consumer choice by limiting access to the larger vehicles that some drivers prefer.[46] The industries and their lobbyists have also argued that the smaller vehicles that fuel economy standards will force consumers to use are less safe than larger vehicles. Public opposition to restrictions on personal use of automobiles, fueled by the opponents of regulation, have contributed to the federal government's inability to restrict commuting by automobile, compel carpooling, and require rigorous vehicle emissions testing.[47]

The environmental regulatory programs that are often at greatest risk tend to be those most easily portrayed as invasive of private property rights. Legislative hearings on the Clean Water Act's dredge and fill permit program have featured small property owners (called at the behest of congressional opponents of the program) who testified that regulation crushed their dreams of owning homes or small businesses. Similarly, the public face of the real estate industry's opposition to the Endangered Species Act's prohibition on habitat modification is not corporate developers or timber companies, whose plans to sell expensive vacation homes or whose logging efforts were upset by regulation. Instead, the campaigns orchestrated by industry lobbyists feature individual small landowners being unfairly treated by big government. Politicians who would never oppose outright the protection of clean water or the value of protecting endangered species may feel comfortable opposing regulation if they can couch their opposition as a crusade to prevent unfair government infringement on sacrosanct private property rights.

V.   Using the Litany to Thwart Efforts to Address Climate Change

The opponents of environmental regulation have not always succeeded in derailing it by invoking the litany. Frequently, however, they provide handy justifications for policymakers antagonistic to regulation. Industry and its political allies have used the same strategy to fight federal climate change policy initiatives. Segments of industry that would be primary targets of climate change regulation, such as the energy industry, have advanced the familiar, sequential, antiregulatory litany. So have government officials who oppose anything other than more study about the risks of climate change. These policymakers have responded to the advice provided in a remarkable document prepared by a Republican Party political consultant, Frank Luntz, which provides a road map for justifying opposition to climate change legislation. The Luntz memorandum is a striking example of an effort to convince politicians to dress antiregulatory policy positions in the garb of the free market liberalism that has well served the opponents of regulation.

VI. Industry Resorts to the Litany to Block Climate Change Regulation

Not surprisingly, industry's first line of defense against climate change regulation has been to deny that the problem exists. Industry's fallback argument has been that, even if the problem exists, humans in general and their own activities in particular are not causing it. One journalist has described a "well-coordinated, well-funded campaign" patterned after the tobacco industry's denial that cigarettes are dangerous. The campaign involved efforts

by contrarian scientists, free-market think tanks and industry [to create] a paralyzing fog of doubt around climate change. Through advertisements, op-eds, lobbying and media attention, greenhouse doubters . . . argued first that the world is not warming; measurements indicating otherwise are flawed, they said. Then they claimed that any warming is natural, not caused by human activities. Now they contend that the looming warming will be miniscule and harmless.[48]

In portraying warming as a fleeting natural phenomenon, these groups claimed that increased energy output from the sun or sunspot activity may be the culprit, and that "sound science" has not yet identified manmade greenhouse gas emissions as the cause, or even as a significant contributing factor.

The public pronouncements of industries targeted by climate change regulation have exemplified this strategy. The Business Roundtable is composed of business leaders (including the energy and auto industries) representing about one-third of the total value of U.S. stock markets. It has recommended "prudence" before addressing climate change because "the science continues to evolve."[49] In particular, it has opposed mandatory emissions controls.

As the existence of climate change and its human causes have become harder to deny, industry has shifted to other elements of the well-worn antiregulatory litany. It has charged that the cost of addressing climate change will be exorbitant. The U.S. Chamber of Commerce has warned that federal climate change legislation would cause sharp increases in energy prices and force U.S. businesses to relocate to countries without regulation. Indeed, legislators have warned that "unilateral" adoption of greenhouse gas controls by the United States would induce China and India to resist controls to enhance their own position in world markets.[50] Coal industry spokespersons have criticized support for climate change legislation among some corporate leaders by charging that they "have demonstrated a willingness to devastate the overall American economy for their own short-term gains."[51]

Industry also has argued that climate change regulation would be unduly intrusive and require sacrifices that would do little to abate climate change. Auto industry representatives have opposed California's controls on greenhouse gas emissions from motor vehicles in these terms. They have called the controls "counterproductive" because they would increase car prices, narrow consumer vehicle choices, sacrifice auto safety, and cause job losses. In addition, they have claimed that there is no proof that California's approach would help slow global warming.[52] Auto industry spokespersons predicted that the Big Three U.S. car manufacturers would have to quit the passenger car and small truck markets entirely if states may adopt their own, disparate mandatory emissions caps.[53]

VII.   The Luntz Memorandum

The arguments against addressing climate change might not have taken root but for the willingness of politicians friendly to industry to endorse the litany in the policy arena. The blueprint for politicians opposed to climate change regulation appears in a blunt memorandum by Republican Party consultant Frank Luntz early during President George W. Bush's first term that was leaked to the press. The memorandum, entitled "The Environment: A Cleaner, Safer, Healthier America," was written to provide advice to Republican candidates to help counter Democratic claims that climate change regulation is imperative.[54] It provided both general and specific guidance on how Republican candidates should justify opposing programs to address climate change.

Notably, the strategy was cast in explicitly ideological terms. It relied heavily on the antigovernment, promarket rhetoric that had allowed the opponents of regulation to pitch positions that otherwise would likely have been unpalatable to the public. The memorandum thus employed framing to make reliance on the litany of industry objections politically feasible.

The Luntz memo urged candidates to emphasize the same pro–free market themes that had characterized opposition to environmental regulation since 1980. It urged candidates to "provide specific examples of federal bureaucrats failing to meet their responsibilities to protect the environment"; to stress the need for freedom, accountability and responsibility; to "specify and quantify the number of jobs lost because of needless, redundant regulation"; to demand that "Washington . . . disclose the *expected cost* of current and all new environmental regulation"; and to emphasize "common sense" and the use of "realistic assumptions."[55] Candidates were urged to "explain how it is possible to pursue a *common sense* or *sensible* environmental policy" that preserves past gains "without going to extremes." "Give citizens the idea that *progress is being frustrated by over-reaching government*."[56] The message was clear: government is the problem, not the solution; out-of-control bureaucrats are irrational zealots with a hidden, self-serving agenda inconsistent with the interests of the general public; and the costs of environmental regulation are unacceptable.

The memo encouraged Republican candidates to portray environmental issues as "compelling stories," and stated that what matters most is "how you frame your argument, and the order in which you present your facts." The objective of storytelling is to convince the public that its salvation lies in acceptance of "the conservative, free market approach to the environment."[57] The memo advised candidates to stress the desirability of a limited role for the federal government in protecting the environment. Although "the public demands at least some federal guidelines, . . . people don't want an intrusive federal bureaucracy dictating local enforcement."[58]

The Luntz memorandum included a separate section entitled "Winning the Global Warming Debate—An Overview." The implication is obvious—the ultimate objective is not to actually prevent the adverse effects of climate change but to "win the debate" by convincing the public that the optimal federal climate change policy is to do nothing. The arguments suggested in the memo were designed to respond to Democratic criticism of President Bush's renunciation of the Kyoto Protocol on climate change in 2001. It described several essential points as the foundation for Republicans' positions on climate change.

The first argument, not surprisingly, was to declare that the existence of global climate change remains unproven:

The scientific debate remains open. Voters believe that there is *no consensus* about global warming within the scientific community. Should the public come to believe that the scientific issues are settled, their views about global warming will change accordingly. Therefore, *you need to continue to make the lack of scientific certainty a primary issue in the debate. . . .*[59]

Similarly, the memo urged its audience to "emphasize the importance of '*acting only with* all *the facts in hand*,' and '*making the right decision, not the quick decision*.'" The major federal environmental laws rest on the premise that environmental policymakers should err on the side of caution by acting to prevent environmental risk in the face of scientific uncertainty. Despite that precautionary thrust, the memo urged Republicans to rely on a version of the "dead bodies" standard—regulation is inappropriate until a pile of dead bodies definitively proves that there is a problem— that had been soundly rejected by both Congress and the courts in the 1970s. To make the argument more palatable, the memo stressed that *"the most important point in any discussion of global warming is your commitment to sound science"* and common sense. It issued an ominous warning, however, that *"the scientific debate is closing [against us] but not yet closed. There is still a window of opportunity to challenge the science."*[60] Thus, the memorandum provided a sound science framing device to justify the first part of the litany, the denial of a problem.

The Luntz memo recommended raising the specter of economic ruin by portraying climate change regulation as another example of big government taxing people to death: "Remember, Americans already think they are an overtaxed people. Treaties such as Kyoto would have been just another tax on an already overburdened population."[61] Nor did the memo neglect the argument that regulation precludes important choices to which U.S. citizens are entitled. It urged its readers to "talk about the real world day-to-day effects that proposed environmental remedies would have on their everyday lives,"[62] and to scare people by predicting that regulation would cause "major lifestyle changes."[63] The attitude was that if climate change, improbably, turns out to be for real, the market would provide the optimal response. Regulation was unnecessary, costly, and would not work.

The memo also suggested playing the "fairness" card by arguing that the United States should not address climate change until nations such as Mexico, China, and India commit to do so. Indeed, the memo characterized the "international fairness issue" as "the emotional home run." Any hint that the U.S. climate change policy should continue the tradition of U.S. leadership on environmental issues was entirely absent. Another fairness argument turned on the disproportionate impacts that climate change regulation would have on the disadvantaged: "Yes, the fact that Kyoto would hurt the economic well being of seniors and the poor is of particular concern."[64]

The Luntz memorandum closed by listing several "principles" of environmental policy and global warming.[65] First, "sound science" must govern decisions on which problems to tackle and how to approach them. Second, it is necessary to identify "real risks" to human health and safety before deciding how to address a problem. Both these principles reflect the most fundamental element of the antiregulatory litany: "Prove it!" Third, "technology, innovation and discovery" are the keys to providing a clean environment. In other words, the market will supply superior solutions to any real environmental problems if left alone. Fourth, environmental policies should take into account the economic impact on the elderly, the poor, and those with fixed incomes. In other words, "It's not fair!" Fifth, "the best solutions are common sense solutions," implying that solutions dictated by the government rather than chosen by the market will be irrational. This point reflects the litany's claim that regulation is too expensive both in absolute terms and in comparison to the resulting environmental benefits. Sixth, "all nations must share responsibility for the environment." In other words, "It's not fair (again)!" Finally, changes in national policy should be "fully discussed in an open forum" with opportunities for public input. In other words, the government can't be trusted and they must be hiding something.

VIII. The Political Response

The advice in the Luntz memorandum found a receptive audience among politicians opposed to government action on climate change. The impact of the memorandum is illustrated by their repeated reliance on the theme that sound science supports neither the assertion that a serious problem exists nor the conclusion that human activities are largely responsible for it if it does. Senator Inhofe, for example, suggested on more than one occasion that global climate change might be "the greatest hoax ever perpetrated on the American people," making the advocates of government action seem no different from those who claim they have been abducted by aliens or seen the Loch Ness monster. Inhofe's position is a particularly crude version of the "Prove it!" strategy.

The Bush administration's approach was slightly more subtle. Vice President Cheney predicted a "big debate" on the question of whether climate change is due to natural climate cycles or human activity.[66] According to two political scientists at the University of Illinois, the Administration sought to generate confusion over the science to argue that scientific uncertainty over the causes of climate change makes regulation premature:

The Bush administration developed statutory and regulatory mechanisms designed to limit the flow of scientific information to the public, and implemented a legal framework to legitimize these mechanisms. The actions of the Bush administration in restricting the public's access to government-sponsored climate change research was unprecedented, affecting the relationship between science and policy in a way that changed the traditionally independent role that scientists have played in the United States. These actions of the Bush administration also negatively affected the media's access to government scientists who are recognized experts in the field.[67]

White House officials edited documents on climate change prepared by government scientists to reinforce the idea that the scientific community has not yet reached consensus on the link between greenhouse gas emissions and global warming. According to a former Republican chief of staff for a congressional science committee, regulatory opponents "settled on the 'science isn't there' argument because they didn't believe they'd be able to convince the public to do nothing if climate change were real."[68] The head of the National Aeronautics and Space Administration in mid-2007 characterized the view that humans should take steps to affect climate as "arrogant" and questioned whether climate change is serious enough to warrant concern among policymakers.[69] According to some reports, the Smithsonian Institution watered down an exhibit on the impact of climate change in the Arctic and avoided any reference to the cause of those changes due to fear of adverse reactions from the Bush administration and Congress.

A. A Change in Corporate Culture?

As the evidence of the dangers of climate change become increasingly irrefutable, all but the most shameless opponents of government action have curtailed their invocation of some elements of the litany. Some corporations have conceded that the problem is real and announced their support for doing something about it. In some cases, businesses such as Wal-Mart have cut their own consumption of electricity and encouraged consumers to purchase energy-efficient products. Other firms, such as Dow Chemical, have invested in research and development of technologies and products intended to reduce greenhouse gas emissions. These positions do not necessarily translate into support for regulation, but some businesses have even supported the adoption of mandatory emissions controls on greenhouse gases. The inducements for supporting either voluntary corporate initiatives or more systematic regulatory programs to address climate change may include taking a socially responsible position or burnishing the corporation's image by placing a green sheen on its activities.

Some businesses have realized that supporting climate change initiatives is in their own self-interest. Some insurance companies, for example, support regulation because unabated climate change will cause them to incur significant liabilities to insureds who have been injured by the consequences of climate change, such as coastal flooding or extreme weather events.[70] Timber companies may benefit from climate change regulation if it allows them to sell credits generated by preserving carbon sinks to industrial emitters of greenhouse gases who wish to avoid making their own reductions.[71] Segments of the energy industry that do not rely on the consumption of fossil fuels clearly have much to gain from restrictions on greenhouse gas emissions. Some companies, such as Dow Chemical, seek to profit from the manufacture and sale of energy-saving products, such as insulation, lightweight plastics, and solar technologies.[72] Others support regulation because they believe they can comply more quickly or efficiently than their competitors, providing them with at least a short-term market advantage.[73] Some support regulation because they have begun lowering their greenhouse gas emissions and stand to profit by selling emission allowances if federal climate change regulation includes an emissions trading regime.

Despite this movement toward support for climate change regulation, industry has not abandoned the litany described in this chapter. Some business support for climate change legislation is based on the fear that delaying its adoption is likely to produce more onerous regulation, either because the evidence of the adverse consequences of climate change will continue to accumulate or because of a change in the balance of political power. Businesses that have reluctantly begun to support regulation for these reasons are likely to invoke some elements of the litany as they push politicians toward policy solutions least likely to adversely affect their interests. Some will assuredly argue, for example, that particular policy options are technologically unrealistic, too expensive, or not worth the costs of compliance. They will also assert that policy options under consideration unfairly require them to make sacrifices not being demanded of other contributors to climate change.

The willingness of portions of corporate America to accept the reality of global climate change and take responsibility for avoiding or mitigating its adverse effects is welcome. It creates unique opportunities for the United States to become a world leader in developing both technological and regulatory solutions to climate change problems. Government programs, whether incentive-based or more traditionally regulatory in character, stand a greater chance of succeeding if the affected industries adopt a cooperative rather than an antagonistic posture.

The abandonment of some elements of the litany by a segment of the business community, however, by no means indicates that the litany has run its course or that the strategies laid out in the Luntz memorandum are no longer relevant to the political discourse on climate change. Some industries—such as segments of the fossil fuel production industry—remain entrenched in their opposition to any government efforts to address climate change. They almost certainly will continue to assert that important scientific questions remain unsettled as to both the existence and causes of climate change and that government programs should await resolution of these questions. If those arguments become even more untenable than they already are, they will likely predict economic ruin to convince environmental policymakers to adopt weak regulation.

B. Government Clings to the Litany

The willingness of some portions of industry to accept the need for meaningful action on climate change is a promising sign that the climate change debate may move beyond the stale rhetoric of free market liberalism. Tragically, at least as of the end of 2008, the federal government had not demonstrated a similar willingness to address the problem constructively. Too many officials seem stuck in the mind-set that the unimpeded free market provides the only legitimate means for protecting Americans against environmental, health, and safety risks. They continue to regard government as the principal problem rather than as a vehicle for enhancing quality of life for the American people by mitigating environmental risks posed by climate change. Some, such as Senator Inhofe, even persist in denying that climate change is due to human activity and that restrictions on greenhouse gas emissions will help mitigate climate change.

These policymakers have stuck to their story, no matter how much it strains credulity. Their story is that climate change is not occurring; that it is not caused by human activity even if it is real; that there is no viable technological fix; that the adverse economic consequences of addressing climate change will be monumental, and certainly not worth the meager benefits (if any) likely to flow from climate change regulation; and that efforts to restrict activities that contribute to global warming and replace them with more environmentally friendly alternatives will unfairly burden helpless Americans and fundamentally alter the American lifestyle for the worse. Little progress can be made in enlisting the assistance of industry in working with government to reduce the risks of climate change and to endorse necessary progressive solutions as long as the free market ideology that has generated these responses controls the debate. Characterizing climate change as the "greatest hoax ever perpetrated on the American people" is hardly the way to craft constructive environmental policy that provides the kind of leadership the United States once provided in dealing with worldwide social problems.

Notes

1. David Vogel, *Fluctuating Fortunes: The Political Power of Business in America* (New York: Basic Books, 1989), pp. 67–69, 72–74 (describing lack of opposition among business community to the early environmental laws and its surprise at the "significant escalation of the federal government's regulatory role"). Cf. Lincoln L. Davies, "Lessons for an Endangered Movement: What a Historical Juxtaposition of the Legal Response to Civil Rights and Environmentalism Has to Teach Environmentalists Today," *Environmental Law* 31 (2001): 229–370 (describing absence of industry presence at hearings on air pollution as a product of industry surprise at popular support for regulation).

2. Richard J. Lazarus, *The Making of Environmental Law* (Chicago: University of Chicago Press, 2004), pp. 75–78.

3. Ibid., p. 69.

4. Martha T. McCluskey, "Efficiency and Social Citizenship: Challenging the Neoliberal Attack on the Welfare State," *Indiana Law Journal* 78 (2003): 783–876.

5. Ibid., p. 784.

6. Ibid.

7. Douglas A. Kysar, "Sustainable Development and Private Global Governance," *Texas Law Review* 83 (2005): 2109–2166.

8. Martha T. McCluskey, "Thinking with Wolves: Left Legal Theory after the Right's Rise," *Buffalo Law Review* 54 (2007): 1191–1297.

9. Sidney A. Shapiro, "Administrative Law after the Counter-Reformation: Restoring Faith in Pragmatic Government," *University of Kansas Law Review* 48 (2000): 689–750.

10. Lazarus, *Making of Environmental Law*, p. 100.

11. Shapiro, "Counter-Reformation," pp. 697, 702.

12. Richard N. L. Andrews, *Managing the Environment, Managing Ourselves: A History of American Environmental Policy* (New Haven, CT: Yale University Press, 1999), p. 257.

13. Lazarus, *Making of Environmental Law*, p. 95.

14. Phillip K. Howard, *The Death of Common Sense: How Law Is Suffocating America* (New York: Warner Books, 1994).

15. Lazarus, *Making of Environmental Law*, p. 97.

16. Shapiro, "Counter-Reformation," p. 702 (citing Vogel, *Fluctuating Fortunes*, pp. 230–231).

17. Thomas O. McGarity, "On the Prospect of 'Daubertizing' Judicial Review of Risk Assessment," *Law and Contemporary Problems* 66 (autumn 2003): 155–225.

18. Thomas O. McGarity, "Our Science Is Sound Science and Their Science Is Junk Science: Science-Based Strategies for Avoiding Accountability and Responsibility for Risk-Producing Products and Activities," *University of Kansas Law Review* 52 (2004): 897–937.

19. *Flue-Cured Tobacco Cooperative Stabilization Corp. v. United States Envtl. Prot. Agency*, 313 F.3d 852 (4th Cir. 2002). See McGarity, "'Daubertizing' Judicial Review," pp. 178–199.

20. William Funk, "Free Market Environmentalism: Wonder Drug or Snake Oil?," *Harvard Journal of Law and Public Policy* 15 (1992): 511–516.

21. Michael R. Bosse, "Comment: George J. Mitchell: Maine's Environmental Senator," *Maine Law Review* 47 (1995): 179–222.

22. Jeff Trask, "Montreal Protocol Noncompliance Procedure: The Best Approach to Resolving International Environmental Disputes?," *Georgetown Law Journal* 80 (1992): 1973–2001. See generally James L. Regens and Robert W. Rycroft, *The Acid Rain Controversy* (Pittsburgh: University of Pittsburgh Press, 1988), pp. 41–47.

23. Robert V. Percival, "Checks Without Balance: Executive Office Oversight of the Environmental Protection Agency," *Law and Contemporary Problems* 54 (autumn 1991): 127–204.

24. Stuart N. Keith, "The EPA's Discretion to Regulate Acid Rain: A Discussion of the Requirements for Triggering Section 115 of the Clean Air Act," *Cleveland State Law Review* 36 (1987–1988): 133–155.

25. See Lazarus, *Making of Environmental Law*, p. 99.

26. Jon D. Hanson and Douglas A. Kysar, "Taking Behavioralism Seriously: Some Evidence of Market Manipulation," *Harvard Law Review* 112 (1999): 1420–1572.

27. Jonathan Miles, "Tobacco Road," *New York Times*, May 6, 2007, Book Review Section, p. 6 (reviewing Allan M. Brandt, *The Cigarette Century: The Rise, Fall, and Deadly Persistence of the Product That Defined America* [New York: Basic Books, 2007]).

28. Thomas O. McGarity, "Proposal for Linking Culpability and Causation to Ensure Corporate Accountability for Toxic Risks," *William & Mary Environmental Law and Policy Review* 26 (2001): 1–65.

29. *United States v. Philip Morris USA, Inc.*, 449 F. Supp. 2d 1, 28 (D.D.C. 2006); stay granted, 2006 WL 4608645 (D.C. Cir. Nov. 1, 2006); order clarified, 477 F. Supp. 2d 191 (D.D.C. 2007).

30. *Lead Industries Ass'n, Inc. v. Environmental Prot. Agency*, 647 F.2d 1130 (D.C. Cir. 1979), cert. denied, 449 U.S. 1042 (1980).

31. See Howard Latin, "Good Science, Bad Regulation, and Toxic Risk Assessment," *Yale Journal on Regulation* 5 (1988): 89–148.

32. Howard Latin, "Real Regulatory Efficiency: Implementation of Uniform Standards and 'Fine-Tuning' Regulatory Reforms," *Stanford Law Review* 37 (1985): 1267–1332.

33. Lazarus, *Making of Environmental Law*, p. 95.

34. *International Harvester v. Ruckelshaus*, 478 F.2d 615 (D.C. Cir. 1973).

35. Thomas O. McGarity, "Regulating Commuters to Clear the Air: Some Difficulties in Implementing a National Program at the Local Level," *Pacific Law Journal* 27 (1996): 1521–1627.

36. Walter Adams and James W. Brock, "The Antitrust Vision and Its Revisionist Critics," *New York Law School Law Review* 35 (1990): 939–967.

37. David Vogel, *National Styles of Regulation: Environmental Policy in Great Britain and the United States* (Ithaca, N.Y.: Cornell University Press, 1986), p. 258 (quoting J. Clarence Davies III and Barbara S. Davies, *The Politics of Pollution* [Indianapolis: Bobbs-Merrill, 1975], p. 53).

38. This set of arguments is often made in conjunction with other litany arguments—nonexistence of a problem, lack of causation, and the infeasibility of fixing the problem—discussed above. Albert Hirschman describes these arguments as the "perversity thesis," the "futility thesis," and the "jeopardy thesis." The first argues that "any purposive action to improve some feature of the political, social, or economic order only serves to exacerbate the condition one wishes to remedy." The second claims that "attempts at social transformation will be unavailing, that they will simply fail 'to make a dent.'" The third holds that "the cost of the proposed change or reform is too high as it endangers some previous, precious accomplishment." Albert O. Hirschman, *The Rhetoric of Reaction: Perversity, Futility, Jeopardy* (Cambridge, MA: The Belknap Press of Harvard University Press, 1991), p. 7.

39. Sidney A. Shapiro and Robert L. Glicksman, *Risk Regulation at Risk: Restoring a Pragmatic Approach* (Stanford, CA: Stanford University Press, 2003), p. 74.

40. Ibid., p. 77.

41. Lazarus, *Making of Environmental Law*, p. 95.

42. Christopher T. Giovanazzo, "Defending Overstatement: The Symbolic Clean Air Act and Carbon Dioxide," *Harvard Environmental Law Review* 30 (2006):

99–163. See also Eban Goodstein, "Polluted Data," *American Prospect* (Nov. 30, 2002), http://www.prospect.org/cs/articles?article=polluted_data.

43. Joseph A. Siegel, "Terrorism and Environmental Law: Chemical Facility Site Security vs. Right-to-Know?," *Widener Law Symposium Journal* 9 (2003): 339–385; David M. Driesen, "Is Emissions Trading an Economic Incentive Program? Replacing the Command and Control/Economic Incentive Dichotomy," *Washington and Lee Law Review* 55 (1998): 289–350.

44. Daniel Cusick, "EPA Ozone Proposal to Face Scrutiny on Hill," *E&E News PM*, June 21, 2007, http://www.eenews.net/eenewspm/2007/6/21.

45. Shapiro and Glicksman, *Risk Regulation*, p. 9.

46. Andrews, *Managing the Environment*, p. 239.

47. See generally McGarity, "Regulating Commuters."

48. Sharon Begley, "The Truth about Denial," *Newsweek*, Aug. 13, 2007, pp. 20, 22.

49. Dean Scott, "Business Roundtable Urges Emissions Curbs, Calls for Expanded Greenhouse Gas Registry," *Environment Reporter* (Bureau of National Affairs) 38 (July 20, 2007): 151.

50. Dean Scott, "Costs Imposed by U.S. Greenhouse Gas Cap May Be Offset by Projected Economic Growth," *Environment Reporter* (Bureau of National Affairs) 38 (March 2, 2007): 481.

51. Coal industry executive Robert Murray, quoted in Margaret Kriz, "Hot Opportunities," *National Journal*, July 7, 2007, pp. 14, 16.

52. John M. Broder, "California Wants Strict Auto Emission Rules," *New York Times*, May 23, 2007, p. A16.

53. Danny Hakim, "Challenge to Emissions Rule Is Set to Start," *New York Times*, Apr. 10, 2007.

54. Frank Luntz, "The Environment: A Cleaner, Safer, Healthier America," http://www.ewg.org/files/LuntzResearch_environment.pdf.

55. Ibid., 131. The memo also urged "talk[ing] about the professions and industries that will be hurt the most." Ibid., p. 140.

56. Ibid., p. 136.

57. Ibid., p. 132–133.

58. Ibid., pp. 135–136.

59. Ibid., p. 137.

60. Ibid., p. 138.

61. Ibid., p. 139.

62. Ibid.

63. Ibid., p. 140.

64. Ibid. The memo also stated: "Stringent environmental regulations hit the most vulnerable among us—the elderly, the poor, and those on fixed incomes—the hardest. Say it." Ibid., p. 139.

65. Ibid., p. 143.

66. Sharon Begley and Andrew Murr, "Which of These Is Not Causing Global Warming Today?," *Newsweek*, July 9, 2007, p. 48.

67. Robert F. Rich and Kelly R. Merrick, "Use and Misuse of Science: Global Climate Change and the Bush Administration," *Virginia Journal of Social Policy and the Law* 14 (2007): 223–252.

68. Begley, "Truth about Denial," p. 24.

69. "NASA Leader: Who Says Warming Is A Problem?," *New York Times*, June 1, 2007, http://www.nytimes/com/2007/06/01/science/earth/01griffin.html?.

70. Peter H. Stone, "Feeling Storm-Tossed," *National Journal*, July 7, 2007, p. 28.

71. Jerry Hagstrom, "Nature's Storage System," *National Journal*, July 7, 2007, p. 31.

72. Kriz, "Hot Opportunities," p. 16.

73. See Elise Zoli and Aladdine Joroff, "Making Silver Linings," *Environmental Forum* 24, no. 3 (May–June 2007): 22–26.

5

The Abandonment of Justice

Amy Sinden

Public policy discussions are increasingly framed (and confined) by the rhetoric, values, and assumptions of economic theory. But with its single-minded focus on efficiency, or aggregate social welfare, economic theory explicitly and self-consciously ignores the distribution of wealth and power in society. These are questions not of efficiency, but of justice—a subject on which classical economic theory has little or nothing to say. Accordingly, framing climate change in economic terms tends to mask important dimensions of the problem. Climate change does reveal a market failure, but that is only part of the problem. Humanity's inability to curb the activities that are contributing to a warming globe has also been driven on several different dimensions by disparities in wealth and power: (1) disparities between the fossil fuel industry and other corporate interests that stand to lose from climate change regulation compared with the largely individual interests that stand to gain; (2) disparities between the developed countries that are largely responsible for causing global warming and the developing countries that are likely to bear the brunt of its effects; and (3) disparities between the present generations that are causing global warming and the future generations that will be saddled with most of its impacts. Ironically, many of the same inequities that are driving the causes of climate change will be exacerbated by the effects of climate change, which will be most devastating to the poor and to future generations.

Recognizing these distributional dimensions of the climate change problem is crucial to crafting effective solutions. But the economic prism through which public policy is now so often filtered has obscured these aspects of the problem. On one level, this results from the fact that economic theory explicitly sets aside distributional issues as outside the scope of its analysis. But the problem runs deeper. In fact, distributional issues do creep into economic analysis and covertly distort its outcomes, skewing public policy even more toward the interests of the powerful and against those of the powerless. First, by measuring welfare in terms of willingness-to-pay, economic analysis implicitly values the interests of the rich over those of the poor. Second, the convention of discounting future costs and benefits dramatically reduces the weight given to the interests of future generations.

I.   Causes: The Three Dimensions of Political Failure

As explained in the introduction to this book, welfare economics evaluates public policies against the standard of Kaldor–Hicks efficiency. A government policy or regulation is "efficient" in the Kaldor-Hicks sense if those who would benefit from the regulation could fully compensate those who would lose and still be better off. Kaldor–Hicks efficiency, then, is a measure of *aggregate* social welfare.[1] Because the hypothetical transfer of wealth from winners to losers need not actually occur, this efficiency standard is entirely insensitive to how welfare is distributed.[2] As long as the welfare of all members of society combined is maximized, it does not matter if some benefit at the expense of others. Thus, a world in which Bill Gates owned all the wealth while others starved and an alternative world in which the same amount of wealth was distributed equally among all individuals could each be equally "efficient" under a Kaldor–Hicks test.[3] Economics, as it is often said, shows us how to produce the largest pie, leaving to politics the task of determining how that pie should be divided up and distributed through tax or welfare programs. Economic theory, then, offers no criteria for deciding distributional questions.[4]

The problem is that to the extent public policy debates frame issues in economic terms, as they frequently do,[5] they risk missing the important distributional aspect of those issues. Viewed through an economic lens, the climate change problem is caused by market failure. It is a classic tragedy of the commons in which each individual, rationally pursuing her self-interest, squanders a commonly held resource to her own and everyone else's detriment. Although this, no doubt, explains an important aspect of the problem, it is not the whole story. Our inability to curb the activities that are contributing to a warming globe is driven not just by market failure, but by a political failure that stems from gross inequities in the distribution of wealth and power. The following pages describe the three axes of inequity that have driven that political failure. These inequities have distorted democratic processes and skewed collective decision making away from the kind of stringent regulation necessary to slow global warming.

A. The Fossil Fuel Industry versus the Public

The politics of climate change has played out against the backdrop of a vast imbalance of power between the interests that stand to gain from climate change regulation and those that stand—in the short run, at least—to lose. Those that stand to lose are those that profit from the extraction and combustion of fossil fuels. These are some of the wealthiest and most powerful corporations in the world. (Exxon-Mobil made over \$39.5 billion in profits in 2006, more than any other corporation worldwide.[6]) These corporations are relatively small in number, and each one stands to suffer substantial, concrete, economic losses in the short run if climate change regulation is enacted.[7] Accordingly, they do not suffer from the collective action and free rider problems that stymie efforts to organize large groups of individuals.

On the other side, those who stand to gain are primarily individual people—the coastal residents from Florida to the Netherlands to Bangladesh whose homes will be inundated by rising seas, the farmers in Africa whose crops will be killed by drought, the children in the tropical and subtropical developing world who will fall ill and die from the spread of malaria, and the Inuit in the Arctic whose homes are already sinking into the melting permafrost. These "gainers" from climate change regulation are enormous in number, widely dispersed around the globe, and have interests that are often hard to measure in precise economic terms. This is just the kind of group that has a particularly hard time organizing politically.[8]

To be sure, there have long been corporate interests on the "gainers" side as well. The insurance industry recognized over a decade ago that by increasing the severity and intensity of storms and flooding, global warming was a likely culprit in the dramatic increase in insurance payouts during the 1980s and '90s.[9] And the alternative energy industry has always clearly stood to gain from the imposition of limits on carbon emissions. But at least until very recently, the power of these companies to influence public opinion and political outcomes has been dwarfed by the enormous wealth and power that the fossil fuel industry has put behind this fight.[10]

This imbalance of power between the fossil fuel industry and the public has contributed to a massive political failure in the United States over the past two decades—a political failure in which our elected representatives at the federal level have acted in direct opposition to the expressed wishes of the electorate. A *New York Times* poll, taken right before the Kyoto accord was reached in 1997, showed 65 percent of Americans saying that the United States should take steps now to cut its own emissions "regardless of what other countries do."[11] Yet just four months earlier the Senate had passed, by a 95 to 0 margin, the Byrd–Hagel Resolution, which said the opposite: that the United States should not sign Kyoto unless the agreement mandated reductions by developing countries as well.[12] And since the treaty that ultimately resulted from the negotiations in Kyoto did not mandate immediate reductions from developing countries, this resolution ultimately marked the death-knell for any attempt to ratify the treaty.[13] This dramatic disconnect between what the American people wanted and what their Senators voted for reflects, at least in part, the overwhelming power and influence of the corporate interests that stand to lose from climate change regulation.[14]

The massive public relations campaign by the fossil fuel industry to, in Robert Glicksman's terms (see chapter 4 of this volume), argue that global warming is not a problem and not its fault, helped cement this political failure.[15] Since the late 1980s, oil companies, car companies, and other industrial interests have formed a whole series of front groups with the mission of creating public doubt about the science behind global warming.[16] These groups have spent millions of dollars on a campaign that included heavy funding of scientists willing to express skepticism about global warming, efforts to publicly smear and discredit scientists on the Intergovernmental Panel on Climate Change, and huge expenditures for advertising and lobbying.[17] In 2005 alone, Exxon-Mobil gave $6.8 million to think tanks like the Competitive Enterprise Institute, whose efforts included the airing of a television ad claiming that carbon dioxide is actually good for the environment, carefully timed to coincide with the release of Al Gore's movie, *An Inconvenient Truth*.[18]

Finally, after nearly two decades, as the evidence of a warming globe has become impossible to refute, the strength of this disinformation campaign is waning. Beginning in the late 1990s with BP and Shell, big companies have gradually been defecting from the strategy of outright denial championed most vigorously by Exxon-Mobil.[19] Even Exxon-Mobil itself has softened its stance, announcing recently that it would stop funding the Competitive Enterprise Institute.[20] And as the political inevitability of mandatory carbon limits becomes undeniable, an increasing number of corporations—including even some of those in the fossil fuel industry—are recognizing that cutting carbon emissions now may ultimately be good for the bottom line.[21] They have come to appreciate that when the carbon limits inevitably come, it will be the details of the legislation—including how credits in a trading scheme are initially distributed—that will determine who wins and who loses. Those who step up early to support the general idea of carbon regulation will gain a seat at the negotiating table and so fare better when the deal is ultimately cut. So it was that Duke Energy and nine other major corporations joined with Environmental Defense and the Natural Resources Defense Council (NRDC) in 2007 to call for nationwide limits to reduce carbon dioxide emissions by 10 to 30 percent over the next fifteen years.[22]

In the face of all of this corporate greening, it's easy to lose sight of the vast power imbalance that has distorted the climate change debate for decades and continues to do so even in the face of overwhelming evidence of the need for regulation. Increasingly, these stories of corporations going green are being spun into a larger cultural narrative of the corporation as redeemed sinner. But it seems safe to say that the power and wealth wielded by the fossil fuel industry succeeded in delaying action on climate change for at least two decades. And it would be a mistake to think that the recent concessions of many in the fossil fuel industry with respect to global warming mean that corporations have suddenly come around to represent the best interests of the general public. In climate change regulation, as in so many matters, the devil is in the details. Depending on where the cap is set, how permits are distributed, and how offsets are designed and monitored, climate change regulation may turn out to be either an effective mechanism that spurs significant reductions in atmospheric greenhouse gas accumulations or a symbolic but empty gesture. As new climate change legislation takes shape, the details the fossil fuel industry pushes will be those that maximize short-term profits. And these will often be the details that move us closer to the second scenario than the first.

B. Developed versus Developing Countries

A similar kind of power imbalance has distorted international negotiations aimed at slowing climate change. Developed countries, of course, have the most power to reduce greenhouse gas (GHG) emissions, both because they are producing more to begin with and because they have more technology and resources to devote to the problem. Yet, the developed world also faces considerable economic incentives to continue to pursue "business as usual." With just 20 percent of the world population, developed countries produced 57 percent of global GNP and 46 percent of global greenhouse gas emissions in 2004.[23] This enormous wealth creates powerful incentives among those who benefit from it to resist any changes to the status quo, including any moves to disturb the well-entrenched infrastructure of fossil fuel extraction, delivery, and consumption. The developed countries, then, have the most power to slow global warming, and yet they face powerful incentives to resist strict limits on GHG emissions. Exacerbating this inertia is the fact that the developed world may escape some of the worst impacts of climate change, at least in the short run. In temperate climates, there is more leeway for temperatures to increase without creating inhospitable conditions. Indeed, at some northern latitudes, crop yields are actually projected to increase.[24] Moreover, the wealth that developed countries enjoy gives them some latitude in adapting to the adverse effects of climate change.

Conversely, those with the most to gain from slowing climate change are those with the least power to do so.[25] As detailed further in part II of this chapter, developing countries are projected to bear the worst of the adverse effects of climate change. And yet they have far less of a capacity to stave off climate change than do developed countries, because they are producing far fewer emissions to begin with. Per capita GHG emissions in the developing world are less than one-sixth what they are in the United States and Canada.[26] Moreover, developing countries have far fewer resources to devote to making the technological changes necessary to slow GHG emissions.[27] As developing countries struggle to develop export industries in which any competitive advantage they have comes from lower costs, forcing their industries to install costly pollution reduction technologies will be difficult.[28]

Sadly, this disparity in wealth and power between the developed and developing worlds and the skewed incentives it generates have derailed efforts to craft a strategy of international cooperation to address climate change. The United States—the most powerful country in the world and the largest contributor of greenhouse gases to the global atmosphere—has consistently refused to agree to binding international commitments to reduce greenhouse gas emissions.

C. Present versus Future Generations

Political decision making about climate change is further distorted by the imbalance of power between current and future generations. Again, there is a mismatch between those who are causing the problem and therefore have the power to fix it, and those who are likely to bear the worst of its effects. Because there's a significant lag time between when heat-trapping gases accumulate in the atmosphere and when the earth's climate reaches a new equilibrium in response to the change, many of the worst effects of the greenhouse gases we are emitting into the atmosphere now won't be felt until decades or even centuries from now.[29] Thus, the political decisions we make now will have profound impacts on future generations.

Yet future generations have no power to affect political decision making in the present. Certainly, we can assume that members of the current political community care about what happens to their children and grandchildren and therefore incorporate the interests of future generations into their preferences and political choices to some degree. But this indirect representation is undoubtedly incomplete. And where the interests of present and future generations conflict—where, for example, imposing irreversible ecological loss or some risk of such loss produces short-term economic benefit (global warming is an obvious example)—the interests of future generations will undoubtedly be less than fully accounted for.[30]

II. Effects: Taking from the Poor

All of these disparities in wealth and power are exacerbated by the fact that the effects of climate change are likely to be inequitably distributed across both space and time.[31] Some of this is simply the luck of geography. A number of the most severe and disruptive impacts of climate change, including drought, sea level rise, and the spread of disease, are projected to be particularly harsh in the developing world.[32] The effects will also be disproportionately severe in the Arctic, where melting ice and permafrost has already begun to displace indigenous communities.[33]

But in other respects, the disparate impacts of climate change are driven by existing inequalities. Poor countries, as well as poor communities within developed countries, are likely to suffer more from climate change because they have fewer resources to devote to adaptation.[34] As Hurricane Katrina all too vividly demonstrated, when natural disaster strikes and existing infrastructure is inadequate, it is the poor—who lack the resources to evacuate, relocate, or rebuild—who suffer the most. Indeed, data have subsequently confirmed what was painfully evident from the news footage and photographs at the time: those displaced by Katrina—the people crowded in the Superdome, stuck out on the streets, and huddled on rooftops—were disproportionately African-American, poor, and unemployed.[35] Although it is impossible to say definitively whether Hurricane Katrina was actually caused by climate change, as sea levels rise and storm intensity increases, we can expect to see similar scenes repeat themselves in low-lying coastal areas around the world.

Finally, climate change will impose disparate impacts across generations. Many greenhouse gases remain in the atmosphere for decades or even centuries. Moreover, there is a delay between when gases first accumulate and when some of the worst effects of climate change will begin to occur.[36] The collapse of the Antarctic and Greenland ice sheets may cause sudden and catastrophic sea-level rise of many meters, but it may take a century or more for this to happen.[37] Accordingly, many of the worst effects of climate change will be borne by future generations who have no power to prevent it.

Thus, climate change is caused not just by market failure but by a massive political failure brought on by the gross disparities in wealth and power described above. In a nutshell, those who bear the largest share of responsibility for having caused the climate change problem are the wealthy and the powerful of present generations. Because the activities that lead to climate change have also generated a substantial share of that wealth and power, those who bear the most responsibility for the problem are reluctant to change their ways. Moreover, their wealth and power allows them to act with impunity even in the face of strong moral claims from the rest of the world. Conversely, those who have the most to lose from climate change and therefore the most to gain from its regulation are disproportionately the poor and powerless, who have little ability to influence those with the most capacity to address the problem.

III. Misconceived Solutions

If we view the problem of climate change through an economic lens, we are likely to misdiagnose the problem and misconceive the solutions. First, because economics obscures the distributional inequities and power imbalances that play such a large role in causing climate change, the solutions it produces inevitably fail to account for this crucial aspect of the problem. A solution that fails to account for the distributional aspects of climate change will be neither just nor workable. Many economists respond to such charges by arguing that equity concerns should simply be considered separately, alongside efficiency considerations. If the problem were simply economic theory's failure to account for distributional concerns, such arguments might have credence. But the problem runs far deeper. Indeed, inequity is embedded in the very logic of welfare economics. Not only does economics ignore the disparities in wealth and power that both drive and are driven by climate change, it exacerbates those disparities. In judging the effectiveness of potential solutions, economics undervalues both the preferences of the poor in relation to those of the rich and the preferences of future generations in relation to those of present generations.

A.   Ignoring Distributional Inequities

Consider first economic theory's standard diagnosis of climate change: Our inability to curb greenhouse gas emissions is caused by a market failure brought on by the tragedy of the commons. Picture Garret Hardin's cattle herders sharing a common pasture.[38] In the parable, each herder is equally responsible for causing the tragedy and each has an equal store of resources and power to devote to fixing it. Responsibility for reversing or preventing the tragedy therefore seems to fall equally on each individual's shoulders. The problem is mutually created, and so is the solution—in Hardin's words, "mutual coercion, mutually agreed-upon."[39]

This conception fundamentally misdiagnoses the problem by casting it as a failure of individual will: If we would all just use energy-efficient lightbulbs and stop driving SUVs, everything would be fine.[40] In this way, the economic lens obscures the role that corporate power plays in distorting political outcomes that might otherwise solve the tragedy of the commons. The corporation's role is recast as that of innocent broker—a neutral facilitator of free market exchange—simply satisfying individual consumer preferences by delivering to consumers the products they demand. Corporations, and the vast power and resources they wield, thus drop out of focus. The problem becomes one not of power imbalance but of consumer as wrongdoer. Under this logic, proposed solutions focus on changing individual consumer behavior rather than reining in corporate power.[41]

Indeed, because it judges potential solutions to the tragedy of the commons against the normative standard of efficiency, economics inevitably masks the pervasive distributional inequities that both cause and are caused by climate change. To measure the efficiency of potential responses to climate change, one must measure the aggregate social costs of reducing greenhouse gas emissions against the aggregate social benefits of preventing some of global warming's effects. In the aggregation, though, all information about the distribution of those costs and benefits among individuals is lost. That's okay, so long as efficiency remains one's only guiding moral principle. Efficiency is itself indifferent to distributional considerations. But to the extent that the distribution of costs and benefits among individuals implicates other important moral or ethical principles, like equity or justice, a strict adherence to efficiency will lead us astray. The efficiency principle, for example, trades off catastrophic consequences for some (including death) for incremental gains spread out among a large group.[42] Thus, the death of a thousand Bangladeshis from sea-level rise would be deemed efficient if it allowed 151 million Americans to each pay a dollar less for electricity.[43]

Additionally, by aggregating costs and benefits, the efficiency principle obscures issues of causation and responsibility. No ethical system sanctions a person causing harm to another person in order to avoid harm to herself. Certainly, the notion that one group of people would cause bodily harm to another group in order to achieve incremental, non-needs-related consumption gains would seem to violate ethical norms under virtually any system.[44] And yet, the efficiency principle sanctions such results.

For example, the regulatory solution that most economists advocate—a globally uniform carbon tax—would achieve efficiency at the expense of equity. To be efficient, the tax rate should be set at the dollar amount of global benefit incurred from each ton of carbon emissions abated. Putting aside the difficulties of generating a meaningful monetary estimate of the marginal benefits of carbon abatement, a tax of this sort would undoubtedly result in a higher rate of abatement—more tons of CO_2 abated per ton of CO_2 emitted—in the developing world than in the developed world.[45] Although the gross amount of emissions per capita is smaller in the developing world, those sources that do exist there tend to employ older technologies and therefore offer more opportunities for low-cost abatement. The incentive that a tax would create for energy producers in the developing world to invest in these low-cost abatement strategies would keep aggregate costs low for the globe as a whole, but it would impose a large share of those costs on developing countries in a way that would seem to many entirely at odds with intuitive notions of equity and justice.[46]

It is, of course, fundamental to the Kaldor–Hicks efficiency criterion that it trades off gains to one set of people for losses to another. The theory is that implementing a policy that is Kaldor–Hicks efficient has the potential to leave all individuals better off than they were before. In a state of Kaldor–Hicks efficiency, it is true by definition that if the winners compensated the losers for their losses, the winners would still have some gains left over. But there is nothing about the Kaldor–Hicks efficiency criterion itself that actually requires such a transfer to take place. Within a domestic political system, the use of Kaldor–Hicks efficiency can be defended on the ground that once policies are implemented to achieve efficiency, the "bigger pie" can be redistributed among members of society according to principles of equity through taxing and spending programs enacted by the government. This argument is problematic, not least because Kaldor–Hicks efficiency often requires trading lives for dollars. But on the global scale, the problem runs even deeper. Because there is no government with authority to redistribute resources across national borders, we can't assume that any inequitable distributions that occur as a by-product of the pursuit of efficiency can be cured.

Because the economic worldview obscures these distributional aspects of the problem, the solutions it generates will inevitably be both unfair and ineffective. They will be unfair because they will ask those with the least resources and the least responsibility for causing the problem to expend large amounts of resources to solve it. They will be ineffective because developing countries are acutely aware of the distributional inequities that permeate the climate change problem and will not be eager to sign on to an international agreement that fails to incorporate principles of fairness aimed at counteracting these inequities.

B. Exacerbating Distributional Inequalities

The problem runs deeper, however. Not only does the efficiency principle ignore disparities in wealth and power, it exacerbates them. Economic theory measures social welfare in a way that undervalues the preferences of the poor in relation to those of the rich and undervalues the preferences of future generations in relation to those of present generations.

1. Undervaluing the poor   Economics measures value in terms of people's willingness to pay. But this presents a host of theoretical difficulties. Chief among these is the problem of *wealth effects*. Since a person's *willingness* to pay depends in part on her *ability* to pay, a poor person's willingness to pay for a particular good generally will be lower than a rich person's, even if the poor person values the good just as much. Therefore, measuring preferences in terms of dollars necessarily undercounts the preferences of poor people relative to rich people.[47]

People living in a coastal village in Bangladesh, for example, might highly value measures to prevent rising sea levels that threaten to inundate their homes; but if their incomes are low, the dollar amount that they would be "willing to pay" to take such measures will also of necessity be low. A number of cost-benefit analyses of climate change regulation acknowledge this problem, but take no steps to account for it.[48] Thus, it is a common practice in such analyses to value the lives of people in the developed world significantly higher than those in the developing world.[49] These differing "values of a statistical life" (VSL) are based on studies in different regions investigating people's willingness to pay to avoid risk (or willingness to accept payment to take on risk). The results of such studies can vary dramatically in different regions of the world. While in the United States, such studies yield a median VSL of approximately $7 million,[50] studies of VSL in the developing world have produced values as low as $20,000.[51] Indeed, the Second Assessment Report of the International Panel on Climate Change (IPCC) created an uproar when it took this approach, suggesting that the lives of people in the developed world should be valued at $3.5 million while the lives of people in the poorest regions of the world were valued at a small fraction of that amount—$120,000 for people in India, for example.[52] Ecological characteristics were also differentially valued. A hectare of wetlands lost in China, for example, was counted at one tenth the value of a hectare of wetlands lost in an OECD country.[53] Some economists propose to correct this problem by using "equity weighting" techniques to weight a person's willingness to pay by some value inverse to her income.[54] But most economists believe that finding a practical way to accomplish such a weighting presents insurmountable barriers.[55]

Stung by the controversy generated by the economic analysis in the Second Assessment Report, the IPCC took a different approach in the Third and Fourth Assessment Reports. It suggested that differing VSLs in different regions of the world should be averaged for purposes of the analysis of climate change.[56] This averaged value comes to one million Euros.[57] Using this figure instead of national values increases the mortality costs associated with climate change by a factor of five.[58]

But even a globally averaged VSL undervalues the interests of the poor, given that most of the costs of climate change mitigation are likely to be borne by the rich. Just as a dollar of benefit provides less utility to a rich person than a poor person, so a dollar of cost imposes less disutility on a rich person than on a poor person. Thus, rich people's dollars aren't directly comparable to poor people's dollars. That means if a cost-benefit analyst measures benefits in dollars that have been partially weighted by poor people's preferences (in the global average VSL) and costs in rich people's dollars, she is still comparing apples to oranges. Each dollar that goes into the globally averaged VSL represents a larger increment of utility than each dollar that goes into rich people's costs.

Therefore, costs measured in rich people's dollars will appear larger than they actually are in utility terms. It's one thing for a poor Bangladeshi to say she's not willing to pay a cost of $20 to avoid a 1 in 1,000 risk of death, because if she doesn't have that $20 to feed her child for the next year, her child will starve. It is quite another thing for a rich American to say that she is not willing to pay a cost of $20 to avoid a 1 in 1,000 risk of death for a Bangladeshi, because if she does not have that $20 to take a cab to the airport next week, she will have to take the bus. Since the costs of climate change mitigation will be paid primarily in rich people's dollars, the benefits (including the VSL) should also be measured in rich people's dollars.

2. Undervaluing future generations   The practice of discounting exacerbates the existing power disparity between present and future generations by undercounting the preferences of future generations vis-à-vis those of present generations. Economists typically apply a discount rate to monetary costs or benefits that will not be realized until some future date.[59] This reflects the time value of money, or the fact that $100 tomorrow is worth less than $100 today, both because of inflation rates and the investment value of money. With a 5 percent discount rate, for example, a $100 cost to be incurred a year from now is converted into $95 "present value."

A discount rate is noncontroversial when applied to money or goods that are easily translated into monetary terms. Based on interest and inflation rates (the opportunity cost of capital), standard discount rates for costs that will not be incurred until some future date are between 4 and 6 percent.[60] But for goods not traded in markets—a human life or a pristine natural area—it is less clear that discounting makes sense. Human lives do not earn interest in bank accounts. It is certainly reasonable to assume that people express time preferences within their own lifetimes—avoiding a risk that may kill me today is worth more than avoiding a risk that won't kill me until ten years from now. When discounting of health or environmental risks is performed over time horizons longer than a few decades, however, it can no longer be thought of as simply trading off risks within particular people's lifetimes. It then has the effect of devaluing the preferences of future generations vis-à-vis present ones.

This problem is particularly salient in the context of climate change. Because of the persistence of greenhouse gases in the atmosphere, many of the worst effects of our actions will not be felt for centuries. But over the course of centuries, even relatively modest discount rates can drastically diminish the weight accorded to harms suffered by future generations. Applying a discount rate of 5 percent to the death of a billion people 500 years from now, for example, yields the conclusion that such an event is less harmful (or costly) than the death of one person today.[61]

Many economists routinely apply a 6 percent discount rate to nonmarket benefits and costs.[62] Some apply a discount rate that declines over time based on evidence that people's time preference is greater in the near term than the long term.[63] But even a declining rate significantly devalues the interests of future generations. Some economists justify the use of discounting for nonmarket benefits and costs on the basis of the opportunity cost of capital (the marginal rate of return on investment).[64] In simple terms, the idea is that we need to set aside less money today to compensate for a death in the future than we would need to compensate for a death today. The problem is that cost-benefit analysis is used not to design trust funds to compensate present and future victims, but to make decisions about whether to take measures to prevent people from being killed in the first place. The conceptual leap—from the idea that compensation for future deaths costs less in today's dollars to the idea that a future person's life is actually worth less than a present person's life—is simply unwarranted.[65]

Others justify the discounting of health and environmental impacts based on "the social rate of time preference."[66] This rate is divided into two separate factors: (1) the expectation that future generations will be richer, and (2) something called "pure time preference."[67] The first factor is accounted for by adjusting the discount rate based on the expected rate of economic growth. The idea is that we should count bad things that happen in the future as less bad, because, as the economy continues to grow, people in the future will be better off and therefore better able to afford the costs of adaptation to or compensation for those bad conditions. The irony is that this is precisely the opposite logic that leads many economists to apply differing VSLs to the rich and the poor. Applying that logic to the comparison of values across generations would require not that we *discount* the lives of future generations, but that we treat them as more valuable than our own. If those living in the future will be richer, then presumably they will also be willing to pay more to avoid the risk of death.[68]

Pure time preference refers to the fact that an individual might value $100 today over $120 next year even if there were zero inflation. In the context of health and environmental impacts to future generations, it is difficult to defend a pure rate of time preference other than zero, except by explicitly claiming that the lives and interests of future generations are worth less than ours—clearly an ethically problematic claim.[69] One can arguably justify a rate of time preference just barely larger than zero on the ground that there is some possibility that future generations will not exist because some catastrophe will destroy most of the human race. But such a rationale can only justify a very small rate. The *Stern Review*, for example, set a pure time preference of 0.1 percent on this basis.[70]

Thus, a number of prominent scholars argue that no discount rate should be applied at all when health and mortality impacts on future generations are at issue.[71] Nonetheless, it is standard economic practice to apply a substantial discount rate to such impacts. That practice is particularly pernicious in the context of climate change, where even small discount rates can dramatically devalue the interests of future generations over the long time horizons involved.

Conclusion

The economic rhetoric that now dominates so much of our public policy discourse has distorted our understanding of the climate change problem. We are so busy hunched over our calculators trying to work out the costs and benefits of a warming globe as a percentage of GDP that we have lost sight of the simple issues of fairness involved. Climate change is both driven by and driving gross disparities in wealth and power. Viewing the problem through an economic lens obscures these issues of distributional equity. But unless we confront these distributional issues directly, we will be unable to craft solutions that are either just or workable.

Notes

1. The Kaldor–Hicks standard assumes that wealth is a proxy for welfare, a problematic assumption, to say the least. See notes 47 to 58 and accompanying text.

2. See Amartya Sen, "The Possibility of Social Choice," *American Economic Review* 89, no. 3 (June 1999): 349–378.

3. Pareto efficiency is also indifferent to distributional issues to the extent that it takes the existing distribution of wealth as a given. See Frank Ackerman and Lisa Heinzerling, *Priceless: On Knowing the Price of Everything and the Value of Nothing* (New York: The New Press, 2004), pp. 32–34. Under an equity weighting approach, the two worlds described above would not be equivalent, because each dollar would be understood to be more valuable to poor people than to rich

people. But such techniques are controversial and fraught with difficulty. See notes 47 to 55 and accompanying text.

4. Warwick J. McKibben and Peter J. Wilcoxen, *Climate Change Policy after Kyoto: Blueprint for a Realistic Approach* (Washington, D.C.: Brookings Institution Press, 2002), p. 67: "Economists are trained to worry about efficiency and to leave matters of equity and distribution to policymakers. With climate change, however, that dichotomy is untenable."

5. For example, in withdrawing from the Kyoto Protocol in 2001, the Bush administration cited the purportedly high cost-benefit ratio associated with participation as the primary reason for its decision. See Kristen Sheeran, "Beyond Kyoto: North–South Implications of Emissions Trading and Taxes," *Seattle Journal of Social Justice 5* (spring–summer 2007): 697–715.

6. See Joe Nocera, "Exxon Mobil Just Wants to Be Loved," *New York Times,* Feb. 10, 2007, C1: "No company in history, not Microsoft, not Wal-Mart, has ever come close to making [this] kind of annual profit."

7. See Mancur Olson, *The Logic of Collective Action: Public Goods and the Theory of Groups* (New York: Schocken Books, 1965), pp. 16–23.

8. Ibid.

9. See Jeremy Leggett, "The Ill Winds of Change: As Hurricane Follows Hurricane, the Trillion-Dollar Insurance Industry Is Now Waking Up to Global Warming," *Guardian,* Oct. 2, 1992, 29.

10. *See* Robert Glicksman, "Anatomy of Industry Resistance to Climate Change: Running the Script," chapter 4, this volume; Andrew C. Revkin and Matthew C. Wald, "Solar Power Captures Imagination, Not Money," *New York Times,* July 16, 2007, A1 (noting that coal industry counts its lobbying budget in "tens of millions" while solar industry counts its lobbying budget in "tens of thousands").

11. James Bennett, "Warm Globe, Hot Politics," *New York Times,* Dec. 11, 1997, 1A.

12. See Byrd–Hagel Resolution, S. Res. 98, 105th Cong. (1997).

13. See generally Michael Grubb et al., *The Kyoto Protocol: A Guide and Assessment* (London: Royal Institute of International Affairs, Energy and Environmental Programme, 1999).

14. "Big U.S. Industries Launch Attack on Warming Treaty—Big Three Auto Makers, Steelmakers, Utilities Are Leading the Charge," *Wall Street Journal,* Dec. 12, 1997, A3. See also Douglas Jehl with Andrew C. Revkin, "Bush in Reversal Won't Seek Cut in Emissions of Carbon Dioxide," *New York Times,* Mar. 14, 2001, A1 (detailing role of pressure from coal industry in Bush's reversal of campaign pledge to regulate CO_2 emissions from power plants).

15. See Donald A. Brown, *American Heat: Ethical Problems with the United States' Response to Global Warming* (Lanham, MD: Rowman and Littlefield, 2002), p. 101 (describing newspaper ads run by Mobil Oil Company in 1990s urging U.S. not to take strong action to mitigate global warming).

16. See generally Union of Concerned Scientists, *Smoke, Mirrors, and Hot Air: How ExxonMobil Uses Big Tobacco's Tactics to Manufacture Uncertainty on Climate Science* (Jan. 2007), http://www.ucsusa.org/news/press_release/ExxonMobil-GlobalWarming-tobacco.html; Sharon Begley, "The Truth about Denial," *Newsweek,* Aug. 13, 2007, 20 (detailing efforts of fossil fuel industry to sow public doubt regarding global warming).

17. See Ross Gelbspan, *The Heat Is On: The Climate Crisis, the Cover-Up, the Prescription* (Cambridge, Mass.: Perseus Books, 1998), p. 34; Matthew F. Pawa and Benjamin A. Krass, "Behind the Curve: The National Media's Reporting on Global Warming," *Boston College Environmental Affairs Law Review* 33 (2006): 485–509.

18. See Joseph V. Amodio, "Al Gore Comes Back, Greener Than Ever," *Newsday,* May 22, 2006, B4; Jeff Nesmith, "Climate Debate Sizzles as Democrats Take Over: ExxonMobil Is Accused of Paying Skeptics," *Atlanta Journal-Constitution* Jan. 4, 2007, 6A; Jennifer 8. Lee, "Exxon Backs Groups That Question Global Warming," *New York Times,* May 28, 2003, C5 (describing Exxon's donations to groups questioning existence of global warming).

19. See Jeffrey Ball, "Digging In—Exxon Chief Makes a Cold Calculation on Global Warming—BP and Shell Concede Ground as Raymond Funds Skeptics and Fights Emissions Caps—A 'Reality Check' on Kyoto," *Wall Street Journal,* June 14, 2005, A1.

20. See David Adam, "Royal Society Tells Exxon: Stop Funding Climate Change Denial," *Guardian,* Sept. 20, 2006, 1.

21. See Daniel C. Esty, "When Being Green Puts You in the Black," *Washington Post,* Mar. 4, 2007, B1. Companies that fail to take action to reduce greenhouse gas emissions in anticipation of future regulation may face difficulty obtaining directors' and officers' liability coverage. See Jeffrey Ball, "Global Warming May Cloud Directors' Liability Coverage," *Wall Street Journal,* May 7, 2003, C1. Indeed, the recent TXU buyout, in which the company reached a well-publicized deal with environmental groups to scrap plans for eight of eleven coal plants, is just one example of a growing trend. See Felicity Barringer and Andrew Ross Sorkin, "Utility to Limit New Coal Plants in Big Buyout," *New York Times,* Feb. 25, 2007, A1.

22. See Steve Lohr, "A Coal Executive with a Clean-up Mission," *New York Times,* Mar. 7, 2007, H2.

23. See Intergovernmental Panel on Climate Change (IPCC), *Climate Change 2007: Mitigation,* ed. Bert Metz et al. (New York: Cambridge University Press, 2007), p. 3.

24. See Intergovernmental Panel on Climate Change (IPCC), *Climate Change 2007: Impacts, Adaptation, and Vulnerability,* ed. Martin L. Parry and Osvaldo Canziani (New York: Cambridge University Press, 2007), p. 11.

25. Brown, *American Heat,* p. 73.

26. IPCC, *Climate Change 2007: Mitigation,* p. 5 (figure SPM 3a). The "developed countries" are those designated as Annex I countries in the U.N. Framework Convention of Climate Change.

27. Brown, *American Heat*, p. 77.

28. Ibid.

29. See Intergovernmental Panel on Climate Change (IPCC), *Climate Change 2007: The Physical Science Basis*, ed. S. Solomon et al. (New York: Cambridge University Press, 2007), p. 17.

30. See Cass R. Sunstein, *After the Rights Revolution: Reconceiving the Regulatory State* (Cambridge, MA: Harvard University Press, 1990), p. 104 (statutes that protect future generations from irreversible losses apt to suffer from inadequate implementation).

31. See Richard S. J. Tol et al., "Distributional Aspects of Climate Change Impacts," *Global Environmental Change* 14 (2004): 259–272, 261 (presenting monetized estimates of regional annual welfare impacts [as percent of GDP]).

32. IPCC, *Climate Change 2007: Impacts*, pp. 294, 317, 383.

33. See Elizabeth Kolbert, *Field Notes from a Catastrophe: Man, Nature, and Climate Change* (New York: Bloomsbury, 2006), pp. 7–10.

34. See Tol et al., "Distributional Aspects of Climate Change Impacts," pp. 264–266.

35. See Center For Progressive Reform, *An Unnatural Disaster: The Aftermath of Hurricane Katrina* (September 2005), pp. 34–35, http://www.progressivereform .org/articles/Unnatural_Disaster_512.pdf; Rick Lyman, "Reports Reveal Hurricanes' Impact on Human Landscape," *New York Times*, June 7, 2006, A16; John R. Logan, "The Impact of Katrina: Race and Class in Storm Damaged Neighborhoods," Brown University Research Paper, http://www.s4.brown.edu/Katrina/ report.pdf.

36. IPCC, *Climate Change 2007: The Physical Science Basis*, p. 17.

37. Hansen et al., "Dangerous Human-made Interference with Climate: A GISS Model E Study," *Atmospheric Chemistry and Physics* 7 (May 2007): 2287–2312.

38. See Garrett Hardin, "The Tragedy of the Commons," *Science* 162 (Dec. 13, 1968): 1243–1248, 1244.

39. Ibid., p. 1247.

40. See Claudia H. Deutsch, "Attention Shoppers: Carbon Offsets in Aisle 6," *New York Times*, Mar. 7, 2007, H1.

41. Much of the public education on climate change recites a litany of the actions individual consumers can take to reduce their carbon footprint. The Web site associated with Al Gore's film, *An Inconvenient Truth*, for example, contains a link entitled "take action" that encourages individuals to buy energy-efficient lightbulbs, turn down their thermostats, replace furnace filters, and so on. See http://www.climatecrisis.net/takeaction/whatyoucando/index.html. In a similar vein, airlines have begun providing links on their Web pages that allow a customer to calculate the carbon footprint of her flight and then purchase offsets from conservation organizations to compensate for those emissions at the same time she books her ticket. See, e.g., http://www.continental.com/web/en-US/ content/company/profile/offset.aspx.

42. See Christian Azar and Thomas Sterner, "Discounting and Distributional Considerations in the Context of Global Warming," *Ecological Economics* 19, no. 2 (November 1996): 169–184, 170; see also IPCC, *Climate Change 2007: Impacts*, ch. 19.5.1 (aggregation of impacts inevitably involves value judgments).

43. Some cost-benefit analysts try to include some description of how costs and benefits are distributed as part of their analysis, but such discussions are inevitably an add-on that cannot be integrated into cost-benefit analysis. See Tol et al., "Distributional Aspects of Climate Change Impacts," pp. 259–272; Aldy et al., "Thirteen Plus One," p. 377.

44. See Azar et al., "Discounting and Distributional Considerations," p. 170.

45. See Sheeran, "Beyond Kyoto," p. 700.

46. See Aldy et al., "Thirteen Plus One," pp. 377, 382.

47. See Duncan Kennedy, "Cost-Benefit Analysis of Entitlement Problems: A Critique," *Stanford Law Review* 33 (February 1981): 387–445, 401–407; C. Edwin Baker, "The Ideology of the Economic Analysis of Law," *Philosophy and Public Affairs* 5, no.1 (autumn, 1975): 3–48, 6.

48. See, e.g., William D. Nordhaus, *Managing the Global Commons: The Economics of Climate Change* (Cambridge, MA: MIT Press, 1994), p. 55; W. R. Cline, *The Economics of Global Warming* (Washington, D.C.: Institute of International Economics, 1992), p. 85.

49. See, e.g., Samuel Fankhauser, *Valuing Climate Change: The Economics of the Greenhouse* (London: Earthscan Publications, 1995), pp. 47–48 (using a statistical value of life in "high income" countries of $1,500,000, in "middle income" countries of $300,000, and in "low income" countries of $100,000).

50. W. Kip Viscusi, "The Value of Life," in *The New Palgrave Dictionary of Economics and the Law*, ed. Peter Newman (New York: Palgrave MacMillan 2008).

51. See, e.g., K. Parikh et al., *Valuing Air Pollution in Bombay* (Bombay: Indira Gandhi Institute of Development, 1994) (cited in Samuel Fankhauser, Richard S. J. Tol, and David W. Pearce, "Extensions and Alternatives to Climate Change Impact Valuation: On the Critique of IPCC Working Group III's Impact Estimates," *Environment and Development Economics* 3, no. 1 (Feb. 1998): 59–81, 67–68.

52. See David W. Pearce, et al., "The Social Costs of Climate Change: Greenhouse Damage and the Benefits of Control," in *Climate Change 1995: Economic and Social Dimensions of Climate Change*, ed. J. P. Bruce, H. Lee, and E. F. Haites (Cambridge: Cambridge University Press, 1995), p. 197.

53. Ibid., pp. 191–192, 204, table 6.5; see also Fankhauser, *Valuing Climate Change*, pp. 32–33.

54. See, e.g., Christian Azar, "Weight Factors in Cost-Benefit Analysis of Climate Change," *Environmental and Resource Economics* 13, no. 3 (April 1999): 249–268; Samuel Fankhauser, Richard S. J. Tol, and David W. Pearce, "The Aggregation of Climate Change Damages: A Welfare Theoretic Approach," *Environmental and Resource Economics* 10, no. 3 (October 1997): 249–266.

55. See Matthew D. Adler and Eric A. Posner, "Rethinking Cost-Benefit Analysis," *Yale Law Journal* 109 (November 1999): 165–247, 189, 193; Intergovernmental Panel on Climate Change (IPCC), *Climate Change 2001: Mitigation*, ed. Bert Metz et al. (New York: Cambridge University Press, 2001), chap. 7.2.2.

56. Ibid., chap. 7.4.4.2; IPCC, *Climate Change 2007: Mitigation*, chap. 2.4.2.4. See also Fankhauser et al., "Extensions and Alternatives," p. 71 (expressing reservations about averaging).

57. Or $1 million USD at 1999 exchange rates.

58. See IPCC, *Climate Change 2007: Impacts*, chap. 8.5.

59. See E. J. Mishan, *Cost-Benefit Analysis* (London: Allen and Unwin, 1971), pp. 175–182.

60. See IPCC, *Climate Change 2001: Mitigation*, chap. 7.2.5.

61. See Derek Parfit, *Reasons and Persons* (Oxford: Clarendon Press, 1984), p. 357.

62. See IPCC, *Climate Change 2001: Mitigation*, chap. 7.2.5 (citing M. Weitzman, "Gamma Discounting for Global Warming," Discussion paper, Harvard University, Cambridge, MA, 1998). Others argue for a much lower discount rate, particularly in the context of climate change, where the relevant time horizons are so long. The *Stern Report*, for example, employed a 1.4 percent discount rate. Nicholas Stern, *The Economics of Climate Change: The Stern Review* (New York: Cambridge University Press, 2007), pp. 52, 183–185, 662–663. This provoked harsh criticism from some economists. See, e.g., William D. Nordhaus, "A Review of the *Stern Review* on the Economics of Climate Change," *Journal of Economic Literature* 45 (Sept. 2007): 686–702. For an analysis of this debate, see Frank Ackerman, *Debating Climate Economics: The Stern Review vs. Its Critics*, Report to Friends of the Earth-UK (July 2007).

63. See IPCC, *Climate Change 2001: Mitigation*, chap. 7.2.5. The UK government's "Green Book," for example, which provides the British government's official guidance on policy analysis, recommends a declining discount rate. See Ackerman, *Debating Climate Economics*, p. 5. Ackerman, however, notes that "such a decline may be less significant than it looks; the first few decades of discounting at higher rates are the most important in terms of evaluation of future costs and benefits" (ibid.).

64. See Azar et al., "Discounting and Distributional Considerations," p. 174.

65. See Douglas A. Kysar, "Climate Change, Cultural Transformation, and Comprehensive Rationality," *Boston College Environmental Affairs Law Review* 31 (2004): 555–590, 580.

66. See Azar et al., "Discounting and Distributional Considerations," p. 174.

67. Ibid.; see also Stern, *The Economics of Climate Change*, p. 662.

68. See Kysar, "Climate Change, Cultural Transformation," p. 579; Lisa Heinzerling, "Regulatory Costs of Mythic Proportions," *Yale Law Journal* 107 (May 1998): 1981–2070, 2051.

69. See Azar et al., "Discounting and Distributional Considerations," p. 176.

70. See Stern, *The Economics of Climate Change*, p. 663. This was based on the arbitrary assumption that the probability of the destruction of humanity is 0.1 percent—that is, that "we are only 99.9% sure that humanity will still be here next year." Ackerman, *Debating Climate Economics*, pp. 4–5.

71. See Richard L. Revesz, "Environmental Regulation, Cost-Benefit Analysis, and the Discounting of Human Lives," *Columbia Law Review* 99 (May 1999): 941–1017, 988–1006; Lisa Heinzerling, "Discounting Our Future," *Land and Water Law Review* 34 (1999): 39–74, 40–41.

6

Neoliberal Instrument Choice

David M. Driesen

Economic theory has profoundly influenced policymakers' thinking about the selection of instruments to effectuate environmental policy goals. And this thinking about the economics of instrument choice has powerfully influenced the United States, leading its government to strongly support environmental benefit trading as an instrument of climate change policy. This chapter will discuss this influence. It begins with a basic explanation of emissions trading, a form of environmental benefits trading, and a short summary of its history. It then recounts the United States' embrace of unrestrained international environmental benefit trading as a climate change remedy and how this has influenced U.S. and international climate change policy. It closes with some analysis of the advantages and disadvantages of the United States' posture in this regard.

Economists have long lamented traditional regulation's inefficiency, referring to it pejoratively as "command and control" regulation (an epithet embraced by many noneconomists as well).[1] They have recommended either pollution taxes or emissions trading in order to remedy this inefficiency, with most of them tending to prefer taxes.[2] President Clinton at one point proposed employing an energy tax to address climate change, which would create an incentive to reduce emissions of carbon dioxide, the principal greenhouse gas. But the rejection of government that Chris Schroeder has described carried with it an extreme aversion to new taxes, and Congress would not support such a tax. Hence, antigovernmental attitudes played a role in limiting even the choices among instruments that economic thought commends.[3]

In the climate change arena, economists' second-choice environmental instrument, emissions trading, gained much more traction. It fit in reasonably well with the prevailing free market ethos and seemed to some policymakers to offer an alternative to government regulation. Accordingly, a brief explanation of emissions trading and its history will prove useful.

I. Emissions Trading Described

U.S. law often relies on uniform performance standards as a means of meeting environmental goals.[4] Such standards require all firms within an industry to reduce emissions by an amount that the government chooses. This leaves firms with some technological flexibility, as polluters may choose any technology that meets the regulatory limit.[5] But it requires each regulated unit within a facility to meet the government-specified target. It is spatially specific regulation.[6]

Economists consider uniform performance standards inefficient. A uniform standard does not produce uniform costs among regulated facilities. Indeed, facilities within an industry commonly encounter widely varying compliance costs when meeting a uniform target. This implies that an industry could meet the same aggregate reduction demanded through a uniform standard more cheaply if facilities facing high marginal control costs made fewer reductions than the uniform standard demands and those facing lower marginal control cost made more reductions than the uniform standard demands. Unfortunately, government officials rarely have sufficient marginal control cost information to fine-tune regulation to match each facility's cost structure. Indeed, governments employ uniform standards precisely because they allow officials to regulate large groups of facilities without having to tailor regulation to each firm's circumstances.

An emissions trading approach allows the owners of regulated facilities themselves to shift around their pollution control obligations to achieve the least-cost allocation of emission reductions. An emissions trading scheme begins with a government regulator setting a uniform standard, just as with traditional uniform performance standards. But when the regulator uses trading, she authorizes owners of pollution sources to forgo a required reduction if they pay other polluters to make extra reductions in their stead. Given the opportunity to trade around compliance obligations in this manner, polluters with high local marginal control cost will presumably forgo local reductions and pay somebody else for extra reductions instead. Conversely, facilities with low marginal control costs will make enough extra reductions to sell them to facilities that would otherwise face high marginal control costs. The polluters themselves rearrange their reduction obligations to achieve the goal the regulator has set for the industry as a whole at lower cost than would happen if each regulated entity met a uniform target. This approach rather ingeniously allows for efficient fine-tuning of regulation without the government having to tailor regulation to each facility's special cost situation.

Trading proponents often claim that emissions trading stimulates innovation more effectively than traditional regulation.[7] Innovation consists of the development and use of a new technique or idea.[8] The idea of newness, an idea at the heart of our concept of innovation, implies that for a technology to be innovative, it must involve a nonobvious departure from prior art. We do not innovate when we employ a pollution-control technique that has been used many times before in a new plant or even a new industry (at least if the applicability is obvious). We innovate when we advance the state of technology by doing more than just making obvious incremental refinements. The end of this chapter will examine the claim that emissions trading more effectively stimulates innovation than traditional regulation. Whatever the claim's merits, it is certainly congruent with market glorification. Indeed, a competitive market's capacity to stimulate innovations bettering our lives constitutes perhaps its most widely admired feature, as evidenced by the laudatory press Apple has received for introducing the iPod. The claim that emissions trading produces superior incentives for innovation helps clothe it with the luster some see in markets generally. This claim is also important to trading's utility in addressing climate change. Scientists now believe that avoiding dangerous climate change will require massive emission reductions, which entails the abandonment of fossil fuels over time.[9] Abandonment of fossil fuels implies a need to innovate to develop cheap and effective substitutes. Innovation can create these substitutes thus making abandonment of fossil fuels technically, economically, and politically feasible. The claim that emissions trading effectively stimulates innovation implies that it stimulates substantial movement in the right direction over time, that is, that it provides a strong impetus to develop technologies capable of substituting for fossil fuels. This claim suggests that emissions trading provides the sorts of economic incentives that will produce a positive economic dynamic. The economic dynamic framework suggests that the suggestion that trading might optimally stimulate innovation is more important than the largely uncontested claim about its static efficiency.

II. Experience with Emissions Trading

The United States began experimenting with emissions trading in the late 1970s, and President Reagan's administration greatly amplified this trend.

The trading programs introduced greater "flexibility" into implementation of the 1977 Clean Air Act Amendments by allowing facilities to escape various reduction obligations if they provided an alternative reduction, usually from a different unit within the same facility. Thus, one unit would use another unit's reductions to offset its emissions. Air pollution experts refer to these early programs as "bubble" programs, because they treated facilities as if they were encased by a giant bubble.[10]

These programs produced very large cost savings, but often these savings came from evasion of pollution control obligations.[11] The program facilitated evasion of reduction obligations because of two fundamental flaws. First, the EPA allowed states to apply the bubble approach to pollutants that could not be well monitored.[12] Second, the EPA did not insist that states cap the emissions of the facilities generating credits. Indeed, the law did not cap the emissions of the facilities purchasing credits either, but it did usually subject them to limitations of their emissions rates.[13] Credits excusing compliance with a local emission limit could be realized through just about any pollution reduction project involving the traded pollutant. The combination of poorly monitored pollution and the lack of caps created enormous complexity that led to lost emission reductions.

The evasions this project-based structure encouraged merit a little explanation, as similar problems may arise in the climate change context. One problem involved giving up an emission reduction at a regulated facility on the basis of a credit reflecting no *additional* pollution reduction. For example, Virginia encouraged siting of a new petroleum refinery within its state by offering it pollution reduction credits that the highway department realized when it switched asphalt formulations. This asphalt switch occurred for economic reasons having nothing to do with pollution control regulations. Without trading, the reduction from the asphalt switch would still have occurred and the refinery would have been required to greatly reduce its emissions and offset the remainder under the Clean Air Act. Because of the trade, the refinery claimed a credit for the asphalt switch and avoided having to reduce its emissions and offset its residual emissions. Thus, the trading caused a loss of emissions reductions that would have occurred had there been no trading for the asphalt credit. Other evasion examples include the "phantom" credits generated by facilities that had shut down; the facilities died but the pollution control credits lived on. Of course shutting down a facility does reduce its emissions. But unless demand slackened, another facility would probably ramp up production and increase emissions to make up for it.

But as no cap existed on the mass of facility emissions, this pollution increase would not be accounted for. Phantom credits justified giving up reductions otherwise required under the Clean Air Act.

President Reagan embraced emissions trading as a piece of his "regulatory reform" program, promising less government and more reliance on markets. In this context, he was loath to recognize that the market he established lacked environmental integrity. And his regulatory reform staff put out reports glowingly praising the "cost savings" the bubble programs had produced, while glossing over the loss of emission reductions otherwise provided for under the Clean Air Act.

The acid rain program that followed, however, would prove more successful. By the end of the 1980s, the acid rain problem had achieved the sort of prominence that global warming achieved around 2006. Regulation seemed inevitable. Both the electric utilities and the Bush administration (the elder Bush) hoped that Congress would employ a flexible cost-saving emissions trading approach to regulation of the sulfur dioxide emissions causing acid rain. They won over the more technocratic environmental groups, such as the Natural Resources Defense Council and Environmental Defense Fund, by capping the mass of regulated facilities' emissions at levels that offered a significant environmental improvement and by generally requiring regulated sulfur dioxide emitters to employ continuous emissions monitors. The combination of a cap and airtight monitoring persuaded technocratic environmentalists that the program would achieve worthwhile goals and ultimately produced the first successful emissions trading program. The program produced the planned reductions quite reliably (indeed early) and significant cost savings. The emission decreases reduced deposition of sulfur dioxide into ecosystems significantly. Reduced deposition, however, did not cure the ecological problem, which had become quite serious during the years when regulators failed to seriously address it. But it is likely that a nontrading program would likewise have failed to completely cure the ecological problem. Only an enormously stringent limit, whether achieved by trading or not, would do that. Overall, the acid rain trading program was a clear success.

III. Trading and the Climate Change Regime

As the acid rain trading program took shape, the United States began to participate in the climate change negotiations that would produce the

Framework Convention on Climate Change and ultimately the Kyoto Protocol. President Bush took a stance fully in keeping with free market ideology, opposing caps on emissions, but supporting trading. This stance ignored the lessons of the acid rain program, which showed that caps are essential to the success of the trading program. And this approach ignored the lessons of the bubble programs, which suggested that project-based trades tended to facilitate evasion of reduction obligations. The United States consistently touted the success of the acid rain program as showing that all emissions trading must be a good idea, thereby ignoring the rather more nuanced and richer lessons a reasonably complete history of emissions trading might offer about program design.

The United States' position on trading during the 1990s and the first years of the twenty-first century remained basically unchanged. The United States wanted broad international environmental benefit trading, not confined to countries willing to cap their emissions or to activities that could be well monitored. I use the term "environmental benefit trading" here, rather than emissions trading, because of the extreme breadth of the United States' position. The United States wanted credits for actions that did not reduce emissions at all, but instead ameliorated climate change by enhancing ecosystems' capacity to act as a carbon sink, absorbing carbon emissions that would otherwise contribute to global warming. For example, the United States wanted credits for tree planting, since trees absorb carbon dioxide. Although the acid rain program succeeded in part because it focused on a single pollutant amenable to reliable monitoring, the United States advocated trades among a basket of greenhouse gases, lumping together those that could be well monitored with those that could not. In this respect, the United States in essence took a position that could duplicate the failure of the bubble program, which focused mostly on an entire category of poorly monitored gases, volatile organic compounds.

This "trading *über alles*" (trading everywhere) position reflected a triumph of economic ideology over sound regulatory practice. Even during the Clinton administration this position continued to command the allegiance of the federal government. Although President Clinton himself was not an ideologue, his administration was well aware that the free market ethos remained very influential in Congress. The administration hoped that its trading *über alles* position would help it win over Republican Senators who liked markets, but detested regulation.

From a free market perspective, this trading position made perfect sense. The broadest possible market maximizes liquidity and trading's cost-savings potential. Thus, this position enjoyed considerable support among both economists and legal academics influenced by the law and economics movement.

From a legal perspective, the position raised considerable concerns. It seemed to ignore the lessons of the bubble experience—that programs reaching poorly monitored activities or relying on project-based credits from noncapped sources tended to produce evasion of reduction obligations, rather than simple cost-effective rearrangements of those obligations.

This position, moreover, troubled delegations from other countries. Representatives of the European Union repeatedly expressed concerns about the environmental integrity of the U.S. approach. They fought hard to limit environmental benefit trading's role in the climate change regime and to build in safeguards to maximize its integrity. Developing countries had even more fundamental concerns about emissions trading. Their representatives tended to view emissions trading as a means of allowing developed countries to escape their moral obligations to address climate change domestically. During climate change negotiations, they frequently noted that developed countries had created this problem, and that they should therefore solve it. And generally, that meant that developed countries should reduce their own emissions. Developing countries' representatives also expressed concerns about trading programs making their future participation in addressing climate change difficult and expensive. Developing countries expected that they eventually would have to deliver emission reductions of their own. If developed countries, who would go first, met their reduction responsibilities by buying up credits in developing countries, the cheap opportunities would be gone when developing countries began to reduce their emissions later in the twenty-first century. Hence, the trading *über alles* position created considerable international tension and greatly complicated ongoing efforts to construct an effective climate change regime.

The United States' neoliberal instrument choice position, whatever its technical merits, had an enormous impact on the evolving climate change regime. At the insistence of the United States, the Framework Convention on Climate Change provided that countries could achieve the Convention's aim, stabilization of emissions at 1990 levels, individually or "jointly." The parties to the Convention probably understood this reference to "joint implementation" as authorizing trading, at least among countries agreeing to aim to stabilize emissions. At the United States' request, the Conference of the Parties to the Framework Convention on Climate

Change (COP) authorized a series of "pilot projects" designed to test the efficacy of international emissions trading during the years between the enactment of the Framework Convention and the completion of the Kyoto Protocol to that convention. Although these projects yielded no clear results and no meaningful evaluation, the United States, predictably in light of the ideology prevailing in Washington, insisted on building broad environmental benefit trading into the Kyoto Protocol.

The extreme U.S. position almost caused the negotiations leading up to the Kyoto Protocol to collapse. The combination of a trading *über alles* position and a refusal to accept meaningful caps infuriated delegates from many countries. Yet, an agreement seemed impossible without the effective participation of the United States, the world's largest greenhouse gas emitter. Finally, the Clinton administration sent Al Gore, a long-time supporter of climate change action, with instructions to broker a compromise. Then Vice President Gore helped broker an agreement that committed the United States to 7 percent reductions below 1990 levels in exchange for an agreement to very broad environmental benefit trading.

Largely as a result of the U.S. position, the Kyoto Protocol contains no less than three emissions trading programs. Only one of these programs limits trades to developed countries with caps. The other two are "project-based mechanisms" that have more in common with the bubble programs than they do with the acid rain program. The first program, Joint Implementation (JI), allows trades with countries (nationals of countries) in Eastern Europe and the former Soviet Union. The second project-based program, the Clean Development Mechanism (CDM), authorizes trades between developed countries (or their nationals) and developing countries. The CDM proposal came from the Brazilian delegation, but its creation and adoption reflect all parties' concern that the United States be brought on board, and the United States strongly supported Brazil's proposal.

The parties to the Kyoto Protocol recognized that these instruments, especially the project-based ones, raised significant problems of monitoring, accounting, environmental integrity, and international coordination. Accordingly, many of the post-Kyoto negotiations have focused on developing governance structures and ground rules for the trading programs. The CDM created the most serious accountability issues, so it generated the most elaborate structures and rules. The COP created a CDM Executive Board consisting of ten country representatives with relevant expertise to oversee CDM implementation. Its duties include approving methodologies for measuring or estimating emission reductions and reviewing individual projects' compliance with ground rules. The CDM also certifies "designated operating authorities," which must estimate the credits a project is supposed to generate and then verify that they actually did produce these credits. In practice, these bodies are usually private consulting firms paid for by project developers. In addition, the host country must approve projects generating credits in its territory. The Kyoto Protocol requires that CDM projects advance sustainable development. The post-Kyoto governance structure assigns the determination of sustainability to host country governments.

One key ground rule, which is stated in the Kyoto Protocol itself, forbids granting credits for projects that do not provide "additional" emission reductions. This rule clearly aims to avoid some of the abuses that afflicted the bubble programs. But it's not an easy rule to administer properly. The regime also creates a process for expert evaluation of credits for sink protection, which remains extremely controversial, partly because of the difficulties in predicting how much carbon reduction value a particular project will generate. These rules provide examples of the many matters that arose because of environmental integrity concerns stemming from the U.S. position and its acceptance in the Kyoto Protocol.

This presentation of the CDM regime does not do justice to its complexity, but it suffices to show that the United States' insistence on broad trading has generated a complex set of institutions and rules. Some JI projects require an approval process similar to that governing CDM. Some can undergo a simpler process. Overall, the project-based mechanisms have created vast potential for avoiding emission reductions and with it, a complex set of rules and procedures to try and limit the potential damage.

Even though the international community included all of these trading programs largely to satisfy the United States (and a few of its allies), the United States did not ratify the Kyoto Protocol. The U.S. failure to ratify the Protocol meant that it could only go into force if another climate skeptic, Russia, ratified it. Russia agreed to ratify the Protocol in exchange for a deal that gave it a lot of emission credits to sell. These "hot air" credits reflect no actual program to reduce greenhouse gas emissions. Instead, these credits reflect the decline in Russian emissions that accompanied post-1990 economic collapse. If Russia sells these credits, then developed countries purchasing the credits can appear to meet their Kyoto targets without actually reducing emissions.

As we have seen, George W. Bush repudiated the Kyoto Protocol outright, in spite of all of the elaborate provisions seeking to cater to Washington's neoliberalism. In other words, after forcing a shotgun marriage between sustainable development and market liberalism, the United States left the bride at the altar.

But the bride soldiered on. The European Union (EU) had been a skeptic of emissions trading and had spent years trying to craft an effective carbon tax regime in keeping with economists' teachings. Faced with an international architecture favoring emissions trading and doubts about whether it could craft an effective carbon tax regime in light of concerns about competitiveness and free trade, it decided to implement an emissions trading scheme. While most analysts refer to this as a cap-and-trade regime, that characterization is too simplistic. The scheme does require EU member states to cap the emissions of certain large greenhouse gas emitters, such as coal-fired power plants. But it authorizes the sources of capped emissions to purchase credits from pollution sources that are not operating under a cap. Indeed, the EU Linking Directive specifically authorizes member states to credit reductions realized through the Kyoto Protocol's project-based mechanisms to the accounts of their regulated facilities. This means, in effect, that this program can lose emission reductions if the project-based mechanisms have integrity problems similar to those that occurred under the project-based bubble programs. Thus the United States' trading *über alles* position ultimately led polities historically quite skeptical of free market extremism to embrace rather broad liberal trading, along with some of the risks to environmental integrity that such a stance implies.

In spite of the Bush administration's repudiation of the Kyoto Protocol, climate change law has begun to emerge in the United States. Many states have come to the conclusion that they simply must act to ameliorate the dangers that climate change poses for their people. California, for example, has become alarmed about the prospect of droughts and other disturbances that climate change promises, and has begun active planning on how to both manage the disasters it can no longer avoid and to do its part to ameliorate climate change itself. And a number of congressmen have introduced a variety of bills in Congress to address global warming; only President Bush's likely veto kept a bill from passing in 2007.

Both the major programs in the most important states to address global warming and the bills pending in Congress rely heavily, and often exclusively, on environmental benefit trading to reduce greenhouse gas emissions. These laws (whether enacted or proposed) vary widely in their scope of coverage and in the amount of emission reductions they demand. But to a remarkable degree, they all contemplate near total reliance on the trading mechanism.

IV. Analysis

Emissions trading does offer an opportunity to cost-effectively achieve environmental goals. And the acid rain program has shown that emissions trading, *if properly designed*, can be effective at achieving some environmental goals. Nevertheless, love of free markets has led the United States to overestimate the value of emissions trading, to underestimate the importance of good design, and to fail to seriously consider more ambitious alternative economic incentives.

A. Efficiency Over Efficacy: The Problem of Overly Broad Design

One major problem with free market ideology's influence over U.S. climate policy involves the direction of trading design. Too much market love may push regulators to design programs too broad for effective enforcement. In this connection, it's helpful to remember that emission trades generally do nothing to advance environmental protection. Decisions about caps by regulators can advance environmental protection. The trades, at best, reallocate the reductions required under a cap in order to reduce their costs. There's nothing wrong with this; rearranging obligations to reduce costs can be desirable. But economists, brokers, and even regulators sometimes evince confusion on this point. They write about how cap-and-trade programs "automatically" produce emission reductions and often evaluate programs using a "more is better" metric; many trades mean a successful program, and few trades indicate failure. The notion that trading "automatically" produces emission reductions is utter nonsense. Trading relies on basically the same mechanisms that traditional regulation uses to generate emission reductions: regulatory decisions about the amount of reductions to require and heavy penalties for noncompliance. Thus, the first phase of the European Union's emissions trading scheme failed to produce any real progress, because the caps European regulators set were lax. Most importantly, the amount of trades has no relationship to the environmental success of a trading program. Lots of trades can indicate lots of fraud, or lots of cost savings while goals are being achieved. It all depends on whether the credit-generating activities have in fact made extra emission reductions of equal value to those foregone by the sources purchasing the credits. And conversely, conformance with the cap without any trading will meet the program's underlying environmental goal.

Free market ideology's view of markets as spontaneously generating benefits tends to obscure the relationship between credit generation and environmental quality in an emissions trading program. In a properly functioning emissions trading market, every time a polluter makes an extra reduction to sell into the market, a purchasing polluter raises its emissions above the amount otherwise required. Polluters, unfortunately, have an economic incentive to exaggerate the value of credits and to understate the value of debits—the amount of undercompliance they financed with a credit purchase. Environmental goals can be realized with few trades or lots of trades. The key question from a regulatory perspective is not whether a lot of trades occurred, but whether the credits traded really were at least as valuable as the debits.

Increasingly, evidence suggests that the broad trading approach the United States has lobbied for has produced lost emission reductions.[14] Emission reduction losses arise when projects lack "additionality"—when credit is awarded for projects that would have reduced emissions even if no polluter had paid for the credit. There is some evidence that the CDM Executive Board has approved projects that differ little from the asphalt project we described above. In one case, it approved a solar energy project for credit, even though the financing was in place long before the possibility of CDM credits existed. The problem is that as long as those purchasing the credits pay some money for them, and a tiny portion of that money reaches those developing the solar project, the project developers can claim that the money was essential to the project's completion. These claims should be regarded as correct when the money earned for the credits account for a very high percentage of the project cost. But such claims appear dubious when the credit revenue accounts for a very low percentage of the project cost, which has been the case with respect to many projects.[15] Renewable energy presents a political problem for the CDM Executive Board. If the CDM Executive Board applied a strict additionality test to relatively expensive projects (like many renewable energy projects), it's possible that no renewables projects would generate credits.[16] To appreciate that this should not be seen as a problem, one must view the trading mechanism analytically, not as magic. If the board disapproves of credits when credit purchases account for a small portion of project revenue, there's a good chance that the project will be built without credit, and therefore without an increase in emissions in the country purchasing the credits. Thus, denial of credits will not cause a loss of renewable energy or other environmental benefit. Under the CDM Executive Board's current approach, we often give up reductions in Europe because of reductions elsewhere that would have occurred even if there had been no credit purchased.

All of these problems arise because of the project-based design. A true cap-and-trade program would produce good overall results in spite of effects like these. But in a project-based program, these sorts of issues can result in lost emission reductions. Hence, the U.S. approach has increased the risk that the emission reductions countries have committed to making will not, in fact, be realized.

B. International Political and Institutional Problems

The potential shortfall in emission reductions could directly worsen climate change, but it also poses a more potent indirect risk. Countries like China and India have so far refused to agree to emission reductions. While they accept the Framework Convention's principle of common but differentiated responsibilities, they believe that developed countries should clean up before they are asked to do so. In future climate change negotiations, they will prove more amenable to reduction commitments if it's clear that developed countries have met their responsibilities under the Kyoto Protocol. The Kyoto Protocol's embrace of virtual compliance—compliance based not on physically achieving targets within the country assuming the target, but on claims about reductions realized elsewhere—may make claimed compliance noncredible. This could add to the larger problem that the United States has created by not trying to comply at all. If the largest emitter did not comply and developing countries have doubts about whether the climate leaders in Europe really complied as well, it may be hard to reach effective agreements to reduce worldwide emissions.

On the other hand, the assumption of these risks has led to the development of governance institutions designed to contain them. Indeed, the creation of expert bodies addressing some of the emissions trading issues under the Kyoto Protocol represents an advance over both the institutional structure governing the bubbles and most, if not all, international environmental law regimes, which often contain weak monitoring and enforcement mechanisms or none at all. Although advances in institutional structure have continued, so far they do not seem to have made up for the deficiencies of such a large, complicated system.

Ample reasons exist for some measured skepticism. The CDM Executive Board has disapproved some projects and reduced the credits claimed for others, so there is evidence that it is willing to counteract some inflated credit claims from project developers. Yet, it may find application of a very strict additionality test politically difficult, as such a test leaves popular measures like solar energy out of the CDM, thereby improving its integrity but diminishing its luster. Project developers generally pay the designated operating authorities to evaluate the project, so notwithstanding the CDM board's accreditation procedures, conflicts of interest may lead designated operating authorities to exaggerate credits or seek certification of dubious projects. And the national governments of developing countries have largely played little role in overseeing CDM projects, which is what resource restraints would lead one to expect.

In spite of all of this, there are some forces limiting the damage potentially coming from Kyoto's overly broad trading schemes. To date, Russia has not undermined the scheme by selling lots of hot air credits. This may reflect decisions on its part that it may profit more by waiting, but it also may reflect a widespread perception that the public in Europe would not accept the use of such credits to undermine Kyoto compliance.

Economic thought has been the driver for assuming these sorts of risk through overly broad trading programs. For economic thought has helped lead the United States to a position seeking the broadest possible trading in order to make sure that private polluters could use the cheapest possible credits for compliance purposes. The possibility that the cheapest credits might prove problematic or fraudulent has had only a minor influence on federal policy, although it has influenced some of the emerging state law more seriously. The Northeastern states, for example, have crafted a Regional Greenhouse Gas Initiative, which features some numerical and qualitative restraints on project-based credits in order to minimize bubble-like problems. In general, love of markets and a lack of serious concern for effective government have led the United States to focus far too much attention on efficient use of private sector resources, and not nearly enough on cost-effective use of very limited government resources. Broad trading programs can exhaust government resources by multiplying the number and types of transactions that the government must monitor in order to assure the legitimacy of any one claimed emission reduction.

C. Trade-offs between Static Efficiency and Long-Term Innovation

Advocates of trading programs under the Kyoto Protocol have predicted that it would create incentives to maximize deployment of renewable energy and energy efficiency. These claims amount to an assertion that emissions trading creates the right economic dynamic.

So far, however, the data from the CDM indicate that emissions trading under the Kyoto Protocol has mostly stimulated end-of-the-pipe controls, not fundamental changes in energy infrastructure. At first glance, these data suggest that emissions trading has stimulated renewable energy and energy efficiency, as most of the projects involve these sorts of measures. But a more careful analysis suggests much more emphasis on end-of-the-pipe approaches than on renewable energy or energy efficiency. End-of-the-pipe approaches have generated the lion's share of credits available in the market.[17] And the number of credits generated provides a more reliable measure of how most reductions get generated. Indeed, hydroflurocarbon (HFC) control projects alone, which have the potential to stimulate emission increases, generated almost half of the total CDM credits generated so far.[18]

Figure 6.1 reflects the distribution of credits sold thus far under the Kyoto Protocol's CDM.[19] It shows end-of-the-pipe controls' predominance, with a relatively small percentage of credits produced by renewable energy and energy efficiency.[20] If one examines somewhat less reliable numbers for projects "in the pipeline" (i.e., not yet fully approved) for CDM only, renewable energy credits rise to about 25 percent by 2012.[21]

Trading also has done absolutely nothing to stimulate nuclear power, which, although controversial, some see as a necessary element of a future largely free of dangerous climate change. The European Union does not

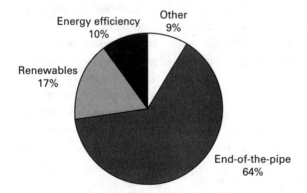

Figure 6.1
Distribution of total CDM credits issued through July 18, 2007.

allow its polluters to use nuclear power credits to satisfy their obligations under its emissions trading scheme. But even without this prohibition in place, nuclear power is too expensive to finance with revenues derived from those seeking low cost abatement.

These results reflect only the early experience with emissions trading under the Kyoto Protocol. The European Union has just completed phase one of a two-phase emissions trading scheme that will produce much of the demand for CDM credits. The second phase will be stricter and could change this picture somewhat, but the credits generated so far reflect the market's anticipation of phase two to some degree.

The experience with broad emissions trading contrasts strikingly with the experience with narrower approaches. Most European countries and several states in the United States have adopted programs aimed specifically at stimulating renewable energy. The most successful programs employ a type of subsidy called a "feed-in tariff" that guarantees renewable energy providers a high price for the energy they produce. In the United States, as we have seen, renewable portfolio standards are more common. Both have been far more effective in stimulating renewable energy than broad-based emissions trading. There is little evidence that maximizing short-term efficiency through adoption of the broadest possible emissions trading program stimulates innovation more effectively than a narrower approach aimed directly at the innovation objective.

The evidence that emissions trading stimulated great reliance on conventional approaches and little fundamental change is consistent with the experience in the U.S. acid rain program. That program produced no renewable energy. Instead, utilities complied predominantly through reliance on two of the oldest and best-understood methods for reducing sulfur dioxide emissions: scrubber installation and use of low-sulfur coal. To be sure, the program did stimulate *some* innovation. It stimulated some advances in scrubber design that won patents. And some analysts described utilities' use of dispatch orders to maximize use of cleaner units as an innovation. But the most thorough review to date of innovation under the acid rain program and its nontrading predecessors addressing the same pollutant from the same sources found that emissions trading produced *less* innovation than traditional regulation.[22] And we have already seen that the bubbles produced a lot more evasion of pollution control obligations than innovation.

A program we have not yet examined, the lead-trading program, did produce fundamental change. But this program required that small refiners phase out lead entirely. It's quite clear that the same phaseout requirement without trading would have produced the same fundamental change. Indeed, the lead-banking program delayed the phaseout somewhat.

Furthermore, the economics literature on trading increasingly expresses skepticism about trading proponents' assertion that trading provides better incentives for innovation than a performance standard of identical scope and stringency.[23] Certainly, it does not reflect the unanimity that prevails with respect to assertions about trading's static efficiency.

Pro–free market policymakers just assume that trading must stimulate innovation better than traditional regulation of identical stringency and scope. But this assumption rests on a fallacy. It assumes that only emissions trading creates markets, and that traditional regulation does not. This assumption is not correct. A traditional performance standard requires reductions in emissions. Once such a standard is established, companies pay contractors, vendors, and/or employees to evaluate pollution-control methods and to purchase and operate pollution-control technologies. A performance standard makes pollution expensive. Once one is promulgated, continuing to pollute at current levels can lead to heavy fines. It therefore creates economic incentives to clean up and a market in technologies capable of assisting in that process. This does not necessarily mean that traditional regulation does a great job at stimulating innovation, either. Indeed, while traditional regulation has, at times, stimulated significant technological innovation, our knowledge of traditional regulation's stimulation of innovation remains woefully incomplete, because of a dearth of postcompliance studies.[24] But the presence of some innovation in both trading and nontrading contexts means that the question of whether emissions trading stimulates significant innovation more effectively than performance standards do is a lot more complicated than many of its proponents have assumed. The tendency to glorify markets has led many in the neoliberal era to treat emissions trading as a panacea with respect to innovation.

A subsequent chapter in this volume will address the question of whether we can do better, and if so, how. Emissions trading's poor track record in stimulating innovation does not necessarily mean that competing mechanisms do better. It does, however, mean that the question of whether we get more innovation by either redesigning emissions trading programs or making use of alternatives merits more discussion than was possible when the neoliberal view dominated.

Conclusion

Glorification of markets has led the United States to favor broad environmental benefit trading. This position led to a climate change regime largely based on this model. The neoliberal instrument choice and design model, however, creates risks of losing planned emission reductions, various institutional failures, and inadequate stimulation of innovation.

None of this means that emissions trading is a poor idea. Indeed, emissions trading constitutes one of the more useful contributions of economic thought to environmental policy, since a well-designed program can help to cost-effectively reduce emissions. But the assumption that just because emissions trading lowers short-term costs, broad environmental benefit trading must be the answer to the climate change problem is an assumption that merits further analysis, which I will provide in a subsequent chapter.

Notes

1. See Nathaniel O. Keohane, Richard L. Revesz, and Robert N. Stavins, "The Choice of Regulatory Instruments in Environmental Policy," *Harvard Environmental Law Review* 22 (1998): 313–367, 313–314 (noting economists' "consistent endorsement" of market-based instruments over "command-and-control" instruments and then explaining the former's cost-effectiveness advantages).

2. Jonathan Baert Wiener, "Global Environmental Regulation: Instrument Choice in Legal Context," *Yale Law Journal* 108 (1999): 677–800, 727–735 (explaining why standard economic analysis tends to favor pollution taxes).

3. Cf. Keohane, Revesz, and Stavins, "Choice of Regulatory Instruments," p. 348 (pointing out that firms will usually prefer grandfathered trading programs to pollution taxes, because only the latter taxes residual emissions).

4. See Bruce A. Ackerman and Richard B. Stewart, "Comment: Reforming Environmental Law," *Stanford Law Review* 37 (1985): 1333–1365.

5. See David M. Driesen, "Is Emissions Trading an Economic Incentive Program? Replacing the Command and Control/Economic Incentive Dichotomy," *Washington and Lee Law Review* 55 (1998): 289–350, 297–298; Robert W. Hahn and Robert N. Stavins, "Incentive-Based Environmental Regulation: A New Era for an Old Idea?" *Ecology Law Quarterly* 18 (1991): 1–42, 5–6; Louis Tornatzky, Mitchell Fleischer, and Alok K. Chakrabarti, *The Processes of Technological Innovation* (Lexington, MA: Lexington Books, 1990), p. 101; Richard Stewart, "Regulation, Innovation, and Administrative Law: A Conceptual Framework," *California Law Review* 69, no. 5 (1981): 1256–1377, 1268; cf. Richard B. Stewart, "Controlling Environmental Risks through Economic Incentives," *Columbia Journal of Environmental Law* 13, no. 2 (1988): 153–169, 158.

6. See Driesen, "Is Emissions Trading an Economic Incentive Program?," p. 303.

7. See Stewart, "Controlling Environmental Risks," p. 160; Keohane, Revesz, and Stavins, "Choice of Regulatory Instruments," p. 314.

8. See David Driesen, "Design, Trading, and Innovation," in *Moving to Markets in Environmental Regulation: Lessons from Twenty Years of Experience*, ed. Jody Freeman and Charles Kolstad (Oxford: Oxford University Press, 2007), pp. 437–438; see generally Adam B. Jaffe, Richard G. Newell, and Robert N. Stavins, "Technological Change and the Environment," in *Handbook of Environmental Economics*, ed. Karl-Goran Maler and Jeffrey Vincent (Amsterdam: Elsevier, 2003), 1: 464–467 (discussing the economists' distinction between "innovation" and "diffusion").

9. See, e.g., H. Damon Matthews and Ken Caldeira, "Stabilizing Climate Requires Near Zero Emissions," Geophysical Research Letters, *Geophysical Research Letters* 35 (2008): L04705.

10. See *Chevron v. Natural Resources Defense Council*, 467 U.S. 837, 840 (1984).

11. See Larry Lohman, *Carbon Trading: A Critical Conversation on Climate Change, Privatisation, and Power* (Uppsala, Sweden: Dag Hammarkjöld Foundation, 2006), pp. 150–151; Driesen, "Is Emissions Trading an Economic Incentive Program?," pp. 314–316; California Air Resources Board and United States Environmental Protection Agency, *Phase III Rule Effectiveness Study of the Aerospace Coating Industry* (1990), p. 4; Richard A. Liroff, *Reforming Air Pollution Regulation: The Toil and Trouble of EPA's Bubble* (Washington, D.C.: Conservation Foundation, 1986); David Doniger, "The Dark Side of the Bubble," *Environmental Forum* 4 (1985): 33–35; Richard A. Liroff, *Air Pollution Offsets: Trading, Selling, and Banking* (Washington, D.C.: Conservation Foundation, 1980).

12. Daniel H. Cole and Peter Z. Grossman, "When Is Command and Control Efficient? Institutions, Technology, and the Comparative Efficiency of Alternative Regulatory Regimes for Environmental Protection," *Wisconsin Law Review* (1999): 887–938, 918–925 (describing how the bubbles of the late 1970s and early 1980s were introduced at a time when pollution could not be monitored).

13. See Byron Swift, "Command without Control: Why Cap-and-Trade Should Replace Rate Standards for Regional Pollutants," *Environmental Law Reporter* 31 (March 2001): 10330–10341.

14. See, e.g., Lambert Schneider, *Is the CDM Fulfilling Its Environmental and Sustainable Development Objectives? An Evaluation of the CDM and Options for Improvement* (Berlin: Oko-Institut, 2007), http://www.panda.org/about wwf/where_we_work/Europe/news/index.cfm?uNewsID=118260; Michael W. Wara, "Measuring the Clean Development Mechanism's Performance and Potential," *UCLA Law Review* 55 (2008): 1759–1803, http://papers.ssrn.com/sol3/papers .cfm?abstract_id=1086242.

15. See Schneider, *Is the CDM Fulfilling Its Objectives?*, p. 42 (showing that CER revenue was a very small part of the projected internal rate of return for 546 of the first 803 projects).

16. Ibid. (showing that CER revenue was generally a very small part of the projected internal rate of return for renewable energy projects).

17. See Kevin A. Baumert, "Note: Participation of Developing Countries in the International Climate Change Regime: Lessons for the Future," *George Washington International Law Review* 38 (2006): 365–407, 386 (noting that gas capture/destruction projects account for 66 percent of expected emission reduction credits); Michael Wara, "Is the Global Carbon Market Working?" *Nature* 445 (February 7, 2007): 595–596, 596 (showing that waste gas projects account for the majority of credits claimed for projects "in the pipeline").

18. Joergen Fenhann, "UNEP Risoe CDM/JI Pipeline Analysis and Database, CDM Pipeline Grouped in Types," http://cdmpipeline.org/cdm-projects-type.htm (showing that HFC projects generated 49 percent of the credits).

19. Ibid.; see also Joergen Fenhann, *Guidance to the CDM/JI Pipeline* (Denmark: Capacity Development for the CDM, 2006), 1, http://cdmpipeline.org/ publications/GuidanceCDMpipeline.pdf (hereafter *CDM/JI Guide*; explaining that data come from UNFCC homepage located at http://cdm.unfccc.int/index.html, including project design documents).

20. I have derived this graph from table 10 of the CDM Pipeline Overview spreadsheet of the UNEP Risoe CDM/JI Pipeline Analysis and Database. See Joergen Fenhann, *CDM Pipeline Overview*, http://cdmpipeline.org/publications/CDMpipeline.xls (table 10 in an Excel spreadsheet of CDM pipeline data; accessed March 12, 2008) (providing analysis of all CDM/JI projects in the pipeline). The "other" category in this chart and the subsequent JI chart denotes technologies that are not known to involve end-of-the-pipe, renewable efficiency, or energy-efficiency technologies. The "other" category includes some projects that might be properly viewed as "end-of-the-pipe" projects, so that the percentage of end-of-the-pipe credits may be understated. The finding that renewables projects generate only a modest percentage of the total credits is broadly consistent with other analysts' conclusions. See, e.g., Wara, "Measuring the Clean Development," p. 26 (stating that renewables have generated 18 percent of the total credits).

21. See Fenhann, *CDM Pipeline Overview* (table 10) (showing that projected renewable energy credits will reach 25 percent in 2012). Furthermore, renewables project developers may face greater risks than developers of cheaper projects of having their projects' emission credits disapproved or reduced. See Lucy Mortimer, "An Uncertain Path," *Carbon Finance* 3 (April 20, 2006): 14, http://www.carbon-financeonline.com (noting that many projects may not make it through the registration process because of financial problems, methodological problems, and uncertainty about the post-2012 carbon market); Ben Pearson, "Market Failure: Why the Clean Development Mechanism Won't Promote Clean Development," *Journal of Cleaner Production* 15, no. 2 (2007): 247–252, 248 (noting that many renewables projects may not meet the Kyoto Protocol's "additionality" criterion). Similarly, the smaller joint implementation mechanism pipeline's renewable energy credits constitute about 19 percent of total projected credits. See Joergen Fenhann, *JI Pipeline Overview*, http://cdmpipeline.org/publi cations/JIpipeline.xls (Excel spreadsheet of JI pipeline data; accessed March 12,

2008), 1. Conversely, analysts expect end-of-the-pipe control's share of future project credits to decline to about 40 percent of the total. See Jane Ellis and Sami Kamel, *Overcoming Barriers to Clean Development Mechanism Projects* (Paris: OECD, 2007), p. 10, http://www.oecd.org/dataoecd/51/14/38684304.pdf; Karan Capoor and Philippe Ambrosi, *State and Trends of the Carbon Market 2007* (Washington, D.C.: World Bank, 2007), p. 28, http://web.worldbank.org/WBSITE/ EXTERNAL/NEWS/0,,contentMDK:21319781~pagePK:64257043~piPK:4373 76~theSitePK:4607,00.html.

22. Margaret R. Taylor, Edward L. Rubin, and David A. Hounshell, "Regulation as the Mother of Invention: The Case of SO_2 Control," *Law and Policy* 27 (2005): 348, 370 (concluding that trading encouraged less innovation than command and control); David Popp, "Pollution Control Innovations and the Clean Air Act of 1990," *Journal of Policy Analysis and Management* 22 (2003): 641 (finding more patenting of scrubber technology under command and control than under the acid rain trading program, but finding a shift in the type of innovation encouraged under trading).

23. See Driesen, "Design," pp. 436–437 and n. 4 (citing sources).

24. Cf. Kurt Strasser, "Cleaner Technology, Pollution Prevention, and Environmental Regulation," *Fordham Environmental Law Journal* 9 (1997): 1–106, 32; U.S. Congress, Office of Technology Assessment, *Gauging Control Technology and Regulatory Impacts in Occupational Safety and Health-An Appraisal of OSHA's Analytical Approach*, OTA-ENV-635, p. 64 (Washington, D.C.: U.S. Government Printing Office, 1995); Nicholas A. Ashford, Christine Ayers, and Robert F. Stone, "Using Regulation to Change the Market for Innovation," *Harvard Environmental Law Review* 9 (1985): 419–466, 440–441; Nicholas A. Ashford and George R. Heaton, Jr., "Regulation and Technological Innovation in the Chemical Industry," *Law and Contemporary Problems*, 46, no. 3 (1983): 109–157, 139–140.

II
Moving Forward

7

Collective and Individual Duties to Address Global Warming

Carl Cranor

Global warming has resulted from too many people and businesses producing too much carbon dioxide and other greenhouse gases, thus disrupting the carbon dioxide balance in the atmosphere. In turn, this imbalance leads to the gradual and possibly catastrophic warming of the planet Earth.

Neoliberalism views such problems in individualistic terms: How can we properly balance people's preferences for goods produced with fossil fuels with their preference for a stable climate? But this problem may be better viewed as a problem in collective morality.

Such collectively caused problems are instances of a generic class of moral problems that are a result of *generalization effects*. Philosophers have addressed generalization effects by means of what they call the *generalization argument*. The almost rhetorical question, "What if everyone did that?" has substantial persuasive power but is not necessarily the best question to ask for all moral issues. However, there are circumstances in which it is quite an appropriate question to ask and answer. This argument typically has the form, "if everyone's doing some act would have undesirable consequences or morally undesirable outcomes, then no one ought to do it." However, this formulation is too simple, as others and I have written elsewhere, because the conclusion simply does not follow.[1] A more nuanced version reveals the complexities of collective moral duties. I explain this below.

In this chapter, I discuss some approaches to what we might call *collective bads*, outcomes that result from too many people doing acts that in the aggregate have collectively bad consequences. A collective bad is analogous to but opposite from a collective good. I discuss this logic for some simpler environmental problems as well as for global warming. After considering the nature of collectively caused harms and some solutions, I discuss four generic lessons from them. (1) Solutions cannot be left to individual choices, even of conscientious moral agents, but require considerable governmental intervention to create and enforce solutions that *coordinate* actions of individuals and governments. (2) There are a variety of approaches consistent with solving collective bads. (3) Some of the most important duties for leaders and citizens alike are morally based political duties. And, (4) given the problems posed by global warming, we must treat both collective and individual duties to reduce it with much greater urgency than we have shown to date.

I. Background

The moral issues that arise from collective bads differ from those of more common moral problems. Philosophers and others are frequently concerned about the conditions under which a promise should be kept or may be broken, whether or not lying is permissible, why it is wrong for an agent to injure or kill others, and so on.[2] The wrongs from broken promises or lying tend to result in harms that fall on particular individuals as a result of the violation. (Of course, there can be broader social and institutional consequences as well, but harm or risk of harm to identifiable others tends to receive the greatest attention.) In many cases, an agent's failure to bear a particular moral responsibility results in a direct harm (or at least a risk) to other individuals. For such cases there is nearly a one-to-one relationship between violation of a duty and a harm or wrong done to others. Call these *direct harm duties* to others, violations of which tend to result in direct harms to others.

The relation between the violation of collective duties and harms is different. If too many people pump water from an underground aquifer, eventually causing it to go dry, or too many people drive cars that pollute the Los Angeles air basin, causing an increase in the incidence of diseases and property damage to fellow citizens, the harmful outcomes only result because too many are doing them. If one person or only a few pump water from an aquifer or drive a car that releases pollution, no one and nothing else likely will be harmed. Indeed there are circumstances in which small numbers of people may do such acts (as long as they are not too frequent) that will be morally permissible. Thus, if there were moral or legal duties not to contribute to collective harms, violation of them would not necessarily cause harm to others. Harm would occur only if too many violated their responsibilities to refrain from contributing to collective harms. This feature of collectively caused harms complicates finding solutions to them.

II. The Logic of Collective Duties

The logic for addressing the consequences of collectively caused harms has several steps and some degree of subtlety that simpler moral issues lack. Applied to generalization effects from greenhouse gases that cause global warming, the picture is roughly as follows. If everyone continues to produce carbon dioxide and other gases that contribute to global warming as they have been, this will result in morally undesirable, even catastrophic outcomes to the environment and the world's human population. The unacceptable outcomes concern not only those in the United States, but peoples and countries around the world. They will include exacerbation of drought in already stressed farming environments, causing greater crop failures and starvation among those who rely on agricultural production. Global warming also appears likely to increase floods and the harms they cause. Seawater will likely flood low-lying areas such as Bangladesh or the U.S. state of Florida, with further quite harmful consequences. It may increase hurricane damage along the eastern seaboard of the United States. Global warming will disrupt many ecosystems around the world with both some good and some bad effects; some ecosystems might merely be changed; others will be destroyed, perhaps forever. This disruption of ecosystems will produce permanent losses of some species. Few of these outcomes at the micro level are certain because of the global nature of the problem and the difficulty of predicting micro effects from a macro phenomenon, but some of the broader environmental effects are predictable (e.g., rising level of the seas, greater droughts and floods).

What follows from collectively caused undesirable outcomes is not that no one's activities should produce greenhouse gases, but that *not all agents should continue to make the same contributions to global warming that they have made in the past.* The activities that collectively cause harmful outcomes must be reduced to ameliorate the problem. *We humans* have a *collective* duty or responsibility not to produce as many greenhouse gas emissions as we have in the past. Past emissions have brought us to the current state of affairs and by themselves may produce catastrophic warming. Continuation of current emission rates portends an even worse future. The prevention of collectively caused problems will require substantial changes in the behavior of all (or a sufficient number) who contribute to the results.

However, solutions to collectively caused problems pose challenges that must be addressed. Two of the most obvious generic issues are the *coordination* problem and the *assurance* problem. (1) Those contributing to the problem (in this case most of the world, but especially the major energy users) must find, as Rawls put it, a "binding collective undertaking that would be best from the standpoint of all."[3] That is, there must be some agreement that reduces the collective bad consequences to some acceptable level and that must be acceptable to those affected by it.[4] This agreement must *coordinate* the behavior of those who contribute to the problem in order to reduce the adverse consequences to some acceptable level. That is, they must behave sufficiently similarly with respect to the unwanted outcome to effectively "solve" the problem. (2) In addition, the agreement must be binding so that there will be ongoing success in reducing the collectively caused harms. There must be assurance that those tempted to cheat on the collective agreement will not do so; in turn, this ensures that the collective solution is stable. This is the *assurance problem*. Since the actions of no one person (or a small number) produces the bad consequences, and typically one person (or a small number) can violate any agreement without significantly worsening the outcome (assuming no threshold effects), each may be tempted to benefit from others' compliance, that is, to free ride. However, free riders treat others unfairly and would be seen to be acting unfairly, tempting fellow citizens to take advantage of the collective enterprise. Consequently, parties to the agreement need some guarantee that by their commitment they are not disadvantaging themselves vis-à-vis others. In short, they must be assured that everyone (or almost everyone) else will abide by the agreement. Typically this guarantee would need to be provided by sanctions of some kind, and typically a sovereign or some other effective agency would apply them. We return to this below.

Merely stating the generalization problem and part of its generic solution does not reveal the full subtlety of the steps needed to achieve the desired result or the complexity of the moral issues involved. The logic of solutions to collectively caused problems requires some further steps, or one might even say some derivative moral decisions. Consider a version of the problem that is somewhat simpler than global warming. Suppose farmers pump water out of a large aquifer underlying several legal jurisdictions, such as states. Suppose further that it is in the self-interest of each to pump more water over time to increase his or her crop yields. At some point the demand on the aquifer will exceed its regeneration or recharge capacity each year. At that point the aquifer will go into decline and the collective benefits to the group of farmers will be less than they would have been if each had pumped less water each year. The solution, of course, is that they need an agreement about the total amount of water that may be pumped annually. And, they must have some arrangement about derivative duties to determine how much water each farmer may pump. In arriving at their chosen solution, they could be guided by a variety of subsidiary moral principles. Each might be permitted to pump equal amounts of water; each might have to reduce water use to levels that existed before the aquifer began to decline. Each might be permitted amounts of water relative to his or her wealth or proportional to the acreage of the farm, and so on. There might be auctionable and tradable rights to pump water. Whatever allocations are decided upon, there must be some procedure for assuring that those who abide by the agreement and only pump their allotment will be protected from others' cheating on the solution. Thus, the coordination and assurance conditions are met.

Choice of derivative duties must satisfy some general principles of justice. It is not merely that *some* principles should guide subsidiary responsibilities, but that at a minimum the solutions should be just. As Rawls argued, justice is the first virtue of institutions and the law: "Laws and institutions no matter how efficient and well-arranged must be reformed or abolished if they are unjust."[5] I do not want to argue for Rawls's or any other particular view of justice, but there are some general considerations to which he has called attention that are important to keep in mind. It is reasonable to expect that representative citizens within a nation will not unduly sacrifice their central interests for the welfare of society as a whole or for particular subsets within it (the problem is to identify those central interests and argue for them). If people are treated in accordance with appropriate principles of justice, such sacrifices would be minimized or brought within a mutually acceptable level. Moreover, one cannot expect compliance with legal or institutional requirements in a sustained manner over a long period of time if the costs of commitment to representative citizens are too great or if they believe they are being treated unjustly. This is especially true with respect to solutions to collective bad problems (and even more true of the long-term collective effort it will take to address global warming), since no particular other person is necessarily harmed when one does not do one's part to reduce contributions to collectively caused harms. *Just* distributions (and ones that are perceived to be just) of derivative duties to reduce collective harms make sustained commitment to the solutions much more acceptable. If citizens were required to make unjust sacrifices, this could plausibly create resentment and temptations to reduce efforts on behalf of collective solutions. Finally, solutions to collective bads will likely be much more stable over time if citizens are treated justly in any sacrifices they are required to make. Consequently, whatever derivative duties are arrived at to reduce collective bads should satisfy these broad considerations of justice in order to ensure the success of the solutions.

Further, a variety of considerations enter into collective solutions. How an agreement is reached and enforced depends on the geographic and other "size" problems of a collective bad. If the aquifer were small enough and the farmers knew each other, a voluntary agreement between them might work, if they could effectively enforce it among themselves. If many farmers are involved, voluntary solutions may not work, and some governmental agency may need to regulate the total amount of water pumped and distribute subsidiary pumping rights.

Those who understand and those who are impacted by the problem will need to see to it that there is an appropriate legal entity (or entities) to create a solution to the problem. This might, for example, involve legislation to create a legal compact coextensive with the region under which the aquifer lies in order to reduce pumping. In short, they have a political responsibility to bring the problem and possible solutions to it to the attention of elected political leaders, who have the authority and legal means to solve it. Political leaders can more effectively address the legal issues that would lead to solutions. Thus, the community will have a morally based *collective political duty* to see to it that elected political leaders who can create legal solutions do so. Political leaders in turn then must *lead* in finding and creating workable solutions. (This will not be easy, because circumstances in which leaders have incentives to continue the present course instead of incurring personal costs in solving the problem invite legislative and other kinds of inaction.) If they fail, they have (a) abrogated their general leadership duties, and (b) abrogated their morally grounded political duties to address the declining aquifer. If political leaders fail, citizens will have good reason to see to it that the leaders carry out their responsibilities or elect someone who will. One aspect of any solution would be some agency to monitor water levels in the aquifer to ensure that the solutions are working. Once solutions have been designed, citizens will have legal duties to abide by the solution and moral responsibilities to abide by their legal duties.

The logic described for overused aquifers applies in outline to global warming. However, since global warming is on a global scale it will involve more actors and more political entities. Morally grounded *political duties* will be especially important in the various communities and for their leaders.

First, to effectively address and reduce global warming, nation-states would need to agree to atmospheric concentration goals of greenhouse gases to sustain the temperature of the planet at some appropriate level to avoid major bad consequences. They would then need to come to a "binding collective undertaking" between themselves for now and into the future to reduce greenhouse gases and eventually cease emitting them, so that global warming would eventually stop. In addition, they would need to solve the assurance problem between nation-states to ensure that there is no cheating on the collective agreement and so that each nation does its part to reduce greenhouse gases. Their collective agreement would involve the assignment of limits to national emissions of greenhouse gases. Amy Sinden argues that these sorts of agreements between countries should also be just and be perceived to be just.[6]

Second, once nation-states have agreed on the requisite contribution each must make to reduce greenhouse gases, each nation then must create policies to allocate responsibilities for citizens and industries within national borders to reduce their contributions. Within a nation where there is an existing organized community of the appropriate size to address the national contribution to the problem and the legal jurisdiction is coextensive with national boundaries, there may be appropriate political institutions with appropriate leaders to design solutions, and distribute derivative duties to reduce a nation's greenhouse gas contribution.[7] For global warming, thus, nation-states, if they have appropriate institutions, will need to take steps to reduce their citizens' contributions to global warming.

If a nation-state does not have appropriate or effective legal institutions for such purposes, these would need to be designed, created, and made efficacious. However, in advanced industrialized countries, the main but not the only contributors to global warming, there already are such institutions. The leaders of countries contributing to global warming would have morally based political responsibilities to address the problem. If they did not, informed citizens would have good reasons to pressure them to do so, or to elect leaders who would.

Consequently, within national institutions there are some special *political responsibilities* that fall on leaders and citizens alike to address collectively caused problems. The relevant community has a collective duty to see to it that the community as a whole reduces its contributions to global warming. This generally implies that each member of the community has a duty to seek appropriate collective action. If there are leaders authorized to act for the community in question, then there are good reasons for the *leaders* to see to it that citizens reduce their production of greenhouse gases. The leaders are in the best position to see to it that the collective duty is carried out and to take steps to prevent the collectively bad consequences. This responsibility rests on a "can implies ought" principle: "Other things being equal, . . . those who have the most power and authority to see to it that a duty be fulfilled ought to do so."[8]

Citizens' carrying out of this political duty is not the only way they can contribute to reducing global warming. They will also have subsidiary or derivative legal and moral duties imposed as part of the nation-state solution. In addition to these, citizens may believe that they have greater moral responsibilities to go beyond what the law requires to reduce global warming. They should be encouraged in this effort. Moreover, the generalization argument can be a guide to actions that collectively would assist in reducing global warming. (If everyone or most acted as the agent does, what would be the effect on greenhouse gases? That is, each person should reasonably think about how their individual actions would affect the production of greenhouse gases and try to reduce or minimize those actions that would increase production.) The political obligation, however, is literally one of the first or primary duties, because it must be carried out to ensure that the nation-state is addressing the problem at all. Thus, for example, if U.S. leaders do not take effective concrete steps to reduce global warming, citizens will have to resort to this primary political duty to elect leaders who will and to pressure those who have political office to take effective action.

Given the growing magnitude of global warming, in what order these steps are taken is perhaps less important than that nation-states reach some agreement to address it and that nations within their borders quickly take steps to reduce greenhouse gases. Part of the negotiation of treaties between nation-states would be some just allocation of the contributions of each to reduce greenhouse gases, as Sinden argues. Moreover, there should be mechanisms for updating the agreements if they are insufficient to achieve the desired goals. Further, each nation will then need to devise national, legally enforceable strategies to meet its targets. Businesses and citizens within each country will then have secondary responsibilities to help implement the overall national strategies. The distribution of secondary duties to citizens within a nation-state would need to be supported first by justice, then by efficiency and other considerations in reaching the national goals. Citizens would rightly have complaints if the national strategies for reducing greenhouse gases violated the broad considerations of justice sketched above. They could also have legitimate complaints if solutions were inefficient or otherwise poorly designed.[9]

The above brief review of collective solutions to collective bads and a reminder of some of the consequences of global warming shows that it is a massive problem that will require myriad strategies at different jurisdictional levels to ensure that nations, legal entities within nations, and finally individuals are appropriately assigned responsibilities to contribute to the solution of the problem and to ensure that the responsibilities are carried out. Within national borders the solutions are easier than between nation-states, but both need attention.

III. Lessons from the Logic of Solving Collective Action Problems

There are at least four major lessons apparent from considering the outline of the arguments concerning collective and individual duties to address global warming: (1) The inadequacy of leaving the solutions to individual choices (or to an unconstrained "market") and the concomitant necessity for governmental action. (2) A wide variety of approaches that might curtail the problem of global warming and a place for a variety of moral considerations constrained by justice to guide allocations of derivative responsibilities for the solution. (3) Major elements of the solution typically would include peculiarly *political duties* on the part of citizens and other actors to ensure that the collective harm is curtailed, and (4), the urgency of individual duties to support the collective duty to reduce global warming. Consider each in turn.

A. The Inadequacy of Individual Choices to Reduce Global Warming and the Necessity of Governmental Action

Solutions to collective action problems are contrary at least to simplified neoliberal views. By "simplified" I mean views that hold that economic markets can reasonably address most social problems, including global warming, together with the view that there is little or no role for governmental involvement. Of course, there likely can be a place for some use of properly constrained markets in creating solutions to the problem (I mention one example below), but there must be governmentally enforceable constraints on any solutions and especially on market solutions in order to ensure that participants abide by the conditions under which markets are permitted.

The logic of collective harms shows why leaving the solutions to individual choices will not work. When there is no *coordinated* collective response to a collective bad, each member or group contributing to the problem would make "decisions on how to act in isolation from the decisions of others." One can show that each person pursuing his or her own long-term self-interest, but at the same time taking into account the actions of others, will act so as to produce collectively bad consequences.[10] Moreover, collective harms do not arise merely from the actions of self-interested agents. That is, since self-interest often leads to wrongful acts, one might suppose that agents committed to acting on moral principle might avoid these problems. However, Miller and Sartorious have argued that there is no defensible moral principle on which individuals can act, making decisions *in isolation* from others (without coordinating with them), that would sufficiently modify behavior to produce a successful solution to collective bads, at least for large-scale problems such as over-population.[11] If these results are correct (at least for large-scale collective problems), the source of collective bads is that agents acting out of self-interest or even out of moral motivations are making decisions *in isolation from one another* and not sufficiently *coordinating their actions*. They are not behaving in a sufficiently constrained manner to reduce bad consequences. *Failure to coordinate behavior* in ways that will solve the problem is a primary difficulty. Coordination requires constraints on or the shaping of individual decisions.

Consequently, unconstrained markets, where agents are making decisions in isolation from one another in pursuit of their own self-interest, will fail to solve problems such as global warming, and almost certainly will exacerbate it. There needs to be some intervention into the decisions of agents who contribute to a collectively bad outcome to ensure that their actions are sufficiently coordinated to modify successfully the collective bad consequences. To the extent that markets can contribute to solving global warming, they must be structured and constrained to ensure appropriately coordinated behavior to reduce warming.

Moreover, solutions to collective bads will involve governmental or quasi-governmental actions in several ways. First, there must be some information-collection agency to monitor the *collective* consequences of actions. A common and credible agency is needed for collecting data to provide a baseline of current concentrations of greenhouse gases and continuing to monitor the success or failure of the chosen solution. Typically it would be an agency of the government with sufficient credibility to ensure that all the appropriate data are gathered, that they are fairly assimilated, not skewed, that they are presented in a balanced and even-handed manner, and that there is a mechanism for complaints about shortcomings in data collection and reporting.[12] Such an agency must continue to faithfully and responsibly gather and report the data, not hide, distort, or "bend" the science as the George W. Bush administration did on global warming.[13]

Second, within national borders, governments would need to enforce collective agreements. There is also a need for assurance that nations will abide by international agreements, but since there is no world government with enforcement power, nations would need to negotiate these issues between themselves with some system of international sanctions and suasion to provide needed guarantees. There are a variety of approaches to coordinating behavior, but all involve sufficiently substantial governmental interventions.

B.   The Variety of Approaches to Curtail Global Warming

Recall that subsidiary steps must be taken to reduce the total production of greenhouse gases. Between nation-states, reduction in total greenhouse gases might occur if only those nations that contributed the most reduced their contributions to achieve the result, if every country made a percentage reduction, if contributing countries made proportional reductions with the largest contributors making the largest reductions (a kind of progressive greenhouse gas reduction as it were [analogous to progressive taxation]), and so on. The point is not to argue for a particular solution but to point out the possibilities for numerous moral and institutional decisions in order to achieve the desired outcome internationally. Such choices belong to the morality of subsidiary solutions to collectively caused problems.

Within nation–states, there are a variety of choices as well that would have to be made to implement compliance with internationally set targets. There could be *governmental mandates*, for example, requiring automobile manufacturers to increase the average gas mileage of the new cars brought into the market or requiring air conditioning and refrigerator manufacturers to create more energy-efficient appliances. Large emitters of greenhouse gases could be mandated to reduce their emissions or sequester the carbon from them, if this is technologically feasible. There can also be *governmentally imposed taxes* on the sale of gasoline in order to discourage the purchase of gas-guzzling cars, to encourage the purchase of hybrids or other highly efficient cars, and to provide incentives for drivers to begin to utilize alternative forms of transportation that on a per-user and per-trip basis emit fewer greenhouse gases. There could be *carbon taxes* on products to try to approximate the true social and environmental costs of the manufacture and use of the products. This would reduce the use of products that involve high carbon emissions and provide a fund that could subsidize efforts to reduce greenhouse gases in areas of our lives not adequately addressed through the tax. Energy producers could be rewarded for motivating their customers to conserve energy. For other activities, there could be subsidies of more benign alternatives in order to encourage them. Choices between possible alternatives must be assessed institutionally and constrained first by justice, and second by efficiency and other considerations for desirability. (Not all of the examples suggested above necessarily satisfy justice conditions.)

Part of a solution to global warming might be the use of appropriately constrained markets. These could take the form of carbon credits that might be purchased at auction and then bought and sold between companies. Those who favor markets would argue both that this maximizes a variety of freedoms to adjust to the socially required goals and that markets are efficient. However, the use of such markets does not eliminate the need for substantial governmental intervention. Quite the contrary. Carbon credits must be legally created by governmental action. They must be constrained in amount so that the total amount of greenhouse gases will reduce the national contribution to global warming. There likely will need to be provisions to further reduce the amount of CO_2 over time if first approximation solutions are not adequate. Once created and sold, or assigned, rights to contribute CO_2 must be enforced. That is, individuals or firms that purchase the right to produce X amount of greenhouse gases must not exceed their allotted amount or the solution will not work. In short, cheating must be prevented even within market solutions. If firms purchase rights to emit CO_2, they may legally do so up to their allocated amount, but must be sanctioned for cheating. In addition, there must be a practical and enforceable mechanism for assessing the emissions of each in order to ensure that each relevant actor is emitting within its rights.

As if to illustrate these points, Ackerman and Stewart in an article published in 1985 point out that markets in pollution credits (analogous to carbon emitting credits) would have the following features.

The reformed system [of marketable pollution credits] we have described involves the execution of four bureaucratic tasks. First, the agency must estimate how much pollution presently is permitted by law in each watershed and air quality region. Second, it must run a system of fair and efficient auctions in which polluters can regularly buy rights for limited terms. Third, it must run an efficient title registry in each region that will allow buyers and sellers to transfer rights in a legally effective way. Fourth, it must consistently penalize polluters who discharge more than their permitted amounts.[14]

They should have added that the total amount of pollution permitted would need to be assessed periodically by an impartial data collection agency after input from scientific committees. Thus, even "market" solutions to global warming will involve several major governmental tasks to create coordinated actions and enforce the solution in just and efficient ways.

C. Morally Based Political Responsibilities to Address Collective Bads

As already discussed, some of the most important moral responsibilities are *political*. Leaders of a country have a political responsibility to see to it that collectively caused problems are addressed and solved. Even in the best circumstances they will have to overcome institutional inertia and political forces that lead in the direction of procrastination. However, when presidential administrations have denied or frustrated steps to recognize and begin to address global warming, they have exhibited substantial failures in their public and moral responsibilities. They not only failed to heed the overwhelming majority of the scientific community that studied the problem, but also manipulated reports showing the problem in order to understate or deny it.[15] They failed miserably to carry out a morally based political duty to see to it that the problem of global warming is addressed.

Citizens of a country have important political responsibilities to see to it that leaders who are in a position to do something about global warming act to reduce and prevent it. In an earlier period when air pollution problems came to public attention, citizens and politicians carried out such political responsibilities. There was considerable political support for addressing the environmental and public health effects of air pollution because scientists and citizens called attention to the problem. Political impetus from the citizenry and informed judgment by some leaders helped to motivate Congress to pass a national law to reduce pollution that targeted particular pollutants of concern. Congress then placed the law under the jurisdiction of a newly created Environmental Protection Agency in order to have one institution responsible for the problem area. The EPA then designed solutions to air pollution consistent with the legislation. This in turn imposed legal duties on states as well as on businesses and citizens who were subject to the laws. And, of course, the laws had to be enforced, too often a shortcoming of agency and congressional behavior.

Moreover, citizens *continue to have morally based political duties.* If presidential administrations or administrative agencies are not addressing global warming, individuals have good reasons to pressure them to do better, to vote to replace elected leaders with those who will address the problems, and so on. This may not be a moral duty that many of us think about, but it is part of the logic of collective duties to prevent environmental harms.

D.   The Urgency of Collective Duties and Their Implementation

There is a final point to be noted, differentiating violations of direct harm duties (DHDs) from violations of collective duties. Identification of violations of DHDs would be comparatively straightforward, and as a result, *moral authority to criticize violations* would also tend to be more obvious and widespread.[16] This is not just because there typically would be a victim (although it helps to see someone harmed as a result of an action over which an individual has quite substantial control), but the relationship between violations and harm to others typically would be comparatively obvious to third parties. This facilitates "seeing" or being aware of the wrong. And, because of the perceptibility of a victim and the harm occurring, this may increase the strength of moral blame and criticism. One might think of this as part of the epistemology of moral wrongness.

Violations of derivative duties that implement the fulfillment of collective duties pose more difficult issues concerning the urgency of the duties and the urgency of blame and criticism when there is failure. When derivative duties to address collective harms are violated, this might not be easily seen. Even if *violations* were comparatively clear, they will less obviously result in harm in general or to particular individuals; the connections between violation and collective harm are greatly attenuated, difficult to identify, or even nonexistent. This could result in a mistaken tendency to moderate the moral force we feel to do our part to prevent collective harms. The attenuation of connections between violations of derivative duties and harm to others or the environment further complicates the morality of collective duties and may (mistakenly) seem to reduce the urgency we have to see to it that collective duties are carried out. It may also tend to reduce criticism of those who fail to do what is required to implement solutions to collectively caused problems. That is, we may feel greater urgency to abide by DHDs and to blame and criticize those who violate them (thus, likely causing harm to others) than the urgency we feel to adhere to duties resulting from a collective duty to prevent harm. We may also feel less urgency to blame and criticize someone who vio- ·

lates a duty derivative to a collective duty that in all likelihood will not necessarily cause harm to identifiable others or the environment (at worst, violation might merely make some minor contribution to a collectively caused harm).

However, we should not give in to these tendencies, if they are there. News and scientific reports almost daily remind us of the serious and probably catastrophic consequences of failing to reduce global warming. Whole ecosystems of the world may change dramatically, never to be seen again in our or our grandchildren's grandchildren's lifetimes, if ever. Millions of fellow human beings are likely to suffer greatly or even die as a result of droughts, torrential downpours, hurricanes, river and sea floods, and so on. We should still act affirmatively and vigorously to see to it that the collective duty to reduce global warming is carried out. And, each of us should feel compelled to carry out the derivative moral duties required to do our fair share in achieving a collective solution. Finally, we should carry out to the utmost of our abilities our political duty to see to it that our leaders, who can do most to craft solutions and enforce them, do so. Failure to act forcefully to hold leaders and others accountable to solve the problem will lead to global and regional calamities. None of this will be easy, but too much is at stake to do otherwise.

Conclusion

Defensible solutions to collectively caused harms pose more complex and subtle moral issues than solutions to simpler moral concerns with which we might be familiar. There may not be a wrong or harm at all, if not too many people perform acts that taken together could result in collective bads. For global warming, the collective wrong results when too many emit greenhouse gases or emit more than the climate of the Earth as we have known it can tolerate without substantial bad consequences. Unfortunately, this is now occurring and will only worsen.

Solutions are not simple, either. Collectively, the world's human populations can no longer emit greenhouse gases at past rates. We must reduce the total amount of greenhouse gases each nation produces. Citizens within nations will need to reduce their emissions on average. There are a variety of just solutions that can be taken to achieve the end result. They will all involve substantial governmental action to legally create solutions, to monitor the degree of success in achieving them, and to enforce them, even when governments employ market-based solutions. Finally, given the magnitude of the problem and its growing urgency, we will need to assign great importance to ensuring compliance with the collective duty to reduce global warming and any derivative duties that are part of the solution. Most importantly, we must hold our political leaders' feet to the proverbial moral fire to ensure that they responsibly address the problem, simply because they can do the most to craft, implement, and enforce solutions.

Notes

1. Edna Ullman-Margalit," The Generalization Argument: Where Does the Obligation Lie?" *Journal of Philosophy* 73, no. 15 (Sep. 2, 1976): 511–522, and Carl F. Cranor, "Collective and Individual Duties to Protect the Environment," *Journal of Applied Philosophy* 2, no. 2 (1985): 243–259.

2. See, e.g., Sissala Bok, *Lying: Moral Choice in Public and Private Life* (New York: Vintage Books, 1979).

3. John Rawls, *A Theory of Justice* (Cambridge, MA: Harvard University Press, 1971). See also Amartya K. Sen, "Isolation, Assurance, and the Social Rate of Discount," *Quarterly Journal of Economics* 81 (1967): 112–124.

4. Rawls appears to articulate a more stringent condition, namely, that the solution must be "best" from the standpoint of all affected by the agreement (but he does not elaborate in *A Theory of Justice* on what this would be). He likely imposes this condition because it would result from the conditions implicit in what he calls the original position. These ensure that everyone affected by a policy must choose it behind a "veil of ignorance" constraining each person to choose only those principles that (roughly) ensure benefits for each.

5. Rawls, *A Theory of Justice*, p. 3.

6. Amy Sinden, "The Abandonment of Justice," chapter 5 in the present volume.

7. Cranor, "Collective and Individual Duties," p. 255.

8. Ibid., p. 252.

9. Rawls, *A Theory of Justice*, p. 3.

10. Mancur Olson, *The Logic of Collective Action* (Cambridge, MA: Harvard University Press, 1971); Edna Ullman-Margalit, *The Emergence of Norms* (Oxford: Oxford University Press, 1977).

11. Frank Miller and Rolf Sartorius, "Public Goods and Population Policy," *Philosophy and Public Affairs* 8 (1979): 148–174.

12. This concern might have seemed merely speculative until the years of the George W. Bush presidential administration, when there were concerted efforts to muzzle governmental scientists, suppress reports, and so on.

13. Tom McGarity and Wendy Wagner, *Bending Science: How Special Interests Corrupt Public Health Research* (Cambridge, MA: Harvard University Press, 2008).

14. Bruce A. Ackerman and Richard B. Stewart, "Comment: Reforming Environmental Law," *Stanford Law Review* 37 (1985): 1333–1365, 1347.

15. Andrew C. Levkin, "Bush vs. the Laureates: How Science Became a Partisan Issue," *New York Times*, October 19, 2004; and Tim Dickinson, "The Secret Campaign of President Bush's Administration to Deny Global Warming," *Rolling Stone* (June 20, 2007).

16. My colleague Coleen Macnamara uses the phrase "authority to criticize," which I borrow from her.

8

Embracing a Precautionary Approach to Climate Change

John S. Applegate

We have seen that the neoliberal framing of climate change relies heavily on cost-benefit analysis, as a proxy for the market, to guide and even to determine appropriate regulatory responses. Cost-benefit analysis implies, however, that we can determine with some accuracy the environmental costs of our free markets, which is a demonstrably false assumption. A precautionary approach, in contrast, accounts explicitly for uncertainty, and therefore it focuses attention on appropriate protective action. It provides a valuable alternative to a market-based approach predicated on cost-benefit analysis.

In common usage, to "take precaution" means to take measures that are calculated to avoid a threatened harmful outcome. In the area of environmental protection, the idea of precaution has additional resonance, because it is widely accepted that the nature and purpose of much environmental regulation is to avoid harm to human health and the non-human environment before such harm comes to pass. This is the *preventive* purpose of environmental regulation. It is also widely understood that preventive regulation must therefore be based on incomplete supporting information, because the inherent complexity and limitations of the relevant science preclude certainty ex ante about causes and consequences. This is the *anticipatory* purpose of environmental regulation, and the idea of precaution embraces both prevention and anticipation.

In order to express the precautionary objectives of environmental regulation, numerous international agreements of the last fifteen or twenty years have adopted the "Precautionary Principle." While its origins are older, the principle received its most commonly cited formulation in the Rio Declaration, a statement of 27 principles that formed the closing document of the 1992 Earth Summit[1] and was signed by 165 nations:

In order to protect the environment, the precautionary approach shall be widely applied by States according to their capabilities. Where there are threats of serious or irreversible damage, lack of full scientific certainty shall not be used as a reason for postponing cost-effective measures to prevent environmental degradation.[2]

The Precautionary Principle is founded on the goal of prevention, and its precise focus is anticipation: "The principle states that in cases of scientific uncertainty '*no evidence of harm*' should not be equated with '*no harm*.'"[3] The principle has become a widely accepted constituent of international environmental law. The United States has expressly accepted it in the Rio Declaration and the United Nations Framework Convention on Climate Change (UNFCCC); and it is therefore entirely appropriate to expect that U.S. policy comport with the Precautionary Principle.

What does it mean to take a precautionary approach to climate change? Because the Precautionary Principle has been the object of an enormous amount of mischaracterization and misunderstanding in the United States, our first task must be to clarify what the Precautionary Principle is *not*. With a few notable exceptions,[4] the American legal literature on the Precautionary Principle has been harshly critical. In fact, the Precautionary Principle has the dubious distinction of being simultaneously attacked as being both extreme and vacuous—that is, both as representing a radical shift in environmental policy toward some kind of neo-Luddism, and as being no more than a truism.[5] Much rubble needs to be cleared away. With that accomplished, we can turn to the actual meaning of the Precautionary Principle. Although it is far from uniformly understood or interpreted, the principle can be said to have four elements, each of which applies quite directly to the problem of climate change. We will find that the Precautionary Principle has especially important things to say about the adequacy of scientific information as a barrier to regulation. Arcuri characterizes this as the "'minimal core' of the Principle: it is meant to justify intervention in the absence of scientific certainty. In other words, uncertainty *per se* should not preclude regulatory actions undertaken to protect human health and the environment."[6] Substantively, the Precautionary Principle points us in a direction quite different from the current neoliberal model, and one that is far more responsive than current U.S. policy is to the current level of understanding of climate science.

I. Critiques of the Precautionary Principle

The Precautionary Principle is not a simple legal concept to describe, because it has been formulated in ways that range between what Arcuri calls α-Precaution (un-precaution, in Wagner's phrase), in which scientific certainty is required before any regulatory action can be taken, to Radical Precaution, which would prohibit any activities that present a potential for significant risk.[7] Scholars have cataloged[8] and compared[9] the various versions in an extensive literature on the subject. In fact, most versions of the principle have coalesced around a fairly moderate or middle-ground version, of the kind that one might imagine would be capable of garnering the support of the 165 nations that signed the Rio Declaration and of being adopted in many other international instruments.[10] Principle 15 of the Rio Declaration articulates the Precautionary Principle as above. The UNFCCC, which was adopted at the same conference, not surprisingly adopted a similar version:

> The Parties should take precautionary measures to anticipate, prevent or minimize the causes of climate change and mitigate its adverse effects. Where there are threats of serious or irreversible damage, lack of full scientific certainty should not be used as a reason for postponing such measures, taking into account that policies and measures to deal with climate change should be cost-effective so as to ensure global benefits at the lowest possible cost.[11]

These versions of the Precautionary Principle (especially the generally applicable Rio Declaration) represent the de facto standard text of the principle. The United States has signed the declaration (as a declaration and not a convention, it is not subject to ratification), and it has signed and ratified the UNFCCC.

A. Neo-Luddism

The most common American caricature of the Precautionary Principle would oppose industrial innovation generally, by prohibiting any economic activity that raises the possibility of even hypothetical environmental adverse effects[12] with no consideration of the severe economic or perverse health and environmental consequences of such a prohibition.[13] Critics of the neo-Luddite version emphasize the impossibility of achieving perfect safety, the utility of many industrial and economic activities despite their hazards, and especially the risk *reductions* that can be attributed even to activities that pose their own risks. Favorite examples include prescription drugs and even fire. The most aggressive form of this argument, that "richer is safer," posits that any failure to encourage economic development amounts to the worsening of the health risks associated with poverty. The rhetorical strategy at work, in other words, is to characterize the Precautionary Principle as Radical Precaution.

Radical Precaution has very few actual (as opposed to imagined) adherents.[14] Undoubtedly a few real neo-Luddites still prowl the Earth, accepting only the risks of a simpler (albeit more dangerous) time.[15] However, such individuals surely represent at most a tiny minority of the population, and they are not likely to be represented at all among the governments that have adopted the Precautionary Principle in international negotiations and national law. Radical Precaution is, in other words, a straw man, but it is worth responding to this criticism so that we can better understand what the Precautionary Principle *is*.

The neo-Luddism criticism asserts, first, that there is in fact no meaningful threshold for the operation of the Precautionary Principle, and, second, that the principle is to be applied in an entirely decontextualized manner. That there is in fact a threshold condition could not be clearer in the standard text. "Where there are threats of serious or irreversible damage" clearly limits the principle's application to a relatively narrow class of dangers to human health and the environment. Although the principle does not define a threshold level of certainty at which a mere concern becomes a "threat," the use of the term "threat" clearly implies a nontrivial degree of likelihood. "Serious or irreversible" may be fairly vague terms, but it is hard to know how a general principle could be much more precise. Certainly the terms are no more vague than the familiar "unreasonable risk"[16] or "high level of protection."[17] It is therefore not the case that virtually any claim of potential damage or any claimed harm will trigger the operation of the Precautionary Principle.

Further, the Precautionary Principle is just that, a principle. It is neither a detailed rule that purports to apply specific standards of conduct to specific circumstances,[18] nor a peremptory norm (like the international prohibitions on slavery or torture) that admits of no derogation or balancing. While the principle announces a clear direction for legal obligations, there is nothing in the text or background of the Precautionary Principle that suggests that it should be applied unthinkingly or without reference to its ultimate goal of protection of human health and the environment or to other, possibly countervailing, concerns. The first sentence of Principle 15 of the Rio Declaration could not be clearer on this point: "In order to protect the environment, the precautionary approach shall be widely applied by States according to their capabilities." It states an overarching goal ("to protect the environment"), two qualifications ("approach"; "widely"), and a countervailing concern ("according to their capabilities"), none of which would be advanced by application out of context or with knowingly perverse results.

The extremism critique assumes, in addition, that there is only one regulatory response envisioned by the Precautionary Principle, and that the response is the wholesale and immediate abandonment of a certain product or activity. Such responses are exceedingly rare in health or environmental regulation of *any* kind, and both the Rio text ("cost-effective measures to prevent") and the UNFCCC text ("cost-effective," "ensure global benefits at the lowest possible cost," "take into account different socio-economic contexts") describe a far more modest, cost-sensitive response. Early versions of the principle and versions in treaties dealing with particularly disfavored materials (like hazardous waste) tend to be worded more strongly, but they have by and large been "tamed" over time.[19] It is not even clear that the Precautionary Principle always places the burden of proving safety with the creator of the potential risk, as some of its supporters have argued.[20]

Despite the persistence of caricatures in the U.S. literature, more recent versions of the Precautionary Principle have added further qualifications that are designed to avoid precisely the excesses that worry some American commentators. The European Commission seeks to cabin the principle by limiting its application to situations where there is a demonstrable lack of knowledge (that is, where a specific data gap has been identified) and by placing it in the larger frame of risk-based regulation and risk management.[21] In the Commission's interpretation, the principle is a specific tool for addressing the specific problem of scientific uncertainty. The Commission's and later versions of the principle also add the element of iteration to the Rio formulation, requiring that reliance on the principle be followed by a concerted effort to resolve the uncertainty that necessitated reliance on the principle in the first place.[22] Iteration confines the Precautionary Principle to serving as a temporary measure to bridge the temporal gap between recognition of a hazard and full understanding of its contours.

B.   A Universal Norm

There are also instances of critics claiming more for the Precautionary Principle than it claims for itself. One is the idea that it is offered as a single universal norm that resolves within a few short words all issues of environmental harm. Sunstein, for example, derides the principle for being "a crude, indirect, and sometimes perverse way of incorporating distributional concerns."[23] This might be true if the Precautionary Principle purported to resolve distributional concerns, but that is patently not its purpose. Although it is undoubtedly a worthy goal to develop universal pronouncements like the Golden Rule, there is no evidence that any of the authors of the several versions of the Precautionary Principle saw themselves as engaged in such an expansive undertaking. Instead, the authors of the Rio Declaration felt that they needed twenty-seven principles to encompass environmental concerns, of which the Precautionary Principle is but one. The UNFCCC lists five principles to guide decisions regarding its still narrower focus.[24] As Arcuri suggests, the Precautionary Principle acts in concert with at least the principles of prevention and of proportionality, and itself addresses primarily one particular and particularly important problem: the temporal relationship of harm to action and of information to regulation.[25]

C. Truisms

Moving from truth to truism, some critics frequently deride the Precautionary Principle as vacuous. It is said to offer little more than platitudes like "look before you leap" or "better safe than sorry," which are axiomatic and of little utility in choosing a course of action in complex situations.[26] Though it might be reassuring to imagine that "look before you leap" is a fixed star in governmental decision making on health, safety, and the environment, experience suggests otherwise. It is simply not the case that governments consistently investigate the environmental consequences of potentially environmentally deleterious actions ("look before you leap") or that they avoid potentially irreversible effects on the environment ("better safe than sorry"). The European Commission filled a lengthy volume, *Late Lessons from Early Warnings*, with tragic failures to follow these maxims.[27] From radiation and benzene to DES and sulfur dioxide, *Late Lessons* had no shortage of examples to draw upon. Environmental impact assessments, the original look before a leap, are still produced only reluctantly and often inadequately. Industrial chemicals are manufactured and sold without any required premarket investigation. (The European REACH legislation, which aims to remedy this, is just coming into effect in 2008.) In other words, what everyone might agree is good practice is by no means universal practice, in the absence of a specific command. Therefore, it hardly seems vacuous to insist, as a matter of general principle, on looking before we leap and being safe rather than sorry. What the Precautionary Principle may lack in intellectual novelty, it more than makes up for in practical necessity.

The Precautionary Principle is also said to represent the truism that environmental regulation (like almost all governmental action) must operate under conditions of uncertainty and imperfect information. If "lack of full scientific certainty" were actually a barrier to regulation, *no* environmental regulation would ever have been imposed—which has obviously not been the case. Therefore, the critics argue, the Precautionary Principle merely states the obvious point that perfect information is never available.

But neoliberal ideology, by demanding that regulation be based on "sound science," has successfully sought to prevent widespread acceptance of scientific uncertainty as an inevitable feature of protective regulation. The "sound science" slogan has served as a framing device for a demand of a high level of proof to justify regulation, proof that can be factored into the quantitative tools of risk assessment and cost-benefit analysis to formulate policy based on the neoliberal model.

The "sound science" slogan highlights the imprecision, incompleteness, and uncertainty that inevitably result from the collision of unrealistically high expectations of scientific analysis with the realities of scientific knowledge. In a governance environment in which bureaucracies seek to rationalize their decisions based on objective criteria, and a cultural environment in which scientific answers are highly respected by the public, the idea that governmental action (especially if it is costly or inconvenient) should be based on comprehensive and certain science has an undeniable allure. The "sound science" frame has become an important way to view the political and analytical landscape of environmental regulation precisely because it is a logical extension of the ideology of quantification and comprehensive rationality.[28]

The shift in framing from precaution to "sound science" plays a large role in neoliberal inaction on climate change. By demanding a level of scientific certainty that is unavailable for preventive action, the rhetoric of "sound science" legitimates the failure to anticipate harmful consequences. The Bush administration consistently avoided regulatory controls by deploying a strategy of highlighting and exaggerating uncertainties, whether or not they are relevant to the decisions that need to be made. To justify its *volte face* on the commitment to ratify Kyoto, the newly inaugurated President George W. Bush asked the National Academy of Sciences to undertake a study of the uncertainties of climate change. The charge to the NAS was patently designed to elicit evidence of uncertainty in the relevant science. Its specific questions concentrated on areas in which certainty was well known not to exist. Nevertheless, the committee responded with a firm statement of the fundamental reality and anthropogenic contribution to climate change. Ignoring the NAS conclusion (so much for "following the science"), Bush continued to speak of "the limits of our knowledge" on climate change, and asserted that "we do not know . . . how some of our actions could impact it."[29]

This was the beginning of the campaign by the White House to refuse to acknowledge the reality or certainty of climate change. As the Union of Concerned Scientists and the House Committee on Oversight and Government Reform recently reported in detailed investigations of political interference in climate change science, the Council on Environmental Quality (CEQ) redacted and rewrote any major administration document that referenced climate change. Changes to one EPA report were so egregious that EPA pulled the entire climate change section rather than publish the authorized version. The redactor-in-chief, Philip Cooney, was a lawyer and former lobbyist for the American Petroleum Institute, and his changes followed precisely the uncertainty line of his former employers.[30] The changes sought to conceal points of agreement among scientists and to exaggerate uncertainties. CEQ not only reviewed and edited all administration testimony on climate change before Congress, it also approved and rejected witnesses based on their commitment to the administration's skeptical position.

D. Indefiniteness

The Precautionary Principle is also less than draconian and more than vacuous because, as a legal principle, it can apply to different situations differently in response to other relevant principles or considerations.[31] Thus the Precautionary Principle has been validly expressed in several forms of words for different applications, and those forms of words are subject to interpretation by different readers and in different circumstances. The Precautionary Principle is not a detailed, highly prescriptive legal rule; it is not intended to be a candidate for the Code of Federal Regulations. As a principle, the Precautionary Principle has neither the specificity nor the all-or-nothing quality (as Dworkin puts it[32]) of a legal rule. Instead, a principle "states a reason that argues in one direction, but does not necessitate a particular decision."[33]

Appropriately, in Article 3 of the UNFCCC (entitled "Principles") the treaty states: "In their actions to achieve the objective of the Convention and to implement its provisions, the Parties shall be *guided*, inter alia, by the following [principles]" (emphasis added). As Fisher says, "Like all legal principles, it is flexible, interrelates with other principles, does not dictate a particular outcome, and can be subject to different interpretations."[34] The Precautionary Principle does not and does not purport to provide *a priori* answers for every case.[35] It may be more familiar to regard the Precautionary Principle as expressing an approach to the many exercises of judgment that are required of environmental policymakers. This is far from trivial. Even as a principle and even in the American legal context, the Precautionary Principle's stance of concern about potential effects and acceptance of residual scientific uncertainty represents a significant but not unbending guide to regulatory action.

E.   Countervailing Risks

A more challenging critique of the Precautionary Principle is that its general command to prevent harm (that is, to avoid risk) provides little guidance in the hard and not infrequent cases in which risk inheres in all sides of a potential action.[36] The emphasis on risk–risk problems has been a hallmark of the neoliberal approach, and has often been used to suggest that government regulation seeking to protect health and safety is futile. As examples, acting to ban DDT in certain parts of Africa would likely increase mortality from malaria; and the development and distribution of genetically modified "golden rice" could reduce vitamin A deficiencies in persons whose diets are dominated by rice, but could have deleterious effects on existing strains of rice. In framing these situations as problems of optimizing competing risks and benefits according to an overarching utilitarian measure, critics of the Precautionary Principle deem it a failure at dealing sensibly with such problems.

The direct answer to this critique is that it misconceives the scope of the Precautionary Principle, certainly as reflected in the Rio and UNFCCC texts. The substantive objective of Principle 15 is "to prevent environmental degradation," which presumably includes threats to human health. It does not deny the existence of countervailing risks, nor does it offer a basis for making substantive judgments about weighing such risks. The function of the principle is, instead, primarily procedural and evidentiary: where serious risks ("threats of serious or irreversible damage") have been identified, they cannot be ignored because of "lack of full scientific certainty." Nor, implicitly, can they be ignored simply because the proposed activity is claimed to have the purpose or effect of reducing other risks. The serious (human health and ecological effects) and irreversible (it is extremely persistent in the environment) dangers of DDT are relevant to a decision whether to ban this highly effective pesticide, even if those dangers are chronic and to some degree uncertain. If, on balance, it appears better to accept those dangers in view of the chemical's utility in combating malaria, the Precautionary Principle offers no substantive objection. In concrete terms, the nuanced treatment of DDT in the Stockholm Convention on Persistent Organic Pollutants—although one of the "dirty dozen," its effectiveness in combating the scourge of malaria in certain parts of the world justifies its continued, though restricted, use in those parts of the world[37]—is by no means precluded by the Precautionary Principle.

It is, however, incomplete to suggest that the Precautionary Principle has nothing to say about risk–risk decisions or that it adopts a stance of strict neutrality. As an initial matter, the Precautionary Principle insists that serious-but-uncertain dangers be included in any calculation of the appropriateness of adopting "measures to prevent environmental degradation." This is not a neutral position. As we have seen, prevention is a substantive choice with respect to the timing of regulatory action, and it is a fundamental element in U.S. environmental law. Seen in its proper context, as a response to the current debates over the role of science in environmental regulation ("shall not be used as a reason"), the Precautionary Principle clearly emphasizes potential environmental and health dangers as an element of the calculation, as opposed to potential economic benefits.

Given the antiregulatory context out of which risk trade-off analysis developed, this is an important corrective.[38] The Precautionary Principle counters the strong tendency of the unregulated market to emphasize the potential benefits of products (which are selling points) and to deemphasize potential harms (which are not). (Indeed, this corrective is often cited as a major justification for environmental regulation generally.[39]) Returning to the genetic modification example, we are all too familiar with claims of remarkable benefits, including environmental benefits, of these products, only some of which have come to pass. Similarly with nanotechnology: nano-scale materials are said to have properties that make them qualitatively more functional than the same material at macro scale, and yet there is little apparent willingness to acknowledge that qualitative differences may operate in harmful ways, as well.[40] If there are threats of serious or irreversible damage, the Precautionary Principle says, they must not be shunted aside by commercial optimism.

The Precautionary Principle might also be said to express a more fundamental skepticism of the optimization analysis that neoliberalism brings to bear on risk–risk decisions.[41] As Kysar has observed, the consequentialist criticism of the Precautionary Principle assumes an overarching measure toward which decisions can be optimized. While cost-benefit analysis remains popular in neoliberal quarters, its theoretical foundations and practical implementation have been sharply criticized[42] as to uncertainty, valuation, discounting, and vision.[43] With respect to uncertainty, the aspect most related to the Precautionary Principle, Kysar argues that the potential for catastrophe as the result of climate change—the effect of incompletely understood physical processes operating within complex, nonlinear systems—renders traditional optimization techniques essentially useless, leaving analysts with either guesses or with an economic principle ("minimax," that is, taking action to minimize the maximum possible loss) that is very consistent with the Precautionary Principle.[44] Economist Martin L. Weitzman, observing that the plausible catastrophic potential of climate change is far greater and more unpredictable than ordinary risks, suggests that a careful weighing of worst-case scenarios (again, a process often associated with the Precautionary Principle) is more appropriate and feasible than quantified consequentialist cost-benefit analyses.[45]

Even putting aside philosophical and methodological objections, one might well conclude that the goal of a truly optimal resolution of risk–risk issues is a mirage anyway. Graham and Wiener, who favor a risk–risk approach, use the analogy of ripples in a pond from a tossed stone: at what point does the analysis end because the relevance or determinacy of the consequences has become too remote?[46] There is no obvious answer. As Hornstein demonstrated in his critique of pesticide regulation, there is little basis for believing that "super synopticism"[47]—thoroughly analyzing every aspect of a problem—is workable as a way of resolving environmental questions.[48] The Precautionary Principle expresses a similar skepticism in its focus on "irreversible damage." In cases where the consequences of an inaccurate optimization analysis cannot be undone, it suggests that extra effort must be made to consider even uncertain evidence of damage in the analysis.

II. A Precautionary Climate Policy

Having determined what the Precautionary Principle is *not*, we can now focus on what it *is*. As described above, the Precautionary Principle addresses a fundamental and for all practical purposes unavoidable problem in environmental policy: a commitment to prevention means that the available evidence to justify regulation will be incomplete, and so, to accomplish prevention, regulation must proceed on an incomplete scientific basis. The Precautionary Principle articulates the core ideas of prevention and anticipation by organizing the way that the environmental regulatory system approaches the unavoidable uncertainties in responding preventively to environmental harms. I have suggested elsewhere that there are four distinct elements embedded in the Rio, UNFCCC, and other leading texts:[49]

a *trigger*, which describes the conditions under which the Precautionary Principle applies;
the *timing* of regulatory action in relation to the available science;
a regulatory *response* to be justified by the Precautionary Principle; and
implicit *iteration*,[50] or revisiting decisions based on uncertainty to determine whether new information should modify prior actions.

Each element gives guidance for addressing environmental harms, and this chapter continues with a discussion of the implications of the elements of the Precautionary Principle for U.S. climate policy.

A. Trigger

The text of the Precautionary Principle expressly identifies two conditions that activate or trigger the principle—"threat" and "serious or irreversible harm"—and it implicitly requires a third—"lack of full scientific certainty" concerning the harm. The existence of a threat indicates some threshold likelihood that an adverse effect will occur. In the text, the degree of likelihood is unspecified, and this could give rise, as critics have pointed out, to demands for action on the basis of largely hypothetical harms. Whatever the merits of the concern about overreaching,[51] this is simply not an issue for climate change. Debates may remain about the timing, nature, and extent of effects, but the fundamental reality of climate change as a global phenomenon is well established.

Likewise, the text does not elaborate on the meaning of "serious or irreversible," though, again, it is no more imprecise than, say, "unreasonable risk" or "substantial endangerment" in U.S. environmental law. It is hard to imagine how global climate change could fail to meet not just one but both criteria. The effects described at the beginning of this volume must be accounted serious by any standard. Moreover, since greenhouse gases (GHGs) reside in the atmosphere for decades, the further impacts of continuing emissions are clearly irreversible in the near term. Indeed, scientists have observed that, in view of the enormous complexity of the global climate system and its interactions with the many ecosystems on earth, the effects of climate change may not proceed in anything like a predictable, linear fashion, and so may result in catastrophic rather than incremental impacts. Even if (as is not the case) neither likelihood nor severity was itself sufficient to trigger the Precautionary Principle, surely their combination (low probability of high consequence, or high probability of low consequence) results in a level of risk that demands precautionary action.

Irreversible harm in fact offers an especially urgent case of prevention. Even a precaution skeptic like Sunstein acknowledges that climate change meets the criteria for what he would regard as an appropriately limited Precautionary Principle, his "Catastrophic Harm Precautionary Principle."[52] Sunstein reaches his conclusions through the use of the same cost-benefit optimization methodology that he uses to criticize the principle in general. He argues that in situations where serious harm is threatened with no room for subsequent correction, or the potential loss is very high even when it is discounted by low probability, the usual economic methods inadequately characterize the risk. In this sense, prevention is an aspect of maintaining flexibility for the future, because serious or irreversible harms cannot be completely undone. As such, the Precautionary Principle also conforms to the insights of economic dynamics.

That uncertainty is a third precondition of the Precautionary Principle was emphasized in the European Union's *Communication on the Precautionary Principle*,[53] and it is implicit in the purpose and structure of the principle.[54] Heinzerling, in fact, argues forcefully in the next chapter that we are *beyond* the Precautionary Principle at this point in the development of our knowledge of climate change.[55] There is much in what she says. At the same time, there remain gaps in our understanding of the nature, degree, speed, and victims (and beneficiaries) of climate change. The precise actions that will need to be taken—especially in areas such as adaptation, which are more location-specific than reducing GHGs—must still be worked out. There is still room, therefore, for a principle that allows us to move beyond consideration of uncertainties to consideration of remedies. For the purposes of deciding the precautionary response to the current state of the evidence, whether one regards such action as precautionary (based on uncertainty) or post-precautionary (based on certainty about the fundamentals) is not decisive. Our growing understanding of climate change consistently reinforces earlier indications of a threat of serious or irreversible harm that demands a vigorous response. As the UNFCCC recognized in incorporating the Precautionary Principle, climate change presents a core application of the principle.

B. Timing

The two central elements of precaution—prevention and anticipation—have in common a statement about temporal relationships: prevention seeks to avoid harms *before* they occur, and anticipation permits regulatory action at an early point in scientific understanding *before* the full extent and causes of harm are certain. Timing is the essence of the Precautionary Principle. The Rio statement of the Precautionary Principle is filled with references to timing:

Where there are *threats* of serious or irreversible damage, lack of full scientific certainty shall not be used as a *reason for postponing* cost-effective measures *to prevent* environmental degradation. (Emphasis added)

The references encompass both prevention and anticipation. The trigger element of "threats" reinforces the temporal aspect, referring to future harm. The Precautionary Principle thus repudiates the "sound science" framing, inasmuch as "sound science" seeks to postpone regulatory action in order to pursue full scientific certainty.

The application to climate change could not be clearer. It is far too late to avoid all of the deleterious effects of climate change in the next few decades, but it is not too late to prevent *further* harm, either for longer periods or of greater intensity. There is, in other words, room for a preventive approach, as well as room to anticipate future effects. It is not appropriate, under the Precautionary Principle, to continue to delay action to control GHGs or to prepare for and mitigate harm, or to limit the response to more research, just because the effects are thought to be uncertain.

A note on burden of proof.   It is frequently asserted, by both supporters and skeptics, that the Precautionary Principle requires that the burden of proof be allocated to the proponent of a product or activity. Supporters see this as a way to turn the problem of uncertainty on its head, to create strong incentives for the private creation of more data, and to resist approval of dangerous activities or products. For supporters, this placement of the burden of proof is the essence of caution.[56] For critics, it would create the impossible task of affirmatively proving safety, depriving society of many useful (even life-saving) products and activities; the health effects of such an allocation could well be perverse. The Precautionary Principle, as such, is not definitive on this matter. Some versions place the burden of proof on proponents of products or activities, some do not, and most are simply silent on the topic, presumably leaving it to existing environmental, health, and safety laws.[57] The Rio and UNFCCC versions fall clearly into the last group. "Shall not be used as a reason" suggests a permissive construction, and specific actions are not mentioned. In the context of climate change, the issue of burden of proof, in any technical sense, is of relatively little consequence. The fundamental outlines of the climate problem, as Glicksman and Heinzerling explain, are clear. At the level of principle (to return to this point again) and in the face of nearly total inaction by the U.S. government, the Precautionary Principle resolves the evidentiary problem by authorizing action despite residual uncertainties.

C. Response

One of the enduring caricatures of the Precautionary Principle is that it requires that any potentially harmful substance or activity be entirely forgone, that it is an all-or-nothing prescription that takes no account of consequences, and that it is all the more destructive because it is so easily triggered. As we have seen, the Precautionary Principle is not nearly so prescriptive. As Fisher has observed, "a fundamental feature of the precautionary principle is that it is not concerned with guaranteeing particular outcomes, but rather with the *process* by which the decision is made."[58] The Precautionary Principle is a *principle*, and as such it states a direction rather than a rule. Thus, it is not intended to obtain inflexible rule-like results,[59] it must always be applied with reference to its underlying purposes, and it is subject to modification by other principles, for instance, the principle of proportionality of response to an environmental threat.[60]

The Precautionary Principle is not, however, infinitely malleable or entirely silent on the question of response. The text of the Rio Precautionary Principle refers to "cost-effective measures," and the UNFCCC version of the Precautionary Principle has even more to say:

taking into account that policies and measures to deal with climate change should be cost-effective so as to ensure global benefits at the lowest possible cost. To achieve this, such policies and measures should take into account different socio-economic contexts, be comprehensive, cover all relevant sources, sinks and reservoirs of greenhouse gases and adaptation, and comprise all economic sectors.[61]

Cost-effectiveness and consideration of hazards, benefits, and consequences guard against overzealousness, but they do not demand actions determined by strict cost-benefit analysis. Cost-effectiveness instead requires the selection of measures that achieve an otherwise established goal at the least cost.

The objective of the Precautionary Principle being to prevent harm by taking early protective action, the short-term irreversibility of global warming makes a particularly strong case for taking strong emissions control and mitigation measures. Irreversible, long-term effects are particularly ill suited to neoliberalism's highly monetized cost-benefit analysis.[62] By reducing the debate to a summation of costs and benefits, cost-benefit analysis tends to obscure the fact that we have irreversible outcomes that may turn out to be nonlinear and worse than we predict. When scientists tell us to expect surprises and that the effects of warming from past emissions are irreversible, the nonquantifiable aspects of the problem, taken together, should play a greater role in our response than the quantifiable costs and benefits—and the Precautionary Principle is consistent with such an approach.

The precautionary model, with its emphasis on the temporal relationships between harm and protective measures, and between evidentiary basis and protective measures, differs importantly from the neoliberal model described in earlier chapters. Precaution has no need for an overarching utilitarian value system by which regulatory action is to be measured, nor does it have any reason to resort to various schemes to quantify life and safety within such a system. As Kysar points out, the Precautionary Principle is readily justifiable on other grounds:

Non-consequentialist theories, for instance, might begin with the existence of an inalienable right held by each generation to the benefit of a minimally stable climate and a corresponding duty on the part of each preceding generation not to act in a manner that jeopardizes the baseline level of climate stability. On this account, the existence of a plausible worst-case scenario in which climate stability is severely and irreversibly disrupted would *in itself* constitute a sufficient reason for restricting greenhouse emissions at least to a level in which the worst case scenario no longer seemed plausible—a course of action that seems precisely to mirror the advice of the precautionary principle.[63]

A precautionary approach also avoids the need to resort to various questionable techniques to provide the numbers that supply the quantitative, "scientific" approach.[64] Precaution has, from this perspective as well, much in common with economic dynamics. It accepts that acting early will mean acting under conditions of uncertainty, that this imposes bounded rationality on decision making, and that our understanding of the relevant facts and science will evolve over time. Such evolution is certainly a reason to choose regulatory responses carefully (in particular, to avoid foreclosing options), but it is not a reason to do nothing.

The Precautionary Principle is consistent with a range of approaches that have been proposed to address climate change, such as wedges, "no-regrets," and adaptation and mitigation. The wedge concept is simple and powerful, the result of Socolow and Pacala's attempt to find ways to make the problem of climate change more tractable. They divide potential actions to reduce GHGs into fifteen distinct wedges (as in a pie chart), from which we can choose seven in their entirety or some portion of all fifteen.[65] They quite rightly do not suggest that these make the problem easy or inexpensive; rather, they show that we have choices in responding to climate change and that they are manageable.

Other observers have offered a no-regrets approach, which addresses climate change through policies that also make sense for other reasons. For example, a substantial increase in automobile fuel efficiency will help to decrease emissions of GHGs, and it will reduce our dependence on a finite natural resource and our subsidy of the extremism that is financed by the petroleum-rich regimes.[66] Many other forms of energy efficiency save more money than they cost, especially in the long run, and so should be welcomed regardless of their contribution to reducing climate change.

Given the near-term irreversibility of climatic effects, a precautionary approach should also include adaptation measures to prevent further harm.[67] Sarewitz and Pielke recommend a range of actions to address the effects of climate change that will occur in the near term, regardless of any action we take now to reduce GHG emissions.[68] For example, the location, intensity, and practices of human occupation are capable of making a significant difference in the severity of the impacts of severe weather events. With or without climate change, it makes good sense to restrict building in threatened areas and floodplains, and yet there seems to be no move to stop subsidizing unsustainable building practices with federal flood insurance. Likewise, serious action to combat deforestation in the developing world, which is both a cause and a magnifier of flood damage, receives little or no attention.

Wedges, no-regrets, and adaptation policies are all clearly precautionary and may be quite appropriate exercises of the Precautionary Principle. Moreover, each offers a greater likelihood of maximizing future options than the current course of continued dependence on carbon-intensive energy. Diversifying energy sources using the wedge concept and greater efficiency in energy use would avoid path-dependence in reducing GHGs, whereas policies that permit continued use of large coal-fired power plants and urban planning that is based on the need for automobile transportation lock us into ever greater GHG emissions.

D. Iteration

In rejecting the rhetoric of "sound science," the Precautionary Principle rejects neither the use of science generally nor the pursuit of excellent science and full understanding of environmental phenomena. Instead, the principle is about the *temporal* relationship between scientific evidence and action. Iteration—the requirement to reexamine actions taken under uncertainty when new evidence comes to light—has developed relatively recently as an explicit part of the Precautionary Principle.[69] The trade-related Sanitary and Phytosanitary (SPS) Agreement is predictably aggressive in this regard: it requires governments that rely on the Precautionary Principle to obtain additional information and to review their decisions in light of it.[70] Other statements of the principle are less mandatory and more flexible.[71] The European Commission asserts that "measures based on the precautionary principle should be maintained so long as scientific information is incomplete or inconclusive. . . . Measures should be periodically reviewed in the light of scientific progress, and amended as necessary."[72] The Cartagena Protocol on Biosafety imposes like requirements.[73]

Although iteration is not universally accepted as integral to the Precautionary Principle, it is in fact implicit in the structure of the principle, as the means for harmonizing prevention and anticipation with a commitment to the use of science in regulation.[74] An early suggestion of iteration in the 1985 Vienna Convention for the Protection of the Ozone Layer offers an apt analogy for climate change. Like the UNFCCC, the Vienna Convention is a framework treaty that was expected to be progressively implemented. The most important of its later protocols, the Montreal Protocol, explains in its preamble that the parties have

Determined to protect the ozone layer by taking precautionary measures . . . with the ultimate objective of their [i.e., ozone-depleting substances] elimination on the basis of developments in scientific knowledge, taking into account technical and economic considerations.[75]

The ozone treaty system thus anticipates that increasing knowledge and technology will indicate adjustments—to be reflected in future protocols—in the actions taken to implement it. It is, like the UNFCCC, structured to be revisited as knowledge develops.

Iteration opens an even more intriguing approach to the evolving understanding of environmental phenomena, advocated by Doremus in natural resources management, which is to think about iteration as a learning process.[76] As the timing element of the Precautionary Principle recognizes, we should expect uncertainties in our understanding of environmental phenomena. As the iteration element recognizes, we should expect to learn more over time, and we should expect that regulatory action taken now can be improved upon when new information becomes available.

The fact that climate change is an extremely long-term phenomenon not only creates the uncertainty that triggers the Precautionary Principle, but it assures that we will learn more as time passes. From this perspective, the Precautionary Principle is a substantive tool for preserving our ability to learn by preventing serious or irreversible harm, and it allows the incorporation of that learning into future decision making by requiring an iterative approach. Addressing climate change will require a long-term commitment to learning, because uncertainties remain and the nature and extent of effects will only reveal themselves over decades. The Precautionary Principle is ideally suited to provide the breathing room to learn, as we go forward, how better to control GHGs for the long term and to create more resilient societies in the near term. Such an approach has the further virtue of advancing a dynamic approach to environmental problems generally and to climate change in particular. An approach that relies on setting direction, preserving options, and adapting to new information conforms to the actual state of our knowledge of the causes and effects of climate change and to the actions that we can take to address it.

The Precautionary Principle is neither radical nor vacuous. It provides meaningful, important guidance for U.S. climate policy, which if followed would take that policy in a different and more active direction. Its core meaning addresses the temporal relationship between harm and protection (prevention) and between scientific knowledge and regulatory action (anticipation). It also addresses the types of harms to be avoided, the appropriate responses, and the need to adapt to new information. But the question of timing remains central, and timing is the central failing of U.S. climate policy. The Precautionary Principle in the Rio Declaration and the UNFCCC speaks directly to the need to avoid future harm from climate change and to take protective action despite lingering uncertainties about the exact effects of climate change; but the United States has consistently followed a policy of further study, delay, and apparent indifference to the consequences of climate change. A precautionary approach does not require particular measures or level of protection, but it does insist on the centrality of prevention and anticipatory action.

Notes

1. Formally, the name of the conference was the United Nations Conference on Environment and Development (UNCED), held in Rio de Janeiro.

2. Rio Declaration of the United Nations Conference on Environment and Development (UNCED), June 14, 1992; Rio Declaration on Environment and Development, Annex 1, Principle 15, U.N. Doc. A/CONF.151/5/Rev. 1 (1992), reprinted in *International Legal Materials* 31 (1992): 874.

3. Elizabeth Fisher, "Precaution, Precaution Everywhere: Developing a 'Common Understanding' of the Precautionary Principle in the European Community," *Maastricht Journal of European and Comparative Law* 9, no. 1 (2002): 9.

4. See, e.g., Robert V. Percival, "Who's Afraid of the Precautionary Principle?" *Pace Environmental Law Review* 23 (2005): 21–81; Mark Geistfeld, "Reconciling Cost-Benefit Analysis with the Principle That Safety Matters More Than Money," *New York University Law Review* 76 (2001): 114–189; Douglas A. Kysar, "It Might Have Been: Risk, Precaution, and Opportunity Costs," *Land Use and Environmental Law* 22 (2006): 1–57; John S. Applegate, "The Taming of the Precautionary Principle," *William and Mary Environmental Law and Policy Review* 27 (2002): 13–78.

5. E.g., Cass R. Sunstein, "Beyond the Precautionary Principle," *University of Pennsylvania Law Review* 151 (2003): 1003–1058; Cass R. Sunstein, *Laws of Fear: Beyond the Precautionary Principle* (Cambridge: Cambridge University Press, 2005) (weak versions "banal"; strong versions dangerous and misguided); Christopher D. Stone, "Is There a Precautionary Principle?" *Environmental Law Reporter* 31 (2001): 10790–10799; John D. Graham, "The Perils of the Precautionary Principle: Lessons from the American and European Experience" (delivered Oct. 20, 2003, at the Heritage Foundation), http://www.heritage.org/Research/Regulation/upload/54513_1.pdf; Frank B. Cross, "Paradoxical Perils of the Precautionary Principle," *Washington and Lee Law Review* 53 (1996): 851–925.

6. Alessandra Arcuri, "The Case for a Procedural Version of the Precautionary Principle Erring on the Side of Environmental Preservation," Global Law Working Paper 09/04 (2007): 1–38, 5, http://ssrn.com/abstract=967779.

7. Ibid. One *actual* strong version is the so-called "Wingspread Statement" of 1998:

We believe there is compelling evidence that damage to humans and the worldwide environment is of such magnitude and seriousness that new principles for conducting human activities are necessary.

While we realize that human activities may involve hazards, people must proceed more carefully than has been the case in recent history. Corporations, government entities, organizations, communities, scientists and other individuals must adopt a precautionary approach to all human endeavors.

Therefore it is necessary to implement the Precautionary Principle: Where an activity raises threats of harm to the environment or human health, precautionary measures should be taken even if some cause and effect relationships are not fully established scientifically.

In this context the proponent of an activity, rather than the public bears the burden of proof.

"Wingspread Statement on the Precautionary Principle," in *Protecting Public Health and the Environment: Implementing the Precautionary Principle*, ed. Carolyn Raffensperger and Joel A. Tickner (Washington, D.C.: Island Press, 1999), pp. 353–354.

8. Nicolas de Sadeleer, *Environmental Principles: From Political Slogans to Legal Rules* (Oxford: Oxford University Press, 2002); Arie Trouwborst, *Evolution and Status of the Precautionary Principle in International Law* (The Hague: Kluwer Law International, 2002); Harald Hohmann, *Precautionary Legal Duties and Principles of Modern International Environmental Law* (London: Graham and Trotman, 1994); *The Precautionary Principle and International Law: The Challenge of Implementation*, ed. David Freestone and Ellen Hey (The Hague: Kluwer Law International, 1996).

9. Applegate, "Taming"; David Vanderzwaag, "The Precautionary Principle and Marine Environmental Protection: Slippery Shores, Rough Seas, and Rising Normative Tides," *Ocean Development and International Law* 33 (2002): 165, 170–173; David Vanderzwaag, "The Precautionary Principle in Environmental Law and Policy: Elusive Rhetoric and First Embraces," *Journal Environmental Law and Practice* 8 (1999): 355, 358.

10. Applegate, "Taming"; Gregory N. Mandel and James Thuo Gathii, "Cost Benefit Analysis versus the Precautionary Principle: Beyond Cass Sunstein's *Laws of Fear*," *University of Illinois Law Review* (2006): 1037.

11. U.N. Framework Convention on Climate Change, art. 3.3, May 29, 1992; 1771 U.N.T.S. 107 (entered into force March 21, 1994), reprinted in *International Legal Materials* 31 (1992): 849 (hereafter UNFCCC).

12. See Arcuri, "Case for a Procedural Version," pp. 9–10, n. 26. As Arcuri points out, this is in fact the version that Sunstein critiques, even though his claim—typical of American critics—is that the Radical version of the principle represents the whole thing. See also Cross, "Paradoxical Perils."

13. Jonathan B. Wiener, "Precaution in a Multi-Risk World," in *Human and Ecological Risk Assessment: Theory and Practice* (New York: Wiley, 2002), ed. Dennis J. Paustenbach, p. 1509; Sunstein, *Laws of Fear*.

14. As Elizabeth Fisher points out in her book review, Sunstein's evidence for the existence of a radical version of the Precautionary Principle is extremely thin, indeed, consisting primarily of exaggerated descriptions by the principle's more vociferous critics. Elizabeth Fisher, "Review of *Laws of Fear: Beyond the Precautionary Principle*, by Cass Sunstein," *Modern Law Review* 69 (2006): 288–292. See also Mandel and Gathii, "Cost Benefit Analysis," p. 1071, n. 187 (calling it a "red herring").

15. Cf. *Whitman v. American Trucking Associations*, 531 U.S. 457 (2001) (Breyer, J. concurring) ("Preindustrial society was not a very healthy society; hence a standard demanding the return of the Stone Age would not prove 'requisite to protect the public health'").

16. See, e.g., Toxic Substances Control Act 15 U.S.C. § 2603(a)(1)(A)(i) (2008).

17. E.g., Treaty on European Union, art. 174(2), April 16, 2003, 2002 O.J. C325; Commission Regulation 1907/2006, art. 1(1), 2006 O.J. L396/1 (hereafter REACH).

18. Fisher, "Precaution, Precaution."

19. Applegate, "Taming the Precautionary Principle."

20. E.g., Raffensperger and Tickner, *Protecting Public Health*; Wiener, "Multi-Risk World," pp. 1513–1516; Applegate, "Taming," pp. 28–29.

21. Commission of the European Communities, *Communication from the Commission on the Precautionary Principle*, COM (Feb. 2, 2000), p. 1 (hereafter *Communication on the Precautionary Principle*). This interpretation underpins some of the most important legislative expressions of the Precautionary Principle, such as the Treaty on European Union, art. 174(2), and the new REACH system of chemical regulation.

22. E.g., Agreement on the Application of Sanitary and Phytosanitary Measures, Jan. 1, 1995, GATT Doc. MTN/FA II-A1A-4 (Dec. 15, 1993) (hereafter SPS Agreement).

23. Cass R. Sunstein, "Irreversible and Catastrophic," *Cornell Law Review* 91 (2006): 841–897, 855.

24. UNFCCC, art. 3.

25. Arcuri, "Case for a Procedural Version"; see also de Sadeleer, *Environmental Principles*, pp. 13–19.

26. Stone, "Is There a Precautionary Principle?"; Graham, "Perils"; Sunstein, *Laws of Fear*.

27. European Environment Agency, *Late Lessons from Early Warnings: The Precautionary Principle 1896–2000*, Environmental Issue Report, no. 22 (Luxembourg: Office for Official Publications of the European Communities, 2001), http://reports.eea.europa.eu/environmental_issue_report_2001_22/en/Issue_Report_No_22.pdf.

28. Hornstein, "Lessons."

29. Sheryl Gay Stolberg, "Bush Proposes Goal to Reduce Greenhouse Gases," *New York Times*, June 1, 2007.

30. House Committee on Oversight and Government Reform, *Political Interference with Climate Change Science Under the Bush Administration*, 110th Cong., 1st Sess., 2007, pp. 16–28; Union of Concerned Scientists, *Scientific Integrity in Policymaking: An Investigation into the Bush Administration's Misuse of Science* (March 2004), pp. 5–8, http://www.ucsusa.org/assets/documents/scientific_integrity/rsi_final_fullreport_1.pdf.

31. Fisher, "Precaution, Precaution."

32. Ronald Dworkin, *Taking Rights Seriously* (Cambridge, MA: Harvard University Press, 1977), p. 24.

33. Ronald Dworkin, "The Model of Rules," *University of Chicago Law Review* 35, no. 1 (1967): 14–46, 26. For example, whereas a core principle established by

the First Amendment unequivocally argues in one direction in the case of governmental prior restraint of a publication, *Near v. Minnesota*, 283 U.S. 697 (1931), its validity as a principle is not undermined by the fact that prior restraint is permitted in extreme cases, *New York Times Co. v. U.S.*, 403 U.S. 713 (1971) (Pentagon Papers Case).

34. Elizabeth Fisher, "Precaution, Law, and Principles of Good Administration," *Water Science and Technology* 52(6) (2005): 19–24, 19.

35. Mandel and Gathii, "Cost Benefit Analysis," p. 1072 (referring to it as a "soft norm").

36. Sunstein, "Beyond the Precautionary Principle"; Sunstein, *Laws of Fear*; Wiener, "Multi-Risk World."

37. Stockholm Convention on Persistent Organic Pollutants, May 17, 2004, reprinted in *International Legal Materials* 40 (2001): 532 (hereafter POPS).

38. Arcuri, "Case for a Procedural Version," p. 21.

39. E.g., Wendy E. Wagner, "Choosing Ignorance in the Manufacture of Toxic Products," *Cornell Law Review* 82 (1997): 773–855; Applegate, "Perils"; Mary L. Lyndon, "Information Economics and Chemical Toxicity: Designing Laws to Produce and Use Data," *Michigan Law Review* 87, no. 7 (1989): 1795–1861.

40. See Albert C. Lin, "Size Matters: Regulating Nanotechnology," *Harvard Environmental Law Review* 31 (2007): 349, 356–361.

41. Applegate, "Taming," pp. 46–48.

42. E.g., Frank Ackerman and Lisa Heinzerling, *Priceless: On Knowing the Price of Everything and the Value of Nothing* (New York: New Press, 2004); David Driesen, "The Societal Cost of Environmental Regulation: Beyond Administrative Cost-Benefit Analysis," *Ecology Law Quarterly* 24 (1997): 545–617; David Driesen, "Regulatory Reform: The New Lochnerism?" *Environmental Law* 36 (2006): 603–649; David Driesen, "Is Cost-Benefit Analysis Neutral?" *University of Colorado Law Review* 72 (2006): 335–403.

43. Douglas A. Kysar, "Climate Change, Cultural Transformation, and Comprehensive Rationality," *Boston College Environmental Affairs Law Review* 31 (2004): 555–590.

44. Ibid., pp. 565–570.

45. Martin Weitzman, "On Modeling and Interpreting the Economics of Catastrophic Climate Change" (Jan. 14, 2008), working paper available at http://www.economics.harvard.edu/faculty/weitzman/files/modeling.pdf (revision of: Martin L. Weitzman, "Role of Uncertainty in the Economics of Catastrophic Climate Change" [May 2007], AEI-Brookings Joint Center Working Paper no. 07-11, available at SSRN: http://ssrn.com/abstract=992873); see also Daniel H. Cole, "Climate Change and Collective Action," available at SSRN: http://ssrn.com/abstract=1069906.

46. John D. Graham and Jonathan Baert Wiener, eds., *Risk vs. Risk: Tradeoffs in Protecting Health and the Environment* (Cambridge, MA: Harvard University Press, 1995).

47. Donald T. Hornstein, "Lessons from Federal Pesticide Regulation on the Paradigms and Politics of Environmental Law Reform," *Yale Journal on Regulation* 10 (1993): 369–446, 386–387.

48. Hornstein (ibid.) advocates a "cause-oriented" approach that seeks out the root of the (pesticide) problem. Driesen, observing the same phenomenon, recommends a "dynamic" approach—rather than seeking an optimal approach now, it is better to establish a direction for policy to move in and make incremental, limited-information decisions along the way. David M. Driesen, *The Economic Dynamics of Environmental Law* (Cambridge, MA: MIT Press, 2003).

49. Applegate, "Taming."

50. Iteration is a relatively new aspect of the understanding of the Precautionary Principle, but it is a logical extension and has been widely adopted. Ibid.

51. Such demands far outnumber actual governmental action, further suggesting that the Precautionary Principle is *in fact* applied in a moderate and even cautious manner.

52. Sunstein, "Irreversible and Catastrophic."

53. *Communication on the Precautionary Principle*, p. 13 (Precautionary Principle is "no longer relevant" once uncertainty has been resolved).

54. Arcuri, "Case for a Procedural Version."

55. See also Lisa Heinzerling, "Climate Change, Human Health, and the Post-Cautionary Principle," *Georgetown Law Journal* 96 (2008): 445–460.

56. See, e.g., "Wingspread Statement."

57. Applegate, "Taming."

58. Elizabeth Fisher, "Risk and Environmental Law: A Beginner's Guide," in *Environmental Law for Sustainability*, ed. Benjamin Richardson and Stepan Wood (Oxford: Hart Publishing, 2006), 97–125, 118.

At their absolute minimum, in fact, the literal command of both the Rio and the UNFCCC versions of the Precautionary Principle is not any specific response, but rather the exclusion of certain kinds of *argument*: "lack of full scientific certainty shall not be *used as a reason* for postponing. . . ." Even such a reading, though highly constrained, would not be vacuous. It expressly rejects the "sound science" framing of climate change. Moreover, the rise of risk assessment and cost-benefit analysis as the preferred justifications for governmental intervention on behalf of the environment places a premium on quantitative modes of argumentation. A rhetorical version of the Precautionary Principle, minimal as it is, counters the fundamental rhetorical assumption of "sound science," that regulatory action must be based on existing scientific knowledge that meets the traditional criteria of scientific validity. The Precautionary Principle has never been seriously understood to be limited to rhetoric, however. Textually, treating the central phrase "shall not be used as a reason" as a mere rhetorical command conflicts with the remainder of the sentence. Both the initial clause, "Where there are threats of serious or irreversible damage," and the concluding clause, "cost-effective measures to prevent environmental degradation" (in the UNFCCC, "taking into account that policies and measures to deal with climate change should be cost-effective so as to ensure global benefits at the lowest possible cost") refer to the actual conditions of decisions and factors in decision making. In other words, though couched as a rhetorical restriction, the text itself indicates a broader intention. This is even clearer in the UNFCCC, which continues, "To achieve this, such policies and measures should take into account different socio-economic contexts, be comprehensive, cover all relevant sources, sinks and reservoirs of greenhouse gases and adaptation, and comprise all economic sectors."

59. Cf. *Tennessee Valley Authority v. Hill*, 437 U.S. 153 (1978). Even if stopping the Tellico Dam seems irrational, the ESA is a rule and clearly requires it.

60. *Communication on the Precautionary Principle*.

61. UNFCCC, art. 3(3).

62. Weitzman, "On Modeling and Interpreting."

63. Kysar, "Climate Change, Cultural Transformation, and Comprehensive Rationality," 555 (emphasis in the original).

64. Kysar succinctly summarizes the intractable difficulties of this enterprise. Ibid.

65. Stephen Pacala and Robert Socolow, "Stabilization Wedges: Solving the Climate Problem for the Next 50 Years with Current Technologies," *Science* 305, no. 5686 (2004): 968–972.

66. Thomas L. Friedman, "The Power of Green," *New York Times Magazine*, Apr. 15, 2007.

67. See Daniel H. Cole, "Climate Change, Adaptation, and Development," *UCLA Journal of Environmental Law and Policy* 26 (2007–2008): 1.

68. Daniel Sarewitz and Roger Pielke, Jr., "Breaking the Global-Warming Gridlock," *Atlantic Monthly*, July 2000.

69. Applegate, "Taming," pp. 31–33, 54–55, 60–61, 75–77.

70. SPS Agreement.

71. European Commission, *Communication on the Precautionary Principle*; Secretariat of the Convention on Biological Diversity, Cartagena Protocol on Biosafety to the Convention on Biological Diversity, Jan. 29, 2000, art. 1, http://www.cbd.int/doc/legal/cartagena-protocol-en.pdf (hereafter Cartagena Protocol), reprinted in *International Legal Materials* 39 (2000): 1027.

72. European Commission, *Communication on the Precautionary Principle*, pp. 5, 20–21.

73. Cartagena Protocol, art. 12(2)–(3).

74. Mandel and Gathii, "Cost Benefit Analysis," pp. 1078–1079. Mandel and Gathii are largely convinced by Sunstein's critiques of the Precautionary Principle, but nevertheless envision a role for the principle, as follows:

The precautionary principle understood as a soft norm would serve to provide a process and opportunity of calling uncertain health and environmental risks to attention without predetermining any particular outcomes. Seen this way, the principle's purpose would be to guide the discretionary powers of decision makers.

Thus its role would not be to justify regulation absolutely, but only contingently or conditionally. Its application would be contingent and conditional because it would be preceded by an awareness of as full a screen of all risks on all sides as possible, as well as paying attention to issues of costs, benefits, values, and distributional effects. Our proposal may not provide the precise guidance or results Sunstein desires, but a system as complex as the universe of real-world threats may not be susceptible to such precision; in this situation, the soft norm of a moderate precautionary principle may provide the optimal level of guidance achievable.

75. Montreal Protocol on Substances That Deplete the Ozone Layer, Preamble, Jan. 1, 1989, reprinted in *International Legal Materials* 26 (1987): 1550.

76. Holly Doremus, "Precaution, Science, and Learning While Doing in Natural Resource Management," *Washington Law Review* 82 (2007): 547–579.

9

Climate Change, Human Health, and the Post-Cautionary Principle

Lisa Heinzerling

In the summer of 2003, at least 20,000 people died in a heat wave that spanned western Europe. France lost the most lives: 14,802, according to a government report produced in the aftermath of the tragedy. Thousands of people also died in Great Britain, Spain, Portugal, Germany, Italy, Belgium, and the Netherlands. The death toll mounted so stealthily, however, that news accounts written fully two weeks into the four-week heat wave focused more on the inconveniences and even economic bonuses of the record-setting temperatures than on their lethal consequences. Eventually the disaster was undeniable: heat-related deaths so overwhelmed French mortuaries, for example, that bodies were stored in refrigerated trucks and warehouses while awaiting burial or cremation.

A study published in the prestigious scientific journal *Nature* in 2004 deemed it "likely" that human-induced increases in atmospheric concentrations of greenhouse gases had "more than doubled the risk of European mean summer temperatures as hot as 2003."[1] The same study found, based on scenarios assuming unmitigated future greenhouse gas emissions, that every other year would be as warm as 2003 in Europe by the 2040s, and that by 2100, a summer like 2003 "would be classed as an anomalously cold summer relative to the new climate."[2]

The European heat wave is a dramatic illustration of the two central factual premises of this Article: climate change harms human health, and we know that climate change is happening. These facts justify a reframing of the public debate on climate change in two ways. First, we should do more to highlight the consequences of climate change for human health. Second, we should recognize that the precautionary moment for action on climate change—the period in which we might have acted based on something less than a scientific consensus on the causes and consequences of climate change—has passed. We are in a post-cautionary world now. Together, the effects of climate change on human health and the undeniable fact that climate change is upon us have several implications for public policy. Perhaps most important, they create a moral imperative for action—dramatic action, *now*—on this problem.

I.   Climate Change and Human Health

There has long been discussion of the implications of climate change for human health, and the link between climate change and human health has been drawn ever more clearly in recent years.[3] But it is also true that widely circulated images of current harms from climate change—melting glaciers, collapsing ice shelves, drowning polar bears—do not have a human face. And it takes some reflection to see the connection between human health and, say, higher water temperatures—reflection that is not always encouraged in our busy world. Thus, although my suggestion that we frame the debate over responses to climate change in terms of effects on human health is by no means original, it is worthwhile to draw, directly and emphatically, the link between climate change and human health, and to think about the consequences of this linkage for policies addressing climate change.

A.   Health Consequences of Climate Change

More frequent and intense heat waves are only one item on the long list of the consequences of climate change that will harm human health. According to the latest scientific research, we can expect the following in our warming world:[4] disease-carrying insects will alter their ranges, appearing in places they have not been before and where humans have not developed immunities, causing more widespread incidence of vector-borne diseases such as malaria; after a slight uptick, crop productivity will decline, causing a concomitant increase in the risk of malnutrition; fish stocks will deteriorate, to the same effect; ground-level ozone will worsen, causing adverse respiratory and cardiovascular events; water supplies will decrease due to reduced snowpack and increased drought; storms will become more frequent and severe, threatening Katrina-like consequences for human health and welfare; flooding will grow more frequent and severe due to storms and rise in sea level; diarrheal disease will increase due to floods and drought; cholera will grow more frequent and toxic due to higher water temperatures; increased pollen production will exacerbate allergies; hunger and malnutrition will rise due to drought and extreme weather events.

Reviewing this list, it appears that there is almost no component of human health that will be untouched by climate change. And the list does not end here. The shrinking resource base of a warming world will also increase the likelihood of refugee crises, violent conflicts, and even wars. In this regard, it is notable that the U.S. Department of Defense appears to have cottoned onto the potentially catastrophic effects of climate change even while the Environmental Protection Agency was fighting hard not to do anything about them. A 2003 report commissioned by the Pentagon—dated a month after the EPA itself declined to regulate greenhouse gases under the Clean Air Act—"imagine[s] the unthinkable" by describing the consequences of an abrupt shift in climate due to slowing of the ocean's thermohaline circulation.[5] The report predicts that shortages in the basic necessities of life—food, water, and energy resources—would result from abrupt climate change, and that these shortages would in turn either cause or exacerbate global conflict. In the event of drastically lowered carrying capacities due to abrupt climate change, the report states bluntly, "Humanity would revert to its norm of constant battles for diminishing resources, which the battles themselves would further reduce even beyond the climatic effects. Once again warfare would define human life."

The Pentagon report deliberately looked at extreme possibilities, noting that "it is DOD's job to consider such scenarios." But the report's dire predictions do not seem so extreme anymore. In April 2007, eleven retired U.S. generals and admirals signed a study, commissioned by the government-funded Center for Naval Analyses, describing the national security consequences of climate change.[6] Calling climate change a "threat multiplier for instability in some of the most volatile regions of the world," the study details the ways in which climate change may push already fragile nations over the brink and put strain on even the most developed nations. "To live in stability," the study observes, "human societies need access to certain fundamental resources, the most important of which are water and food." Yet, as the study makes clear, these basic resources—and thus the stability on which national security depends—are threatened by climate change. Armed conflict, mass migration, and even terrorism are among the national security consequences the study associates with climate change. The seriousness of these consequences, and their link to climate change, were highlighted just one day after this study was published, when the United Nations Security Council met for the very first time to discuss climate change as a security issue.[7]

The human health consequences of climate change are not just worries for the remote future; they are happening here and now. In addition to the research on the relationship between Europe's disastrous heat wave and climate change, other studies have also found a probable connection between current adverse health consequences and climate change.[8] Already, for example, researchers have found that the changing climate has likely influenced the geographic range of disease-carrying insects.[9] Perhaps more remarkably, climate change has also been cited as an underlying cause of current armed conflict. The genocide in Darfur, for example, is now regarded as having arisen at least in part from territorial disputes caused by persistent drought conditions associated with a warming world.[10]

As if all this were not bad enough, the health consequences I have described will almost certainly be the worst for the poorest among us, who are least able to fend off or bounce back from such stressors. The world's poorest nations already suffer from the kinds of food and water shortages that will only worsen in the coming years; their capacity to handle further scarcity is limited. They also lack the resources (such as funds for relocation necessitated by rising sea levels) and services (such as health care) that will be necessary in any effort to mitigate the effects of climate change. Adding insult to injury, the poorest countries are also those that have contributed the least to the present problem. This inequity might itself lead to a further downward spiral in human welfare by fueling conflicts, perhaps even armed conflicts, between the climate haves and have-nots.

B.   Policy Consequences of Health Consequences of Climate Change

What are the consequences, for public debate and public policy, of framing the problem of climate change in terms of human health? I believe framing the problem this way has at least three implications: motivating political action, enlarging the number and kinds of governmental institutions involved in the problem, and creating a strong moral case for action.

First, and most pragmatically, "environmental" threats rarely capture the attention of the public and policymakers unless and until they are linked to human health. People are worried about the polar bear, to be sure, but it is doubtful that the polar bear's plight alone—or even the added plight of the many other species threatened by climate change—will prompt the kinds of large changes necessary to address climate change. To take an example from early in the environmental era, many studies connected the pesticide DDT with harm to wildlife, even to harm to the beloved bald eagle, but it was not until DDT was tied to cancer risk in humans that the federal government decided to ban the substance. The same basic story holds for the regulation of many other pollutants. Speaking in purely practical terms, therefore, it makes a great deal of sense to highlight the consequences of climate change for human health.

Second, emphasizing the consequences of climate change for human health will also affect the way we think about responses to this problem. If we think of climate change as purely an "environmental" problem, we will likely turn, in the United States, to the EPA for an answer. But as important as the EPA is, domestically, with respect to this problem, I believe it is equally vital that we turn to other, nonenvironmental institutions for assistance. Framing climate change as a human health threat naturally encourages resort to agencies charged with a traditional public health mission, such as the Centers for Disease Control and the National Institutes of Health. It also prompts attention to even less obvious institutions, like the United Nations Security Council. The point is that we will think differently about solutions to climate change, as an institutional matter, if we frame the problem of climate change as a human health problem.

Finally, recognizing the current and future consequences of climate change for human health makes the moral case for aggressive action on climate change unimpeachable. If we were simply talking about a more uncomfortable climate, or even destruction of other species, it might be easier to dismiss the moral imperative of action on climate change. But humans are dying and falling ill due to our collective actions, and will continue to do so in even larger numbers if we do nothing. Emphasizing the human dimension of climate change brings a moral clarity to the problem that is not matched by worries about the polar bear.

II. The Post-Cautionary Principle

The recognition that climate change is upon us, and harming us, now, leads me to suggest one other way to reframe public discourse on this issue. We should cease discussing responses to climate change in terms of the "Precautionary Principle" and should begin to think instead in terms of a "post-cautionary" approach.

For a long time, climate change has been *the* exemplar for application of the Precautionary Principle. This principle has taken many forms over the years, but in its simplest, and perhaps most common, formulation, it stands for the idea that we should not wait for scientific certainty before acting on a threat. The motivating principle is that we are better off being safe than being sorry.

At this moment in history, discussing climate change in terms of the Precautionary Principle is, I believe, a serious mistake. As I discuss below, we probably blew past our precautionary opportunity sometime in the 1980s. We are now, and have been for some time, in a post-cautionary world. The scientific debate over whether climate change is happening, and whether it will hurt us, is over; the important questions are when it will get worse, and by how much. I suggest, therefore, that we begin to discuss climate change in terms of a post-cautionary principle. Recognizing that we have hurtled past precaution into a post-cautionary world has several important implications for public policies concerning climate change.

A.   Climate Change's Precautionary Period

In this section, I ask two famous questions, but about climate change rather than cover-ups: what did we know, and when did we know it?[11] My aim here is not to identify a single precautionary moment for climate change. My aim, instead, is to argue that climate change had not just a precautionary moment but a precautionary period, in which the evidence of an impending catastrophe was strong enough, and the signs of even greater future calamity clear enough, that the precautionary principle, properly applied, should have inspired us to take aggressive action. I believe that period passed in the late 1980s.

To early climate scientists, the idea of significant "climate change" was something of an oxymoron. Climate was, by definition, *stable*. Indeed, one of the great puzzles for early climate scientists was the cause and course of the ice ages: how could such a dramatic change in climate have happened, and how long did it take? Perhaps ironically, scientists' search for the answer to the mystery of the long-ago ice ages helped spur the research that led to the "discovery" of climate change in our own time.

Scientific understanding of the past and present climate proceeded fitfully at best during the nineteenth and early twentieth century, yet several discoveries from the nineteenth century were seminal in the study of climate. In the early 1800s, Joseph Fourier, likening the Earth's atmosphere to a "hothouse," speculated that the gases in the atmosphere prevented the sun's radiation from escaping entirely back into space. In 1859, John Tyndall found that carbon dioxide was opaque to infrared radiation, and thus trapped some of the Earth's infrared radiation in the atmosphere. In

1896, the Swedish scientist Svante Arrhenius undertook a computational project fit for a modern computer when he calculated the potential effect on average global temperature of changing the level of carbon dioxide (CO_2) in the atmosphere. His calculations were based, of necessity, on a highly simplistic view of the drivers of climate. Remarkably, however, his estimate of the effect of a doubling of CO_2 in the atmosphere—an increase in average global temperature of 9 to 11° Fahrenheit—was not far off from today's estimates. Nevertheless, Arhennius's work slipped into obscurity, picked up here and there by other climate scientists in the first half of the twentieth century, but not seriously pursued.

Scientific findings that would lead to the discovery of climate change in our time began to steadily appear in the mid-twentieth century. In 1957, Roger Revelle and Hans Seuss published a paper concluding that the then-widely accepted view that the oceans could be counted upon to absorb any amount of CO_2 we belched into the atmosphere was mistaken; most of the CO_2 that ended up in the oceans "would promptly be evaporated."[12] At about the same time, another turning point in the development of climate science occurred when Charles David Keeling received funding to measure atmospheric concentrations of CO_2 at the Mauna Loa Observatory in Hawaii and in Antarctica. With the exception of a brief hiatus in these studies as a result of a funding cutoff in the early 1960s, Keeling's measurements provided us with the first careful and consistent record of actual, year-by-year CO_2 concentrations in the atmosphere at a specific location. What they showed proved indispensable to the development of modern climate science: CO_2 concentrations were on a steady upward path.

Climate scientists also began to apprehend how quickly climate could change. Early climate scientists were loath to admit that the climate could change significantly over a short period of time; they thought in terms of geological time, with changes occurring over tens of thousands of years. Ice core samples from Greenland tested and eventually debunked this long-held assumption of stability. A study published in 1972, for example, reported that a cold spell that happened some 12,000 years ago—dubbed the Younger Dryas—had happened in as little as one or two centuries. Ice core samples also bore evidence of rapid warming and cooling periods. Studies such as these upended the comfortable assumption of climate scientists (and perhaps the rest of us) of a stable climate, changeable only over many millennia.

Another venerable assumption of climate scientists was that of a balance of nature, which would lead the climate to take self-correcting actions tending in the direction of stability rather than instability. Scientists in the second half of the twentieth century began serious study of the possibility of bad as well as good feedbacks; in this system, a rise in temperature could, for example, cause melting of ice, which would increase the albedo effect of the oceans, which in turn would lead to further warming, and so on. In this world, spiraling bad effects, rather than self-correcting reactions tending toward stability, would make a bad situation even worse.

By the late 1980s, then, this much was clear. The greenhouse effect was a plausible scientific theory. Manmade greenhouse gas emissions were increasing. Atmospheric concentrations of greenhouse gases were increasing. The world was getting warmer. Climate could change abruptly. Once the climate started to change, it might deteriorate rapidly due to positive feedback effects.

Other important points were less clear. Was the world's present warming a result, at least in part, of man's greenhouse gas emissions? What did the future hold? Answers to these questions were complicated by scientists' growing recognition that we might not discern the effects of climate change until they were upon us, and more drastic future effects had become inevitable.

In discussing scientific research spanning a century or more, involving many thousands of researchers and untold numbers of studies, it is risky to pinpoint any one moment of clarity. But in a scientific field as fraught with political meaning as climate science is, one can perhaps identify moments when existing scientific research made its way into the public consciousness in such a way that public policy might have reacted to the emerging understanding. I believe such a moment happened, among other times, in the summer of 1988. That summer, which saw terrible droughts in the U.S. Midwest and unprecedentedly hot weather in the Northeast, veteran NASA scientist James Hansen came before Congress and announced that global warming was upon us and that the greenhouse effect was likely the cause.[13] It was time to "stop waffling so much," he said in an interview after his testimony, and to "say that the evidence is pretty strong that the greenhouse effect is here."[14] That same summer, the United National Environmental Program and Canada sponsored a conference in Toronto, at which participants called for an international convention on climate change.[15]

Congress did not act on Hansen's advice. It passed laws authorizing more research on climate change,[16] but did nothing to regulate the causes of climate change. Indeed, instead of bringing aggressive action on climate change, the years following Hansen's testimony witnessed what I regard as a retrenchment in climate policy. Scientists retreated to the newly formed Intergovernmental Panel on Climate Change (IPCC) to develop carefully worked out consensus statements on climate change and its effects. The fossil fuel industry began to wage a years-long, multimillion dollar effort to persuade the public of the shakiness of climate science.[17] Scientific ignorance became official government policy.[18]

Into this stew of an emerging scientific consensus and a growing political backlash stepped the international environmental community. In 1992, at the Earth Summit in Rio, nations agreed to the United Nations Framework Convention on Climate Change, which for the first time officially linked responses to climate change to the precautionary principle. Article 3 of the Convention, setting forth the "principles" of the document, stated that "The Parties should take precautionary measures to anticipate, prevent or minimize the causes of climate change and mitigate its adverse effects. Where there are threats of serious or irreversible damage, lack of full scientific certainty should not be used as a reason for postponing such measures, taking into account that policies and measures to deal with climate change should be cost-effective so as to ensure global benefits at the lowest possible cost."[19] Similarly, the Rio Declaration, agreed to at the same time, stated: "In order to protect the environment, the precautionary approach shall be widely applied by States according to their capabilities. Where there are threats of serious or irreversible damage, lack of full scientific certainty shall not be used as a reason for postponing cost-effective measures to prevent environmental degradation."[20] In the years following the Earth Summit, public discourse on climate change and public discourse on the precautionary principle almost inevitably merged: climate change policy, said the government of Canada in a typical recent formulation, should be developed with the Precautionary Principle as a guiding framework.[21]

The irony, even tragedy, in this is that the Precautionary Principle swept onto the climate change scene almost at the same moment it could have, and should have, departed the field. Before the Earth Summit, the IPCC—the largest peer-reviewed scientific collaboration in the history of the world—had already declared that the world was warming and that it was likely that additional warming of several degrees would occur by 2050.[22] This statement that the world was indeed warming was exactly the kind of scientific consensus the Precautionary Principle declared unnecessary to justify action on an impending threat of potentially grave proportions. By 1995, of course, the IPCC had gone further and identified a "discernible human influence" on the climate, and the long battle over the basic outlines of climate change science could have been declared over.

Yet things only got worse from there. The U.S. Senate in 1998 announced its intention to reject any international agreement on climate change that did not include binding requirements for developing nations,[23] and in 2001 the Bush administration withdrew from the Kyoto Protocol entirely. President George W. Bush himself dismissed a 2002 report by his own agencies, linking anthropogenic greenhouse gas emissions and climate change, as a "report put out by the bureaucracy."[24] In 2003 the White House edited out all save one reference to climate change in what was billed as a comprehensive report on the environment.[25] At the same time, critics of government regulation seized on the Precautionary Principle as a misguided, even dangerous, idea[26]—thus moving the battlefield over climate policy from the scientific arena, where all but a few, mostly industry-funded,[27] skeptics accepted the ever-more dire predictions of a coming climate catastrophe, to the abstract realm of organizing principles for public policy. Perhaps, hinted the critics between the lines, one could reject action on climate change by rejecting the Precautionary Principle—without ever taking a close look at the scary scientific consensus on the subject.

If my account is correct, then the Precautionary Principle as applied to climate change was, at best, an anachronism as soon as it was adopted. At worst, it inadvertently played into the hands of critics of swift and aggressive action on climate change, feeding the industry-funded view that the science of climate change was too uncertain to justify such action.

Subsequent reports of the IPCC, and subsequent events in the world, including the collapse of Antarctic ice sheets, melting of glaciers, and thawing of Arctic permafrost, have only deepened the case for my argument that we have moved from a precautionary to a post-cautionary period. I close with a brief discussion of several implications of this development for public policy.

B.   Public Policy and Private Conduct for a Post-Cautionary World
Acknowledging that we have passed the precautionary moment with respect to climate change has several implications for public policy.

First, stressing the now-inevitable human health consequences of climate change makes untenable certain arguments that have been raised against doing much of anything at all to address this problem. All around us appear scare stories about what will happen to our economy, and even to our way of life, if we act aggressively against climate change.[28] But, as we have seen, the consequences of *not* acting are terrible indeed. As the renowned climate researcher James Hansen has put it, if we continue on our present course with respect to greenhouse gas emissions, we will soon, quite simply, live on "a different planet."[29] Fixing on the human consequences of climate change reveals the dangerous ludicrousness of industry's calls for "business as usual"—and their frequent suggestion that this scenario bears zero costs. Climate change is having and will have profound effects on the economy, with enormous costs. It is a lie to pretend that inaction on climate change is a "no-cost" scenario—for anyone.

Second, acknowledging our post-cautionary status means that we cannot hope that reduction of greenhouse gas emissions alone will avert the harmful consequences of climate change. We must also adapt to the consequences that we cannot now avoid. Some environmentalists have eschewed the idea of adapting to climate change, preferring instead to talk only in terms of mitigating the problem through the reduction of greenhouse gases. They worry, apparently, that if we talk about adapting to climate change, we will have less motivation to address the problem in a more preventive and fundamental way. But the problem is upon us, causing harm now. We no longer have the luxury of choosing between adaptation and mitigation; we must do both.

Third, it means that we cannot afford to discard any of the actions we are already taking to reduce greenhouse gases. In the United States, in the absence of any federal action on the matter, states and local governments have adopted numerous laws and policies aimed at reducing greenhouse gases.[30] As Congress debates its own potential responses to the issue of climate change, it must be careful not to undo any of the steps states and local governments have already taken. It would be easy enough, in a period when the Supreme Court has expanded its preemption jurisprudence,[31] for Congress even inadvertently to displace state and local laws on climate change. I would go so far as to say that unless Congress is willing to pass a very aggressive law (or laws) on greenhouse gases, it should simply stay out unless it also enacts language unmistakably disclaiming any preemptive intent. If Congress were to pass a weak law that at the same time is held (by the current conservative Supreme Court) to preempt state and local efforts on climate change, it would be worse than not acting at all.

Fourth, in making public policy on climate change, especially in a post-cautionary world, we must not make the best the enemy of the good. Many academics have devoted loving attention to exactly which kind of regime—international or domestic, market-based or technology-based—is ideal for the problem of climate change. We do not have the luxury of waiting for the ideal solution now, especially when the likely favorite among theoreticians—an international trading regime with participation by the United States and developing countries such as China—would entail a significant lead time. In this setting, we may do well to use nonobvious second-best solutions, including state and local actions to reduce greenhouse gases. Indeed, time appears to be so short for effective action on climate change that I believe we should even stop waiting around for the government to act on this issue, and take the matter into our own hands. We are all implicated in climate change. We drive cars, switch on the lights, turn up the AC, boot up our computers, and so on. We don't have to wait for action on climate change; we can use our own *inaction*—less driving, less electricity use—to start tackling the problem.

Finally, and most important, passing from a precautionary to a post-cautionary world has large consequences for the moral status of the debate over climate change. In the first part of this chapter, I described how gravely human life and health are and will be affected by climate change. In this part of the chapter, I have explained that we now *know* that humans will die and fall ill as a result of this problem. The first describes a consequence; the second describes our knowledge of its occurrence. Knowledge that death and suffering will result from our actions uncontroversially leads to a moral obligation to change our behavior. Knowing killing is, in the United States, condemned in criminal laws in all fifty states, in modern regulatory laws at the federal level, and in civil jury awards in tort cases.[32] These laws embody a moral commitment against knowing killing that, in traditional criminal contexts, is uncontroversial. It should be no more controversial when it occurs on a global scale.

Neoliberalism is at the heart of attempts to justify knowing killing despite the deeply entrenched norm against it. Economic analysis of policies aimed at protecting humans from disease and death proceeds on the assumption that the relevant victims are "statistical persons"—persons unidentified in advance and most likely even after the fact. Economic analysis could not proceed without the contrivance of "statistical persons" and the attendant premise that such persons have consented to the consequences they will bear. The contrivance fails when real people fall ill or die, and the consent is a fiction encouraged by the neoliberal belief that decisions made in private markets—such as a decision to accept a riskier job in exchange for a higher wage—reflect humans' true desires, in all contexts, at all times.

Conclusion

Climate change is a public health threat of the highest order. Almost every facet of human health is being or will be affected by this phenomenon. Unfortunately, we long ago frittered away climate change's precautionary period. We are at a stage, now, when we can expect large-scale human health consequences from a warming world. Perhaps the worst of these consequences can be avoided. We have a moral imperative to try.

Notes

This chapter was originally published in the *Georgetown Law Journal* in 2008.

1. Peter A. Stott, D. A. Stone, and M. R. Allen, "Human Contribution to the European Heatwave of 2003," *Nature* 432, no. 7017 (Dec. 2004): 610.

2. "Europe Heatwave Killed Some 19,000," *China Daily*, September 26, 2003; Catherine Brahic, "Med to Get Five Times as Many Dangerously Hot Days," *New Scientist*, June 18, 2007, http://environment.newscientist.com/channel/earth/dn12086.

3. A. J. McMichael et al., eds., *Climate Change and Human Health: Risks and Responses* (Geneva: World Health Organization, 2003).

4. The discussion in this paragraph relies on the 2007 report of the Intergovernmental Panel on Climate Change (IPCC), *Climate Change 2007: Impacts, Adaptation, and Vulnerability*, Contribution of Working Group II to the Fourth Assessment Report of the Intergovernmental Panel on Climate Change, edited by Martin L. Parry and Osvaldo Canziani, Summary for Policymakers (New York: Cambridge University Press, 2007), http://www.ipcc-wg2.org/.

5. Peter Schwartz and Doug Randall, *An Abrupt Climate Change Scenario and Its Implications for United States National Security* (San Francisco, CA: GBN Global Business Network, October 2003). The thermohaline circulation is the "conveyor belt" that moves warm water "from the tropics toward the poles," warming Europe. Elizabeth Kolbert, *Field Notes from a Catastrophe: Man, Nature, and Climate Change* (New York: Bloomsbury Publishing, 2006), pp. 56–57.

6. The C.N.A. Corporation, *National Security and the Threat of Climate Change* (April 2007), http://securityandclimate.cna.org/report/.

7. U.N. Security Council, Department of Public Information, "Security Council Holds First-Ever Debate of Impact of Climate Change on Peace, Security, Hearing Over 50 Speakers," news release, April 17, 2007, http://www.un.org/News/Press/docs/2007/sc9000.doc.htm/.

8. World Health Organization, *The World Health Report 2002* (Geneva: WHO, 2002), p. 72, http://www.who.int/whr/2002/en/.

9. Stephen Y. Liang, K. J. Linthicum, and J. C. Gaydos, "Climate Change and the Monitoring of Vector-borne Disease," *Journal of American Medical Association* 287, no. 17 (May 2002): 2286.

10. C.N.A. Corporation, *National Security and the Threat of Climate Change*, p. 15; and Stephan Faris, "The Real Roots of Darfur," *Atlantic Monthly* 299, no. 3 (April 2007): 67.

11. For this account of the development of the scientific understanding of climate change, I am indebted to the following sources: Spencer R. Weart, *The Discovery of Global Warming* (Cambridge, MA: Harvard University Press, 2003); Elizabeth Kolbert, *Field Notes from a Catastrophe*; James Rodger Fleming, *Historical Perspectives on Climate Change* (New York: Oxford University Press, 1998); Tim Flannery, *The Weather Makers: How Man Is Changing the Climate and What It Means for Life on Earth* (New York: Atlantic Monthly Press, 2005); and David M. Hart and David G. Victor, "Scientific Elites and the Making of US Policy for Climate Change Research," *Social Studies of Science* 23, no. 4 (November 1993): 643.

12. Roger Revelle and Hans E. Suess, "Carbon Dioxide Exchange between Atmosphere and Ocean and the Question of an Increase of Atmospheric CO_2 During the Past Decades," *Tellus* 9 (1957): 18.

13. *Greenhouse Effect and Global Climate Change, Part 2: Hearing Before the S. Comm. on Energy and Natural Resources*, 100th Cong. 43 (1988), Statement of James E. Hansen; and Statement of Hon. J. Bennett Johnston ("The greenhouse effect has ripened beyond theory now. We know it is fact.").

14. Philip Shabecoff, "Global Warming Has Begun, Expert Tells Senate," *New York Times*, June 23, 1988.

15. Neil Carter, *The Policy of the Environment: Ideas, Activism, Policy* (Cambridge: Cambridge University Press 2007), pp. 250–251.

16. Global Change Research Act of 1990, Pub. L. No. 101-606, 104 Stat. 3096; Food, Agriculture, Conservation and Trade Act of 1990, Pub. L. No. 101-624, Title XXIV, 104 Stat. 3359; Energy Policy Act of 1992, Pub. L. No. 102-486, Title XVI, 106 Stat. 2776.

17. Ross Gelbspan, *The Heat Is On* (Reading, MA: Perseus Books, 1998), pp. 33–61; Spencer R. Weart, *The Discovery of Global Warming* (Cambridge, MA: Harvard University Press, 2003), p. 168.

18. Ross Gelbspan, *Boiling Point* (New York: Basic Books, 2004), pp. 37–61; Chris Mooney, *The Republican War on Science* (New York: Basic Books, 2005), pp. 78–101.

19. U.N. Framework Convention on Climate Change, art. 3(3), May 9, 1992, S. Treaty Doc. No. 102-38, 1771 U.N.T.S. 107.

20. United Nations Conference on Environment and Development, Rio Declaration on Environment and Development at annex 1, princ. 15, U.N. Doc. A/CONF .151/5/Rev.1, reprinted in *International Legal Materials* 31: 874, 879.

21. Office of the Auditor General of Canada, *2006 Report of the Commissioner of the Environment and Sustainable Development to the House of Commons,* http://www.oag-bvg.gc.ca/domino/reports.nsf/html/c20060900se01.html.

22. Intergovernmental Panel on Climate Change (IPCC), *IPCC Second Assessment: Climate Change 1995,* http://www.ipcc.ch/pdf/climate-changes-1995/ipcc-2nd-assessment/2nd-assessment-en.pdf.

23. Byrd–Hagel Resolution, S. Res. 98, 105th Cong. (1997).

24. Katherine Q. Seelye, "President Distances Himself from Global Warming Report," *New York Times,* June 5, 2002.

25. Gelbspan, *Boiling Point,* p. 42.

26. Cass R. Sunstein, "Beyond the Precautionary Principle," *University of Pennsylvania Law Review* 151, no. 3 (2003): 1003.

27. Chris Mooney, "Some Like It Hot," *Mother Jones* 30, no. 3 (May-June 2005): 36.

28. For a recent example, see Eric Peters, "Seppuku for the U.S. Auto Industry," *American Spectator,* July 6, 2007, http://www.spectator.org/dsp_article .asp?art_id=11687.

29. Andrew C. Revkin, "Climate Expert Says NASA Tried to Silence Him," *New York Times,* January 29, 2006.

30. For discussion, see Kirsten H. Engel and Scott R. Saleska, "Subglobal Regulation of the Global Commons: The Case of Climate Change," *Ecology Law Quarterly* 32, no. 2 (2005): 183.

31. David C. Vladeck, "Preemption and Regulatory Failure," *Pepperdine Law Review* 33, no. 1 (2005): 105–110.

32. Lisa Heinzerling, "Knowing Killing and Environmental Law," *New York University Environmental Law Journal* 14, no. 3 (2006): 521–526.

10

The Cost of Greenhouse Gas Reductions

Thomas O. McGarity

The debate over whether greenhouse gas (GHG) emissions contribute to global warming is over. Although large uncertainties continue to cloud the science related to the relationship between particular GHGs and the pronounced elevation in global temperatures during the last century and the extent to which cumulative emissions contribute to climate change, the range of the uncertainties has narrowed considerably. All but the most committed skeptics and a few demagogues in Congress now accept that human activities have contributed to global warming and both that something must be done to reduce GHG emissions in the near term and that even greater efforts will have to be undertaken in the intermediate term between 2010 and 2020 to stabilize GHG emissions.

The history of past great debates over environmental policy suggests that the debate over global warming will now shift from the realm of science to the realm of economics, as activists and defenders of the status quo argue over how much it will cost to achieve particular levels of GHG reduction and whether we are willing to pay those costs. Following the historical pattern, the headlines of major stories about climate change began to shift from the science to the economics of global warming in mid-2007. A front page article in the July 15, 2007, issue of the *Washington Post* headlined "Climate Change Debate Hinges on Economics" quoted the head of a conservative think tank to say that the question now is: "Will Congress get in place a larger architecture that sends a signal to the economy that accelerates change?"[1] Congressman John Dingell, no fan of GHG controls (especially as they relate to the automobile industry that dominates his district), introduced a bill providing for a carbon tax because he "sincerely doubt[ed] that the American people will be willing to pay what this is really going to cost them."[2] And the editorial board of the *Wall Street Journal* chortled its agreement with the long-time congressman in an editorial entitled "Truth in Global Warming."[3]

Many former global warming skeptics have now become GHG reduction pessimists, arguing that the technologies needed to reduce GHGs to 1990 levels are simply not available at what they regard to be a reasonable cost. The CEO of American Electric Power Company, a company that plans to take no serious steps to reduce its very large GHG emissions inventory until the government actually mandates action, predicted that the company simply could not deliver significant GHG reductions until at least 2020 and, even then, only by raising energy prices 50 percent.[4] The industry-funded Electric Power Research Institute has concluded that it will take until 2025 or 2030 to reduce emissions to 1990 levels, even in the unlikely event that the industry increases nuclear power production by 60 percent, doubles wind and solar energy production, and develops cost-effective carbon capture technologies.[5] Citing studies indicating that reducing GHG emissions in 10 years would cost more than 4 percent of the gross domestic product (GDP), the Cato Institute advocates delaying any action for up to 20 to 30 years.[6] Reasoning that "wealthier is healthier," some extreme pessimists even claim that spending resources on reducing GHG emissions will result in hundreds of "statistical deaths" from reduced incomes of low-income workers.[7]

The truth of the matter is that the actions that Americans must take to reduce GHG emissions to the levels required to slow down the alarming trends in global warming might well be expensive and inconvenient. Moreover, it may well be that a carbon tax of the sort proposed by Congressman Dingell is the most efficient vehicle for inducing the necessary changes. The good news is that technologies already in existence or that will be available in the very near future are capable of meeting reasonable GHG reduction goals if we have the political will to do the job and the wisdom to create the right incentives to take action in both the near and intermediate terms. Although uncertainties comparable in magnitude to those that once plagued climate change science now befuddle the economics of GHG controls, there are good reasons to believe that gloomy predictions that implementing these technologies will result in huge costs that may disrupt the U.S. economy are overblown. At the same time, rosy predictions that the change can be accomplished in a way that is essentially cost-free may be unduly optimistic.

This chapter will provide an overview of several approaches that economists have recently used to estimate the costs of GHG reductions. Economists have recently refined these approaches in the debates over the California GHG reduction initiatives. Focusing particularly on two of these studies, this chapter will highlight the speculative nature of the economic forecasting that goes into cost estimates, the room that such necessary speculation provides for outcome-oriented manipulation, and the subtle way that the assessments themselves become tools for advocating particular policy approaches. Finally, it will identify several opportunities for improving GHG reduction cost assessments to make them more accurate and more useful to policymakers in the future.

I. Predictions, Uncertainties, and Assumptions

The most striking aspect of past efforts to estimate GHG reduction costs is the exceedingly large range over which such estimates vary.[8] For example, a comprehensive survey undertaken by the World Resources Institute (WRI) of GHG reduction costs that the United States would have incurred to meet the Kyoto Protocol examined 162 predictions from 16 models and found a variation over a huge range, from a negative impact of around 3 percent of GDP using "worst case" assumptions to a positive impact of 2.5 percent of GDP using "best case" assumptions.[9] A more recent study undertaken by a working group of the Intergovernmental Panel on Climate Change (IPCC) estimated that the costs would range between a 3 percent decrease and a "small increase" in GDP.[10] Even the worst-case estimate identified in these two studies came in a full percentage of GDP below the estimate of 4.2 percent of GDP prepared by Department of Energy's Energy Information Administration using still another model.[11] Using the 2006 GDP as expressed in 2000 dollars, these estimates extend from a net loss to the economy of $470 billion to a net gain of $282 billion, a range of around $750 billion.[12]

The huge variance is attributable to the fact that the estimates in turn require highly uncertain predictions about how companies, government institutions, and individuals will go about implementing GHG reduction goals.[13] A proper cost estimate requires two major predictions. The analyst must first predict the "baseline" state of the world that would exist in the absence of the proposed regulatory intervention. The analyst must then compare that prediction to a second prediction of the state of the world that would exist if the regulatory intervention were undertaken.[14] The baseline prediction, in turn, includes a number of predictions, including, for example, predictions about how the supply and demand for energy will evolve in the absence of regulatory action and predictions about how other unrelated regulatory interventions will increase

or decrease emissions of GHGs.[15] Cost estimates are thus always hypothetical because they are essentially comparisons of two hypothetical
states of the world.[16]

GHG reduction cost estimates involve speculative predictions over
long time horizons. GHGs have been accumulating in the atmosphere for
the past century, and they will continue to build up for as long as emissions of GHGs exceed equilibrium levels.[17] This cumulative aspect of
global warming has at least two important implications for cost assessment. First, it means that any efforts to deal with global warming must
necessarily be long-term in nature. Second, it means that even though
achieving the ultimate stabilization goal lies in the rather distant future,
short-term savings incurred by putting off GHG reductions today may
result in much larger expenditures in the long term. To the extent that
cost assessments ignore this implication or paper it over with rosy assumptions about the availability of better technology some time in the future,
they will underestimate the overall costs of achieving the goal.

Pressed to find ways around the inability of even the most sophisticated economic models to capture the enormous complexities inherent in
assessing costs incurred by multiple sectors of the economy over a very
long time horizon, analysts tend to substitute huge simplifying assumptions for nonexistent information. Because the time horizons are large
and GHG reduction technologies are in their infancy, the analysts must
necessarily incorporate assumptions about how quickly technologies will
emerge and how rapidly the economy will grow. Since the energy sector
is a major contributor to GHGs, analysts must also make Herculean
assumptions about how individuals will react to changes in energy prices
and the extent to which higher prices will induce consumers of energy to
adopt available approaches to energy conservation and approaches that
may become available in the future. Furthermore, since many observers
believe that the government will adopt a cap-and-trade approach toward
implementing GHG reduction goals, cost analysts must predict how
effectively the broad choice between purchasing credits and installing
technology or conserving energy will result in sufficient action being
taken across all of the relevant actors to achieve the GHG reduction
goals by the prescribed deadlines. Other prominent cost estimates assume
that all relevant governmental entities implement GHG reductions by
enacting a simple emissions tax, which most economists assume to be the
most efficient approach of all.

Finally, rather than attempting to place a dollar value on their estimates, the analysts tend to express them in gross terms like the percent-

age of a country's GDP. This has several advantages, including its comprehensiveness and the fact that it is a standard concept that allows comparisons across different countries. Because the costs incurred and GDP levels are contemporaneous, percent GDP also has the considerable advantage of avoiding arguments over the appropriate discount rate to apply, thereby permitting intertemporal comparisons.[18] GDP does have the not insignificant disadvantage of excluding less tangible considerations like the nonmarket value of environmental quality.[19] Since the focus is on costs, and not on cost and benefit comparisons, however, this is not a major drawback.

II.   The Impact of Differing Approaches and Assumptions

Not surprisingly, GHG cost estimates are highly dependent on the assumptions that the analysts employ.[20] This section of the chapter examines some of the more important of these assumptions.

A.   Base Case Assumptions
The starting point for a GHG cost estimate is the "base case" prediction of the way that technologies and the economy would evolve in the absence of the relevant regulatory intervention. The difference between the base case state of the world and the hypothetical state of the world that would exist if the intervention takes place obviously depends on whether base case estimates of GHG emissions, the availability of energy technologies, and rate of economic growth are optimistic or pessimistic.[21] In an analysis undertaken for the Pew Center on Global Climate Change of dozens of runs from 14 different models, the base case predictions of U.S. carbon emissions by 2010 ranged from a 20 percent increase to a 75 percent increase.[22] Obviously, mitigation measures taken to offset an additional 75 percent baseline increase in emissions (in addition to those needed to reduce emissions from current levels to achieve the stabilization goal) will be more costly than measures needed to offset an additional 25 percent increase.

B.   Top-Down versus Bottom-Up Approaches
Probably the most significant distinction among the existing climate change cost-assessment approaches is between "top-down" and "bottom-up" approaches. Top-down models are "aggregate models of the whole economy that represent the sale of goods and services by producers to households and the reciprocal flow of labor and investment funds from

households to industries."[23] Top-down models in turn come in two varieties. "Macroeconomic" top-down models base predictions about future economic behavior on past macroeconomic behavior, rather than on the assumption that consumers always act efficiently. "General equilibrium" top-down models assume that consumers behave rationally and optimize the costs and benefits of their choices, and therefore assume that consumers will eventually respond efficiently to any external stimulus, like the increase in price for a unit of energy.[24] Bottom-up models "examine the technological options for energy savings and fuel-switching that are available to individual sectors of the economy" and then aggregate the costs of implementing those options over all of the relevant sectors.[25]

Top-down models extrapolate the potential for technological change from past experience and assumptions about consumer behavior; bottom-up models focus on the technologies that are currently available or could be made available within the relevant time horizon and predict how consumers will react to the availability of technologies at various price levels.[26] Top-down models highlight the constraints on the availability of capital and risk aversion and resistance to change on the part of consumers and managers; bottom-up models highlight inefficiencies in existing patterns of energy use and opportunities for technological change. Top-down models are by nature cautious about change and pessimistic about the potential for improvement. They tend to assume, like many conservative economists, that if available alternatives really are more efficient, consumers and companies would already have adopted them.[27] Thus, they are not optimistic about the ability of regulation-induced price increases to stimulate innovation in the direction of a movement away from existing patterns of fossil fuel use. Bottom-up models are skeptical about the "magic of the marketplace" and optimistic about the possibilities for change through technological improvement. Not surprisingly, top-down models tend to yield higher GHG reduction costs than bottom-up models.[28]

Since assumptions about the potential for technological innovation tend to be one of the largest sources of uncertainty in predicting GHG reduction costs,[29] the debate over the relative virtues of top-down and bottom-up approaches is difficult to resolve as an empirical matter. Predicting the nature and pace of regulation-induced technological innovation is by no means an easy task, and for that reason, neither top-down nor bottom-up models focus heavily on the potential for regulation (whether in the form of taxes or direct governmental requirements) to bring about dramatic reductions in costs. Yet, history teaches that this frequently happens in the real world. For example, the automobile industry's original estimates in the mid-1970s for the cost of installing airbags would be about $1,100 per vehicle. By the mid-1980s, however, the National Highway Traffic Safety Commission estimated that technology had progressed so rapidly that its estimated cost was about $320 per vehicle.[30] A more recent assessment of the cost based on twenty years' experience is $278 in 2003 dollars.[31] The fact that predicting the impact of regulation on innovation is difficult does not suggest, however, that it should be ignored, as most top-down and many bottom-up analyses do.[32]

C. Ancillary Benefits

The mitigation measures that companies, institutions, and individuals take to reduce GHG emissions will often result in reductions in other environmental pollutants at the same time. For example, greater reliance on alternative energy production technologies like solar and wind energy will reduce emissions of sulfur dioxide, nitrogen dioxide, and particulate matter from power plants at the same time that they reduce emissions of carbon dioxide. Many GHG reduction cost estimates therefore include an estimate cost of removal of nongreenhouse pollutants that would otherwise be incurred to meet pollution reduction goals for those pollutants as "ancillary benefits" of reducing GHGs.[33] Others have attempted to place a dollar value on the ancillary environmental improvements, and they tend to yield very high offsets. For example, one study estimated that the ancillary benefits alone could offset 50 to 100 percent of the costs of the greenhouse reduction efforts.[34] Like the estimates of GHG reduction costs, estimates of ancillary benefits are highly complex and plagued by large uncertainties, but they are rarely insignificant.[35]

D. Economic Incentives versus Technology-Based Standards

Most economists take it as a matter of faith that economic incentives will bring about technological change in a more cost-effective way than technology-based standards, to which they assign the pejorative "command and control."[36] They therefore assume that it will be less costly to achieve GHG reduction goals through incentive-based interventions like carbon taxes and cap-and-trade regimes than by "technology-forcing" regulatory requirements.[37] The Environmental Protection Agency and many environmental advocacy groups agree with this assessment in general if not in all the particulars.[38] And this assumption permeates most GHG reduction cost models. The top-down studies therefore tend to support the conclusion that implementing GHG reduction goals through a carbon tax or emissions trading regime will substantially reduce estimated costs.[39] For example, one comprehensive modeling exercise undertaken during the late 1990s on the costs of meeting the Kyoto Protocol goals in the United States yielded estimates of $76 to $322 per ton of CO_2 without trading compared to $44 to $135 per ton with trading.[40]

E. Recycling Revenues

To the extent that GHG reductions are induced through carbon taxes, the overall economic impact of the program can be offset to a considerable degree by "recycling" the revenues from the taxes back into the economy to sponsor low-carbon technologies or income tax cuts, rather than simply adding them to the U.S. Treasury to be spent on wealth redistribution or national defense.[41] The assumption underlying this proposition is that taxes "discourage savings, work, or investment by lowering after-tax returns to those activities." By offsetting the carbon tax with reductions in other taxes, the government can put into place a program that is neutral with respect to such disincentives. For example, one study estimates that the GDP cost of a carbon tax of $25 per ton could be reduced by 40 to 55 percent by offsetting revenues with cuts in the marginal tax rates on personal incomes.[42] A similar result would be attained if a cap-and-trade program allocated initial entitlements via an auction and recycled the revenues from the auction back into the economy.[43] This benefit of returning revenues to the economy accounts for much of the variance in top-down models of GHG reduction costs. Some analysts have even argued that recycling revenues from GHG taxes could more than offset the cost of reducing GHGs, thereby yielding a "double dividend" for the economy.[44] The question whether any particular plowback represents an "efficient" return to the economy or merely another opportunity for "inefficient" government expenditure is, of course, highly controversial.[45]

F. Timing of Reductions and Safety Valves

As with most economic activity, timing can have a large impact on compliance costs. Putting off the day of reckoning can significantly reduce the estimated costs of taking action necessary to achieve GHG reduction goals because it allows affected entities to spread the cost of their efforts across broader time horizons, retire existing equipment as scheduled, and generally adjust their overall planning accordingly.[46] Most economists agree that "rapid, unplanned and unexpected adjustment is likely to be much more costly than slow, planned and expected change."[47] They further agree that "adopting an explicit long-term target for atmospheric concentrations and then choosing policies to achieve the most efficient time path for emissions reductions to meet the target could significantly lower the economic impact."[48]

On the other hand, since the extent of global warming depends on the total amount of GHGs in the atmosphere, the longer it takes to reach the GHG emission reduction goals, the warmer the planet will get and the more difficult it will be for societies to deal with the adverse consequences of global warming. Moreover, if the regulatory program demands more from sources of GHGs in the distant future than in the near term, they may decide to wait it out in the hope that new information or changing politics will render more drastic action unnecessary.[49] To discourage such companies from putting off necessary investments in the near term, it is therefore critical that the long-term goal be credible and close enough in time to affect the decisions of current economic actors. Otherwise, sources will fail to plan for and invest in the more drastic long-term measures in the near term and the program will fail to meet the long-term goals.[50]

Some analysts have suggested that GHG reduction programs should contain a "safety valve" that would in essence call a "time out" in progress toward the relevant GHG reduction goal when it became apparent that the costs of attaining the goal by the predetermined deadline were going to be too high.[51] In the context of a cap-and-trade program, for example, such a safety valve would establish a trigger price for a tradable unit (e.g., a ton of CO_2 emissions) that would never be exceeded.[52] The implementing agency would accomplish this by making as many additional units available at the trigger price as necessary to clear the market at that price. The price would be set "low enough that it is not considered punitive, but rather as an assurance by the government that it would not consider control costs above that level to be desirable as a normal course of events."[53] This in turn would allow regulated entities to make investment decisions with confidence and provide some assurance that the market would not be so volatile as to threaten the overall economy.[54] Not surprisingly, the affected industries are big fans of safety valves.[55]

III.   Estimating the Costs of Complying with California's Greenhouse Reduction Programs

On June 1, 2005, Governor Arnold Schwarzenegger of California signed an executive order requiring the state to achieve 2000 levels of GHGs by 2010 and 1990 levels by 2020. Beyond that, the state must reduce emissions to 80 percent below 1990 levels by 2050.[56] Soon thereafter, the California Climate Change Center at the University of California at Berkeley undertook a study of the policies that the state could adopt to achieve the governor's goals.[57] The results of that study were cautiously optimistic and, not surprisingly, controversial. The bottom line was that meeting the goals would require "a profound refashioning of the economy, comparable to the shift that was triggered by the energy crisis of the early 1970s, or the shift that is still occurring following the introduction of micro-computers in the late 1980s and the internet in the 1990s."[58] At the end of the day, however, the state was likely to have a higher gross state product (GSP) if it undertook the "profound refashioning" than if it adhered to the baseline scenario.[59]

Two years later, the consulting firm CRA International prepared a similar study for the Electric Power Research Institute (EPRI) on the achievability of reaching the targets of Governor Schwarzenegger's Executive Order as well as a statute requiring enforceable interim emissions limits as of 2012 and a gradual reduction thereafter to the emissions target of the 2005 Executive Order—1990 levels by 2020.[60] That study concluded, somewhat less optimistically, that "the proposed emission limits can, indeed, be achieved, but . . . the costs involved will vary widely depending upon the eventual approaches chosen to implement specific policy goals."

The Berkeley study employed a general equilibrium top-down framework to model the economic costs of meeting the 2020 target.[61] It did, however, incorporate a great deal of bottom-up information about individual sectors of the state economy that were significant contributors to GHG emissions. It included both technologies identified in engineering studies for various sectors of the economy as well as mitigation measures, such as replacing agricultural land with CO_2-consuming forests. Based on multiple runs of the Berkeley Energy and Resources model, the report concluded that "ambitious mitigation targets can probably be met without unduly adverse effects on aggregate economic growth." Indeed, "well designed [GHG] reduction policies can be economically expansionary if they are based on appropriate incentives, limit administrative costs, and promote the innovation and adoption behavior that has delivered historical improvements in emission efficiency."[62]

This result was attained because "some of the most prominent policies" that the model analyzed "have the potential to help meet the state's ambitious [GHG] reduction objectives, while at the same time stimulating aggregate economic growth by increasing productivity and efficiency." Thus, "many policies under active consideration in California actually *save money* and *increase employment* overall because the indirect effects are so important."[63] Moreover, "although some sectoral policies might individually occasion small reductions in GSP or state employment, the entire basket of policies stimulates the state economy."[64] Two of the indirect gains, however, may be unique to California. The report noted that the state "has a high degree of import dependence in its energy demand," and energy expenditures therefore "represent a leakage from the state economy." To the extent that the money that would otherwise pay for imported energy stays in the state, it represents a gain in the state's GSP.[65] In addition, since a significant part of California's economic growth derives from "its status as a first-tier innovation economy," climate change policies that "promote technology adoption and innovation" will enhance the state's private sector productivity. These benefits can in turn "transmit themselves across the entire economy, increasing competitiveness, profitability, and living standards."[66]

The EPRI study examined twenty hypothetical scenarios using a model that it characterized as a "top down–bottom up" model because it combined a top-down general equilibrium model with a bottom-up model that was limited to the electricity sector, which accounted for the majority of emissions factored into the model.[67] To the extent that bottom-up analysis of other sectors had a large impact on California's GHG emissions (e.g., the transportation and building construction sectors), the model relied on its general equilibrium assumptions about consumer behavior. The general conclusion of the study was that the 2020 goal of returning to 1990 emissions levels in California could be achieved with existing technology, but getting there could be quite costly if the implementing agencies did not adopt efficient approaches to reducing GHG emissions.[68]

Unlike the Berkeley study, the EPRI study concluded that "all policies that significantly reduce [GHG] will entail costs to the California economy" and those costs would "appear as reductions in economic welfare, consumption, and Gross State Product."[69] In particular, the cost of reaching the 2020 goal of a return to 1990 emissions would range from $104 billion to $367 billion.[70] The state could meet the goal in a more cost-effective manner if it adopted a cap-and-trade approach than if it imposed "sector-specific command-and-control" requirements (an approach that the electric power industry had long opposed for the electricity sector). In addition, "an allowance price safety valve could enhance a cap-and-trade plan's cost-effectiveness by allowing regulators to sell as many permits as demanded at a pre-specified price."[71] The report predicted that a suitable safety valve could "reduce the economic costs by over 40%, if the state's . . . reduction targets should prove to rest on over-optimistic low-cost assumptions about abatement costs."[72]

The EPRI report highlighted at several points the cost-saving advantages of a safety valve. In addition to dramatically reducing the cost of the program, a safety valve would "dampen the sharp allowance price fluctuations" caused by "weather, the business cycle, or shifting energy markets" that "have proven to be an expensive feature of other cap-and-trade programs."[73] The report acknowledged in passing that "if the safety valve is triggered, the emission targets will not be met as anticipated," but it did not attempt to probe in any detail the adverse consequences of missing the 1990 target by 2020.[74] Instead, it optimistically predicted that "since only cumulative emissions over long time periods matter for climate risk," any shortfall "could be made up in future years, especially if some form of banking provides an incentive to make larger emission reductions in years when costs are low."[75]

Although the EPRI study did not attempt to explain the difference between its estimates and those of the Berkeley study, the primary difference appears to flow from the Berkeley study's emphasis on the indirect effects of the program, effects that were in fact very similar to those predicted by "recycling" scenarios of other modeling exercises. In addition, the EPRI study did not consider the positive impact on the state's economy of reduced energy imports, a consideration that is not easily generalized to the nation as a whole or even to other states. To a large extent, however, the reasons for the differences in outcomes are hidden in the models themselves and not easily accessible to lay observers. The discretion that the analyst has in choosing the assumptions that drive the models provides an opportunity to shape the analysis to support particular policy outcomes. Whereas the Berkeley study's results highlighted the ease with which the state's economy could absorb the changes necessary to meet the goals of the statute and executive order, the EPRI study's results supported what looked very much like a brief for the cap-and-trade approach with a relatively easily invoked safety valve.

IV. Lessons from Past Cost Estimates

The foregoing description and analysis of past GHG reduction cost assessments suggest that several opportunities exist to improve upon past assessments. Since the federal government has still not embarked on a clear path toward sustainable emissions of GHGs, there is still time to take advantage of these opportunities in crafting this country's much-needed climate change policies. This section of the chapter briefly explores some of those opportunities.

A. Transparency with Respect to Assumptions

Since cost estimates vary widely and since those wide variations depend largely on the assumptions that drive the models upon which the estimates are based, it is critical that the analysts who prepare such estimates make those assumptions available to users in language that is accessible to lay persons.[76] While some of the existing GHG reduction cost assessments have been good about laying out the primary assumptions underlying the estimates, the assumptions driving other assessments "are difficult to tease out because they are embedded in detailed aspects of the model's structure."[77] Because the choice among assumptions can depend as much on the analyst's policy preferences (or those of the study's sponsor) as on objective considerations, the failure to make those assumptions explicit can mask the extent to which the results are policy-dominated. Particularly in controversial areas of public policy like the debates over the steps that government should take to address global warming, analysts face great pressures to employ the assumptions necessary to make advocacy documents look like objective-looking economic projections. Transparency with respect to outcome-determinative assumptions can reduce the potential for nonobjective cost assessments to sway the debate.

B. Caution about Market-Based Approaches

As discussed earlier, many studies simply assume that the government will implement GHG reduction programs with a simple carbon tax because that is the most efficient way to achieve any particular emissions reduction goal. To the extent that cost assessments reflect that assumption, these predictions may be unrealistically low for the simple reason that it is highly unlikely that the United States Congress will enact such a program.[78] Republicans have been railing against "tax and spend" Democrats for the past thirty years with such success that it would take a courageous politician of either party to support a bill that called for a massive tax on all energy consumers. This political reality holds even though there may be general agreement among the experts that more intrusive regulatory programs will ultimately impose even greater costs on consumers indirectly through increased prices. It may be possible to make a carbon tax more politically palatable by clearly linking it to an income tax cut designed to recycle the revenues back into the economy, but even this is a highly unlikely political scenario.

Because economists of both political parties have advocated cap-and-trade programs as an alternative to traditional technology-based regimes since the mid-1970s, it is highly likely that Congress will enact such a program to implement GHG reduction goals. The California program is based on the cap-and-trade model, and most proposed federal legislation incorporates cap-and-trade as well. Policymakers should be cautious, however, about accepting rosy predictions of greatly reduced costs by cap-and-trade regimes. If, for example, the government makes the initial allocations of credits by simply assigning them to existing emitters, rather than selling them in an auction (a very likely possibility, given the political realities of interest group politics), then any assumptions about recycling the proceeds into productive economic uses must be abandoned. Furthermore, advocates of cap-and-trade regimes tend to belittle the high administrative costs of implementing such regimes. For example, such regimes cannot easily be extended to small emitters (whose contributions to the aggregate emissions inventory may be quite large) and to emitters whose emissions are not easily monitored or accurately calculated from easily monitored surrogate measures.[79] Finally, since tradable emissions credits look a lot like property rights, it may be difficult politically or legally to "cancel" those rights when it later becomes apparent that emission reduction goals are in jeopardy.[80] In sum, unless cost estimates based on the cap-and-trade implementation assumption allow for the realities of regulatory failure, they are likely to be unrealistically low.

C.   If It Sounds Too Good to Be True, It Probably Is
There are good reasons to be skeptical about conclusions that measures required by regulations aimed at reducing GHGs will make money for the polluters. The Berkeley study and others that yield negative impacts on GDP from meeting GHG reduction goals are based on the implicit assumption that the baseline economy is not performing optimally, an assumption that most top-down models refuse to make.[81] In a political economy that has historically subsidized both coal and ethanol produc-

tion, provided a host of tax benefits to the oil and gas industry, and even allowed wealthy businesspersons to write off gas-guzzling Hummer vehicles, the proposition that the economy is not performing optimally is hardly far-fetched. At the same time, the assumption that a carbon tax or cap-and-trade GHG reduction regime will wring many of these imbedded inefficiencies out of the economy may require a leap of faith that realistic policymakers may be unwilling to take. A prominent critique of the Berkeley study argues that "the costs of a policy that targets potentially cost-saving measures can be underestimated (i.e., savings from that policy can be overestimated) by failing to account for the reality that some of those cost savings would be realized even without the policy."[82] For example, some consumers may have purchased fuel-efficient automobiles even without government-mandated fuel economy standards, and such purchases should properly be assumed to reduce baseline emissions, rather than to reflect the implementation of the standards.[83]

Optimistic estimates of the extent to which the relevant economic actors will adopt inexpensive mitigation measures are likewise suspect. For example, cost estimates based on the assumption that lands with marginal agricultural value will be purchased for the purpose of planting forests may underestimate the extent to which long-time farmers will be reluctant to part with their land at what economists regard to be a "reasonable" price.[84] Furthermore, to the extent that mitigation measures are not easily quantified and accurately measurable, they may not in fact be real. How much of the GHG reduction gains may appropriately be assigned to some aggressive carbon sequestration techniques, for example, is a controversial subject in need of much further analysis. Indeed, until such techniques are better understood, analysts should probably discount cost-savings estimates attributable to mitigation measures to some extent to reflect the very real possibility that some aggressive marketers of mitigation may in fact oversell their techniques, thereby leaving the emissions unmitigated and in need of future reduction or mitigation.

Other aspects of negative cost estimates also warrant careful scrutiny. For example, the potential of recycling revenues from a carbon tax or cap-and-trade program into the economy through an income tax cut is highly controversial. More importantly, recycling is probably not a politically viable option. First, as previously discussed, any solution that sounds like a tax is probably dead on arrival in Congress. Second, while virtually all economists agree that the most efficient way to allocate initial entitlements in a cap-and-trade regime is an auction,[85] the affected industries are uniformly opposed to a universal auction as a vehicle for allocating entitlements, preferring instead a scheme that spreads them among existing sources in some equitable fashion.[86] Since the industries that are large carbon emitters are also economically and politically powerful actors, it may be necessary to "bribe" them with a free initial allocation of GHG emission permits to secure their support for any cap-and-trade program.[87]

D. Safety Valves

Virtually all observers agree that despite the undeniable need to take prompt action to reduce GHG emissions, a regulatory regime that attempts to move very rapidly to an ambitious emissions reduction goal will impose far higher costs than a more gradual approach "in which existing technologies and infrastructures are gradually replaced by low carbon options as they come to the end of their working lifetimes."[88] The bipartisan "compromise" bill introduced in the summer of 2007 by Senators Jeff Bingaman and Arlen Specter therefore contains a cap-and-trade provision that would set the 2020 cap at 2006 emissions levels and provides a safety valve that would require the implementing agency to sell as many permits as needed to maintain the price of carbon dioxide emissions at no more than $12 per ton, even if that would in turn allow emissions that would exceed the modest 2006 cap.[89] Currently, the price on world markets for the right to emit a ton of carbon dioxide as of December 2008 is $29.[90] Former Secretary of Energy John M. Deutch estimates that carbon capture technology, one of the more promising GHG reduction techniques for power plants and industrial boilers, will not become economically viable until the cost of carbon dioxide approaches $30 per ton.[91]

Safety valves have some very serious disadvantages. Most importantly, to the extent that the safety valve is invoked, allowable emissions will exceed the cap. Unless the program calls for measures to offset "safety valve emissions" before the relevant deadline, this would mean that the GHG reduction program would fail to meet its goal and global warming would continue unabated. If the cost of installing effective GHG technology is $30 per ton and the safety valve is set at $12 per ton, then the government will sell a lot of credits, the technology will go unused, and the GHG reduction goal will be missed.

Even if the safety valve is set at levels above the cost of some existing technologies, to the extent that safety valves provide wiggle room for future adjustment, the program's credibility may suffer, and "skeptical investors may adopt a wait-and-see attitude toward taking near term steps to reduce GHG emissions."[92] The assurance that a safety valve provides that the price of a ton of CO_2 will not exceed a specified price may encourage sources simply to factor that price into their future operating expenses and forgo capital investments. Then, when the day of reckoning arrives, little action will have been taken to reduce emissions, the undiminished demand for credits will cause the implementing agency to sell emissions credits beyond the cap, and the program's goals will go unmet. An emissions tax would avoid this problem if it included a one-way ratchet that precluded the implementing agency from lowering taxes and forced the agency to raise the tax periodically for as long as the emissions reduction target remained unmet.[93] Sources could write the tax into operating expenses, but when the tax increased as companies failed to take action, the incentive to take action instead of paying the higher tax would grow.

The advocates of "safety valves" stress that if the cost of reaching GHG reduction goals is as low as some predict, then policymakers should not be reluctant to include "safety valves" in the program. If the optimistic estimates are correct, they argue, then the safety valves will never be used. Policymakers may land us in the worst of all possible worlds if they accept rosy estimates of the costs of achieving GHG reduction goals and conclude from those estimates that an easily triggered safety valve is warranted on the ground that it will probably never be invoked. If the rosy estimates turn out to be far off-base, for example, then we may wind up in a situation in which a very large proportion of the available credits are traded at the low safety valve price, the government is forced to sell more and more credits at that price as energy use goes up, and the GHG reduction goals are quietly ignored as the deadlines slip by.

Conclusions

The hundreds of estimates of the costs of reaching various GHG reduction goals by various deadlines have produced an extremely wide variety of results, because they are all based on modeling exercises in which the analysts cover large gaps in available information with broad and often unverifiable assumptions. The wide variance in the existing estimates of GHG reduction costs suggests that policymakers should take all such estimates with a large grain of salt and avoid relying heavily on any single estimate.[94] The very real possibility that a study's conclusions reflect unconscious bias warrants additional caution. On the other hand, when estimates from different models tend to converge on a single conclusion, they may provide useful information to policymakers who are starving for guidance in a sea of uncertainty.

When expressed as a percentage of GDP, most of the past estimates converge on a fairly consistent conclusion that "the costs of mitigating climate change would be small in relation to the level of GDP and would not be disruptive of economic growth" so long as the powers that be do not attempt to rush matters too quickly.[95] This conclusion is indeed comforting, but we should not interpret it to mean that long time horizons and safety valves are necessary to avoid disruption. A carbon tax that is pegged to near-term and medium-range emissions goals and is programmed to ratchet upward when goals are not met may be the best way to ensure both that the emissions reductions will take place in the real world and that the effort will not be unduly inefficient.

Notes

1. Steven Mufson, "Climate Change Debate Hinges on Economics," *Washington Post*, July 15, 2007, A1.

2. Edmund L. Andrews, "Counting on Failure, Energy Chairman Floats Carbon Tax," *New York Times*, July 7, 2007, A9.

3. Editorial, "Truth in Global Warming," *Wall Street Journal*, July 10, 2007, A15.

4. Rebecca Smith, "Inside Messy Reality of Cutting CO_2 Output," *Wall Street Journal*, July 12, 2007, A1.

5. Ibid.

6. Thomas G. Moore, *Climate of Fear: Why We Shouldn't Worry about Global Warming* (Washington, D.C.: Cato Institute, 1998), p. 157.

7. Frances B. Smith, "The Human Costs of Global Warming Policy," in *The Costs of Kyoto*, ed. Jonathan Adler (Washington, D.C.: Competitive Enterprise Institute, 1997), pp. 39–48.

8. John P. Weyant, *An Introduction to the Economics of Climate Change Policy* (Arlington, VA: Pew Center on Global Climate Change, 2000), p. 4; Robert Repetto and Duncan Austin, *The Costs of Climate Protection: A Guide for the Perplexed* (Washington, D.C.: World Resources Institute, 1997), p. 12, fig. 1.

9. Repetto and Austin, *The Costs of Climate Protection*. See also Terry Barker, Jonathan Kohler, and Marcelo Villena, "Costs of GHG Abatement: Meta-Analysis of Post-SRES Mitigation Scenarios," *Environmental Economics and Policy Studies* 5 (2002), 135–166 (extending the analysis to published and reaching similar conclusions).

10. Intergovernmental Panel on Climate Change (IPCC), *Climate Change 2007: Mitigation of Climate Change*, Contribution of Working Group III to the Fourth

Assessment Report on the Intergovernmental Panel on Climate Change, ed. B. Metz et al., Summary for Policymakers (New York: Cambridge University Press, 2007), p. 16, http://www.ipcc.ch/pdf/assessment-report/ar4/wg3/ar4-wg3-spm.pdf.

11. Terry Barker and Paul Ekins, "The Costs of Kyoto for the US Economy," *Energy Journal* 25 (2004): 53–71; Barker, Kohler, and Villena, "Costs of GHG Abatement." See also Dennis Anderson and Matt Leach, "The Costs of Mitigating Climate Change," *World Economics* 6 (2005): 71–90 (citing estimates of costs ranging from – 1 percent to 4.5 percent of GDP).

12. The estimate used a 2006 GDP estimate of $11.29 trillion.

13. Barker, Kohler, and Villena, "Costs of GHG Abatement," p. 136 (noting that the "estimation of the economic impact of global warming is subject to a great deal of uncertainty and economic analyses have produced widely differing estimates of the economic implications of policies . . . for emissions reduction").

14. See Thomas O. McGarity and Ruth Ruttenberg, "Counting the Cost of Health, Safety, and Environmental Regulation," *Texas Law Review* 80 (2002): 1997–2058; Office of Management and Budget, *Economic Analysis of Federal Regulations Under Executive Order 12866* (1996), http://www.whitehouse.gov/omb/inforeg_riaguide/.

15. See Office of Management and Budget, *Economic Analysis.*

16. Barker and Ekins, "The Costs of Kyoto," p. 55.

17. IPCC, *Climate Change 2007: Mitigation*, Summary for Policy Makers, p. 3.

18. Barker and Ekins, "The Costs of Kyoto," p. 55.

19. Ibid.; Repetto and Austin, *The Costs of Climate Protection*, p. 11.

20. Barker, Kohler, and Villena, "Costs of GHG Abatement," p. 157 (explaining that much of the variation in dozens of predictions from a score of different models "can be explained by choice of assumption").

21. Weyant, *Introduction to the Economics of Climate Change Policy*, pp. 8–10.

22. Ibid., p. 2.

23. Repetto and Austin, *The Costs of Climate Protection*, p. 6. See also IPCC, *Climate Change 2007: Mitigation*, Summary for Policy Makers, p. 10.

24. Repetto and Austin, *The Costs of Climate Protection*, p. 6.

25. Ibid. See also IPCC, *Climate Change 2007: Mitigation*, Summary for Policy Makers, p. 10; Robert N. Stavins, Judson Jaffe, and Todd Schatzki, "Too Good to Be True? An Examination of Three Economic Assessments of California Climate Change Policy," http://ssrn.com/abstract-973836.

26. Repetto and Austin, *The Costs of Climate Protection*, p. 6.

27. See Stavins, Jaffe, and Schatzki, "Too Good to Be True," p. 14 (asking "if opportunities truly exist to reduce costs while reducing emissions, why would potential beneficiaries of these opportunities not undertake them voluntarily?"). Top-down models also tend to "assume away energy subsidies that may encourage excessive fuel use and must be financed through higher levels

off economically burdensome taxes." Repetto and Austin, *The Costs of Climate Protection*, p. 18.

28. IPCC, *Climate Change 2007: Mitigation*, Summary for Policy Makers, pp. 11–13; Barker and Ekins, "The Costs of Kyoto," p. 54; Repetto and Austin, *The Costs of Climate Protection*, pp. 6–7.

29. See Andrew Dressler and Edward Parson, *The Science and Politics of Global Climate Change* (New York: Cambridge University Press, 2006), chap. 4.

30. David Bollier and Joan Claybrook, *Freedom from Harm* (Washington, D.C.: Public Citizen, 1986), 81.

31. Leonard Evans, "Airbag Benefits, Airbag Costs" (Washington, D.C.: SAE International, 2003), http://www.scienceservingsociety.com/p/155.pdf.

32. See Nicholas Stern, *The Economics of Climate Change: The Stern Review* (Cambridge: Cambridge University Press, 2007), p. 262; David Driesen and Amy Sinden, "The Missing Instrument: Dirty Input Limits," *Harvard Environmental Law Review* 22 (2009): 65–116.

33. Barker and Ekins, "The Costs of Kyoto," p. 63. See also Repetto and Austin, *The Costs of Climate Protection*, p. 8.

34. Repetto and Austin, *The Costs of Climate Protection*, pp. 28–29. See also IPCC, *Climate Change 2007: Mitigation*, Summary for Policy Makers, p. 17.

35. Barker and Ekins, "The Costs of Kyoto," p. 64. See also Dallas Burtraw et al., "Ancillary Benefits of Reduced Air Pollution in the US from Moderate GHG Mitigation Policies in the Electricity Sector," *Journal of Environmental Economics and Management* 45 (2003): 650–673.

36. See, e.g., Robert W. Hahn and Robert N. Stavins, "Incentive-Based Environmental Regulation: A New Era from an Old Idea?" *Ecology Law Quarterly* 18 (1991): 1–42; Stephen Breyer, "Analyzing Regulatory Failure: Mismatches, Less Restrictive Alternatives, and Reform," *Harvard Law Review* (1979): 549–609.

37. CRA International, Program on Technology Innovation, *Economic Analysis of California Climate Change Initiatives: An Integrated Approach* (Electric Power Research Institute, 2007), p. 1-6, http://www.epa.state.il.us/air/climatechange/documents/california-climate-study-final-report.pdf; Judith M. McNeill and Jeremy B. Williams, "The Economics of Climate Change: An Examination of the McKibbin–Wilcoxen Hybrid Proposal for a Carbon Price for Australia" (U21Global Working Paper No. 005/2007, 2007), p. 15; Dallas Burtraw, Testimony of Dallas Burtraw, Resources for the Future before the Subcommittee on Energy and Air Quality of the House Committee on Energy and Commerce, 110th Cong., 1st Sess. (March 29, 2007).

38. See Brian McLean, Testimony of Brian McLean, Director, Office of Atmospheric Programs, Office of Air and Radiation, Environmental Protection Agency, before the Subcommittee on Energy and Air Quality of the House Committee on Energy and Commerce, 110th Cong., 1st Sess. (March 29, 2007); Fred Krupp, Testimony of Fred Krupp, Environmental Defense, before the Subcommittee on Energy and Power, of the House Committee on Energy and Commerce, 110th Cong., 1st Sess. (February 13, 2007).

39. Repetto and Austin, *The Costs of Climate Protection*, p. 1; Weyant, *Introduction to the Economics of Climate Change Policy*, p. 12.

40. Barker and Ekins, "The Costs of Kyoto," p. 60 (analyzing the influential series of studies applying an Energy Modeling Forum exercise and published in 1999).

41. IPCC, *Climate Change 2007: Mitigation*, Summary for Policy Makers, p. 16 (stating that modeling studies indicate that costs may be substantially lower under the assumption that revenues from carbon taxes or auctioned permits under an emission trading system are used to promote low-carbon technologies or reform existing taxes); Weyant, *Introduction to the Economics of Climate Change Policy*, p. 12 (reporting that "theoretical work indicates that the costs of carbon taxes can be significantly reduced by using the revenues to finance cuts in the marginal rates of existing income taxes, as compared with returning the revenues to the economy in a 'lump sum' fashion"); Repetto and Austin, *The Costs of Climate Protection*, p. 7.

42. Barker and Ekins, "The Costs of Kyoto," p. 65.

43. Repetto and Austin, *The Costs of Climate Protection*, p. 35.

44. Weyant, *Introduction to the Economics of Climate Change Policy*, p. 12.

45. Barker and Ekins, "The Costs of Kyoto," p. 66.

46. Organisation for Economic Cooperation and Development and International Energy Agency, *Climate Policy Uncertainty and Investment Risk* (Paris: OECD, 2007), p. 14; Weyant, *Introduction to the Economics of Climate Change Policy*, p. 14.

47. Barker and Ekins, "The Costs of Kyoto," p. 61. See also Anderson and Leach, "Costs of Mitigating Climate Change," p. 80 (concluding that "if the transition to a low-carbon economy were to be pushed to extremes over a very short period, then costs would indeed by high").

48. Repetto and Austin, *The Costs of Climate Protection*, p. 21.

49. McNeill and Williams, "The Economics of Climate Change," p. 14; Organisation for Economic Cooperation and Development and International Energy Agency, *Climate Policy Uncertainty*, p. 15.

50. See Michael A. Toman, Richard D. Morgenstern, and John Anderson, "The Economics of 'When' Flexibility in the Design of GHG Abatement Policies," *Annual Review of Energy and the Environment* 24 (1999): 431–460.

51. Organisation for Economic Cooperation and Development and International Energy Agency, *Climate Policy Uncertainty*, p. 17.

52. Toman, Morgenstern, and Anderson, "Economics of 'When' Flexibility," p. 453; Warwick J. McKibbin and Peter Wilcoxen, "A Better Way to Slow Climate Change" (Brookings Policy Brief no. 17, 1997); Burtraw, Testimony; Anne E. Smith, Testimony of Anne E. Smith, Vice-President, CRA International, before the Subcommittee on Energy and Air Quality of the House Committee on Energy and Commerce, 110th Cong., 1st Sess. (March 29, 2007).

53. Smith, Testimony.

54. Ibid.

55. See, e.g., Ralph Izzo, Testimony of Ralph Izzo, Chairman and Chief Executive Officer-Elect, Public Service Enterprise Group Inc., before the Subcommittee on Energy and Air Quality of the House Committee on Energy and Commerce, 110th Cong., 1st Sess. (March 29, 2007); James E. Rogers, Testimony of James E. Rogers, Chairman, President and CEO, Duke Energy Company, before the Subcommittee on Energy and Air Quality of the House Committee on Energy and Commerce, 110th Cong., 1st. Sess. (March 20, 2007); Michael G. Morris, Testimony of Michael G. Morris, Chairman, President and Chief Executive Officer, American Electric Power, before the Subcommittee on Energy and Air Quality of the House Committee on Energy and Commerce, 110th Cong., 1st. Sess. (March 20, 2007); David L. Sokol, Testimony of David L. Sokol, Chairman and CEO, Mid-American Energy Holdings Company, before the Subcommittee on Energy and Air Quality of the House Committee on Energy and Commerce, 110th Cong., 1st. Sess. (March 20, 2007); John G. Rice, Testimony of John G. Rice, Vice Chairman, General Electric Company, before the Subcommittee on Energy and Power, of the House Committee on Energy and Commerce, 110th Cong., 1st Sess. (February 13, 2007).

56. Michael Hanemann and Alexander E. Farrell, *Managing GHG Emissions in California* (Berkeley: California Climate Change Center at UC Berkeley, 2006), p. 1-3.

57. Ibid.

58. Ibid., p. 1-4.

59. Ibid., p. 2-4.

60. CRA International, Program on Technology Innovation, *Economic Analysis of California Climate Change Initiatives*, p. 1-2.

61. Hanemann and Farrell, *Managing GHG Emissions in California*, pp. 2–46.

62. Ibid.

63. Ibid., pp. 2–4.

64. Ibid.

65. Ibid., pp. 2–12.

66. Ibid.

67. CRA International, *Economic Analysis of California Climate Change Initiatives*, p. 4-2.

68. Ibid., p. 1-2.

69. Ibid., p. 1-6.

70. Ibid.

71. Ibid., p. 1-7.

72. Ibid.

73. Ibid., p. 3-9.

74. Ibid., p. 3-8.

75. Ibid., p. 3-11.

76. Barker, Kohler, and Villena, "Costs of GHG Abatement," p. 157 (taking the position that choices about assumptions "should be made explicit when reporting results").

77. Weyant, *Introduction to the Economics of Climate Change Policy*, p. 2. See also Repetto and Austin, *The Costs of Climate Protection*, p. 3 (noting that "the underlying economic models may contain dozens of complicated equations that are nearly impenetrable to all but trained econometricians").

78. John Hawksworth, *The World in 2050: Implications of Global Growth for Carbon Emissions and Climate Change Policy* (New York: PricewaterhouseCoopers, 2006), p. 10 (observing that "despite their theoretical attractions, carbon taxes have faced both political and practical difficulties that have often either blocked their introduction entirely, or led to exemptions that significantly blunt their impact on carbon emissions"); Repetto and Austin, *The Costs of Climate Protection*, p. 2.

79. See Repetto and Austin, *The Costs of Climate Protection*, p. 2.

80. Ibid.

81. IPCC, *Climate Change 2007: Mitigation*, Summary for Policy Makers, p. 16.

82. Stavins, Jaffe, and Schatzki, "Too Good to Be True," p. 23.

83. Ibid., p. 24.

84. Ibid., p. 23.

85. Burtraw, Testimony.

86. Morris, Testimony; Rogers, Testimony.

87. McNeill and Williams, "The Economics of Climate Change," p. 14.

88. Anderson and Leach, "The Costs of Mitigating Climate Change," p. 81.

89. Steven Mufson, "Climate Change Debate Hinges on Economics," *Washington Post*, July 15, 2007, A1.

90. Ibid.

91. Ibid.

92. Repetto and Austin, *The Costs of Climate Protection*, p. 22.

93. Ibid.

94. Weyant, *An Introduction to the Economics of Climate Change Policy*, p. ii.

95. Anderson and Leach, "The Costs of Mitigating Climate Change," p. 87.

11

Toward Distributional Justice

Amy Sinden and Carl Cranor

As we saw in chapter 5, the problem of climate change is permeated with inequity. Neither responsibility for causing global warming nor vulnerability to its effects is distributed equally across space or time. With just 20 percent of the world's population, the developed countries have contributed 80 percent of total accumulated greenhouse gases currently in the atmosphere.[1] This is not surprising, since greenhouse gas emissions are generally correlated with consumption levels and wealth. The wealthy drive big cars, fly in airplanes, heat and cool large houses and offices, and generally consume large quantities of manufactured goods. Moreover, most of the increase in greenhouse gases that is driving climate disruption has occurred just since the mid-twentieth century.[2] Indeed, fully half of the increase in atmospheric concentrations of CO_2 since 1750 has occurred in the last three decades.[3] Thus, it is the wealthy and powerful of present generations who are responsible for the vast bulk of the greenhouse gases currently accumulated in the atmosphere. Conversely, it is the poor and future generations—those with the least culpability in causing the problem—who will bear the brunt of its effects.

As we have also seen, the tendency of U.S. policymakers to frame the climate change issue in the language and logic of welfare economics obscures this aspect of the problem while simultaneously exacerbating it. Yet, any just and workable solution must confront the question that economics ignores: how should the burdens of responding to climate change be distributed across the globe and across generations? These are questions of fairness and ethics, on which the efficiency principle offers no guidance. As we explore below, however, certain fundamental principles that are widely shared across cultures, religions, and ethical systems can provide guideposts for resolving these questions.[4] If the United States is to regain credibility in international negotiations, we must recognize the limitations of the efficiency principle and instead take these principles of justice as our starting point in crafting a new climate change policy.

In the following pages we discuss these principles and offer some ideas about what form a new climate change policy shaped by them might take. Our focus here is primarily on the costs of mitigation—efforts to reduce emissions of greenhouse gases or increase sequestration of such gases in natural or human-made carbon sinks. Specifically, we consider what a just distribution of these costs might look like. (We leave the question of adaptation costs primarily to chapter 13.) Part I considers how the burdens of mitigation should be distributed within present generations, and part II considers how these burdens should be distributed between present and future generations.

I. Equity within Present Generations

There is now a broad international consensus that anthropogenic climate disruption is occurring and that global emissions of greenhouse gases must be reduced in order to mitigate its effects.[5] We begin from that premise. Given that global emissions must be reduced, what is a fair distribution of the burden of emissions reduction among individuals or countries?

One argument is that everyone around the world should reduce their emissions by the same percentage. This is effectively the position the United States took when it refused to ratify the Kyoto Protocol in 1997, asserting that the United States should not have to agree to binding emissions cuts until the developing world did the same.[6] During the 2000 presidential campaign, George W. Bush reiterated the same position:

I'll tell you one thing I'm not going to do is I'm not going to let the United States carry the burden for cleaning up the world's air like the Kyoto treaty would have done. China and India were exempted from that treaty. I think we need to be more even handed.[7]

This is also the position of many economists, who advocate either a globally uniform emissions tax or an emissions trading program that allocates allowances on the basis of existing emissions.[8] A globally uniform tax would induce roughly the same percentage of emissions reduction around the world, assuming that it cost polluters in different countries roughly the same amount to reduce emissions levels.[9] If every country imposed a tax of \$20 per ton of CO_2, for example, we might expect that to result in emissions reductions of roughly 15 percent in each country.[10] Under such a scenario, the United States would bear the costs of reducing its emissions from 7 to 6.3 billion tons, and India would bear the costs of reducing its emissions from 1.5 to 1.35 billion tons.[11] An emissions trading program that allocated allowances among countries based on existing emissions levels would distribute costs in a similar fashion, requiring roughly the same percentage of emissions reductions from each country.[12]

Would such a distribution of the costs of mitigation be fair? Those who promote such arrangements often frame them in terms of the principle of equality, as George W. Bush did when he argued that demanding emissions reductions from the developing world would be more "even handed." In a similar vein, Eric Posner and Cass Sunstein argue that "[a globally] uniform greenhouse gas tax has a great deal to recommend it . . . nations and their citizens will in an important sense be treated the same."[13]

On a superficial level, requiring an equal percentage of emissions reductions from each country does comport with the principle of equality. However, a deeper question is whether that particular equal treatment of countries is a just solution to the mitigation problem. The equality principle articulated by George W. Bush really only superimposes a veneer of equal treatment on an otherwise vastly unequal situation. The percentage reduction being demanded of each country is equal, but the amounts being emitted by each country to begin with vary wildly. And when we look at per capita emissions, the inequity becomes even more apparent. Requiring equal percentage reductions might, for example, allow an American who has been emitting 20 tons of greenhouse gases each year to continue to emit 16 tons per year, while asking an Indian who emits only 1.2 tons per year to ratchet her emissions down to 0.96 tons.[14] Or, as Peter Singer puts it, "if to meet the limits set for the United States, taxes or other disincentives are used that go no further than providing incentives for Americans to drive more fuel efficient cars, it would not be right to set limits on China that prevent the Chinese from driving cars at all."[15] In sum, the equal percentages approach contains a hidden assumption that the preexisting distribution of emissions is somehow legitimate. While this aspect of the argument is usually left unspoken, those advocating such an arrangement should be called on to defend the legitimacy of the preexisting distribution of emissions.

A. Distributional Equity: Prospective Equal Shares

In general, when a group of people takes a resource that was previously held in common as an undifferentiated whole and divides it up among the individual members of the group, the default assumption is that the resource should be allocated to each individual in equal shares.[16] This assumption is fundamental and intuitive. A parent gives a chocolate bar to two children. Generations of children have approached the situation with a time-honored approach that ensures the bar is divided into two equal portions: "You break it, I choose." From behind a Rawlsian veil of ignorance, representative parties would no doubt also agree to divide commonly held resources according to an equal shares approach.[17]

In the absence of some good reason to give some people a larger share than others,[18] the equality principle requires that we distribute to each individual on the planet an equal share in the absorptive capacity of the atmosphere.[19] This approach respects the equal right of each human being to a share in this undifferentiated natural resource. Such an allocation would be recognized as just from an impartial point of view before the absorptive capacity had been substantially used up.[20] No agent or representative person would agree to freely give up her stake in the absorptive capacity of the atmosphere (and gratuitously sacrifice her interests to others), nor could she expect that others would freely sacrifice their absorptive capacity to her. Thus, each having an equal stake in the absorptive capacity of the atmosphere seems the obvious principle from an impartial point of view.

Ideally, an equal shares approach would allocate allowances or shares directly to each individual on Earth.[21] But in light of the fact that international relations rest fundamentally on a system of mutual respect for national sovereignty, any global solution to climate change will have to begin with an agreement to allocate the costs of mitigation among sovereign nations rather than among individuals. Below we describe such a system, understanding, of course, that it does not address the significant and politically messy challenge of ensuring a just distribution of mitigation costs within nations.

An equal shares approach could be used to accomplish an allocation of mitigation costs among nations in the following manner: First, a global cap on total worldwide greenhouse gas emissions per year would be set. Second, the global cap would be divided by world population (as of some specified date) to derive an individual yearly greenhouse gas emissions quota. Third, each country would be allocated an annual emissions allowance derived by multiplying their population (on the specified date) by the individual quota. Fourth, these allowances would be made tradable. If the United States, for example, wanted to emit more than its quota, it could buy excess allowances from a country with spare capacity, say, India. Allowing trading would help to ensure that emissions reductions were made cost-effectively.[22] Individuals in the developed world might well continue to emit more greenhouse gases than those in the developing world, but only to the extent those in the developing world chose to trade their right to emit for cash. Finally, effective monitoring and enforcement mechanisms would be crucial to ensure that no cheating occurred.[23]

The question of what population statistics to use raises some difficult issues. If each country's budget were adjusted each year to reflect changes in population, this would create a perverse incentive, effectively rewarding those countries with the fastest-growing populations. This problem could be solved by arbitrarily picking a date and using that global population distribution to allocate national allowances.[24] Some have proposed using 1990 population numbers.[25] Peter Singer argues for using estimates of future population levels at some agreed-upon date several decades in the future, in order to avoid penalizing those countries with younger populations.[26] But such an approach would arguably have the effect of penalizing countries that have already taken steps to limit population growth. China, for example, now has a relatively old population as a result of its one-child policy.[27]

A number of academics and policy analysts have proposed some version of this idea. The Global Commons Institute has been advocating it in international climate negotiations since 1990, under the name "Contraction and Convergence."[28] Under their proposal, the developed nations would be given an adjustment period of several decades during which time they would "contract" their emissions until the world finally "converged" on a uniform per capita allocation.[29] Their proposal has been endorsed by a number of governmental and nongovernmental organizations, including the European parliament[30] and India.[31] The general approach has been endorsed by German Chancellor, Angela Merkel,[32] among others.[33]

B. Accounting for History

None of the above analysis, of course, takes account of history. Some principles of justice are historical—asking how resources originally came to be owned and subsequently transferred in order to determine whether the current distribution is just. But others take a "time-slice" approach, looking at a particular moment in time and asking whether the existing distribution comports with some principle of fairness or justice.[34] The "prospective equal shares approach" described above is of this latter type; it looks at the distribution of the absorptive capacity of the atmosphere at the present moment in time and asks how it might be fairly distributed.

But in the context of climate change, history matters a lot. Greenhouse gases can remain in the atmosphere for centuries or even millennia after they are emitted,[35] and it is the total accumulation of greenhouse gases in the atmosphere that drives the greenhouse effect, rather than the flow of emissions into the atmosphere at any given time.[36] Accordingly, we can think of the greenhouse gases emitted over the last century as having already begun to "use up" the available absorptive capacity of the atmosphere. The United States, for example, with less than 5 percent of the world's population, is responsible for well over 25 percent of the greenhouse gases currently accumulated in the atmosphere.[37]

One way to try to account for history would be to imagine going back in time and applying the prospective equal shares approach at the moment that the resource first came into being, before anyone started using it up. In this instance, that would not be the moment at which the atmosphere was first created, but rather the point at which human activity first began "using up" the absorptive capacity of the atmosphere by emitting greenhouse gases in substantial amounts. We might, for example, imagine dividing the absorptive capacity of the atmosphere into equal shares two centuries ago, at the eve of the Industrial Revolution. We could then use this accounting to hold the developed countries responsible for the atmospheric debt that they have accrued over the last two hundred years.

Such a scheme would raise two conceptual difficulties, however. First, since many of the people among whom the allocations would be made were not even alive at the time that these past emissions occurred and since many of those who were alive at that time are now dead, attributing responsibility for these past emissions among the present generation is conceptually problematic.[38] To the extent we allocate allowances to countries on a per capita basis, we might reason that present generations in a given country continue to reap the benefits of the economic development that their ancestors achieved by generating greenhouse gases. But this is clearly less than a perfect fit. Second, it might seem unfair to penalize developed countries for emissions that occurred before it was reasonably foreseeable that such emissions might lead to global warming.[39]

These objections could be largely diffused by beginning the historical accounting at some date by which it is reasonable to say that the scientific understanding of climate change was clear. We might say 1990—the date of the IPCC's First Assessment Report.[40] Alternatively, we could pick 1992, the year negotiations were completed on the U.N. Framework Convention on Climate Change. Or we could pick 1997, the year the Kyoto Protocol was negotiated.

Once a starting date is agreed on, a historical equal shares approach might take the following form: First, the total amount of global greenhouse gas emissions that occurred between the start date and the present date would be calculated. Second, that number would be divided by the average world population during that period to get an individual entitlement. Third, the individual entitlement would be multiplied by each country's average population during that period to get a country allowance. Fourth, each country's actual emissions during the period would be estimated. Fifth, the amount by which each country's total emissions during the period exceeded (or fell short of) their allowance would be calculated. Those countries whose total emissions exceeded their allowance would be required to buy down their excess historical emissions by purchasing credits from those whose total emissions were less than their allowance. Since there is very little difference between a ton of CO_2 emitted twenty years ago and a ton of CO_2 emitted today, these credits could be treated as equivalent to the credits under the prospective equal shares scheme so that the two markets could be combined.

The other way to account for history is to simply look at past events from the standpoint of the present day and apply broadly shared historical principles of justice to determine how resources should be redistributed in the present to account for past events. The following three principles of justice are widely shared across cultures, religions, and ethical systems. Many people argue that the fairness of climate change policy should be measured against them:

Corrective justice One who causes harm to another should pay to remedy (or prevent) the harm.[41]

Unjust enrichment One who profits at another's expense has a duty to compensate the other for her losses.[42]

Equalizing burdens Where a group engages in a common enterprise for the benefit of all, those with more than enough resources (i.e., the ability to pay) should contribute more.[43]

Indeed, these principles are already incorporated in international agreements governing climate change and environmental protection generally. The first and second are reflected in the in the oft-cited "polluter pays" principle, memorialized in Principle 16 of the Rio Declaration:

National authorities should endeavor to promote the internalization of environmental costs and the use of economic instruments, taking into account the approach that *the polluter should*, in principle, *bear the cost of pollution*, with due regard to the public interest and without distorting international trade and investment.[44]

The first and third principles are incorporated in the U.N. Framework Convention on Climate Change, under which the developed nations agreed to:

Protect the climate system . . . on the basis of equity and in accordance with their *common but differentiated responsibilities and respective capabilities*. Accordingly, *the developed country Parties should take the lead* in combating climate change and the adverse effects thereof.[45]

An equal shares approach, whether purely prospective or prospective and historical, comports with all three of these principles. It comports with the principle of corrective justice, because under an equal shares allocation, those in the developed world who are causing the problem of climate change by emitting levels of greenhouse gases that exceed the carrying capacity of the atmosphere would pay the lion's share of the costs of reducing those emissions.[46] Assuming a cap that decreases over time, at the initial stages, at least, developing countries would have per capita emissions that were below (or equal to) the individual quota. Accordingly, they would not have to reduce emissions at all and, unless they increased emissions dramatically, would also have excess allowances to sell. If and when the cap approached zero, of course, all countries would have to reduce emissions, but by this time the vast majority of the total reduction costs would already have been borne by the developed world.[47] Accordingly, the equal shares approach is consistent with principles of corrective justice.

Similarly, an equal shares allocation comports at least roughly with the principles of justice that underlie the doctrine of unjust enrichment. Those in the developed world have benefited from the economic growth and material comforts that the unsustainable emission of greenhouse gases has enabled them to achieve. These profits, it turns out, will be at the expense of many in the developing world who will suffer the effects of drought, food shortages, increased disease, and flooding as a result of climate change. The developed countries, therefore, which in effect have been unjustly enriched, have a duty of restitution, to compensate those in the developing world for their losses. As noted above, under an equal shares allocation, the developed world is likely to bear most, if not all, of the costs of mitigation. This will involve a substantial transfer of wealth from the developed to the developing world, as in order to continue producing even a fraction of the greenhouse gases they currently emit, developed countries will have to purchase unused credits from the developing world. To the extent that such an allocation will induce the payment of substantial sums of money by the developed world to the developing world, it is roughly compatible with the principle of unjust enrichment.[48]

Finally, an equal shares allocation comports with the principle of equalizing burdens. This principle requires that a larger share of the burden of a common enterprise be borne by those who have more resources, at least if they have more than enough to meet their basic needs. An equal shares approach to climate change mitigation imposes the lion's share of the burden on those in the developed world, who clearly meet this criterion.

In sum, an equal shares approach to the distribution of the costs of climate change mitigation is consistent with fundamental and broadly shared notions of justice, including equality, corrective justice, and unjust enrichment.

II. Intergenerational Equity

The climate change problem raises issues of temporal as well as spatial distribution. Thus, in addition to the questions raised above about how the costs of mitigation should be distributed among those currently living, there are questions about how the burdens of mitigation should be distributed between present and future generations. This of course raises the question of how stringent a cap on global emissions we should impose now, rather than the question (addressed above) of how that cap should be distributed among the individuals now living. The more stringent a cap we impose on current emissions, the lower the costs of mitigation and adaptation we will impose on future generations. As discussed more fully in chapter 5, neoliberalism, with its single-minded focus on the efficiency principle, provides no compass for assessing the profound questions of intergenerational equity that are inextricably bound up with the cap-setting problem. Indeed, by reducing the question to a mechanistic aggregation of the present generation's preferences and discounting future impacts, neoliberalism actually tends to exacerbate the intergenerational inequity spawned by climate change.

One way to step outside of the reach of the efficiency principle and find a just principle for distributing the burdens of climate change mitigation between generations is to adopt a deliberative position for thinking about the issue that provides a fair vantage point for assessing the responsibilities among different generations. We can approximate one such impartial position or vantage point by imagining decision makers behind a "veil of ignorance,"[49] a well-known theoretical device for ensuring a considerable degree of impartiality in a normative judgment. This veil would preclude the imaginary participants from knowing to what generation they belonged (though they would know that, barring some catastrophe, there would be future generations), from what country they came, whether their country was rich or poor (though they would know that there would be both extremely rich and extremely poor countries), and so on. The important point for reasoning about how to distribute responsibility for addressing global warming would be the recognition that a decision maker in the deliberative position did not know to what generation she belonged.

Under these circumstances, what principle would decision makers adopt for addressing global warming? Among those applying the veil-of-ignorance device to intergenerational equity, there is wide agreement that since a decision maker behind the veil would not know to what generation she belonged and would neither acquiesce in unduly sacrificing for future generations nor expect other generations to sacrifice for her generation, the appropriate principle would be one that left the planet in the condition in which one's generation inherited it.[50] That is, once a person finds oneself in a particular generation, one should work for policies that ensure future generations will inherit a planet in as sound an environmental condition as the one inherited from the previous generation.

John Rawls has not addressed the problem of global warming directly, but he has addressed issues of intergenerational justice more generically by asking how much one generation needs to save for future generations in order to achieve the social minimum required by defensible principles of justice.[51] He concludes:

Justice does not require that early generations save so that later ones are simply more wealthy. Saving is demanded as a condition of bringing about the full realization of just institutions and the equal liberties [required of justice. Appropriate savings within each generation would be] designed to improve the standard of life of later generations of the least advantaged, thereby abstaining from the immediate gains which are available. By supporting these arrangements the required saving can be made, and no representative man in any generation of the most disadvantaged can complain of another for not doing his part.[52]

Rawls's formulation of an appropriate just savings rate between generations has some application to intergenerational equity concerning global warming. One could regard preserving the climate of the planet in the same condition in which present generations inherited it as part of just savings for future generations. Insofar as extreme global warming would adversely affect the worst-off groups in the worst-off societies undermining their prospects for just treatment, Rawls's argument would provide support for stabilizing planet temperature or greenhouse gas concentrations at or close to current levels or perhaps for setting aside monetary capital to help compensate the least-advantaged in future generations for effects of global warming (if such a strategy could provide any commensurate response to deterioration of the planet).

Edith Brown Weiss, using a similar original position heuristic, comes to a similar conclusion. Arguing that "each generation is both a custodian and user of our common natural and cultural patrimony,"[53] she argues that

[each] generation would want to inherit the common patrimony of the planet in as good condition as it has been for any previous generation and to have as good access to it as previous generations. This requires that each generation pass the planet on in no worse condition than it received it and provide equitable access to its resources and benefits.[54]

The arguments utilized by both Rawls and Brown Weiss result from similar strategies.

It is useful to contrast Brown Weiss's principle with an alternative she describes in her book: the "opulent model." Under this model, "the present generation consumes all that it wants today and generates as much wealth as it can either because there is no certainty that future generations will exist or because maximizing consumption today is the best way to maximize wealth for future generations."[55] This model bears some resemblance to proposals by neoliberals. They argue that current generations should not unduly impoverish themselves for future generations that will be richer than us. However, this argument does not seem plausible. Current generations' wealth has resulted from the use of fossil fuels and a favorable climate, but both are disappearing. Consequently, on these dimensions, future generations will be poorer than the current generation. Moreover, monetary or other financial capital in the form of wealth is not likely to be fungible with the losses that will accompany climate change—the human illnesses and deaths, the destruction of eco-systems, and the loss of stable climate. In short, money can neither purchase a better climate nor compensate for the losses climate change will bring.

If we adopt a principle recommending that any generation convey a global environment in as good a condition as the present and previous generations found it, what are the implications for climate change policy? Does such a principle obligate us to pass on a planet with the same average temperature as the one we inherited, or a planet with no worse a concentration of greenhouse gases in the atmosphere? If we take seriously Brown Weiss's proscription to leave the planet in "as good condition" as we found it, presumably we are thereby obligated to pass on a planet with the same average global temperature as the one we inherited. We might call this the *strong version* of Brown Weiss's formulation.

But the long lag time between when emissions occur and when the Earth's temperature adjusts in response to the change arguably makes the intergenerational calculus more complicated. Some of the increase in global temperatures occurring during our lifetimes is the result of greenhouse gases released into the atmosphere by prior generations. Should we be held responsible for the delayed effects of prior generations' actions?

We might alternatively read Brown Weiss's formulation as bound up with notions of causation and responsibility. Perhaps her formulation holds each generation responsible for the degraded conditions that occur during that generation's tenure because it assumes that those conditions were caused by that same generation. Indeed, before we came to understand the science of climate change, that was probably a safe assumption. If this is so, then perhaps in the context of climate change, Brown Weiss's formulation is best rephrased as a duty on each generation to cause no further harm to the environment (a sort of Hippocratic Oath to the Earth). Thus, the current generation would have a duty not to exacerbate the warming that has already been set in motion by the actions of previous generations. We might call this the *weak version* of Brown Weiss's formulation.

Unfortunately, this conundrum is really only academic. We are long past the point of being able to hand the planet to the next generation with the same climate we found when we got here. The Earth has already warmed by more than a tenth of a Celsius degree per decade over the past fifty years,[56] and is projected to warm by another two tenths of a degree per decade over the next twenty years even if we begin to curb emissions substantially right now.[57] Indeed, even if we reduced emissions (and increased sinks) enough to stabilize the concentration of greenhouse gases in the atmosphere tomorrow, we would not wash our hands of culpability. Under that scenario, anthropogenic warming and sea level rise would still continue for centuries.[58] And thus our continuing emissions, even at a drastically reduced rate, would still be contributing to the warming of the planet.

The only way we can avoid contributing to further global warming is by reducing our emissions to "nearly zero."[59] If we do that quickly, recent studies show that we may be able to prevent global temperatures from rising more than 2° above preindustrial levels.[60] Thus, if we can accomplish zero emissions, we may at that point begin to be in compliance with the weak version of Brown Weiss's duty to future generations—her admonition not to cause further harm. We will not be making up for the harm our generation has already caused, however. And we *will* be passing on a planet with a worse climate than the one we inherited. Compliance with the strong version of Brown Weiss's duty to future generations—passing on the global environment in as good condition as we found it—is already out of reach.

Conclusion

We can no longer deny that unless we drastically reduce emissions of greenhouse gases on a global scale, climate change threatens our planet with unprecedented catastrophic consequences. The cost of making the necessary reductions will not be cheap, requiring no less than a full-scale reconfiguration of the carbon-based economy that now dominates the globe. Yet in order to move ahead with the dramatic mitigation efforts that are so urgently needed, we must confront the thorny issue of who should pay. Although appeals to the efficiency principle and the logic of welfare economics have come to dominate our public policy debates, efficiency offers no guidance on problems of distribution. We must instead look to principles of justice to guide us in developing a scheme to distribute the costs of climate change mitigation.

In the preceding pages we have tried to sketch the outlines of a just approach. Among current generations, multiple, fundamental, noncontroversial, and widely shared principles of justice point toward a per capita distribution of the right to emit greenhouse gases. Between generations, imagining the decision-making process that would occur behind a Rawlsian veil of ignorance produces the conclusion that the current generation owes a duty to future generations to pass on a global environment in as good a condition as we found it—or, at least, to do no further harm to the environment during our tenure here. According to the latest science, this implies, at a minimum, a duty of breathtaking urgency—to reduce emissions to nearly zero as soon as possible. It goes without saying that if we are to have any hope of meeting that obligation to the future, we must move quickly to build consensus on a global scheme for climate change mitigation. But only a scheme that distributes the costs of mitigation among current generations according to broadly shared principles of justice will have any hope of success.

Notes

1. See P. Harrison and F. Pearce, "AAAS Atlas of Population and Environment," (2001), http://www.ourplanet.com/aaas/pages/atmos02.html (accessed October 23, 2007).

2. See Susan Solomon et al., *Climate Change 2007: The Physical Science Basis* (New York: Cambridge University Press, 2007), p. 135, figure 1.

3. Ibid., p. 137.

4. See Henry Shue, "Climate," in *A Companion to Environmental Philosophy*, ed. Dale Jamieson (Malden, MA: Blackwell Publishers, 2001), pp. 449, 457 ("Climate change, fortunately, is a case in which ethical reality is much less messy than ethical theory").

5. See Intergovernmental Panel on Climate Change (IPCC), *Climate Change 2007: Synthesis Report*, Contribution of Working Groups I, II, and III to the Fourth Assessment Report of the Intergovernmental Panel on Climate Change (Geneva: IPCC, 2007).

6. See Byrd–Hagel Resolution, S. Res. 98, 105th Cong. (1997); Donald A. Brown, *American Heat: Ethical Problems with the United States' Response to Global Warming* (Lanham, MD: Rowman and Littlefield, 2002), pp. 37–39, 70.

7. From Bush's statement in the second of the three televised debates during the 2000 campaign, quoted in Peter Singer, *One World: The Ethics of Globalization* (New Haven, CT: Yale University Press, 2002), p. 26.

8. See William Nordhaus, *The Challenge of Global Warming: Economic Models and Environmental Policy* (2007), pp. 121–124, http://nordhaus.econ.yale.edu/dice_mss_072407_all.pdf; Eric A. Posner and Cass R. Sunstein, "Climate Change Justice," John M. Oline Law and Economics Working Paper No. 354 (Aug. 2007), p. 8, http://papers.ssrn.com/sol3/papers.cfm?abstract_id=1008958 (citing a "consensus" that any global effort to reduce greenhouse gas emissions should take the form either of a globally uniform emissions tax or a Kyoto-style cap-and-trade system, in which "existing emissions levels provide the foundation for initial allocations" of emissions rights).

9. Specifically, this assumes that polluters in different countries face similar marginal abatement cost curves. To the extent marginal abatement costs differ, it is actually likely that they are generally lower in developing countries. This would

mean that a globally uniform tax would actually induce higher rates of abatement in the developing world than in the developed world (and higher rates of spending in relation to total greenhouse gas emissions), since the older technologies used in the developing world probably offer greater opportunities for low-cost abatement strategies.

10. See Nordhaus, *Challenge of Global Warming*, pp. 121–124.

11. See Energy Information Administration, *Emissions of Greenhouse Gases in the United States 2005* (2005), p. ix, http://www.eia.doe.gov/oiaf/1605/ggrpt/pdf/executive_summary.pdf (reporting greenhouse gas emissions in U.S. of 7.147 billion metric tons in CO_2 equivalents in 2005); Subodh Sharma, Sumana Bhattacharya, and Amit Garg, "Greenhouse Gas Emissions from India: A Perspective," *Current Science* 90 (2006): 326, 328 (reporting greenhouse gas emissions in India of 1.485 billion metric tons in CO_2 equivalents in 2000).

12. See Posner and Sunstein, "Climate Change Justice," p. 34 (noting the similarity between a uniform tax and a cap-and-trade program that distributes allowances on the basis of existing emissions: "both take existing emissions rates as the starting point"). This is the general form that the Kyoto Protocol took, at least with respect to those countries that took on binding emissions reduction targets. Those targets were tied to existing emissions levels, with most countries agreeing to reduce emissions by 8 percent from 1990 levels. See Kyoto Protocol to the United Nations Framework Convention on Climate Change, Dec. 10, 1997, U.N. Doc. FCCC/CP/197/L.7/Add. 1, art. 3.1 and Annex B.

13. Posner and Sunstein, "Climate Change Justice," p. 33.

14. See United Nations Statistics Division, Millennium Development Goals Indicators, Carbon Dioxide Emissions (CO_2), metric tons of CO_2 per capita (last updated Aug. 1, 2007), http://mdgs.un.org/unsd/mdg/SeriesDetail.aspx?srid=751&crid=.

15. Singer, *One World*, p. 38.

16. H. Peyton Young, *Equity in Theory and Practice* (Princeton, N.J.: Princeton University Press, 1994), p. 163 ("every distributive rule begins with some conception of equality").

17. See John Rawls, *A Theory of Justice* (Cambridge, MA: Harvard University Press, 1999).

18. See Young, *Equity*, pp. 79–80.

19. See Anil A. Agarwal and Sunita Narain, *Global Warming in an Unequal World: A Case of Environmental Colonialism* (New Delhi: Center for Science and Environment, 1991); Singer, *One World*, p. 43; Henry Shue, "Avoidable Necessity: Global Warming, International Fairness, and Alternative Energy," in *NOMOS XXXVII: Theory and Practice*, ed. Ian Shapiro and Judith Wagner DeCew (New York: New York University Press, 1995), pp. 239, 257–258; Brian Barry, *Why Social Justice Matters* (Malden, MA: Polity Press, 2005), pp. 267–268; Aubrey Meyer, *Contraction and Convergence: The Global Solution to Climate Change* (Totnes, Devon: Green Books, 2000); Brown, *American Heat*, pp. 213–215.

20. One could utilize something like Rawls's original position to suggest such impartial choice conditions. Rawls, *A Theory of Justice*.

21. Some have proposed that national governments could administer systems of personal carbon entitlements that would be tradable, but such schemes obviously present formidable logistical challenges. See, e.g., Mayer Hillman, "A Modest Proposal to Save the Planet," *Independent Review* (May 28, 2004).

22. But see Shue, "Climate," p. 455 (arguing that each individual should be entitled to the minimum share of emissions rights necessary to survival and that this minimum share should be nontradable: "A society in which food is available only for payment is a brutal and uncivilized place. What is suggested here is merely the equivalent of food stamps on the global level for vital emissions").

23. Deciding which emissions to attribute to each country for accounting purposes is not necessarily as straightforward as it might seem. Who, for example, should be held responsible for the emissions produced by a factory in China that produces a toy bought by a consumer in the United States? While the standard approach is to hold countries responsible for all the emissions *produced* within their borders, a system that allocated emissions based on consumption instead might arguably be more consistent with principles of causation in which notions of responsibility are ultimately grounded. The choice of how to attribute responsibility for these emissions embodied in the consumer goods that are traded across international borders is not trivial. Indeed, a recent study found that the carbon embodied in U.S. imports from China in 2003 represented 6 percent of total U.S. CO_2 emissions. See B. Shui and R.C. Harriss, "The Role of CO_2 Embodiment in U.S.–China Trade," *Energy Policy* 34 (2006): 4063–4068.

24. See Barry, *Social Justice*, pp. 257, 267 (arguing that current population statistics should be used).

25. See Brown, *American Heat*, p. 215.

26. See Singer, *One World*, p. 36.

27. Arguably, China ought to get some credit under such a scheme for the fact that it has already limited its population growth. Indeed, China takes the position that its one-child policy is part of its climate change policy and has had the effect of preventing 1.3 billion tons of annual CO_2 emissions that otherwise would have occurred. See National Development and Reform Commission, People's Republic of China, "China's National Climate Change Programme" (June 2007), p. 11, http://en.ndrc.gov.cn/newsrelease/P020070604561191006823.pdf.

28. Meyer, *Contraction and Convergence*.

29. The Global Commons Institute has suggested setting a deadline of either 2020 or 2050 for reaching an equal shares allotment ("convergence"). See Global Commons Institute, "GCI Briefing: Contraction and Convergence," http://www.gci.org.uk/.

30. European Parliament, Resolution on Climate Change in the Run Up to Buenos Aries (November 1998), adopted Sept. 17, 1998 ("re-iterat[ing] and re-emphasis[ing] once again [the European Parliament's] view that a set of common principles will have to be based on, inter alia: . . . initial distribution of emissions

rights according to the Kyoto targets [with] progressive convergence towards an equitable distribution of emissions rights on a per capita basis by an agreed date in the next century"), http://www.europarl.europa.eu/pv2/pv2?PRG=CALDOC &FILE=980917&LANGUE=EN&TPV=DEF&LASTCHAP=1&SDOCTA=6& TXTLST=1&Type_Doc=FIRST&POS=1.

31. See Brown, *American Heat*, p. 213 (describing argument for equal per capita shares in atmosphere made by Indian representative at global warming negotiations in Geneva in 1991).

32. "The Isolation of America," *Spiegel Online* (Aug. 31, 2007) (Merkel advocates equalizing worldwide per capita greenhouse gas emissions), http://www.spiegel .de/international/germany/0,1518,503176,00.html.

33. If, in fact, the global cap on greenhouse gas emissions must ultimately be reduced to zero, or near zero, as we suggest in part II of this chapter (see notes 57 to 59 and accompanying text), trading in allowances will eventually slow down and then stop altogether. As per capital emissions allowances begin to converge with the existing level of per capita emissions in the poorest countries, there will be fewer and fewer allowances available for trade. Eventually, there will no longer be enough allowances to create a functioning market. At that point, the program would operate like a traditional regulatory permit scheme.

34. See Robert Nozick, *Anarchy, State, and Utopia* (New York: Basic Books, 1974), pp. 153–155.

35. See A. Montenegro et al., "Long Term Fate of Anthropogenic Carbon," *Geophysical Research Letters* 34, L19707 (2007): 1–5, 1 (concluding that "25% [of CO_2 emissions] have lifetimes much longer than 5000 years").

36. Solomon et al., *Climate Change 2007: The Physical Science*, p. 17.

37. See Jim Hansen, "The Threat to the Planet: Actions Needed to Avert Dangerous Climate Change," talk delivered to SOLAR 2006 Conference on Renewable Energy, Denver, Colorado (July 10, 2006) (27.8 percent of global cumulative global CO_2 emissions between 1750 and 2005 attributable to U.S.), http://www .columbia.edu/~jeh1/2006/solar_threattalk_20060905.pdf.

38. See Edward A. Page, *Climate Change, Justice, and Future Generations* (Northhampton, MA: Edward Elgar, 2006), p. 169.

39. Ibid.

40. See Lisa Heinzerling, "Climate Change, Human Health, and the Post-Cautionary Principle," *Georgetown Law Journal* 96 (January 2008): 445–460, reprinted as chapter 9 in this volume (arguing that scientific consensus on climate change became clear in the late 1980s or early 1990s).

41. See Page, *Climate Change and Future Generations*, pp. 167–170; Matthew D. Adler, "Corrective Justice and Liability for Global Warming," *University of Pennsylvania Law Review* 155 (2007): 1859.

42. See Henry Shue, "Global Environment and International Inequality," *International Affairs* 75 (1999): 531; Daniel A. Farber, "Adapting to Climate Change: Who Should Pay?" *Journal of Land Use and Environmental Law* 23 (fall 2007):

1–37. This in turn might be seen as resting on a principle of fairness according to which, while one is entitled to the benefits that accrue to one through one's activities, even adventitious and accidental benefits, one should in fairness bear the costs, even adventitious and accidental costs, that one's activities impose on others. In this instance, pollution or excessive use of the absorptive capacity of the atmosphere are the costs of one's activities that in fairness should be internalized. See A. M. Honore, "The Morality of Tort Law—Questions and Answers," in *Philosophical Foundations of Tort Law*, ed. David G. Owen (Oxford: Clarendon Press, 1995), p. 79.

43. See Shue, "Global Environment"; Page, *Climate Change and Future Generations*, pp. 170–172. See also Shue, "Climate," p. 457 (citing all three principles as "the most familiar" grounds for the distribution of the mitigation costs of climate change: (1) contribution to the problem [causal responsibility], (2) "benefit from the processes that have caused climate change," and (3) ability to pay).

44. United Nations, Rio Declaration on Environment and Development, U.N. Doc. A./CONF 151/26, 31 I.L.M. 874 (Aug. 12, 1992) (emphasis added).

45. United Nations Framework Convention on Climate Change, U.N. Document A/CONF. 151/26, art. 3, Paragraph 1 (May 9, 1992).

46. See Brown, *American Heat*, p. 214.

47. This might strike some as unfair: Since the developing countries are also emitting greenhouse gases, shouldn't they also have some (albeit smaller) obligation to reduce from the outset? But arguably, an individual who is emitting less than her equal share quota is by definition not *causing* the problem. A man in India who pedals a rickshaw for a living and lives in a house without heat or air conditioning can legitimately say that had everyone in the world emitted at his rate all along, there would be no climate change problem.

48. To the extent that the principles of unjust enrichment and corrective justice would also call for payments for adaptation to and compensation for unavoided harms from climate change, those would have to be handled through a separate scheme, as discussed in chapter 13.

49. See Rawls, *A Theory of Justice*, pp. 11, 17, 118–123. Rawls is a well-known proponent of this approach and he has been followed by Edith Brown Weiss. See Edith Brown Weiss, *In Fairness to Future Generations: International Law, Common Patrimony, and Intergenerational Equity* (Dobbs Ferry, NY: Transnational Publishers, 1988), p. 24. However, many other philosophers and theorists across different traditions and fields have endorsed a similar device, even though they have not called it a "veil of ignorance"; see, e.g., Immanuel Kant, *The Critique of Practical Reason*, trans. and ed. Lewis White Beck (Chicago: University of Chicago Press, 1947), pp. 68–72; R. M. Hare, *The Language of Morals* (Oxford: Oxford University Press, 1952); J. C. Harsanyi, "Cardinal Utility in Welfare Economics and in the Theory of Risk-Taking," *Journal of Political Economy*, 61 (1953), to name just a few.

50. Rawls, *A Theory of Justice*, p. 251; Brown Weiss, *Fairness*, p. 24.

51. Rawls, *A Theory of Justice*, p. 251.

52. Ibid., pp. 257–258.

53. Brown Weiss, *Fairness*, p. 21.

54. Ibid., p. 24; see also p. 348 (suggesting that the same principle applies to the problem of climate change).

55. Ibid., p. 23.

56. Solomon et al., *Climate Change 2007: The Physical Science Basis*, pp. 5, 10 (reporting a linear warming trend of 0.13°C per decade of past 50 years and that "most of [this] observed increase in global average temperature . . . is very likely due to the observed increase in anthropogenic greenhouse gas concentrations").

57. Ibid., p. 12.

58. Ibid., p. 16; H. Damon Matthews and Ken Caldeira, "Stabilizing Climate Requires Near-Zero Emissions," *Geophysical Research Letters*, 35 L04705 (2008): 1–5, 1.

59. Matthews and Caldeira, "Stabilizing," pp. 4–5: "Avoiding future human-induced climate warming may require policies that seek not only to decrease CO_2 emissions, but to eliminate them entirely."

60. Ibid.

12

Toward Sustainable Technology

David M. Driesen

We should think of environmental policy as a means of stimulating sustainable technology—technologies that will enable us to meaningfully address global warming while achieving other societal goals.[1] We must fundamentally change how we think about instrument choice in order to create a positive economic dynamic that will take us where we need to go in the long term.

This chapter will first explain why relentless pursuit of short-term efficiency through broad environmental benefit trading is in tension with the goal of maximizing investment in our long-term future and explore briefly one of the many options for improving trading's design. It will then put forward two alternatives to Kyoto-style trading. The first alternative, a *dirty input limit*, stimulates fundamental change by limiting the use of fossil fuel. The second alternative, an *environmental competition statute*, aims to stimulate a race to develop the best possible technologies to limit greenhouse gas emissions. Together, they illustrate that adoption of an economic dynamic leading to sustainable development can productively and creatively improve environmental law, even in the realm of instrument choice, where efficiency-based thinking has made useful contributions.

I. Environmental Benefit Trading: Short-Term Efficiency and Long-Term Environmental Goals

Measures maximizing short-term efficiency do not necessarily maximize long-term welfare, because lower short-term costs do not stimulate higher long-term benefits.[2] Economists implicitly recognize that short-term cost savings do not aid technological innovation in their pollution tax models. These models assume that a tax rate increase augments innovation rates.[3] This makes sense. Innovation is often costly and almost always uncertain. To develop something new, one must invest in investigating an idea that might not work out. Therefore, people tend to choose to innovate when not innovating is costly enough to make innovation seem worthwhile.[4] This idea that high costs motivate innovation is consistent with the induced innovation hypothesis that economists often employ in analyzing innovation,[5] which holds that producers tend to innovate in response to scarcity, which raises costs. To put it more simply, necessity is the mother of invention.[6]

Economists' assumption that high costs stimulate innovation is at war with the assumption that broad emissions trading stimulates innovation more effectively than a traditional performance standard of identical scope and stringency. Emissions trading lowers the cost of employing conventional control techniques by permitting polluters to reallocate their reduction responsibilities to minimize costs. It follows that emissions trading reduces innovation levels below what would occur with the same regulatory limits in place without trading.[7]

As a corollary, a broad emissions trading design, which increases the number of sources potentially generating credits, provides less powerful incentives for innovation than a narrow design.[8] A broad design maximizes cost savings, permitting a wide variety of conventional techniques to generate credits. A narrow design limits the number of conventional technological options that can reduce emissions, thereby increasing pressures for innovation. The California Air Resources Board recognized this corollary explicitly when it established its carbon dioxide standards for new vehicles. It refused to permit offset credits from outside the transportation sector to count toward meeting its standard, because of the desirability of encouraging technological innovation in vehicle design. It recognized that allowing manufacturers to offset rather than reduce vehicle emissions would cause the manufacturers to avoid innovative vehicle design in favor of paying for credits reflecting cheaper and more conventional techniques for realizing emission reductions.[9] It did, however, employ a narrower form of trading to increase flexibility and lower cost, allowing vehicle manufacturers to comply with the carbon dioxide standard on a fleet-wide average basis, rather than requiring each and every vehicle to meet the standard.

The idea that emissions trading encourages more innovation than traditional regulation comes from a woefully incomplete evaluation of economic incentives. Trading proponents point out that trading creates an incentive to go beyond compliance.[10] But this is correct only with respect to sellers of credits. Trading creates an incentive for about half of the pollution sources, the ones with the lowest marginal control costs, to go beyond compliance. It follows that trading provides superior incentives for those enjoying low marginal control costs to innovate.

Unfortunately, trading also creates an incentive going in the opposite direction. It encourages half of the polluters to stop short of compliance—to emit more than they would have under a performance standard regime. Trading decreases innovation incentives for about half of the polluters, the undercomplying buyers, to innovate.

One cannot analyze trading's effect on innovation by focusing only on the sources that overcomply, any more than one could analyze it by focusing only on those that undercomply. Polluters that do not reduce emissions locally buy credits to make up the shortfall. In a trading program, undercompliance by some finances overcompliance by others. The economist David Malueg pointed out almost two decades ago that trading reduces innovation incentives for half the sources.[11] But trading proponents often neglect this point.

Since trading decreases innovation rates for about half the sources and increases them for another half of the sources, the right question is: What is the net effect of trades shifting reductions from high-cost to low-cost sources?

Most importantly, trading decreases the net incentive for high-cost innovation, relative to the incentives that a traditional performance standard of identical scope and stringency would provide. Under a traditional performance standard, the polluters facing the highest marginal control cost would have incentives to adopt any innovation costing less than their high marginal cost. Under trading, they have no incentive to adopt such innovations. Instead, they will pay polluters with low marginal control costs to make reductions in their stead. The only innovations that will prove worthwhile in a trading program are those lower than the equilibrium price for abatement established by the permit market. And that price will be lower than the marginal control costs of polluters facing high costs under a traditional regulation—substantially lower in many cases. Trading eliminates all incentives to make innovations costing more than the relatively low cost of conventional pollution reductions established by the trading market.

This destruction of incentives for relatively high-cost innovation matters, because development of technologies that can significantly increase our capacity to address a major problem like global warming will tend to cost a lot, at least initially. It's not an accident that broad environmental benefit trading programs have done little to promote renewable energy and nothing to promote nuclear power. Development of nuclear power or renewable energy will likely prove more costly than the cheapest conventional approaches for reducing emissions. By referring to nuclear power, I do not mean to express any view on its desirability. But some people believe that we will need to deploy nuclear power to adequately address global warming and that the risks are manageable. If governments wish to use nuclear power to address global warming, they will have to do more than just allow it to generate credits in emissions trading schemes. For an emissions trading scheme gives priority to low-cost abatement and does not secure investment in high-cost abatement with huge carbon dioxide reduction potential.

Many technological innovations that have significantly improved our lives involved costly investments that ultimately delivered significant welfare benefits at lowered cost. Manufacturers introduced automobiles as luxury goods commanding a high price. Mass production later lowered vehicles' prices sufficiently to enable their regular use for personal transportation, building on investments previously made in high-cost motoring. Similarly, personal computers followed investment in expensive supercomputers, which only large institutions could afford. In these cases, and many others, high-cost investment ultimately led to lower cost and significant improvements in our lives.

Investments that make it possible to address global climate change will likely follow a similar pattern. In the short run, many investments that help create technologies that can eventually provide cost-effective substitutes for fossil fuels will likely prove costly. These investments, however, will lower prices and improve the effectiveness of the technologies involved. Indeed, this has happened with just about all forms of renewable energy, because of policies put in place specifically to stimulate these costly investments.[12] We desperately need these investments on a massive scale if we hope to cope with the challenge global warming poses.

Emissions trading, however, will usually stimulate such expensive innovations only when all other cheaper options have been exhausted. Private actors in emissions trading markets tend to purse the least-cost abatement options. They will typically not consider the positive spillovers from investments in new approaches that make them desirable for society at large. For positive spillovers, by definition, are advantages that do not benefit the party investing in the technology that is generating the positive spillover. For example, an investment in new solar technology can produce ancillary benefits for society that justify its high cost. Such an investment may build knowledge that will allow other producers to make additional advances that reduce solar energy's price or increase its utility (for example, making it more viable in cloudier climates). Since market actors cannot predict these positive spillovers in advance and some of these spillovers may benefit competitors, rather than the company making the investment, project developers will tend to underinvest in this sort of innovation. This idea, that markets often produce an underinvestment in innovation because the investor cannot capture the positive spillovers and innovation is an uncertain process, is well recognized in the economics of innovation generally.[13] These lessons suggest, at a minimum, that emissions trading markets, like markets generally, will prove suboptimal in stimulating valuable innovation.

Faith in emissions trading's capacity to encourage innovation stems, in part, from the myth that emissions trading provides continuous incentives for innovation, something that traditional regulation does not do. In fact, to the extent emissions trading encourages innovation, the duration of that incentive precisely matches that provided by a traditional performance standard. Both traditional regulation and emissions trading's innovation incentive continues until the compliance deadline arrives and then subsides. The incentive to reduce emissions in a trading program comes from governmental commands to reduce emissions by a set amount by a date certain. Polluters are willing to pay for emission reductions, because they must purchase them in order to comply by the deadline, unless they reduce locally by the deadline. Some polluters will overcomply, because polluters with high compliance costs will pay for a limited amount of credits, the amount necessary for them to avoid local compliance, and no more. It follows that rational credit sellers will only pay to produce enough credits to meet this limited demand, as no substantial market exists for credits not needed for compliance purposes. Once a polluter has met its compliance obligation, either by purchasing credits or by complying locally, no incentive exists to continue reducing emissions.

Trading programs, of course, can lengthen the duration of incentives for innovation by lengthening the compliance period. But a traditional regulation can do the same. The compliance period can be short or long, and the compliance deadline extinguishes incentives for innovation in both cases.

Of course, if regulators could be counted on to continually and predictably tighten their regulatory limits, then a continuous incentive to reduce emissions and to innovate might exist. But this would be true whether or not regulators use emissions trading as the mechanism to meet these continually revised limits. In practice, however, polluters frequently lobby and litigate to delay or weaken limits, including limits to be met through emissions trading. And regulators often find it difficult to tighten limits for a variety of reasons.

The limits of my claim about trading and innovation require some emphasis. I am not saying that trading never encourages innovation. I am merely pointing out that trading produces less powerful incentives for valuable high-cost innovation than traditional regulation of *identical scope and stringency*. I am also claiming that emissions trading does not produce optimal innovation.

One can address trading's weakness in stimulating innovation by increasing the cap's stringency. A trading program reducing pollution by X tons encourages expensive innovation less well than a performance standard providing for X tons of reduction. But if one establishes an innovation premium in the cap, call it P, such that the cap requires $X + P$ tons of reduction, the trading program would stimulate more innovation, presumably, than a trading program under a cap of X tons. In order for a trading program achieving a reduction of $X + P$ to produce as much high-cost innovation as a performance standard requiring X tons of reduction, however, $X + P$ must raise marginal control costs so that they equal the marginal control costs of achieving X through performance standards. Since trading significantly lowers marginal control costs, the innovation premium (P) necessary to meet this condition will usually prove quite high.

It is unlikely that the political economy advantages of trading will make it feasible to adopt a cap with an innovation premium sufficient to offset the innovation losses from trading (for expensive innovation). The increased stringency deprives polluters of the cost savings that trading would otherwise provide. Moreover, since polluters will likely have little or no information about the marginal cost of reductions at others' facilities that they might purchase, they may evaluate a proposed cap of $X + P$ in terms of the cost of making all of the reductions at their own facilities, attributing little or no cost reduction to the market. Their local abatement costs will be much higher for limit $X + P$ than for limit X. And vigorous industry opposition to a more stringent cap decreases the likelihood of the government compensating for innovation lost through increased stringency. An innovation premium is a good idea, but it may be difficult to obtain a sufficiently ambitious premium.

In keeping with the prevailing practice in the literature, I've framed this discussion as a comparison between traditional regulation and environmental benefit trading. This approach simplifies my effort to analyze the central tendencies of neoliberal instrument choice and to reorient our thinking. But a serious effort to address climate change may require more creative use of economic incentives to produce an economic dynamic favoring sustainable development. To do this, however, we must not assume that desirable innovation is an inevitable by-product of mechanisms designed to maximize short-term efficiency.

Instead, we must design instruments specifically to encourage the innovations that will make it possible to phase out fossil fuels. We have seen that carbon dioxide constitutes about 80 percent of global-warming-potential-weighted greenhouse gases currently emitted.[14] For that reason, when scientists analyze the question of how one would technically avoid dangerous climate change, they focus almost entirely on analyzing the capacity of various alternative fuel sources and energy efficiency improvements to displace fossil fuels.[15] Furthermore, absent a phaseout of these fuels by the end of this century, scientists expect global warming to be very dangerous.[16] Accordingly, scientists have been accompanying calls for a phaseout by the end of this century with a call for a 50 percent cut below 1990 levels by 2050.[17] Because developing countries will not cut emissions unless developed countries show good faith and provide technological leadership by going first, developed countries probably need cuts in the order of 80 percent by 2050 as a prelude to a complete phaseout.[18] Yet, perhaps because of a psychological aversion to squarely confronting the need for such a significant change, most of the instrument-choice debate focuses on abstract "carbon abatement" policies, like emissions trading, which address the idea of a fossil fuel phaseout only obliquely.[19]

We will stop using fossil fuels eventually, no matter what we decide. Oil will run out at some point, and eventually, so will coal. These are nonrenewable resources in limited supply. The question is whether we will phase out these substances before or after absolute scarcity forces enormous price increases and then makes them simply unavailable for any purpose. Replacing fossil fuels as soon as possible will yield enormous benefits. Every year that we continue burning fossil fuels we add carbon dioxide to the atmosphere, which accumulates and remains there for more than a century, committing us to more future warming. Fossil fuels also lie at the root of most of our most serious conventional pollution problems. Phasing out fossil fuels would lessen or eliminate particulate pollution (associated with tens of thousands of annual deaths in the United States), ozone (associated with asthma and other lung disease), hazardous air pollution (associated with cancer, birth defects, and neuro-logical defects), oil spills, non-point source pollution, and destruction of land and water from coal mining. We do not know how quickly oil prices will rise or how quickly the price of renewables will fall. But we do know that the right direction for society is to phase out fossil fuels over time. The economic dynamic theory emphasizes that we should move in the right direction even when the costs and benefits of doing so cannot predicted with reasonable accuracy.

II. Dirty Input Limits

We saw in chapter 6 that environmental benefit trading under the Kyoto Protocol has tended to encourage end-of-the-pipe solutions. This is not surprising, because emissions trading focuses on end-of-the-pipe control. It limits a particular pollution output. In this respect, it follows the pre-vailing model of traditional regulation, which also focuses on end-of-the-pipe limits, albeit without the trading possibility. This section explores the idea of limiting the inputs that cause global warming instead of the pollution outputs that constitute the symptoms. I refer to laws that limit the use or production of an input generating pollution as a dirty input limit, or DIL.[20]

The climate change regime's focus on end-of-the-pipe solutions is in tension with the teachings of the pollution prevention literature. This literature points out that often pollution prevention—reducing or elimi-nating undesirable inputs into polluting processes—can reduce multiple pollutants at once, often in several different media. By contrast, end-of-the-pipe control can transfer pollution from one medium to another. For example, carbon capture and storage, an end-of-the-pipe approach under consideration to address climate change, poses some risks of ground-water contamination, because it involves transfer of carbon dioxide from air to land. Methods that avoid generation of carbon dioxide in the first place, however, prevent pollution and contaminate neither medium. The literature also points out that pollution prevention is often cheap.

Pollution prevention tends to involve fairly fundamental technological changes. A focus on pollution prevention challenges firms to change their processes—to change how they produce goods and services valued by society. Firms tend to like output-based regulation, because end-of-the-pipe control does not require creative changes in fundamental processes.

We can require pollution prevention by imposing limits on the inputs that create pollution, rather than the resulting pollution output. In particular, we could limit the carbon content of all fuels, which would stimulate a move away from fossil fuels with high carbon content like coal and oil. Or we could simply limit the amount of oil and coal that the United States uses. Furthermore, we could create allowances to use or produce these inputs, and make the allowances tradable, thereby reducing cost and improving flexibility.

Although this may seem radical, we have used DILs in the past. Indeed, they figure prominently in our most well-known environmental success stories, the reduction and eventual phaseouts of lead and of key ozone-depleting substances. In the case of lead, the EPA first created DILs to reduce gasoline's lead content and then gradually phased lead out. This phaseout produced a public health triumph, as lead from gasoline played a large role in elevating blood lead levels and associated neurological problems. Ozone-depleting chemicals threatened to deplete the stratospheric ozone layer, which shields us from ultraviolet radiation. This would allow ultraviolet radiation to increase skin cancers, disorder our immune systems, and wreak ecological havoc. The United States led the world to an agreement to limit the production of key ozone-depleting chemicals under the Montreal Protocol on Ozone Depleting Substances. A few years later, the world agreed to phase out key ozone depleters entirely. The United States, and the rest of the world, used DILs to accomplish this phaseout. Although a hole had already opened up in the ozone layer before the world acted, these DILs were very successful, and scientists now expect the ozone layer to heal.

These DILs unleashed significant technological changes, causing the reformulation of gasoline and vast changes in a variety of processes using ozone-depleting substances. Thus, many analysts credit these DILs with effectively stimulating innovation.

Although the Montreal Protocol provided some authority to trade, no trades actually occurred.[21] The later stages of the lead phaseout, however, involved a quite active trading and banking program, using tradable DILs, rather than tradable emission output allowances. The EPA authorized small refiners phasing out lead to bank credits if they phased out lead more quickly than required and to purchase allowances authorizing increased lead content from those who overcomplied. Although this arrangement delayed the phaseout somewhat,[22] it lowered the small refiners' costs and increased flexibility.

DILs unleash technological innovation and therefore may produce significant cost savings, because they focus producers on changing the fundamental inputs into production processes. Indeed, the ozone DILs unleashed so much cost-saving innovation that in hindsight we think of the phaseouts of key ozone depleters as easy accomplishments. But when the United States started to address ozone-depleting chemicals, they were used ubiquitously as solvents, refrigerants, propellants, foams, and pesticides, and experts believed that finding substitutes was either expensive or simply impossible.[23] Moreover, the DILs spurred significant technological advances even before the phaseouts came into effect.[24] So, a DIL can catalyze innovation even if it does not involve a phaseout.

Most analysts will tend to assume that a DIL phasing out fossil fuels, however, will prove outlandishly expensive, because currently few cheap substitutes for fossil fuels exist. The United States, however, need not phase out fossil fuels in the near term. It could establish a firm target modestly cutting their overall use or just permitting no further increases in their use. This approach would send a powerful signal that industry needed to innovate to find alternative fuels, especially in light of the possibility of future cuts or phaseouts. It would likely provoke some innovation and might therefore prove less costly than expected. Moreover, regulators could then use the cost experience from implementing a modest DIL to evaluate how much further we could go without undue hardship.

The advantages of a fossil fuel DIL are most acute in the transportation sector. Because output-based limits are so difficult to administer, output-based trading schemes arising under the Kyoto Protocol to date have focused exclusively on imposing limits on power plants and large industrial pollution sources. In the United States, however, transportation accounts for about one third of greenhouse gas emissions. Both in the United States and in many other countries these emissions have risen rapidly, because of increased driving. Yet, output-based cap-and-trade for transport is not feasible, because we cannot track each driver's carbon dioxide output in order to set up a tradable allowance system focused on outputs. As a result, trading schemes enacted as of this writing have not included transport emissions, and this sector's emissions remain uncapped.

A DIL would permit capping fossil fuel use in the transport sector, guaranteeing a reduction in the total mass of emissions within the polity employing the DIL. For example, the EPA could calculate the total carbon content burned in the United States in a recent year. It could then auction off allowances reflecting 90 percent of the total carbon content of fuel emitted to refiners and fuel importers.

This DIL, like all DILs, would create a ripple effect beyond the sector possessing allowances. Because a DIL constricts output that forms part of a production stream, it limits production and use of the limited input at every stage, from material extraction to end use. Fuel manufacturers would have to change fuels in order to stay within the DIL's limits and still supply the drivers with sufficient fuel. The gasoline scarcity this creates would cause vehicle manufacturers to innovate as well, as fuel-efficient and "flex fuel" vehicles would become a necessity. If the innovation this unleashed contains costs sufficiently (vehicle efficiency improvements, in particular, would likely have that impact), then consumers would not be affected. If costs rose, this would put pressure on drivers to use public transport, ride a bike, or live closer to work, and would therefore put pressure on governments to fund mass transit.

Because producers of pollution inputs are usually less numerous than end users, DILs usually will prove much easier to administer than output-based programs. In the United States, a program limiting the carbon content of transportation fuels could be administered by auctioning tradable permits to refiners, owners of natural gas pipelines, and fuel importers. This is a smaller group of entities than those successfully regulated under the acid rain trading program. Expanding the program to include coal processors, allowing rather comprehensive regulation of fossil fuels would only produce about 2,000 regulated entities.[25] Such a program is a lot simpler than the output-based trading mechanisms under Kyoto, which could, in principle, reach not just the handful of suppliers of dirty inputs, but all of the downstream users of those inputs where pollution outputs are released. And it would be far easier to administer than the piecemeal program of output-based measures that have struggled to address the transportation sector's emissions in the past.

A fossil fuel DIL would provide a wide variety of benefits going beyond climate protection. Limits on fossil fuel production or use would ameliorate environmental damage throughout the production stream. Oil extraction, transportation, and refining damage land and water and pollute the air. More air and water pollution occur when the fuel is added to gasoline tanks and then burned. Similarly, coal mining destroys water and land. When the coal is burned, the power plants emit many more harmful pollutants than just carbon dioxide. The U.S. regulatory system has struggled for many years to separately regulate all of the pollution outputs stemming from fossil fuel use on a piecemeal basis. It would be far more efficient to simply limit fossil fuel production at the source, thereby simultaneously addressing all of these problems.

Adoption of a DIL will require a change in our thinking. If one's only goal is to reduce private polluters' control costs for a single pollutant, then an output-based trading approach makes sense. After all, polluters generally have the option of using a pollution-prevention approach if it meets their output-based limit. For example, under an output-based approach, power plant operators complying with a limit on their carbon dioxide emissions could choose to switch to natural gas—that is, to change inputs. But operators of coal plants will prefer to have the option of employing carbon capture and storage—an end-of-the-pipe control— if it proves cheaper (regardless of whether it's safe and effective). If one accepts the prevailing quick-fix mentality, then the polity should clearly permit this choice, and DILs would not be applied in this sector. Carbon capture and storage, however, will not reduce the impacts of coal mining on land and water, which have been devastating; coal-mining firms have removed whole mountaintops to get at coal. Carbon capture and storage only addresses global warming, not the particulate, nitrogen oxide, and mercury emissions emanating from coal-fired power plants. By addressing each of these problems piecemeal we complicate long-term planning for industry and strain the capacity of regulators. And carbon capture will not prepare us for the day, admittedly long in the future, when coal runs out.

DILs make sense if your goals include sustainable development, long-term technological development, and efficient use of government resources devoted to addressing serious environmental problems, not just achieving a single environmental goal at the lowest possible short-term costs. They offer a far more positive economic dynamic than output-based trading, as they are far more likely to stimulate fundamental technological change than an output-based system, which accommodates, rather than fights, technological lock-in.

DILs' capacity to challenge the status quo, of course, may create political obstacles to their enactment. Leaders determined to seriously address climate change, however, may overcome these challenges. Some states, such as California, may find such a reform congenial, because they see themselves as environmental leaders. And if more Katrina-like disasters unfold, the political climate may come to favor the most effective solutions, even on the federal level. Finally, effective political leaders may find that some firms, those with substantial investments in alternatives to fossil fuels, can become their allies in seeking to effectively change the status quo.

Yet, government timidity in demanding changes that may require substantial innovation has limited our achievements under a host of environmental instruments, and this problem may well impose some limit on the scope and effectiveness of DILs as well. The next section addresses an approach specifically designed to allow private sector initiative in environmental innovation to prosper even in the face of government timidity in setting limits.

III. An Environmental Competition Statute

We have achieved a number of advances in material welfare because entrepreneurs seek to get rich by developing and introducing innovations. Examples include the cellular phone, the personal computer, and various uses of the Internet. Innovators' ability to gain market share through productive change is limited only by their imagination and capabilities in meeting potential demand. Unfortunately, the free market rarely encourages innovations improving the environment, because they usually benefit the public as a whole, rather than particular consumers paying for favorable environmental changes.

An environmental competition statute aims to stimulate a race to the top, a competition to develop and deploy environmentally superior technology. In order to stimulate this race, an environmental competition statute authorizes those producing products or services with relatively low carbon emissions to collect two fees from competitors with higher emissions. The law would require that the first fee fully compensate the lower emitting facility owner for the full cost of using and developing an environmentally superior approach. The second fee would provide a guaranteed profit for these investments. The government would establish the rate of profit in the statute, by setting a premium above the cost of achieving lower emissions. This premium would assure a reasonable profit to any producer who achieved lower emissions than a competitor on top of the basic costs recouped from that competitor. For example, if the government set a 10 percent premium and a coal-fired power plant spent a million dollars on carbon capture and storage, the owner of that plant could demand that the owner of a power plant with higher carbon dioxide emissions pay her $1,100,000, the cost incurred in lowering emissions plus the premium.

For climate change purposes, Congress (or a state legislature) could authorize all power producers with low emissions to recoup the costs they incurred in achieving these low emissions from any power plant they choose that has higher emissions, along with the government-set premium. The legislature should require emissions measurement on a tons-per-kilowatt-hour produced per year basis. Normalizing emissions by production volume will avoid a perverse problem that might otherwise arise. A small, very dirty coal-fired power plant might have lower total emissions than a clean, but very large, natural gas power plant serving many more customers if a simple mass-based metric were employed. By normalizing emissions according to production, the scheme would make sure that dirtier operators paid cleaner operators, not vice versa. This scheme implies that a solar power plant owner, which would have zero emissions, could collect her construction costs from a coal-fired power plant with high emissions.

We could apply the same approach to the automotive industry. Manufacturers achieving low carbon dioxide emissions per vehicle per mile for the entire passenger car lineup could collect a fee reflecting the full costs of improving their carbon emissions performance from whichever competitor they'd like to target.

An environmental competition statute has the potential to encourage contests to improve environmental quality comparable to the ongoing competition to realize other sorts of improvements. It aims to allow the capabilities of innovators free rein in improving environmental quality. It makes it possible for anybody reducing pollution to realize a profit from doing so. It seeks to emulate the economic dynamics of competitive markets, instead of the efficiency posited in economic modeling exercises.

The statute also creates risks for those who fail to advance and innovate, comparable to the risks faced by noninnovators in competitive markets for nonenvironmental goods and services. Just as makers of mainframe computers must adapt to the threat posed by PCs or risk losing market share, those who fail to adopt the latest environmental technology should lose money to faster-moving competition. This statute allows environmental innovators to prosper at the expense of environmental laggards, thereby allowing environmental markets to function like other competitive markets. In short, an environmental competition statute encourages competition to improve the environment.

Absent government regulation, free markets permit polluters to externalize the costs pollution creates. Exxon, for example, will not bear the full costs of global warming that its gasoline caused. The rising seas will inundate Bangladesh and, closer to home, Florida, and homeowners there will pay the costs, if they live. While Exxon externalizes its pollution costs, it must internalize (pay) all costs incurred to limit carbon emissions. Therefore, if Exxon wished to devote most its resources to developing alternative fuels, it would bear these costs itself. No wonder that markets by themselves have failed to produce significant progress on global warming, even though some companies have voluntarily improved energy efficiency—a move that usually has no net costs. An environmental competition statute permits facilities to systematically externalize pollution control costs, even significant costs, just as they now systematically externalize pollution costs—that is, the environmental and public health harms that pollution causes.

Most existing law allows the timidity of government officials to limit our environmental achievements. The law authorizes federal and state officials to limit the amount of pollution that facilities can emit. The officials administering these laws usually must take the costs environmental law might impose on our most antiquated facility owners into account in thinking about mandating environmental change. They rarely, however, actively consider the economic benefits those with newer technologies might realize from substantial positive environmental change when establishing new standards. As a result, even when modernization would generate new jobs and greatly improve the environment, government regulations only rarely demand significant changes in approach.

Government officials often feel obliged when setting standards for an entire industry to make sure that every company in an industry can meet the standards it sets. Although the law authorizes and sometimes requires regulations based on the achievements of the best performers, government officials tend to avoid aggressive regulation because of the political and legal problems that tough standards might create. Whereas in other areas competition tends to make the best performers the trend setters, in environmental law, laggards have a big influence on the quality of environmental performance.

This feeling of obligation and pressure from the judiciary leads to standards not reflecting the full capabilities industry possesses to improve environmental performance. Government officials often base their regulations on the technical capabilities of pollution-control technology. Government officials often, however, have limited knowledge of industry capabilities to improve environmental performance. As a result, they tend to demand relatively modest improvement based on well-understood technology. This has been the case, to some degree, even under statutory provisions designed to force technology.

Many policymakers associate this problem of government regulation failing to encourage substantial innovation with command-and-control regulation. But this timidity problem also limits the achievements of emissions trading programs. Emissions trading programs require, as we have seen, that government officials limit the amount of pollution that regulated facilities emit. Government officials develop these limits with the costs to old established industry of making changes very much in mind. They therefore usually make demands that do not require basic technological changes significantly improving societal welfare. So, trading has not functioned to produce the kind of wide-open competition that has enriched people with new ideas providing material benefits to consumers.

The same problem of government timidity would limit the efficacy of pollution taxes. If the traditional U.S. antipathy toward taxes abated sufficiently to allow them to be passed at all, government officials would have to choose the tax rates to apply to pollution. They would probably find it politically difficult to set rates sufficiently high to stimulate significant innovation in environmentally friendly technologies. A tax program would provide a continuous incentive to innovate, but only for a limited class of innovations, those with marginal costs less than the marginal tax rate. Taxes would not provide good incentives for important cutting-edge technologies that would require significant investments putting their marginal costs above marginal tax rates, even if such investments would lower costs and improve environmental quality in the long run.

The legislation should also forbid communication about how firms plan to respond to the environmental competition statute among competitors. Otherwise, they might agree to do nothing, thereby eliminating the incentives to compete. Absent such conspiracies, some companies with advanced environmental capabilities will likely seize the opportunity to extract payments from competitors, thereby starting the race to the top. Firms who do not view themselves as environmentally advanced may start beefing up their emission-reducing activities out of fear of becoming a target.

The legislation should also seek to minimize litigation by providing a dispute-settlement mechanism, perhaps through mandatory arbitration. Disputes may arise about who is a competitor and who has the lowest emissions. A dispute-settlement mechanism can prevent these quarrels from becoming too distracting, even though actions taken to reduce pollution in order to get transfer payments or to avoid becoming a payer of one can prove productive even if final settlement is delayed.

This approach can either address greenhouse gas emissions neglected by other schemes or supplement them. It's possible, for example, to use DILs to require as much movement away from fossil fuels as government regulators feel comfortable in requiring, while using an environmental competition statute to accelerate the innovation process to produce the newer, better, cheaper, technology that would make stricter DILs than would otherwise be plausible in the near future. Or, for that matter, one could continue with the current output-based approach and at the same time use an environmental competition statute to pave the way for stricter future limits.

Those who think that environmental law should above all make sure that we do not spend too much on pollution control will not find the environmental competition statute very congenial. It gives free rein to entrepreneurial effort to reduce emissions, but apparently does little to constrain costs. In practice, however, some cost restraint would exist. In order to be a competitor in one of these markets with a legal right to demand payment, the entrepreneur reducing emissions would also have to continue to make and sell a product. If the firm spends so much reducing carbon that it goes bankrupt or has no customers, it's not a competitor and can't collect a fee. So, a polluter cannot spend infinite amounts of money on carbon reduction under this scheme, only as much as is feasible while meeting society's needs for the goods or services produced.

Yet, this approach, by design, contains less *a priori* cost constraints than typical government-led regulation. The relative lack of restraint helps this mechanism generate the rapid improvement in environmental technology that we will need to address the daunting challenges of global warming. We are not in any imminent danger of doing too much to avoid dangerous climate change. We desperately need mechanisms that can move us beyond the slow plodding limits of government decision making through cumbersome and oft-litigated administrative law proceedings.[26]

IV. Some Concluding Thoughts about Instrument Choice

Allegiance to the neoliberal economic efficiency ideal has proven neither efficient nor efficacious. We ought not assume that measures designed to maximize short-term efficiency will maximize long-term welfare with climate change looming on the horizon. Since we have locked-in infrastructure that destabilizes the climate, the most cost-effective moves from this decidedly inefficient baseline will tend to perpetuate the lock-in. We should instead aim to create an economic dynamic that moves us away from fossil fuels to a future of much cleaner technology. Recognition of the tension between relentless pursuit of short-term cost-effectiveness and mechanisms that will produce the needed investments and experiments to produce a more sustainable future should inform U.S. climate change law, as we finally move to meet the challenge we have so long neglected.

The mechanisms introduced here—the DILs and environmental competition statutes—present some fruits of the more creative thinking that a focus on positive economic dynamics can produce. But other mechanisms also have value. Renewable portfolio standards, for example, have encouraged more use of renewable energy. Policymakers should focus hard on the question that this chapter puts front and center—what are the best mechanisms for speeding a shift away from fossil fuel use? Policymakers should employ an economic dynamic framework in answering this question and seriously consider the proposals advanced in this chapter as part of the answer. They should ask how they can create incentives for rapid technological innovation and deployment, taking into account the full range of incentives and institutional considerations that this chapter and this book highlight.

Notes

1. See generally Markin Jaenicke and Claus Jacob, "Ecological Modernization and the Creation of Lead Markets," in *Towards Environmental Innovation Systems,* ed. Matthias Weber and Jens Hemmelskamp (Berlin-Heidelberg: Springer, 2005), pp. 175–194.

2. See generally David M. Driesen, *The Economic Dynamics of Environmental Law* (Cambridge, MA: MIT Press, 2003), p. 4; F. M. Sherer, "Schumpeter and Plausible Capitalism," in *Economics of Technical Change,* ed. Edwin Mansfield and Elizabeth Mansfield (Brookfield, VT: Edward Elgar, 1993), p. 183.

3. See, e.g., Francesco Ricci, "Environmental Policy and Growth When Inputs Are Differentiated in Pollution Intensity," *Environmental and Resource Economics* 38 (2007): 297–298.

4. Margaret R. Taylor, Edward L. Rubin, and David A. Hounshell, "Regulation as the Mother of Invention: The Case of SO_2 Control," *Law and Policy* 27 (2005): 348–378.

5. Patrick Matschoss and Heinz Welsch, "International Emissions Trading and Induced Carbon-Saving Technological Change: Effects of Restricting the Trade in Carbon Rights," *Environmental and Resource Economics* 33 (2006): 172; Richard G. Newell, Adam B. Jaffe, and Robert N. Stavins, "The Induced Innovation Hypothesis and Energy Saving Technological Change," *Quarterly Journal of Economics* 114 (1999): 941–975.

6. Taylor, Rubin, and Hounshell, "Regulation as the Mother of Invention."

7. See Taylor, Rubin, and Hounshell, "Regulation as the Mother of Invention"; David M. Driesen, "Is Emissions Trading an Economic Incentive Program: Beyond the Command and Control/Economic Incentive Dichotomy," *Washing-*

ton and Lee Law Review 55 (1998): 289–350; David M. Driesen, "Does Emissions Trading Encourage Innovation?" *Environmental Law Reporter* 33 (2003): 10106; David Wallace, *Environmental Policy and Industrial Innovation: Strategies in Europe, the USA, and Japan* (London: Royal Institute of International Affairs, Energy and Environmental Programme, 1995), p. 20; Nicholas A. Ashford, Christine Ayers, and Robert F. Stone, "Using Regulation to Change the Market for Innovation," *Harvard Environmental Law Review* 9 (1985): 419–466, 440–441; Nicholas A. Ashford and George R. Heaton, "Regulation and Technological Innovation in the Chemical Industry," *Law and Contemporary Problems* 46, no. 3 (1983): 109–157, 139–140.

8. See David M. Driesen, "Sustainable Development and Market Liberalism's Shotgun Wedding: Emissions Trading Under the Kyoto Protocol," *Indiana Law Journal* 83 (2008): 21–69.

9. California Environmental Protection Agency, Air Resources Board, *Staff Report: Initial Statement of Reasons for Proposed Rulemaking*, Public Hearing to Consider Adoption of Regulations to Control Greenhouse Gas Emissions from Motor Vehicles (2004), p. vii (prohibiting use of credits from nonvehicle measures or for measures outside of California to avoid diluting carbon reduction regulations' technology-forcing effect).

10. See, e.g., Adam B. Jaffe, Richard G. Newell, and Robert N. Stavins, "Environmental Policy and Technological Change," *Environment and Resource Economics* 22 (2002): 51.

11. David A. Malueg, "Emissions Credit Trading and the Incentive to Adopt New Pollution Abatement Technology," *Journal of Environmental Economics and Management* 16 (1987): 52–57.

12. Axel Michaelowa and Sonja Butzengeiger, "EU Emissions Trading: Navigating between Scylla and Charybdis," *Climate Policy* 5 (2005): 3; Jeffrey Greenblatt et al., "Baseload Wind Energy: Modeling the Competition Between Gas Turbines and Compressed Air Energy Storage for Supplemental Generation," *Energy Policy* 35 (2007): 1474 (attributing a 30 percent annual increase in installed wind capacity to a "twofold drop in capital costs between 1992 and 2001" and "government initiatives"); Commission of the European Communities, *The Share of Renewable Energy in the EU: Commission Report in Accordance with Article 3 of Directive 2001/77/EC, Evaluation of the Effect of Legislative Instruments and Other Community Policies on the Development of the Contribution of Renewable Energy Resources in the EU and Proposals for Concrete Actions* (Brussels: 2004), p. 12; see also, e.g., "Sunlit Uplands: Wind and Solar Power Are Flourishing, Thanks to Subsidies," *Economist*, June 2, 2007.

13. Brett M. Frischman and Mark A. Lemley, "Spillovers," *Columbia Law Review* 107 (2007): 257–301, 258–261; Gregory N. Mandel, "Promoting Environmental Innovation and Intellectual Property Innovation: A New Basis for Patent Rewards," *Temple Journal of Science, Technology, and Environmental Law* 24 (2005): 51–69, 56 (explaining that if a person "builds a better mousetrap," others may copy it); Richard A. Posner, *Catastrophe: Risk and Response* (New York: Oxford University Press, 2004), 123–124.

14. Daniel A. Lashof and Dilip R. Ahuja, "Relative Contributions of Greenhouse Gas Emissions to Global Warming," *Nature* 344 (April 5, 1990): 529–531; see also H.-Holger Rogner et al., "Introduction," in Intergovernmental Panel on Climate Change (IPCC), *Climate Change 2007: Mitigation of Climate Change*, Contribution of Working Group III to the Fourth Assessment Report of the Intergovernmental Panel on Climate Change, ed. Bert Metz et al. (Cambridge: Cambridge University Press, 2007), pp. 102–103.

15. See, e.g., Bert Metz and Detlef van Vuuren, "How, and at What Costs, Can Low-Level Stabilization be Achieved?—An Overview," in *Avoiding Dangerous Climate Change,* ed. Hans Joachim Schellnhuber (Cambridge: Cambridge University Press, 2006), pp. 337–345; Ken Caldeira, Atul K. Jain, and Martin I. Hoffert, "Climate Sensitivity Uncertainty and the Need for Energy without CO_2 Emission," *Science* 299 (March 28, 2003): 2052–2054; Daniel P. Schrag, "Confronting the Climate-Energy Challenge," *Elements* 3 (June 2007): 171–178.

16. See Schrag, "Confronting the Climate-Energy Challenge"; James Hansen et al., "Dangerous Human-Made Interference with Climate: A GISS ModelE Study," *Atmospheric Chemistry and Physics* 7 (2007): 2287–2312; Martin I. Hoffert et al., "Advanced Technology Paths to Global Climate Stability: Energy for a Greenhouse Planet," *Science* 298 (November 1, 2002): 981–987.

17. Michel den Elzen and Malte Meinshausen, "Multi-Gas Emission Pathways for Meeting the EU 2°C Climate Target," in *Avoiding Dangerous Climate Change*, ed. Hans Joachim Schellnhuber et al. (New York: Cambridge University Press, 2006), pp. 299–309.

18. Ibid.

19. See, e.g., Robert R. Nordhaus and Kyle W. Danish, "Assessing the Options for Designing a Mandatory U.S. Greenhouse Gas Reduction Program," *Boston College Environmental Affairs Law Review* 32 (2005): 97–163; Robert N. Stavins, *Policy Instruments for Climate Change: How Can National Governments Address a Global Problem?* (Washington, D.C.: Resources for the Future, January 1997).

20. See David M. Driesen and Amy Sinden, "The Missing Instrument: Dirty Input Limits," *Harvard Environmental Law Review*, 22 (2009): 65–116.

21. Ibid.

22. See David M. Driesen, "Is Emissions Trading an Economic Incentive Program? Replacing the Command and Control/Economic Incentive Dichotomy," *Washington and Lee Law Review* 55 (1998): 289–350, 316–317 and n. 131.

23. Edward A. Parson, *Protecting the Ozone Layer: Science and Strategy* (Oxford: Oxford University Press, 2003), p. 9.

24. Ibid., pp. 40, 183–191.

25. Center for Clean Air Policy, "U.S. Carbon Emissions Trading: Description of an Upstream Approach" (1998), p. 6, http://www.ccap.org.

26. See generally Thomas O. McGarity, "Some Thoughts on 'Deossifying' the Rule-Making Process," *Duke Law Journal* 41 (1992): 1385–1462.

13

Adaptation, Economics, and Justice

Robert R. M. Verchick

International efforts to combat the threat of global warming correctly emphasize greenhouse gas reduction. But for developing countries, whose communities could be wiped out by one sustained drought or misplaced hurricane, the long road to abatement is not enough. Developing countries must begin *adapting* to climate change—now. The poorest and most vulnerable nations, however, lack resources to erect the dams, levees, insurance markets, and health clinics that adaptation requires. Northern industrialized countries' efforts to aid southern countries' adaptation have been meager at best. Although the North recognizes a utilitarian argument for engaging the developing world in emissions reductions, it lacks a compelling rationale for helping the South survive the climate threats we cannot stop. We are like Phoebe in the television show *Friends*, who, when asked by a neighbor to help move furniture, replies, "I wish I could, but I don't want to."

But just wishing we could help is not enough. This chapter argues that although we in the North are not yet serious about helping our neighbors to the South, we should be. Our focus on narrow, short-range market interests has distracted us from an opportunity to act justly and thereby engage the developing world in reducing greenhouse gases (GHGs) for the benefit of all. Global warming is, to quote the *Stern Review*, "the biggest market failure in the world."[1] But the problem goes far beyond market failure. Global warming is also about inequality—inequality based on wealth, race, geographic location, and geopolitical power. Understanding this inequality is the key to understanding the moral and practical justifications for an aggressive effort to aid developing countries in adaptation efforts and helps us to imagine what a successful worldwide adaptation program might look like.

This chapter has four parts. The first part briefly revisits predictions about the effects of climate change, with an emphasis on global inequality and the need for adaptive measures. The second part shows why the United Nations' and the United States' efforts to enhance global adaptation efforts have been insufficient. Their initiatives fall short, in large part, because they are based on a neoliberal model of problem solving, which blinds global leaders to higher moral obligations and to more practical strategies for international cooperation. Part III calls for a stronger moral foundation for adaptation aid, which market economics cannot provide. Part IV offers a moral justification for adaptation aid. Drawing from international relations literature on fairness and trust, this section finds both philosophical and practical reasons for supporting a moral view beyond what the market perspective alone can justify. Based on that discussion, the section then begins to speculate about what a "serious" global adaptation initiative might look like.

Before moving on, I should define two terms, *mitigation* and *adaptation*. *Mitigation* refers to actions taken either to reduce GHG emissions or to enhance the sequestration of such gases in "carbon sinks." Mitigation includes energy conservation, use of renewable energy, forest enhancement, and carbon capture and storage.

Adaptation refers to the responses a society takes to better *cope with* or *adjust to* climate change impacts. Such responses include building a seawall, restoring a barrier island, or improving the regional insurance system. Some initiatives, like better zoning near shore, address dangers of "exposure." Others, like malaria prevention and micro-lending programs, seek to reduce *vulnerability* and enhance societal *resilience*. As one example of the term's breadth, the U.N. Development Programme catalogs global adaptation programs under headings like "Agriculture/Food security," "Public Health," "Disaster Risk Management," and "Coastal Zone Management."[2]

According to the Intergovernmental Panel on Climate Change (IPCC), adaptation by itself will never be enough to cope with all climate change effects, particularly the loss of biodiversity and the disintegration of ice sheets and glaciers.[3] The effectiveness of any given strategy is highly particularized and will depend on geographic risk, the social capital of the community involved, and political and financial constraints. No one knows what "full" adaptation would even cost. Estimating the cost of an effective levee system—as residents of New Orleans are now finding—is hard enough. How do you predict the cost of agricultural reform in drought-prone Africa? Or the relocation of millions of people in Bangladesh? In one of the few estimates available, the World Bank speculates that it would cost $10 billion to $40 billion annually for the world to substantially adapt to climate change.[4] When you consider that the cost of restoring Louisiana's coast, alone, might cost $1 billion annually over the next thirty years, this estimate seems low.

I. Mapping Vulnerability

In chapter 1, Christopher Schroeder and Robert L. Glicksman show that climate change threatens the basic elements of human welfare across the globe.[5] But the predicted exposure of societies to such damage is not uniform. Countries in tropical areas are more likely to be hit harder. Tropical nations already endure climatic disturbances like cyclones, monsoons, and the El Niño and El Niña cycles. There is persuasive evidence that global warming could extend or intensify these events.[6] Agricultural productivity in the tropics has always presented special geographic challenges, a fact that has contributed to overall slower economic growth. Such challenges include extreme weather, poorer soils, the presence of pests, and higher crop respiration rates. Climate change will augment these problems. In the blunt words of the *Stern Review*: "Climate change will have a disproportionately damaging impact on developing countries due in part at least, to their location in low latitudes, the amount and variability of rainfall they receive, and the fact that they are already too hot."[7]

As the 2004 Asian tsunami demonstrated, people in the developing world are least able to cope with sudden disasters when they do occur because of substandard infrastructure, poor emergency response, and insufficient medical services. Indeed, deaths from natural disaster are generally linked to a nation's economic welfare and its degree of income inequality.[8] Developing countries will also show greater sensitivity to climate change because of their economic reliance on agriculture and fragile ecosystems. In sub-Saharan Africa, for instance, 64 percent of people are employed in the rural farming sector.[9] The percentage is nearly the same in South Asia.[10] People in developing countries also rely more heavily on subsistence goods and services drawn from the environment, such as fish, vegetables, firewood, fiber, and drinking water.

In developing countries, climate victims will be mainly people of color. A large share will be infants and children, elderly people, and the disabled.[11] This means more work for women and girls, who generally care for the children, the elderly, and the infirm.[12] Women and girls, who in many cultures also grow the food and collect the water, will also find these chores consuming more of their time, leaving less time for education and vocational training.[13] By pushing girls out of school, climate change is expected to increase female illiteracy.[14]

Wealthy countries, like the United States, Japan, and the original members of the European Union, will also face serious climate-related problems, including sea-level rise and more intense droughts and storms. In the United States, state governments and private research centers have begun documenting a troubling array of climate-induced harms expected in California, the Pacific Northwest, and the Northeast. As Hurricane Katrina demonstrated in 2005, the effects of climate disaster, even in a rich country, will most seriously harm a society's most vulnerable—the children, the elderly, the poor, and the infirm.[15]

II.   Current Efforts to Address Adaptation

A.   International Efforts
The U.N. Framework Convention on Climate Change (UNFCCC) acknowledged the need for adaptation strategies from the very beginning, although it was short on details. Article IV, for instance, requires parties to "cooperate in preparing for adaptation to the impacts of climate change."[16] Article III urges parties to expand development assistance to foster "sustainable economic growth and development in . . . developing country Parties, thus enabling them better to address the problems of climate change."[17]

Convention parties have since created four programs to promote adaptation. Two specifically target the poorest countries. The Least Developed Countries Fund (LDC Fund) assists needy countries in preparing National Adaptation Programmes of Action (NAPAs), reports that identify actions and priorities important to adaptation efforts. A second fund, the Adaptation Fund, will provide more significant funding for projects in poor countries. This program, which comes online in 2010, is partially funded by the sales of certified emissions reduction units to richer countries. Two other programs are nominally open to all member nations. One, the Strategic Priority on Adaptation (SPA) fund, supports projects that enhance vulnerable ecosystems and produce "global environmental benefits."[18] The other, the Special Climate Change Fund (SCC Fund) supports adaptation, disaster-risk management, coastal zone planning, and other long-range activities.

The programs are nothing if not ecumenical. There is something for nations with globally important eco-assets and for those scraping by on almost nothing. Some, like the LDC Fund and the SCC Fund, focus on institutional and developmental needs; others, like the SPA fund, want to see change in the physical landscape. All suggest that need and geographic diversity are important. But however broad in scope, the UNFCCC's funding programs are, at this point at least, just a drop in a very big bucket. All programs require the recipient nation to share costs, sometimes on a fifty–fifty basis, as a means of demonstrating local commitment. And while the U.N. optimistically puts the total cost of climate adaptation at "tens of billions of dollars," the sum of all UNFCCC adaptation funds now pledged tops out at a few hundred million dollars.[19]

These arrangements will be eagerly debated as the international community negotiates a successor agreement to the Kyoto Protocol, which expires in 2012. As this book goes to press, the UNFCCC is hoping to lay the groundwork for such an agreement at the fifteenth Conference of the Parties, to be held in Copenhagen, Denmark, in December 2009. At that meeting, and those that follow, the question of binding emissions reductions for large developing countries will take center stage. And as nations like India and China have made clear, those commitments will be tied directly to the willingness of richer nations to help poorer ones implement green technology and adapt to a more volatile climate.

B. National and Local Efforts

In the United States, federal adaptation policy makes for short discussion. The American Bar Association's 2007 book on American climate change policy—which is nearly 800 pages long—covers adaptation in two pages, with room for photos.[20] The climate change legislation proposed in 2009, while historic, deals mainly with mitigation (by way of a cap-and-trade system) and is relatively vague on adaptation. On the international side, U.S. behavior has obstructed multinational adaptation efforts more than it has helped, although this may change as President Barack Obama's climate agenda advances. The U.S. decision to quit Kyoto under the second Bush administration pulled at an already sensitive rift between North and South that to this day threatens cooperation on issues of mitigation and adaptation. To its credit, the United States does contribute to UNFCCC adaptation funds. Over the last decade, it has pledged hundreds of millions of dollars to the Global Environmental Facility (GEF), which in addition to other development initiatives, manages the UNFCCC's LDC and SPC funds.[21]

Yet the United States has been criticized recently for trying to push the GEF away from a need-based allocation system in favor of a "performance-based" system, which would reward countries judged to be political, economic, and environmental reformers, while withholding aid from those that are not.[22]At the 2004 Conference of the Parties in Buenos Aires—the so-called Adaptation COP—the United States fiercely resisted an adaptation plan offered by Argentina, though the plan eventually passed. Also in Buenos Aires, the United States raised hackles when it supported Saudi Arabia's plea that adaptation funds be made available to oil-producing nations whose economies would be harmed by green technologies.[23] That proposal temporarily derailed negotiations at the Adaptation COP, although such aid has since been incorporated into the Special Climate Change Fund.

On the domestic side, U.S. adaptation efforts lag significantly behind those of other countries. Unlike Great Britain, for instance, whose ambitious Climate Impacts Program establishes new construction guidelines and aids communities in future planning, the U.S. federal government has no national adaptation policy and no apparent plans to develop one. Some federal agencies have begun to factor climate change into their projects. One of the most dramatic examples concerns the rebuilding of New Orleans after Hurricane Katrina. Having acknowledged serious flaws in the construction and design of the federal levee system, the U.S. Army Corps of Engineers is now combining stricter design standards with state-of-the-art computer models that aim to project the effects of global warming on storm surge, storm frequency, and sea-level rise. The Corps's long-term efforts to restore Louisiana's endangered coastal wetlands (some of the most productive in the world) will similarly include ongoing assessments of climate change effects.

States and cities are also stepping up to the plate. In 1988, Maine began incorporating projections of sea-level rise due to climate change into some of its coastal building codes.[24] City building codes in New Orleans, informed by federal flood maps, now also incorporate the effects of climate change. California, a domestic leader in climate change efforts, has launched a major initiative to study the state's vulnerability to drier weather, shrinking aquifers, and rising tides.[25] States like Washington and New York have begun similar efforts. Yet, such efforts still trail behind those of many European cities and Canadian provinces.[26]

III. Adaptation and Economics

There are several reasons for the North's slow response to global adaptation needs and for the United States' nearly defiant neglect. Automakers, Big Oil, and the coal industry have all helped subdue public calls for more aggressive climate policy nationally and internationally. President George W. Bush's distrust of climate science and sometimes abrasive style also stymied progress on this topic. (President Obama has promised a more diplomatic and science-friendly approach.)

But another barrier to adaptation policy concerns free-market orthodoxy, or what David M. Driesen in the introduction to this volume calls "the neoliberal model."[27] Recall some of the characteristics that Driesen associates with neoliberalism. It is an approach that favors market-based solutions and distrusts government-based ones. It measures desirable outcomes in terms of "objective" indicators of combined social wealth, without formal concern for less measurable values like distributional fairness or restorative justice. In addition, we might add that neoliberalism promotes an ethic—some would say "virtue"—of self-sufficiency and the stoic acceptance of unfortunate consequences. That is, individuals are expected to assume the risk of participating in the market and to adapt to changing landscapes.

Market fundamentalism of this kind sets a poor foundation for adaptation policy. There are simply too many diverse places facing too much risk with too little cash to solve this problem through "self-sufficiency" and "market forces" alone. The UNFCCC's four adaptation programs seem, at first glance, to move beyond the neoliberal approach. The LDC and Adaptation Funds, for instance, target "need" rather than "economic value." And all four funds seek geographic and other forms of diversity that could not be justified with market values alone. But elsewhere market thinking is creeping back in, as in the UNFCCC's matching funds requirements and U.S. efforts to introduce performance-based allocations into the GEF fund. In addition, some economists are urging policymakers to approach adaptation in terms of more generalized aid, as a way of maximizing social welfare and avoiding government intrusion. These influences could weaken future adaptation programs.

A. Matching Funds

Since neoliberalism relies on an individualist model, its stance toward adaptation tends to rely as heavily as possible on "self-reliance." This notion leads to demands that nations receiving development aid agree to pay a portion of the costs. The idea is not unreasonable. Matching creates an incentive for the host country to implement the program efficiently and responsibly. In particular, holding the beneficiary at least partly responsible for cost may reduce wasteful pork-barrel politics (rent-seeking) and locals' overreliance on foreign bailouts (moral hazard).

But a system too dependent on matching grants distorts aid distribution and can significantly slow it down. It can distort aid distribution by making it impossible for the societies most vulnerable to climate change to get aid, since they cannot pay a significant share of the costs. It can significantly slow down aid because of the political difficulty of negotiating cost-sharing arrangements. Some domestic examples make the point. After Hurricane Andrew devastated the Florida coast in 1992, the White House immediately waived the traditional 10 percent matching funds requirement for federal assistance out of recognition that the recovery would otherwise be delayed. (The requirement was again waived for New York City following the events of 9/11.) But after Hurricane Katrina and subsequent levee failures flooded 80 percent of New Orleans, the White House enforced the requirement for more than a year before finally giving in, a delay that significantly slowed rebuilding efforts in the city.

At the very least, matching funds must be set at affordable levels, which take into account a country's available resources. It may be that the affordable level is not enough to combat rent-seeking or moral hazard. If that is so, other means must be devised to address those issues, without endangering the poor. A second point is that matching funds make the most sense where their use will lead recipients to make better choices. Requiring matching funds for projects that donors have already chosen is less justifiable. This issue will resurface in the next section when I discuss fairness and a recent controversy over who should pay for the South's mandatory NAPA reports.

B. Performance-Based Allocations

The United States' attempt to steer SCC and LDC funds toward "performance-based" allocations is generally viewed by both supporters and critics as a way to promote more liberalized trade. In fact, the United States' GEF proposal closely resembles the second Bush administration's Millennium Challenge Account, which was developed around the same time. This "performance-based" fund provides development aid on the basis of national indicators intended to measure a country's commitment to good government, citizen welfare, and "economic freedom," the last being an umbrella phrase intended to imply open markets, sparse regulation, and other neoliberal values.

The tendency to use it to promote economic orthodoxy can be damaging. Development programs associated with the World Bank and International Monetary Fund, for instance, are often criticized for their tendency to favor development projects that increase the production and exports of needy countries but degrade essential cultural and environmental resources. Performance-based assistance programs, like the Millennium Challenge Account or the U.S. proposal for GEF allocation, raise questions about a donor county's commitment to helping people in immediate need. Such programs also drive a wedge between countries favored with aid and those that are not. As one German representative to the GEF explained in his opposition to the U.S. position, "To implement a GEF funded project according to *national* indicators would be to undermine the unique global character of the GEF. To forsake a project just because the host country is a bad economic or political performer could affect the whole [of] mankind in a negative manner."[28]

C. Competing Strategies

In addition to the UNFCCC funds, there is a growing discussion about the use of general development programs as a means of enhancing adaptive capacity. Recall that poor people, because they lack basics like medical care and safe shelter, are much more likely to suffer from environmental disaster than rich people. Economists Gary Yohe and Richard Tol estimate that "for every percent of economic growth [in a country] vulnerability falls by a percent."[29] For this reason, many have begun to follow the lead of economist and Nobel laureate Douglass North, who contends that general and targeted development aid to poor countries should be the highest priority in international adaptation policy.[30] The Copenhagen Consensus Center, an economics-based think tank in which North participates, goes even further. In a highly publicized report, the group suggested that liberalizing trade was more important than responding to global warming at all, whether through mitigation or adaptation.[31] Such prescriptions are appealing to a market view because they minimize governmental involvement (which neoliberals distrust) and purport to maximize social utility.

But as international leaders ponder the next stage of adaptation policy, it would be a mistake to substitute either aid or trade for a comprehensive adaptation strategy. Sure, prosperity is good. But general advancement does not necessarily serve the same constituency as more tailored adaptation programs. The millions of farmers in flood-prone deltas or African dustbowls need lifesaving infrastructure *now*, in the form of dikes, reservoirs, insurance networks, and other projects. Development aid, nearly by design, has a longer time line. In a generation, such aid might deliver farmers from the delta to cities with working sewage systems and better jobs. But meanwhile the next monsoon season is already on its way. As for more liberalized trade, it is true that pulling down trade barriers will lead to larger aggregate growth. But the benefits and costs of globalization have always been unevenly distributed. Even with today's relatively free markets, just 6 percent of foreign investment goes to Africa, while the 47 poorest countries receive only 2 percent.[32]

From a market-based perspective, these distributional differences do not matter so much. Because neoliberalism focuses on combined social welfare, an aggregate rise in wealth is a success regardless of which rice farmers are helped in what poor country. But to those with a more holistic view, distribution matters very much. If one of the goals of adaptation policy is to help people in the South whose lives are endangered by energy policies of the North, the proposals of aid and trade fall short. In addition to these arguments, there is one last objection to using general aid as a substitute for a more ambitious adaptation policy. The idea dangerously confuses the concepts of charity and justice, a topic considered more fully in the next section.

IV. Adaptation and Justice

Over two centuries ago, early feminist Mary Wollstonecraft roared, "it is justice, not charity, that is wanting in the world!"[33] While everyone recognizes that the world's response to climate change must effectively target adaptation (along with mitigation), the world has tended to view adaptation funding as a charity, rather than a requirement of justice. Wealthy nations—looking through a neoliberal lens—do not see global adaptation as an urgent need or at least do not see it as benefiting them in any important economic way, and so tend to treat it like an inefficient charity. Thus they underfund it. Viewing adaptation funding as a moral obligation grounded in justice principles would lead to a more robust response to the global adaptation needs. We need a broader sense of national purpose anchored in a theory of global justice. The move from "charity" to "justice" requires a reframing of the issues. Charity is what a Samaritan does when she feels sorry for you and wants to help. Justice is what a society owes to you because of your membership in a shared community.

Justice is important for both philosophical and practical reasons. In many philosophical traditions, the point of identifying shared ethical values is to bring people and societies together. This end is inherently good, as it fulfills an innate human need to connect to others, to care for others, and to be cared for. On the practical side, justice promotes altruism, reciprocity, and cooperation. All of these things promote community and enable long-term survival. To ground an adaptation strategy in something more durable than market preference will require a commitment to a model of justice that appeals both to philosophical principles and realistic concerns. In the remainder of this chapter, I hope to start a discussion about an appropriate model of justice to guide adaptation policy.

A. Justice for Philosophers

Adaptation strategy should begin with the moral commitment that society owes to the least advantaged. In political theory the idea is perhaps best expressed as a version of distributive justice, made famous by philosopher John Rawls in his pathbreaking *A Theory of Justice*. Seeking a standard of wealth distribution among members of a single society, Rawls imagined how members would define their interests at the formation of a hypothetical "social contract." He concluded that members of this new society, if shorn of information about their eventual "class position or social status,"[34] would choose distributional principles that maximize the position of the persons least well off.

Years later, in *The Law of Peoples*, Rawls modified the theory to apply it to distributions of wealth among societies. There, Rawls declined to extend his earlier rule in full, but instead argued that privileged societies have the duty to aid their poorer neighbors at least up to the point that their neighbors can "manage their own affairs reasonably and rationally and eventually . . . become members of the Society of well-ordered Peoples."[35] Once the target is reached, "further assistance is not required, even though the now well-ordered society may still be relatively poor."[36] Significantly, redistributions of wealth may be unequal (the poorest get more). For Rawls, the principles of allocation are based in a theory of international community.

Rawls's views are concerned with a strand of theory called *distributional justice*. But it is also possible to justify aid to the world's poor in terms of *compensatory justice*, which addresses how those inflicting harm should compensate those that they injure. Under this theory, LDCs would argue that their need for adaptation aid arises from historical injury visited on them by their more industrialized neighbors.

There is truth in this charge. Recent empirical studies using materials-flow analysis show that natural capital in southern countries is sacrificed to feed consumption in the North. Pointing to such analyses, economists J. Timmons Roberts and Bradley Parks argue that "from both an import and export perspective . . . core economies are draining ecological capacity from extractive regions by importing resource-intensive products and have shifted their environmental burdens to the South through the export of waste."[37] As but one example, they note that the original fifteen EU nations import, in *physical terms*, more than *four times* what they export; but that the *money value* of what they export is *four times* that of what they import.[38] This unequal exchange of natural capital, what some call "environmental imperialism," is fueling enormous resentment among developing countries and has become a significant stumbling block in climate negotiations.

B. Justice for Realists

When put into practice, a sound theory of justice leads to practical improvements in individual and political life. Justice helps define human goals and adds muscle to flabby social policies. In times of crisis—a war, natural disaster, or social upheaval—a commitment to justice can unite those with shared interests and stiffen resolve. Today the world faces a series of existential red alerts, from global warming, to nuclear proliferation, to Islamist jihad. The challenges are too broad for any regional bloc or even hemisphere to address. They require cooperation among nations in the North and South.

There are many ways to encourage poor countries to join industrialized countries in efforts to address important global problems. The use of "soft" power through the practice of justice is one important element. Sometimes powerful countries enlist other countries into global initiatives through moral suasion and "leading by example." Since World War II, such strategies were significant to human rights initiatives, including the official rejection of torture by most thoughtful nations; the importance of setting a just example explains the alarm expressed by many Americans upon hearing reports of abusive CIA interrogation tactics under the second Bush administration. Nations also attempt to encourage cooperation among nations through trade and aid programs. The strategy can be successful if targeted correctly. One could imagine encouraging nations like Indonesia or Brazil to participate in mitigation efforts in return for, say, adaptation aid. The philosopher will object that aid, if already justly deserved, should not be conditioned on future acts. But such carrot-dangling is nearly inevitable in real-world politics. It may be defended on pragmatic grounds *if* such policies produce a significant net benefit for receiving countries and *if* local governments and civil society are included in the development of those policies.

A sometimes overlooked benefit of practicing justice is the fostering of community through trust. Today the bonds of trust between rich and poor nations are badly frayed. A significant reason is that the South believes the North has built its flashy culture and plus-sized economy on the backs of equatorial peoples. Half a millennium ago, the North enriched itself by stealing the South's labor and natural resources. Today it has stolen the climate and shows comparatively little concern for tropical and subtropical nations left to resist rising tides and sun-baked fields.

Thus, in the second televised presidential debate in 2000, then-candidate George W. Bush had this to say about what he would do in response to climate change: "I'll tell you one thing I'm not going to do is I'm not going to let the United States carry the burden of cleaning up the world's air, like the Kyoto treaty would have done. China and India were exempted from that treaty. I think we need to be more even-handed." Year's earlier, Bush's father, George H. W. Bush, had caused considerable stir at the Rio Earth Summit when, as president, he expressed a similar skepticism for targets and timetables by insisting that "the American lifestyle is not open to negotiation."[39]

These statements reveal important points about fairness and community, respectively. George W. Bush's concern for an "even-handed" approach suggests a theory of justice based on straight egalitarianism, without regard to a nation's resources or culpability. His father's refusal to consider any concession that might threaten "the American lifestyle" suggests that fairness has its limits. Specifically, the elder President Bush appeared to suggest that these needier nations lay *outside* the community to which the United States owes much responsibility. He thus appeared to question the very existence of a Rawlsian social contract among nations.

But the elder Bush, a veteran of World War II, surely understood the necessity of a social contract among today's nation-states. Even neoliberals, riding on the comet's tail of globalization, promote the role of institutional togetherness through the World Trade Organization, the World Bank, the European Union, and other entities. Even President George W. Bush, typically seen as a go-it-alone president, speaks persuasively for a world committed to global security, where countries fight terrorism not only for their own national security but for the national security of others.

Climate change is likewise a serious threat to global security that requires extraordinary cooperation among nations. Everyone agrees that stabilizing GHG emissions cannot happen without help from the largest developing countries. Even if the North were capable of completely adapting to climate change (a goal it could never approach), it would still be wise to attend to the South. As a U.N. development report noted earlier this decade, "In the global village, someone else's poverty very soon becomes one's own problem: of lack of markets for one's products, illegal immigration, pollution, contagious disease, insecurity, fanaticism, terrorism."[40]

It is tempting to hope that enlightened self-interest will push poor countries to enlist in the struggle to mitigate GHGs and join regional adaptation efforts with neighboring countries. But the scenario is unlikely due to lack of trust. A less powerful actor can rationally justify a refusal to join a mutually beneficial campaign if it perceives its partners as untrustworthy. In this case, the South's lack of confidence rests in a deep-seated resentment over what the South views as injustices perpetrated by the North. These perceived wrongs include experience with colonialism, inequalities in resource exchange, and climate injustice.

To illustrate how neoliberal values can hamper trust and cooperation, Roberts and Parks point to the 2004 COP-10 meeting in Buenos Aires in which the issue of "matching funds" for required national adaptation plans threw the climate negotiations into a tailspin. After noting that adaptation plans for the forty-eight LDCs could have all been fully financed for $11 million—which was *less* than the amount already on hand for such purposes—the authors express disbelief at some Western countries insistence on matching funds. The money at stake, they write,

was a pittance compared with the cost of having developing countries believe that the developed countries are indifferent to their circumstances. Issues like this could provide opportunities to build social capital that underpins long-term cooperation, but in the hands of short-sighted negotiators following hard-line mandates ... events like this can just as easily drive a downward spiral of distrust.[41]

The upshot, of course, is that LDCs are still required to contribute to adaptation plans, beyond their reasonable ability to pay, simply to indicate "buy in." Situations like these suggest the need for a kind of targeted magnanimity, in which wealthier nations set the foundation for long-term cooperation by viewing their poorer neighbors, not as Hobbesian brutes, but as members of a moral community in which *no one* succeeds without mutual trust. We in the developed world can no longer afford to sweat the small stuff.

In short, anyone thinking that climate risk, alone, will lead poor, populous countries to negotiate GHG reductions had better think again. "No matter how important a nation is ecologically or how vulnerable it currently is," write Roberts and Parks, "other factors tend to lead to adoption of environmental treaties."[42] Those "other factors," which include democratic structures and meaningful foreign assistance, challenge the current U.S. approach, which underfunds initiatives and rhetorically appeals to "even-handedness." Overtures to the developing world may someday have strings attached. But a successful approach must also acknowledge the moral dimension of the global warming debate. This will mean moving away from some market-based ideas like "the beneficiary pays" or "most bang for the buck," and toward agreements favoring aid to "the least advantaged" or the "least culpable."

C. A Marshall Plan for the South?

Climate change now demands an unprecedented political and economic commitment. It suggests the need for a kind of twenty-first-century Marshall Plan. Economist Thomas Schelling has thoughtfully argued that global reductions of GHG emissions require strategies reminiscent of the United States' successful effort to revive war-torn Europe.[43] But perhaps the more compelling application is to *adaptation* rather than mitigation.

As in the era following World War II, we face a group of nations that have an aching need for technical and economic assistance. Their plight is not the result of war but of another destructive force that, though less direct, threatens to erode the economic, political, and cultural stability of billions of people. The moral imperative is there. To stand by while a generation of innocents slips into chaos cannot be justified. Similarly, the rehabilitation and protection of this vulnerable community is essential for the long-term political and economic stability of the rest of the world.

What would a "serious" adaptation program, patterned after the Marshall Plan, look like? For starters it would be bold and well funded. The Marshall Plan, begun in 1947 and bankrolled by the United States, eventually distributed more than $12 billion in technical and economic assistance to nearly twenty European countries.[44] A serious adaptation plan must over the course of a decade be expected to distribute tens of billions of dollars to perhaps fifty of the neediest countries. Like the Marshall Plan, a serious adaptation plan would go for the deep pockets. In 1947, the United States correctly understood that although it had not caused the war, its booming economy had put it in a unique position to help dress the wounds. It also understood that European markets and political stability were an important part of the national interest. Today OECD nations are similarly in a position of enormous comparative wealth and have a compelling interest in global environmental, economic, and political stability. In addition, they have all profited immensely from the carbon economy and thus should be expected to contribute to global adaptation efforts.

Like the Marshall Plan, a serious adaptation program would focus on allocating funds quickly. In the first years of the Marshall Plan, the U.S. government did not bother with highly uncertain cost-benefit surveys. Indeed, in the latter years of the program, the United States required receiving nations, themselves, to allocate U.S. funds, which they eventually did with the help of arbitration. (As it turns out, the final allocation of Marshall Plan funds roughly tracked a per capita distribution pattern.) Adaptation funds should not be allocated this loosely, but should ideally target need and population base, while including a strong role for participants in major allocation decisions.

Unlike the Marshall Plan, which focused only on Europe and excluded Japan and Hong Kong, a new adaptation fund would be geographically diverse and focus primarily on need. Targeting the fifty poorest nations would be a good start. A serious adaptation plan would emphasize physical infrastructure and a more precise targeting of programs to make sure that money reached the most needy people within countries. In this way, the adaptation program would differ from the Marshall Plan, which was more concerned with developing trade and consumer markets than it was with promoting environmentally sustainable economies.

The details will require a balance between the philosophical and realist notions of global justice. The philosophical side argues for aid with few conditions, premised either on one's membership in the global community or on one's subjection to unjust harm. The side of the realist is concerned not only with justice as an *end*, but also with justice as a *means*—in this case, a means toward cooperative efforts to fight climate change. This suggests the eventual need for development assistance with real strings attached in order to nudge countries like India, China, and Brazil toward serious mitigation and adaptation efforts.

The ideal adaptation plan would include a mix of methodologies. But the overriding goal would be to build trust between North and South. Industrial countries must promote policies that show concern for the real threats now facing developing countries. In the beginning, this may mean transfers of need-based aid without concern for political or economic policies. Eventually, aid must be tied to reform; but those reforms should be targeted primarily to enhance the conditions that make poorer nations most amenable to engaging in environmental cooperation. Future aid would thus help poor nations diversify resource-based economies and encourage a strengthening of civil liberties and an acceptance of civil society.

"Climate change," write Roberts and Parks, "is fundamentally an issue of inequality."[45] Addressing that inequality is fundamental to any future progress on climate change. As long as the North views southern desperation as largely irrelevant to its own interest, adaptation aid will continue to be a mission of charity only—help that we wish we would give, but don't want to. Seeing climate threats as issues of inequality and unfairness enables us to move from charity to justice and, as it turns out, from altruism to long-range self-interest.

Notes

1. Nicholas Stern, *The Economics of Climate Change: The Stern Review*, (Cambridge: Cambridge University Press, 2007), p. 1 (hereafter *Stern Review*).

2. U.N. Development Programme, UNDP's Adaptation Portfolio, http://sdnhq .undp.org/gef-adaptation/projects.

3. Intergovernmental Panel on Climate Change (IPCC), *Climate Change 2007: Impacts, Adaptation and Vulnerability*, Contribution of Working Group II to the Fourth Assessment Report of the Intergovernmental Panel on Climate Change, ed. Martin L. Parry and Osvaldo Canziani (New York: Cambridge University Press, 2007), p. 781.

4. Ibid., p. 734 (citing World Bank, *Clean Energy and Development: Toward an Investment Framework*, Annex K [Washington, D.C.: World Bank, 2006]).

5. Chris Schroeder and Robert Glicksman, "The United States' Failure to Act," chapter 1 in this volume.

6. Ibid., p. 32.

7. *Stern Review*, pp. 94–95 (internal quotation marks omitted).

8. See Matthew E. Kahn, "The Death Toll from Natural Disasters: The Role of Income, Geography, and Institutions," *Review of Economics and Statistics* 87, no. 2 (2005): 271–284, 271.

9. *Stern Review*, pp. 32, 52.

10. Ibid.

11. Ibid., pp. 110, 114.

12. Ibid., p. 114.

13. Ibid.

14. Ibid.

15. See Robert R. M. Verchick, "Risk, Fairness, and the Geography of Disaster," *Issues in Legal Scholarship*, Symposium on Catastrophic Risks: Prevention, Compensation, and Recovery (2007); article 6, http://www.bepress.com/ils/ iss10/art6.

16. United Nations Framework Convention on Climate Change, art. IV, opened for signature May 29, 1992, S. Treaty Doc. No. 102-38 (1992), 1771 U.N.T.S. 107.

17. Ibid., art. III.

18. Global Environmental Facility, United Nations Development Programme, "Strategic Priority on Adaptation (SPA): Guidelines," http.//www.undp.org/gef/adaptation/funds/04c_i.htm#spa.

19. Oxfam International, *Financing Adaptation: Why the U.N.'s Bali Climate Conference Must Mandate the Search for New Funds* (Dec. 4, 2007), p. 5, table 1, http://www.oxfam.ca/news-and-publications/publications-and-reports/financing-adaptation-why-the-un2019s-bali-climate-conference-must-mandate-the-search-for-new-funds/file.

20. See John C. Dernbach, "U.S. Policy," chap. 3 in *Global Climate Change and U.S. Law*, ed. Michael B. Gerrard (American Bar Association: Chicago, 2007), pp. 61–100, 80–82.

21. Susan R. Fletcher, *Global Environmental Facility: Overview*, Oct. 28, 2005, http://leahy.senate.gov/issues/foreign%20policy/PDFS/GlobalEnvironmentFacility.pdf; Global Environmental Facility, *Climate Change Adaptation*, http://www.gefweb.org/interior.aspx?id=264.

22. J. Timmons Roberts and Bradley C. Parks, *A Climate of Injustice: Global Inequality, North–South Politics, and Climate Policy* (Cambridge, MA: MIT Press, 2007), pp. 227–228.

23. Hermann E. Ott, Bernd Brouns, Wolfgang Sterk, and Bettina Wittneben, "It Takes Two to Tango—Climate Policy at COP 10 in Buenos Aires and Beyond," *Journal For European Environmental and Planning Law* 2 (2005): 84–91, 86.

24. Beth Daley, "U.S. Lags on Plans for Climate Change," *Boston Globe*, April 5, 2007, p. 1A.

25. California Environmental Protection Agency, *Climate Action Team Report to Gov. Schwarzenegger and the Legislature*, March 2006, http://www.climatechange.ca.gov/climate_action_team/reports/2006report/2006-04-03_FINAL_CAT_REPORT.PDF.

26. See Daley, "U.S. Lags," p. 1A.

27. See Driesen's introduction to the present volume.

28. Quoted in Roberts and Parks, *A Climate of Injustice*, p. 228.

29. Gary Yohe and Richard S. J. Tol, "Indicators for Social and Economic Coping Capacity: Moving toward a Working Definition of Adaptive Capacity," *Global Environmental Change* 12 (2002): 25–40, 29.

30. Douglass C. North, *Institutions, Institutional Change, and Economic Performance* (Cambridge: Cambridge University Press, 1990), pp. 80–82.

31. Copenhagen Consensus 2004, Press Release, "HIV/AIDS, Hunger, Free Trade and Malaria Top Experts' List" (undated), http://www.copenhagenconsensus.com/Files/Filer/CC/Press/UK/CLOSINGPR1.pdf; *How to Spend $50 Billion to Make the World a Better Place*, ed. Bjørn Lomborg (Cambridge: Cambridge University Press, 2006).

32. See James Gustave Speth, "Development Assistance and Poverty," chap. 7 in *Stumbling toward Sustainability*, ed. John C. Dernbach (Washington, D.C.: Environmental Law Institute, 2002), pp. 163–72, 167–168.

33. Mary Wollstonecraft, *A Vindication of the Rights of Women*, ed. Carol H. Poston (New York: Norton, 1975), p. 71.

34. John Rawls, *A Theory of Justice* (Oxford: Oxford University Press, 1973), pp. 302–303.

35. John Rawls, *The Law of Peoples* (Cambridge, MA: Harvard University Press, 1999), p. 111.

36. Ibid.

37. Roberts and Parks, *A Climate of Injustice*, p. 168 (citations omitted).

38. Ibid. (citing Stefan Giljum and N. Eisenmenger, "North–South Trade and The Distribution of Environmental Goods and Burdens: A Biophysical Perspective," *Journal of Environment and Development* 13, no. 1 [2004]: 84).

39. Quoted in Roberts and Parks, *A Climate of Injustice*, p. 3.

40. U.N. General Assembly, Fifty-fifth Session, Official Records, Agenda item 101, *High-Level International Intergovernmental Consideration of Financing for Development: Final Report*, prepared by the United Nations Secretary-General, A/55/1000, p. 3, 2001, www.un.org/esa/ffd/a55-1000.pdf.

41. Roberts and Parks, *A Climate of Injustice*, pp. 212–213.

42. Ibid., p. 209.

43. Thomas C. Schelling, "What Makes Greenhouse Sense?" *Foreign Affairs* 81 (May–June 2002): 2–9.

44. Herbert Giersch, Karl-Heinz Paque, and Holger Shmieding, "Openness, Wage Restraint, and Macroeconomic Stability: West Germany's Road to Prosperity 1948–1959," chap. 1 in *Postwar Economic Reconstruction and Lessons for the East Today*, ed. Rudiger Dornbusch, Wilhelm Nölling, and Richard Layard (Cambridge, MA: MIT Press, 1993), pp. 1–28, p. 15.

45. Roberts and Parks, *A Climate of Injustice*, p. 23.

Conclusion: Toward a Fresh Start

David M. Driesen

This book shows how neoliberalism led to the United States' failure to adequately address global climate change. In doing so, this book shows that environmental policy does not function, as is sometimes supposed, as simply an arcane policy domain of its own. Rather, general economic thought exerts a profound influence on how we respond to a complex phenomenon like global warming.

The presidential election of 2008 appears to reflect some recognition of neoliberalism's inadequacy. For President Obama won the election by blaming the economic collapse of 2008 on the Bush administration's preference for unfettered markets over adequate regulation. And both candidates supported meaningful action on global warming, with the winning candidate having the stronger position on that issue. Yet, it would be a mistake to assume that this election settled every question about neoliberalism or, perhaps more importantly, about constructing adequate alternatives. Therefore, this book offers much-needed guidance for constructing a new framework and better climate change policy at a time when a real possibility of significant change has arisen, even though some of the worst failures that it chronicles belong to the past.

In particular, even the less ideological supporters of neoliberalism will likely continue to embrace cost-benefit analysis and market mechanisms with an insufficient appreciation of their weaknesses, too much concern about temporary economic equilibriums, and too little recognition of the importance of economic dynamics. Thus far President Obama has not rescinded the Executive Order bequeathed by prior administrations that emphasizes cost-benefit analysis, and he has endorsed climate change bills that contain some of the overly broad approaches to trading that this book has criticized. Nor has Congress suddenly rejected neoliberal economic thought.

The continued embrace of neoliberalism, albeit with some adjustments, may seem strange. For the collapse of the subprime mortgage market constitutes such a stunning example of the importance of change over time and the insignificance of short-term economic efficiency. Subprime lenders employed cost-benefit analysis to rationally calibrate how much extra interest (benefit) would compensate for the predicted default rate among low-income borrowers (costs). Because of rising housing prices, some actors miscalculated, assuming that even defaulting borrowers would not hurt them too much. But still, they engaged in a form of cost-benefit calculation. Wall Street firms also used cost-benefit analysis to construct derivative securities based on these loans. In both cases, it is now clear that reliance on this core neoliberalist construct fueled myopic delusions, because this sort of cost-benefit analysis exhibits the hubris all too reminiscent of the conceits Frank Ackerman finds in the cost-benefit analysis of climate change. The most important elements of their calculations involved substantial uncertainties, such as the direction of future housing prices and the likely rates of default under new underwriting standards (or lack of standards) that had never existed before. Like writers of environmental cost-benefit analysis who are confronting nonquantifiable ecological effects (like climate change feedback loops), these devotees of rational analysis ignored or gave insufficient weight to the soft variable.

More fundamentally, the short-term efficiency that all this securitization and variable rate lending spawned turned out to matter not at all. What mattered was the failure to choose adaptively efficient institutional arrangements, which could respond effectively (perhaps by renegotiating mortgages quickly) to unpredictable costs (defaults during a collapse of housing prices). This failure to employ precaution in the face of uncertainty led to an unfavorable direction of change over time (financial collapse). Yet, the apparent rationalism of cost-benefit analysis continues to beguile many and will continue to appeal to those who are not comfortable bravely facing, instead of wishing away, uncertainty. And faith in markets has not vanished in government and academic circles, even if it has vanished among investors; no major political figure has endorsed the end of securitization of mortgages, and few leaders seem prepared to heed many economists' call to nationalize the banks in light of the experience of other countries with similar types of financial crises. When President Obama said that nationalization is "contrary to our traditions," he was referring to the role of neoliberalism, the faith in markets and the tradition of distrust of government that Chris Schroeder and Robert Glicksman discussed.

The election of Barack Obama apparently heralds the beginning of some effort to address global climate change, but we have a long way to go before neoliberalism recedes and an economic dynamic approach that is responsive to justice takes its place. The Obama administration, and future administrations, will have to cope with the challenge of making wise decisions about how to address climate change made irretrievably worse by the extreme neoliberalism prevalent in past years.

Perhaps the increased participation in the 2008 election suggests a public willingness to assume the moral commitments inherent in the collective duties Carl Cranor outlines with respect to climate change. It remains to be seen whether voters preoccupied with their own dwindling economic prospects will remain active generally and assume the moral commitments that Cranor calls for. But his call provides a refreshing alternative to the moral complacency and the emphasis on pursuit of self-interest that has largely displaced ideals of moral civic engagement in recent years.

Embrace of precaution will be critical to effective action, lest even in a post-precautionary world that understands climate changes, remaining uncertainties about the magnitude of the consequences defeat an adequate response. Surely Lisa Heinzerling shows that doing nothing is irrational in light of the lack of uncertainty about the scientific fundamentals and the existence of substantial human-caused warming. And Robert Glicksman's discussion of climate disruption's consequences also reinforces this point. Yet John Applegate's call for embrace of precaution remains important, because uncertainties will always remain about the precise magnitude, timing, and location of consequences. Indeed, recent data showing sea-level rise exceeding that predicted by climate change researchers highlight the danger of insufficiently vigorous action in the face of uncertainty.

Discussion of costs and benefits, the subject of Frank Ackerman's and Tom McGarity's respective chapters, continues to play a significant role in the selection of near-term targets for both emerging federal and state programs addressing climate change. We should approach these tasks with an appreciation of the history of overestimating costs that McGarity highlights and the need to avoid the hubris that Ackerman discusses.

Once targets are established, policymakers should set up mechanisms to retrospectively collect actual cost information from real experience. This approach can pave the way for decisions more responsive to reality and less responsive to uncertain projections in the future. And, as Ackerman suggests, we need a central focus on uncertainty, a regard for the future, and recognition of costs in economic dynamic terms, as part of a choice about what path to follow, rather than simple negatives to be avoided.

We must also remain vigilant about the extent to which the neoliberal narrative, with its emphasis on aggregate social welfare, masks the profound inequities in power and wealth that both drive and are driven by global warming, as Amy Sinden's chapter explores. As laid-off workers watch bailed-out bank executives take multimillion dollar bonuses, the financial crisis has laid bare the fault lines between rich and poor in this country. But even after the financial meltdown triggered a new skepticism about free-market ideologies, our continuing tendency to describe the climate crisis in economic terms—as a market failure requiring solutions that carefully balance aggregate costs and benefits—threatens to subtly divert our attention from, and exacerbate, the distributional inequities that are at its core.

Of course, even as the new administration and the new Congress move forward to address global climate disruption, some special interests will continue to deploy a version of the litany Robert Glicksman described to resist changes needed to address it effectively. Neoliberalism's diminished luster in light of its failure in the area where its prescriptions seem most apt—financial markets—may make government officials less responsive to the litany than they had been when a thoroughgoing faith in neoliberalism appeared plausible. But learning the hard lessons about our failed climate change policy that this book teaches may help create the climate of ideas necessary to support a more effective policy.

It will be interesting to see whether the fossil fuel industry can keep the flow of economic benefits usually bestowed upon them in the past, as described by Joe Tomain. Fossil fuel favoritism seems more vulnerable to attack than ever before, because of the increased salience of climate change, the runaway federal deficit, and the decline of free-market ideology that has, strangely, helped lead to government support of fossil fuel companies in the past.

The issues I have highlighted about emissions trading remain central to debates going forward. In 2008, the weaknesses of carbon offset markets in generating real emission reductions became more widely apparent. Accordingly, policymakers have begun to study and adopt methods for limiting the amount of offsets allowed into trading markets, through qualitative and quantitative controls. My chapter shows that this approach not only improves environmental integrity, but can also boost innovation.

Yet, we will need more creative thinking about how to better stimulate innovation if we hope to effectively address climate disruption that has become more inexorable with every passing year. The dirty input limits (DILs) mechanism has begun to play a role in debates about climate change instrument choice. Congress has found that it is not practical to address transport emissions without going "upstream." Accordingly, regulation of the transport sector in bills seeking to impose an economy-wide cap regulate the carbon content of fuels, thereby imposing a DIL. But these DILs limit the mechanism's promise for innovation by allowing producers to exceed input limits if they pay for output-based controls on greenhouse gas emissions. So, these bills represent a hybrid between DILs and more conventional end-of-the-pipe approaches and will therefore spur less innovation than a pure DIL would.

An environmental competition statute can provide a model for future efforts to stimulate serious innovation, but has not yet gained traction in the policymaking sphere. This proposal and other serious ideas for spurring innovation will only make progress in the United States after we and our leaders embrace the creation of a favorable dynamics for innovation and reject short-term efficiency as the major guiding principle of regulation.

The failure to fully embrace an economic dynamic approach to innovation has impoverished the debate about economic stimulus, even though the desire for sound climate change policy has played a role in that debate, primarily in supporting recommendations for investment in renewable energy and increased energy efficiency. Yet, when automakers came looking for a bailout, nobody seriously considered funding fledgling car companies now making much more environmentally advanced vehicles than General Motors and Chrysler produce. Although politically difficult, it is quite possible that such investments would generate more jobs and prosperity in the long run than further investments in failed companies. Of course, this suggestion highlights one of the difficulties in embracing positive long-term economic dynamics—the difficulty of change. It might be necessary, as a matter of justice, for government to finance retraining or transportation of displaced workers, fund health care for stranded employees of defunct automakers, and assume substantial pension costs in order to make such a proposal a political possibility. Even though difficult, the idea of using economic stimulus to cultivate the new rather than to resuscitate the old deserves serious discussion. As we move forward with economic stimulus measures to revive the economy, we may need much more emphasis on investments offering positive long-term economic dynamics and much less on quixotic efforts to revive failed companies.

Careful thinking about climate justice has a role to play in the domestic sphere, but it must also be part of the effort to restore the United States' place in the world. With respect to justice, we see some hopeful signs, but no major shift in U.S. thinking yet. Ideals of distributional justice have played a big role in post-Kyoto international climate change negotiations and will continue to do so. Developing countries' insistence on adherence to the "common but differentiated responsibilities" principle in the U.N. Framework Convention on Climate Change—a key principle that recognizes that developed countries must lead by example in light of their historic contributions to global warming and their capacity to address it—means that developed countries have to address distributional justice concerns in order to secure mitigation commitments from developing countries. But U.S. leaders need to embrace justice principles and explain them to the American public in order to make them an integral part of U.S. climate change policy. Too many members of Congress and a significant segment of the public remain convinced that we should not move aggressively unless India and China do so *at the same time*. Of course, we need to get China, India, and other developing countries on board. But we can only bring them along if we respect justice principles that are important to them, which implies that we must implement effective climate change policies that demonstrate some responsibility in this matter *before* demanding cleanup from those with less capability and less historical responsibility.

Sensitivity to the distributional justice principles Carl Cranor and Amy Sinden discuss must play a large role in U.S. policy toward developing countries in the climate change context and in other contexts as we move forward. Congress remains anxious about the United States adopting firm targets for greenhouse gas reductions without concrete commitments from China, India, and other competitors in global markets. Accordingly, bills creating federal cap-and-trade programs to address global warming contain various forms of what we might loosely call "countervailing duty" provisions.[1] These provisions provide that after some time has lapsed our trading partners must either regulate to address climate change or purchase allowances in global carbon markets if they wish to export energy-intensive goods to the United States. Economists have begun to analyze whether these provisions prevent leakage—an increase in emissions abroad triggered by policies decreasing emissions at home. So far, little evidence exists that these policies reduce leakage.[2] While this sort of analysis is surely helpful, we can make serious errors if we do not examine these measures through a justice lens as well. Having just caused an economic crisis around the world, the United States could easily alienate developing countries in a way that hinders progress on climate change if it does not consider whether a countervailing duty program treats developing countries fairly. Thus, there is an urgent need to examine these proposals from a justice perspective in terms of the principles of fair distribution of burdens that Cranor and Sinden lay out. And if, as is likely, Congress adopts some countervailing duty proposal, we will need a justice-based analysis of proposals on how to use the discretion likely to be afforded the executive branch in implementing these programs in a just manner.

Unfortunately, the United States' failure to address climate change means that some significant climate change has become inevitable, and countries around the world must adapt. Now that we have spurred an economic collapse in developing countries as well as made a major contribution to climate disruption, Robert Verchick's call for just policies to aid developing countries' adaptation programs has become more urgent. The economic collapse means that developing countries have even fewer resources available to fund their own adaptation programs or to respond to demands for matching grants than had before. Poverty increases from a global recession make climate change's likely effect on people in developing countries more severe. Unfortunately, the need for adaptation assistance from developed countries has become more urgent at a time when an economic collapse has made response to this urgency with U.S. dollars more difficult than ever. Hence, it may require a real revolution in our thinking to move forward along the lines Verchick indicates. But as time goes on, some positive developments may emerge. Recently, a trend has developed favoring auctioning of allowances for cap-and-trade programs. This has been made part of the Regional Greenhouse Gas Initiative, the first U.S. cap-and-trade program, and has also figured in bills proposing a federal cap-and-trade program. Using some of the funds from these auctions to fund adaptation in developing countries may become a possibility in the future.

More broadly, the need for justice may become more of an imperative during a time of economic stress. In the past, economic calamities combined with perceptions of injustice have led to violent conflicts. Hence, the need for justice may have increased even as the temptations to forgo its demands may have increased.

While *Economic Thought and U.S. Climate Change Policy* teaches valuable lessons about fundamental issues that will remain with us for some time to come, it also raises additional questions that merit research. This book argues that economic thought has played a role in creating failed U.S. climate change policy, while not denying the effects of special interest influence and framing. Indeed, we have argued that policy framing translated fairly abstract economic concepts into fairly simple rubrics that rendered neoliberalism concrete and attractive. We have shown that economic thought has played a major role in shaping U.S. climate policy, but the precise relationship between economic thought, special interest influence, framing, and events influencing public opinion is surely a complex subject, which needs more research.

We do not suppose that this book provides the last word on neoliberalism or on how to apply a more realistic and just economic dynamic approach to future efforts to address global climate change. Our book suggests numerous questions, both big and small, that require further research. For example, an economic dynamic approach focuses on a desirable direction of change over time. How often is a general desirable direction easily identifiable? In doubtful cases, what principles should inform the identification of desirable directions? With respect to justice, we need more thinking about the role of justice and self-interest in policymaking, both in the climate change arena and elsewhere. We need more research into how to make adaptation assistance effective. Robert Verchick's case for justice demanding that we fund adaptation assistance is compelling. But in some countries that deserve our help real concerns exist about whether any form of international aid will be wisely spent.

More specifically, if we should not place too much stock in cost-benefit analysis, how should we establish goals for regulation? Several of the authors contributing to this volume have addressed this question, with David Driesen defending feasibility analysis,[3] Chris Schroeder (along with Sid Shapiro, who did not write for this book) offering "Pragmatic Regulatory Analysis,"[4] and Amy Sinden showing that a cost-blind approach helps overcome special interest influence on environmental law.[5] In practice, international discussion of goals for climate change programs these days follows the Sinden approach most closely. Most governments have supported ambitious overall goals reflecting, more or less, the amount of reductions scientists tell us we need to make to have a reasonable chance of avoiding very dangerous climate change. But when governments actually implement climate change programs, elements of the feasibility approach and the pragmatic approach enter the picture. In any case, we need further research and analysis of alternatives to cost-benefit analysis in the climate change context, building on this work and Frank Ackerman's and Tom McGarity's insights herein about how to think about costs and benefits.

A related question involves the proper role of standard economic techniques like cost-benefit analysis. If we accept Frank Ackerman's call for more honesty and less hubris, does this imply that academic economists should carry out cost-benefit analysis as a means of studying programs, but that policymakers should never consider such analysis as it is simply too unreliable to play any role at all in policy debates? Or should we instead consider several different cost-benefit studies in the legislative process with due regard for their limitations? I have argued elsewhere that cost-benefit analysis, though dysfunctional in administrative processes, has a role to play in legislative processes, where its limitations can be subject to public scrutiny. Ackerman's convincing argument should play a huge role in curing the neoliberal tendency to treat a particular cost-benefit study as authoritative information, rather than as what it is: a compendium of limited information quantified according to the analysts' preferred assumptions. But this argument should spur more debate on how precisely we respond to these insights.

More indirectly, this book raises profound questions about the proper role of government. Chris Schroeder and Robert Glicksman point out that environmental law arose in an era of confidence in government's ability to solve environmental problems through regulation, an era that ended as climate change emerged as a serious issue. While we have entered a new era where reliance on free markets has been discredited, it is not clear that faith in government has been restored. As we craft climate change policy, we will have to grapple with questions about government's role. Should government only provide incentives for fundamental change through economic incentive programs? Or should it single out especially promising clean technologies for government subsidies? Should government engage in climate-related research and development directly, as it did when creating the atom bomb? Questions like these implicate the broad themes of this book. We now know that complete reliance on markets is a dead end. But that recognition leads to further questions about the proper role of government in an era when we realize that we do need a stronger government role than we've seen in the past.

In short, neoliberalism contributed significantly to the United States' failure to address global climate change. We need instead to construct a response that fosters favorable economic dynamics and respects justice.

While this book offers both concrete thinking about governing principles for the new era and specific policy ideas, it also raises questions requiring further analysis and research.

Notes

1. Carolyn Fischer and Alan K. Fox, *Comparing Policies to Combat Emissions Leakage: Border Tax Adjustments versus Rebates* (2009), p. 1, http://www.rff.org/RFF/Documents/RFF-DP-09-02.pdf.

2. Ibid., p. 14 (finding that countervailing duties and similar policies do not necessarily reduce global emissions or leakage).

3. David M. Driesen, "Distributing the Costs of Environmental, Health, and Safety Protection: The Feasibility Principle, Cost-Benefit Analysis, and Regulatory Reform," *Boston College Environmental Affairs Law Review* 32 (2005): 1–95.

4. See Sidney A. Shapiro and Christopher H. Schroeder, "Beyond Cost-Benefit Analysis: A Pragmatic Reorientation," *Harvard Environmental Law Review* 32 (2008): 433–501.

5. Amy Sinden, "In Defense of Absolutes: Combating the Politics of Power in Environmental Law," *Iowa Law Review* 90 (2004): 1405–1511.

Bibliography

Ackerman, Bruce A., and Richard B. Stewart. "Comment: Reforming Environmental Law." *Stanford Law Review* 37 (1985): 1333–1365.

Ackerman, Frank. *Debating Climate Economics: The Stern Review vs. Its Critics.* Report to Friends of the Earth–UK, July 2007, http://www.ase.tufts.edu/gdae/Pubs/rp/SternDebateReport.pdf.

Ackerman, Frank. "Hot, It's Not: Reflections on *Cool It,* by Bjørn Lomborg." *Climate Change* 89, no. 3–4 (2008): 435–446.

Ackerman, Frank, and Ian Finlayson. "The Economics of Inaction on Climate Change: A Sensitivity Analysis." *Climate Policy* 6, no. 5 (2006): 509–526.

Ackerman, Frank, and Lisa Heinzerling. *Priceless: On Knowing the Price of Everything and the Value of Nothing.* New York: The New Press, 2004.

Adam, David. "Royal Society Tells Exxon: Stop Funding Climate Change Denial." *Guardian,* Sept. 20, 2006: 1.

Adams, Walter, and James W. Brock. "The Antitrust Vision and Its Revisionist Critics." *New York Law School Law Review* 35 (1990): 939–967.

Adler, Matthew D. "Corrective Justice and Liability for Global Warming." *University of Pennsylvania Law Review* 155 (2007): 1859–1868.

Adler, Matthew D., and Eric A. Posner. "Rethinking Cost-Benefit Analysis." *Yale Law Journal* 109 (Nov. 1999): 165–247.

Agarwal, Anil A., and Sunita Narain. *Global Warming in an Unequal World: A Case of Environmental Colonialism.* New Delhi: Center for Science and Environment, 1991.

Agreement on the Application of Sanitary and Phytosanitary Measures. Jan. 1, 1995, GATT Doc. MTN/FA II-A1A-4 (Dec. 15, 1993).

Aldy, Joseph E., Scott Barrett, and Robert N. Stavins. "Thirteen Plus One: A Comparison of Global Climate Policy Architectures." *Climate Policy* 3 (2003): 373–397.

Amodio, Joseph V. "Al Gore Comes Back, Greener Than Ever." *Newsday,* May 22, 2006: B4.

Anderson, Dennis, and Matt Leach. "The Costs of Mitigating Climate Change." *World Economics* 6 (2005): 71–90.

Andrews, Edmund L. "Counting on Failure, Energy Chairman Floats Carbon Tax." *New York Times*, July 7, 2007: A9.

Andrews, Edmund L. "House Votes to Rescind Oil Drillers' Tax Breaks." *New York Times*, Jan. 19, 2007.

Andrews, Edmund L. "Inspector Finds Broad Failures in Oil Program." *New York Times*, Sept. 26, 2007.

Andrews, Edmund L. "U.S. Agency To Review Oil Royalties." *New York Times*, Nov. 2, 2006.

Andrews, Edmund L. "U.S. Drops Bid Over Royalties from Chevron." *New York Times*, Oct. 31, 2006.

Andrews, Richard N. L. *Managing the Environment, Managing Ourselves: A History of American Environmental Policy.* New Haven, CT: Yale University Press, 1999.

Applegate, John S. "The Taming of the Precautionary Principle." *William and Mary Environmental Law and Policy Review* 27 (2002): 13–78.

Arcuri, Alessandra. "The Case for a Procedural Version of the Precautionary Principle Erring on the Side of Environmental Preservation." Global Law Working Paper (09/04, 2007): 1–38, http://ssrn.com/abstract=967779.

Arrow, Kenneth J. *Social Choice and Individual Values.* New Haven, CT: Yale University Press, 1963.

Ashford, Nicholas A., Christine Ayers, and Robert F. Stone. "Using Regulation to Change the Market for Innovation." *Harvard Environmental Law Review* 9 (1985): 419–466.

Ashford, Nicholas A., and George R. Heaton, Jr. "Regulation and Technological Innovation in the Chemical Industry." *Law and Contemporary Problems* 46, no. 3 (1983): 109–157.

Associated Press. "Bush: Kyoto Treaty Would Have Hurt Economy." June 30, 2005, http://www.msnbc.msn.com/id/8422343/.

Association of Metropolitan Water Agencies. *Implications of Climate Change for Urban Water Utilities.* Dec. 2007, http://www.docuticker.com/?p=18394.

Azar, Christian. "Weight Factors in Cost-Benefit Analysis of Climate Change." *Environmental and Resource Economics* 13, no. 3 (1999): 249–268.

Azar, Christian, and Stephen H. Schneider. "Are the Economic Costs of Stabilizing the Atmosphere Prohibitive?" *Ecological Economics* 42 (2002): 73–80.

Azar, Christian, and Thomas Sterner. "Discounting and Distributional Considerations in the Context of Global Warming." *Ecological Economics* 19, no. 2 (1996): 169–184.

Baer, Paul. "The Worth of an Ice-Sheet: A Critique of the Treatment of Catastrophic Impacts in the *Stern Review*." December 23, 2006, http://www.postnormaltimes.net/blog/archives/2006/12/the_worth_of_an_1.html.

Baker, C. Edwin. "The Ideology of the Economic Analysis of Law." *Philosophy and Public Affairs* 5, no.1 (1975): 3–48.

Ball, Jeffrey. "Digging In—Exxon Chief Makes a Cold Calculation on Global Warming—BP and Shell Concede Ground as Raymond Funds Skeptics and Fights Emissions Caps—A 'Reality Check' on Kyoto." *Wall Street Journal*, June 14, 2005: A1.

Ball, Jeffrey. "Global Warming May Cloud Directors' Liability Coverage." *Wall Street Journal*, May 7, 2003: C1.

Bamberger, Robert L., and Carl E. Behrens. *Energy Policy: Comprehensive Energy Legislation (H.R. 6, S. 10) in the 109th Congress.* Washington, D.C.: Library of Congress, Congressional Research Service, July 29, 2005.

Barker, Terry, and Paul Ekins. "The Costs of Kyoto for the US Economy." *Energy Journal* 25 (2004): 53–71.

Barker, Terry, Jonathan Kohler, and Marcelo Villena. "Costs of GHG Abatement: Meta-Analysis of Post-SRES Mitigation Scenarios." *Environmental Economics and Policy Studies* 5 (2002): 135–166.

Barrett, Scott. *Environment and Statecraft.* Oxford: Oxford University Press, 2005.

Barringer, Felicity, and Andrew Ross Sorkin. "Utility to Limit New Coal Plants in Big Buyout." *New York Times*, Feb. 25, 2007: A1.

Barry, Brian. *Why Social Justice Matters.* Malden, MA: Polity Press, 2005.

Battin, James, Matthew W. Wiley, Mary H. Ruckelshaus, Richard N. Palmer, Elizabeth Korb, Krista K. Bartz, and Hiroo Imaki. "Projected Impacts of Climate Change on Salmon Habitat Restoration." *Proceedings of the National Academy of Science USA* 104, no. 16 (2007): 6720–6725.

Baumert, Kevin A. "Note: Participation of Developing Countries in the International Climate Change Regime: Lessons for the Future." *George Washington International Law Review* 38 (2006): 365–407.

Baumol, William J., Robert W. Crandall, Robert W. Hahn, Paul L. Joskow, Robert E. Litan, and Richard L. Schmalensee. "Regulating Emissions of Greenhouse Gases Under Section 202(a) of the Clean Air Act." October 2006, http://www.aei-brookings.org/admin/authorpdfs/page.php?id=1336.

Baxter, William F. *People or Penguins: The Case for Optimal Pollution.* New York: Columbia University Press, 1974.

Begley, Sharon. "The Truth about Denial." *Newsweek*, Aug. 13, 2007: 20–29.

Begley, Sharon, and Andrew Murr. "Which of These Is Not Causing Global Warming Today?" *Newsweek*, July 9, 2007: 48.

Bennett, James. "Warm Globe, Hot Politics." *New York Times*, Dec. 11, 1997: 1A.

"Big U.S. Industries Launch Attack on Warming Treaty—Big Three Auto Makers, Steelmakers, Utilities are Leading the Charge." *Wall Street Journal*, Dec. 12, 1997: A3.

Bok, Sissala. *Lying: Moral Choice in Public and Private Life.* New York: Vintage Books, 1979.

Bollier, David, and Joan Claybrook. *Freedom from Harm*. Washington, D.C.: Public Citizen, 1986.

Bosse, Michael R. "Comment: George J. Mitchell: Maine's Environmental Senator." *Maine Law Review* 47 (1995): 179–222.

Brahic, Catherine. "Med to Get Five Times as Many Dangerously Hot Days." *New Scientist* (June 2007): 18, http://environment.newscientist.com/channel/earth/dn12086.

Breyer, Stephen. "Analyzing Regulatory Failure: Mismatches, Less Restrictive Alternatives, and Reform." *Harvard Law Review* 92, no. 3 (1979):549–609.

Broder, John M. "California Wants Strict Auto Emissions." *New York Times*, May 23, 2007: A16.

Brown, Donald A. *American Heat: Ethical Problems with the United States' Response to Global Warming*. Lanham, MD: Rowman and Littlefield, 2002.

Brown Weiss, Edith. *In Fairness to Future Generations: International Law, Common Patrimony, and Intergenerational Equity*. Dobbs Ferry, NY: Transnational Publishers, 1988.

Bruce, James P., Hoesung Lee, and Erik F. Haites, eds. *Climate Change 1995: Economic and Social Dimensions of Climate Change*. Cambridge: Cambridge University Press, 1996.

Buchanan, James M., and Gordon Tullock. *The Calculus of Consent: Logical Foundations of Constitutional Democracy*. Ann Arbor: University of Michigan Press, 1962.

Burtraw, Dallas, Alan Krupnick, Karen Palmer, Anthony Paul, Michael Toman, and Cary Bloyd. "Ancillary Benefits of Reduced Air Pollution in the US from Moderate GHG Mitigation Policies in the Electricity Sector." *Journal of Environmental Economics and Management* 45 (2003): 650–773.

Burtraw, Dallas. Testimony of Dallas Burtraw, Resources for the Future before the Subcommittee on Energy and Air Quality of the House Committee on Energy and Commerce, 110th Cong., 1st Sess., March 29, 2007.

Byrd–Hagel Resolution, S. Res. 98, 105th Cong., 1997.

Caldeira, Ken, Atul K. Jain, and Martin I. Hoffert. "Climate Sensitivity Uncertainty and the Need for Energy without CO_2 Emission." *Science* 299 (March 28, 2003): 2052–2054.

California Air Resources Board and United States Environmental Protection Agency. *Phase III Rule Effectiveness Study of the Aerospace Coating Industry*. 1990.

California Environmental Protection Agency. *Climate Action Team Report to Gov. Schwarzenegger and the Legislature*, March 2006, http://www.climatechange.ca.gov/climate_action_team/reports/2006report/2006-04-03_FINAL_CAT_REPORT.PDF.

California Environmental Protection Agency, Air Resources Board. *Staff Report: Initial Statement of Reasons for Proposed Rulemaking*. Public Hearing to Consider Adoption of Regulations to Control Greenhouse Gas Emissions from Motor Vehicles, 2004.

Capoor, Karan, and Philippe Ambrosi. *State and Trends of the Carbon Market 2007*. Washington, D.C.: World Bank, 2007.

Carter, Neil. *The Policy of the Environment: Ideas, Activism, Policy*. Cambridge: Cambridge University Press, 2007.

Center for American Progress. *Progressive Priorities: An Action Agenda for America*. Washington, D.C.: Center for American Progress, 2005, http://www .americanprogress.org/projects/progressivepriorities/prog_priorities.pdf.

Center for Clean Air Policy. "U.S. Carbon Emissions Trading: Description of an Upstream Approach." 1998, http://www.ccap.org

Center for Health and the Global Environment, Harvard Medical School. *Climate Change Futures: Health, Ecological and Economic Dimensions*. Ed. P. Epstein and E. Mills, Nov. 2005, http://www.climatechangefutures.org/report/ index.html.

Center for Progressive Reform. *An Unnatural Disaster: The Aftermath of Hurricane Katrina*. September 2005, http://www.progressivereform.org/articles/ Unnatural_Disaster_512.pdf.

Chevron v. Natural Resources Defense Council, 467 U.S. 837, 840 (1984).

Clark, John G. *Energy and the Federal Government: Fossil Fuel Policies, 1900–1946*. Urbana: University of Illinois Press, 1987.

Cline, W. R. *The Economics of Global Warming*. Washington, D.C.: Institute of International Economics, 1992.

C.N.A. Corporation. *National Security and the Threat of Climate Change*. April 2007. http://securityandclimate.cna.org/report/.

Cole, Daniel H. "Climate Change, Adaptation, and Development." *UCLA Journal of Environmental Law and Policy* 26 (2007–2008): 1–18.

Cole, Daniel H. "Climate Change and Collective Action." http://ssrn.com/abstract= 1069906.

Cole, Daniel H., and Peter Z. Grossman. "When Is Command and Control Efficient? Institutions, Technology, and the Comparative Efficiency of Alternative Regulatory Regimes for Environmental Protection." *Wisconsin Law Review* (1999): 887–938.

Commission of the European Communities. *Communication from the Commission on the Precautionary Principle*. COM (00)0001.

Commission of the European Communities. *The Share of Renewable Energy in the EU: Commission Report in Accordance with Article 3 of Directive 2001/77/EC, Evaluation of the Effect of Legislative Instruments and Other Community Policies on the Development of the Contribution of Renewable Energy Resources in the EU and Proposals for Concrete Actions*. Brussels: 2004.

Commission Regulation 1907/2006, art. 1(1), 2006 O.J. L396/1.

Copenhagen Consensus 2004. Press Release. "HIV/AIDS, Hunger, Free Trade and Malaria Top Experts' List" Undated, http://www.copenhagenconsensus.com/Files/Filer/CC/Press/UK/CLOSINGPR1.pdf.

Cowan, Robin, and Staffan Hultén. "Escaping Lock-in: The Case of the Electric Vehicle." *Technological Forecasting and Social Change* 53, no. 1 (1996): 61–79.

Coward, Howard, and Thomas Hurka, eds. *Ethics and Climate Change: The Greenhouse Effect.* Waterloo, Ontario: Wilfrid Laurier University Press, 1993.

CRA International, Program on Technology Innovation. *Economic Analysis of California Climate Change Initiatives: An Integrated Approach.* Electric Power Research Institute, 2007. http://www.epa.state.il.us/air/climatechange/documents/california-climate-study-final-report.pdf

Cranor, Carl F. "Collective and Individual Duties to Protect the Environment." *Journal of Applied Philosophy* 2, no. 2 (1985): 243–259.

Cross, Frank B. "Paradoxical Perils of the Precautionary Principle." *Washington and Lee Law Review* 53 (1996): 851–925.

Cudahy, Richard D. 1996. "Deregulation and Mergers: Is Consolidation Inevitable?" *Public Utilities Fortnightly* (Oct.15, 1996): 46, http://www.pur.com/pubs/1921.cfm.

Cusick, Daniel. "EPA Ozone Proposal to Face Scrutiny on Hill." *E&E News PM*, June 21, 2007, http://www.eenews.net/eenewspm/2007/6/21.

Dales, J. H. 1968. *Pollution, Property, and Prices.* Toronto: University of Toronto Press.

Daley, Beth. "U.S. Lags on Plans for Climate Change." *Boston Globe*, April 5, 2007: 1A.

Daly, Herman E. "Economics in a Full World." *Scientific American* 293, no. 3 (2005): 100–107.

Dasgupta, Partha. "Comments on the *Stern Review*'s Economics of Climate Change." Revised December 12, 2006, http://www.econ.cam.ac.uk/faculty/dasgupta/STERN.pdf.

Davies, Lincoln L. "Lessons for an Endangered Movement: What a Historical Juxtaposition of the Legal Response to Civil Rights and Environmentalism Has to Teach Environmentalists Today." *Environmental Law* 31 (2001): 229–370.

DeFina, Robert. 1977. "Public and Private Expenditures for Federal Regulation of Business." St. Louis, November 1977. Working Paper No. 27, Center for the Study of American Business.

De Miguel, Carlos, Xavier Labandeira, and Baltasar Manzano, eds. *Economic Modeling of Climate Change and Energy Policies.* Cheltenham: Edward Elgar, 2006.

den Elzen, Michel, and Malte Meinshausen. "Multi-Gas Emission Pathways for Meeting the EU 2°C Climate Target." In *Avoiding Dangerous Climate Change*, ed. Hans Joachim Schellnhuber et al., 299–309. New York: Cambridge University Press, 2006.

Department of Energy Organization Act. 42 U.S.C. § 7101 *et seq.*

Department of the Interior, Office of Inspector General. *Audit Report: Mineral Management Service's Compliance Review Process.* Report No. C-IN-MMS-0006-2006, December 6, 2006.

Dernbach, John C. "U.S. Policy." Chap. 3 in *Global Climate Change and U.S. Law*, ed. Michael B. Gerrard, 61–100. Chicago: American Bar Association, 2007.

de Sadeleer, Nicolas. *Environmental Principles: From Political Slogans to Legal Rules.* Oxford: Oxford University Press, 2002.

Deutsch, Claudia H. "Attention Shoppers: Carbon Offsets in Aisle 6." *New York Times*, Mar. 7, 2007: H1.

Devaney, Earl E. Investigative Report: Memorandum from Inspector General Earl E. Devaney to Secretary Dirk Kempthorne. Sept. 19, 2007, Washington, D.C., http://www.doioig.gov/upload/Qui%20tam.pdf.

Dickinson, Tim. "The Secret Campaign of President Bush's Administration to Deny Global Warming." *Rolling Stone*, June 20, 2007. http://www.rollingstone.com/politics/story/15148655/the_secret_campaign_of_president_bushs_administration_to_deny_global_warming. Accessed July 31, 2007.

Dietz, Simon, Chris Hope, Nicholas Stern, and Dimitri Zenghelis. "Reflections on the *Stern Review* (1): A Robust Case for Strong Action to Reduce the Risks of Climate Change." *World Economics* 8, no. 1 (January–March 2007): 121–168.

Doniger, David. "The Dark Side of the Bubble." *Environmental Forum* 4 (1985): 33–35.

Doremus, Holly. "Precaution, Science, and Learning While Doing in Natural Resource Management." *Washington Law Review* 82 (2007): 547–579.

Dornbusch, Rudiger, and James M. Poterba, eds. *Global Warming: Economic Policy Responses.* Cambridge, MA: MIT Press, 1991.

Downing, Thomas E., Alexander A. Olsthoorn, and Richard S. J. Tol, eds. *Climate, Change, and Risk.* London: Routledge, 1999.

Dressler, Andrew, and Edward Parson. *The Science and Politics of Global Climate Change.* New York: Cambridge University Press, 2006.

Driesen, David M. "Design, Trading, and Innovation." In *Moving to Markets in Environmental Regulation: Lessons from Twenty Years of Experience*, ed. Jody Freeman and Charles Kolstad, 437–438. Oxford: Oxford University Press, 2007.

Driesen, David M. "Distributing the Costs of Environmental, Health, and Safety Protection: The Feasibility Principle, Cost-Benefit Analysis, and Regulatory Reform." *Boston College Environmental Affairs Law Review* 32 (2005): 1–95.

Driesen, David M. "Does Emissions Trading Encourage Innovation?" *Environmental Law Reporter* 33 (2003): 10094–10108.

Driesen, David M. "Is Cost-Benefit Analysis Neutral?" *University of Colorado Law Review* 72 (2006): 335–403.

Driesen, David M. "Is Emissions Trading an Economic Incentive Program? Replacing the Command and Control/Economic Incentive Dichotomy." *Washington and Lee Law Review* 55 (1998): 289–350.

Driesen, David M. "Regulatory Reform: The New Lochnerism?" *Environmental Law* 36 (2006): 603–649.

Driesen, David M. "Sustainable Development and Market Liberalism's Shotgun Wedding: Emissions Trading Under the Kyoto Protocol." *Indiana Law Journal* 83 (2008): 21–69.

Driesen, David M. *The Economic Dynamics of Environmental Law*. Cambridge, MA: MIT Press, 2003.

Driesen, David M. "The Societal Cost of Environmental Regulation: Beyond Administrative Cost-Benefit Analysis." *Ecology Law Quarterly* 24 (1997): 545–617.

Driesen, David M., and Charles Hall. "Efficiency, Economic Dynamics, and Climate Change: A Critical Look at the Neoclassical Paradigm for Environmental Law." *Digest: National Italian American Bar Association Law Journal* 13 (2005): 1–33.

Driesen, David M., and Amy Sinden. "The Missing Instrument: Dirty Input Limits." *Harvard Environmental Law Review* 22 (2009): 65–116.

Dworkin, Ronald. *Taking Rights Seriously*. Cambridge, MA: Harvard University Press, 1977.

Dworkin, Ronald. "The Model of Rules." *University of Chicago Law Review* 35, no. 1 (1967): 14–46.

Ebi, Kristine L., Gerald A. Meehl, Dominique Bachelet, Robert R. Twilley, Donald F. Boesch, et al. *Regional Impacts of Climate Change: Four Case Studies in the United States* (Dec. 2007), http://www.pewclimate.org/regional_impacts.

Edsall, Thomas. *Building Red America*. New York: Basic Books, 2006.

Ellis, Jane, and Sami Kamel. *Overcoming Barriers to Clean Development Mechanism Projects*. Paris: OECD, 2007, http://www.oecd.org/dataoecd/51/14/38684304.pdf.

Energy Future Coalition. *Challenge and Opportunity: Charting a New Energy Future*. Washington, D.C.: Energy Future Coalition, http://www.energyfuture coalition.org/pubs/EFCReport.pdf.

Energy Information Administration. *Emissions of Greenhouse Gases in the United States 2005*, 2005, http://www.eia.doe.gov/oiaf/1605/ggrpt/pdf/executive_summary.pdf.

Energy Information Administration. "Impacts of the Kyoto Protocol on U.S. Energy Markets and Economic Activity." 1998. http://www.eia.doe.gov/oiaf/kyoto/kyotorpt.html.

Energy Information Administration, and U.S. Department of Energy. *Annual Energy Review 2006*. Washington, D.C.: GPO, June 2007. http://www.eia.doe.gov/aer/pdf/aer.pdf.

Energy Information Administration, and U.S. Department of Energy. *Annual Energy Outlook 2007: With Projections to 2030*. Washington, D.C.: GPO (February 2007).

Energy Information Agency, and U.S. Department of Energy. *International Energy Annual 2004*, "World Primary Energy Production, 1980–2004." July 2006. http://www.eia.doe.gov/pub/international/iealf/tablef1.xls.

Energy Policy Act of 1992. Pub. L. No. 102-486, Title XVI, 106 Stat. 2776.

Energy Policy Act of 2005, 42 U.S.C. §§101–237.

Energy Security Act. Pub. L. No. 96-294, 1980.

Engel, Kirsten H., and Scott R. Saleska. "Subglobal Regulation of the Global Commons: The Case of Climate Change." *Ecology Law Quarterly* 32, no. 2 (2005): 183–233.

Entman, Robert M. "Reporting Environmental Policy Debate: The Real Media Biases." *Harvard Inteternational Journal of Press/Politics* 1, no. 3 (1996): 77–92.

"Environment: A Cleaner, Safer, Healthier America." http://www.prwatch.org/node/1765/print.

Environmental Defense Fund v. Duke Energy Corp. 127 S.Ct. 1423 (2007).

Esty, Daniel C. "When Being Green Puts You in the Black." *Washington Post*, Mar. 4, 2007: B1.

Esty, Daniel C., and Andrew S. Winston. *Green to Gold: How Smart Companies Use Environmental Strategy to Innovate, Create Value, and Build Competitive Advantage*. New Haven, CT: Yale University Press, 2006.

European Environment Agency. *Late Lessons from Early Warnings: The Precautionary Principle 1896–2000. Environmental Issue Report*, no. 22, Luxembourg: Office for Official Publications of the European Communities, 2001, http://reports.eea.europa.eu/environmental_issue_report_2001_22/en/Issue_Report_No_22.pdf.

European Parliament. *Resolution on Climate Change in the Run Up to Buenos Aries*. November 1998. Adopted Sept. 17, 1998. http://www.europarl.europa.eu/pv2/pv2?PRG=CALDOC&FILE=980917&LANGUE=EN&TPV=DEF&LASTCHAP=1&SDOCTA=6&TXTLST=1&Type_Doc=FIRST&POS=1.

"Europe Heatwave Killed Some 19,000." *China Daily*, Sept. 26, 2003.

Evans, Leonard. "Airbag Benefits, Airbag Costs." Washington, D.C.: SAE International, 2003. http://www.scienceservingsociety.com/p/155.pdf.

Fankhauser, Samuel. *Valuing Climate Change: The Economics of the Greenhouse*. London: Earthscan Publications, 1995.

Fankhauser, Samuel, Richard S. J. Tol, and David W. Pearce. "Extensions and Alternatives to Climate Change Impact Valuation: On the Critique of IPCC Working Group III's Impact Estimates." *Environment and Development Economics* 3, no. 1 (Feb. 1998): 59–81.

Fankhauser, Samuel, Richard S. J. Tol, and David W. Pearce. "The Aggregation of Climate Change Damages: A Welfare Theoretic Approach." *Environmental and Resource Economics* 10, no. 3 (Oct. 1997): 249–266.

Farber, Daniel A. "Adapting to Climate Change: Who Should Pay?" *Journal of Land Use and Environmental Law* 23 (fall 2007): 1–37.

Farber, Daniel A., and Philip Frickey. "The Jurisprudence of Public Choice." *Texas Law Review* 65 (1987): 873–927.

Faris, Stephan. "The (1987) Real Roots of Darfur." Atlantic Monthly 299, no. 3 (April 2007): 67.

Faure, Michael, Joyeeta Gupta, and Andries Nentjes, eds. *Climate Change and the Kyoto Protocol: The Role of Institutions and Instruments to Control Global Change*. Cheltenham: Edward Elgar, 2003.

Feely, R. A., Christopher L. Sabine, and Victoria J. Fabry. "The Pew Charitable Trust Science Brief: Carbon Dioxide and Our Ocean Legacy." April 2006. http://www.pewtrusts.org/uploadedFiles/wwwpewtrustsorg/Reports/Global_warming/carbon_dioxide_ocean_legacy.pdf.

Fenhann, Joergen. *Guidance to the CDM/JI Pipeline*. Denmark: Capacity Development for the CDM, 2006. http://cdmpipeline.org/publications/Guidance CDMpipeline.pdf.

Fenhann, Joergen. *CDM Pipeline Overview*. http://cdmpipeline.org/publications/ CDMpipeline.xls.

Fenhann, Joergen. *JI Pipeline Overview*. http://cdmpipeline.org/publications/ JIpipeline.xls.

Fenhann, Joergen. "UNEP Risoe CDM/JI Pipeline Analysis and Database, CDM Pipeline Grouped in Types." http://cdmpipeline.org/cdm-projects-type.htm.

Fiorna, Morris P. *Congress: Keystone of the Washington Establishment*. New Haven, CT: Yale University Press, 1989.

Fischer, Carolyn, and Alan K. Fox. *Comparing Policies to Combat Emissions Leakage: Border Tax Adjustments Versus Rebates*. Feb. 2009. http://www.rff.org/ RFF/Documents/RFF-DP-09-02.pdf

Fisher, Elizabeth. "Precaution, Law, and Principles of Good Administration." *Water Science and Technology* 52, no. 6 (2005): 19–24.

Fisher, Elizabeth. "Precaution, Precaution Everywhere: Developing a 'Common Understanding' of the Precautionary Principle in the European Community." *Maastricht Journal of European and Comparative Law* 9, no. 1 (2002): 7–28.

Fisher, Elizabeth. "Review of *Laws of Fear: Beyond the Precautionary Principle*, by Cass Sunstein." *Modern Law Review* 69 (2006): 288–292.

Fisher, Elizabeth. "Risk and Environmental Law: A Beginner's Guide." In *Environmental Law for Sustainability*, ed. Benjamin Richardson and Stepan Wood, 97–125. Oxford: Hart Publishing, 2006.

Flannery, Brian P., and Charlotte A. B. Grezo, eds. *IPIECA Symposium on Critical Issues in the Economics of Climate Change*. London: IPIECA, 1997.

Flannery, Tim. *The Weather Makers: How Man is Changing the Climate and What It Means for Life on Earth*. New York: Atlantic Monthly Press, 2005.

Fleming, James Rodger. *Historical Perspectives on Climate Change*. New York: Oxford University Press, 1998.

Fletcher, Susan R. *Global Environmental Facility: Overview*. (Oct. 28, 2005). http://leahy.senate.gov/issues/foreign%20policy/PDFS/GlobalEnvironmentFacility .pdf.

Flue-Cured Tobacco Cooperative Stabilization Corp. v. United States Envtl. Prot. Agency, 313 F.3d 852 (4th Cir. 2002).

Food, Agriculture, Conservation and Trade Act of 1990. Pub. L. No. 101-624, Title XXIV, 104 Stat. 3359.

Freestone, David, and Ellen Hey, eds. *The Precautionary Principle and International Law: The Challenge of Implementation*. The Hague: Kluwer Law International, 1996.

Friedman, Thomas L. "The Power of Green." *New York Times Magazine*, Apr. 15, 2007.

Frischman, Brett M., and Mark A. Lemley. "Spillovers." *Columbia Law Review* 107 (2007): 257–301.

Frumhoff, Peter C., James McCarthy, Jerry Melillo, Susanne Moser, and Donald Wuebbles, *Confronting Climate Change in the U.S. Northeast: Science, Impacts, and Solutions*. July 2007. http://www.climatechoices.org/assets/documents/ climatechoices/confronting-climate-change-in-the-u-s-northeast.pdf.

Funk, William. "Free Market Environmentalism: Wonder Drug or Snake Oil?" *Harvard Journal of Law Public and Policy* 15 (1992): 511–516.

Galbraith, John Kenneth. *American Capitalism: The Concept of Countervailing Power*. Boston: Houghton Mifflin, 1952.

Galbraith, John Kenneth. *The New Industrial State*. Boston: Houghton Mifflin, 1967.

Geistfeld, Mark. "Reconciling Cost-Benefit Analysis with the Principle That Safety Matters More Than Money." *New York University Law Review* 76 (2001): 114–189.

Gelbspan, Ross. *Boiling Point*. New York: Basic Books, 2004.

Gelbspan, Ross. *The Heat Is On: The Climate Crisis, the Cover-Up, the Prescription*. Cambridge, MA: Perseus Books, 1998.

Gelbspan, Ross. *The Heat Is On: The High Stakes Battle Over Earth's Threatened Climate*. Reading, MA: Addison-Wesley, 1997.

Gerrard, Michael B., ed. *Global Climate Change and U.S. Law*. Chicago: ABA Publishing, 2007.

Giersch, Herbert, Karl-Heinz Paque, and Holger Shmieding. "Openess, Wage Restraint, and Macroeconomic Stability: West Germany's Road to Prosperity 1948–1959." Chap. 1 in *Postwar Economic Reconstruction and Lessons for the East Today*, ed. Rudiger Dornbusch, Wilhelm Nölling, and Richard Layard, 1–28. Cambridge, MA: MIT Press, 1993.

Giljum, Stefan, and N. Eisenmenger. "North–South Trade and the Distribution of Environmental Goods and Burdens: A Biophysical Perspective." *Journal of Environment and Develeopment* 13, no. 1 (2004): 73–100.

Giovanazzo, Christopher T. "Defending Overstatement: The Symbolic Clean Air Act and Carbon Dioxide." *Harvard Environmental Law Review* 30 (2006): 99–163.

Global Change Research Act of 1990. Pub. L. No. 101-606, 104 Stat. 3096.

Global Commons Institute. "GCI Briefing: Contraction and Convergence." http://www.gci.org.uk/.

Global Environmental Facility. *Climate Change Adaptation.* http://www.gefweb.org/interior.aspx?id=264.

Global Environmental Facility, and the United Nations Development Programme. "Strategic Priority on Adaptation (SPA): Guidelines." http://www.undp.org/gef/adaptation/funds/04c_i.htm#spa.

Goodstein, Eban, and Hart Hodges. "Polluted Data." *American Prospect* (Nov. 1997). http://www.prospect.org/cs/articles?article=polluted_data.

Graham, John D. "The Perils of the Precautionary Principle: Lessons from the American and European Experience." http://www.heritage.org/Research/Regulation/upload/54513_1.pdf.

Graham, John D., and Jonathan Baert Wiener, eds. *Risk vs. Risk: Tradeoffs in Protecting Health and the Environment.* Cambridge, MA: Harvard University Press, 1995.

Greenblatt, Jeffrey, Samir Succar, David C. Denkenberger, Robert H. Williams and Robert H. Socolow. "Baseload Wind Energy: Modeling the Competition Between Gas Turbines and Compressed Air Energy Storage for Supplemental Generation." *Energy Policy* 35 (2007): 1474–1492.

Greenhouse Effect and Global Climate Change, Part 2: Hearing Before the S. Comm. on Energy and Natural Resources. 100th Cong. 43, 1988, Statements of James E. Hansen and Hon. J. Bennett Johnston.

Griffin, James M., ed. *Global Climate Change: The Science, Economics and Politics.* Cheltenham: Edward Elgar, 2003.

Grubb, Michael Christian Vrolijk, and Duncan Brack,*The Kyoto Protocol: A Guide and Assessment.* London: Royal Institute of International Affairs, Energy and Environmental Programme, 1999.

Gupta, Joyeeta. *The Climate Change Convention and Developing Countries: From Conflict to Consensus?* Dordrecht: Kluwer Academic Publishers, 1997.

Hagstrom, Jerry. "Nature's Storage System." *National Journal (Wash.)* (July 7, 2007): 31.

Hahn, Robert W., and Robert N. Stavins. "Incentive-Based Environmental Regulation: A New Era for an Old Idea?" *Ecology Law Quarterly* 18 (1991): 1–42.

Haines, Andy, and Jonathan A. Patz. "Health Effects of Climate Change." *Journal of the American Medical Association* 291, no. 1 (2004): 99–103.

Hakim, Danny. "Challenge to Emissions Rule Is Set to Start." *New York Times*, Apr. 10, 2007.

Hall, Darwin C., and Richard B. Howarth eds. *The Long-Term Economics of Climate Change: Beyond a Doubling of Greenhouse Gas Concentration.* Vol. 3 of *Advances in the Economics of Environmental Resources.* Amsterdam: Elsevier, 2001.

Hanemann, Michael, and Alexander E. Farrell. *Managing GHG Emissions in California.* Berkeley, CA: California Climate Change Center at UC Berkeley, 2006.

Hansen, James. "The Threat to the Planet: Actions Needed to Avert Dangerous Climate Change." Talk delivered to SOLAR 2006 Conference on Renewable Energy, Denver, Colorado, July 10, 2006. http://www.columbia.edu/~jeh1/2006/solar_threattalk_20060905.pdf.

Hansen, James, Makiko Sato, Pushker Kharecha, David Beerling, Robert Berner, Valerie Masson-Delmotte, Mark Pagani, Maureen Raymo, Dana L. Royer and James C. Zachos. "Target Atmospheric CO_2: Where Should Humanity Aim?" *Open Atmospheric Science Journal* 2 (2008): 217–231.

Hansen, James, M. Sato, R. Ruedy, P. Kharecha, A. Lacis, R. Miller, L. Nazarenko, K. Lo, G. A. Schmidt, G. Russell, I. Aleinov, S. Bauer, E. Baum, B. Cairns, V. Canuto, M. Chandler, Y. Cheng, A. Cohen, A. Del Genio, G. Faluvegi, E. Fleming, A. Friend, T. Hall, C. Jackman, J. Jonas, M. Kelley, N. Y. Kiang, D. Koch, G. Labow, J. Lerner, S. Menon, T. Novakov, V. Oinas, Ja. Perlwitz, Ju. Perlwitz, D. Rind, A. Romanou, R. Schmunk, D. Shindell, P. Stone, S. Sun, D. Streets, N. Tausnev, D. Thresher, N. Unger, M. Yao, and S. Zhang. "Dangerous Human-Made Interference with Climate: A GISS ModelE Study." *Atmospheric Chemistry and Physics* 7 (2007): 2287–2312.

Hanson, Jon D., and Douglas A. Kysar. "Taking Behavioralism Seriously: Some Evidence of Market Manipulation." *Harvard Law Review* 112 (1999): 1420–1572.

Hardin, Garrett. "The Tragedy of the Commons." *Science* 162 (Dec. 13, 1968): 1243–1248.

Hare, R. M. *The Language of Morals.* Oxford: Oxford University Press, 1952.

Harrison, P., and F. Pearce. "AAAS Atlas of Population and Environment." 2001. http://www.ourplanet.com/aaas/pages/atmos02.html

Harsanyi, J. C. "Cardinal Utility in Welfare Economics and in the Theory of Risk-Taking." *Journal of Political Economy* 61, no. 5 (1953): 434–435.

Hart, David M., and David G. Victor. "Scientific Elites and the Making of US Policy for Climate Change Research." *Social Studies of Science* 23, no. 4 (Nov. 1993): 643–680.

Harvey, David. *A Brief History of Neoliberalism.* Oxford: Oxford University Press, 2005.

Hawksworth, John. *The World in 2050: Implications of Global Growth for Carbon Emissions and Climate Change Policy.* New York: PricewaterhouseCoopers, 2006.

Hayes, Peter, and Kirk Smith, eds. *The Global Greenhouse Regime: Who Pays? Science, Economics, and North–South Politics in the Climate Change Convention.* Tokyo: United Nations University Press, 1994.

Heinzerling, Lisa. "Climate Change, Human Health, and the Post-Cautionary Principle." *Georgetown Law Journal* 96 (2008): 445–460.

Heinzerling, Lisa. "Discounting Our Future." *Land and Water Law Review* 34 (1999): 39–74.

Heinzerling, Lisa. "Knowing Killing and Environmental Law." *New York University Environmental Law Journal* 14, no. 3 (2006): 521–526.

Heinzerling, Lisa. "Regulatory Costs of Mythic Proportions." *Yale Law Journal* 107 (May 1998): 1981–2070.

Helmer, Martins, Rice & Popham. "Several Major Oil Companies Repay Royalties Owed to United States of Nearly One Half Billion Dollars." http://www.fcalawfirm.com/cases/case003.html. Accessed April 14, 2008.

Hibbing, John, and Elizabeth Theiss-Morse. *Congress as Public Enemy.* New York: Cambridge University Press, 1995.

Hillman, Mayer. "A Modest Proposal to Save the Planet." *Independent Review* (May 28, 2004).

Hirschman, Albert O. *The Rhetoric of Reaction: Perversity, Futility, Jeopardy.* Cambridge: The Belknap Press of Harvard University Press, 1991.

Hoffert, Martin I., Ken Caldeira, Gregory Benford, David R. Criswell, Christopher Green, Howard Herzog, Atul K. Jain, Haroon S. Kheshgi, Klaus S. Lackner, John S. Lewis, H. Douglas Lightfoot, Wallace Manheimer, John C. Mankins, Michael E. Mauel, L. John Perkins, Michael E. Schlesinger, Tyler Volk, and Tom M. L. Wigley. "Advanced Technology Paths to Global Climate Stability: Energy for a Greenhouse Planet." *Science* 298, no. 5595 (Nov. 1, 2002): 981–987.

Hoffman, Andrew J., ed. *Global Climate Change: A Senior-Level Debate at the Intersection of Economics, Strategy, Technology, Science, Politics, and International Negotiation.* San Francisco: New Lexington Press, 1998.

Hohmann, Harald. *Precautionary Legal Duties and Principles of Modern International Environmental Law.* London: Graham and Trotman, 1994.

Honore, A. M. "The Morality of Tort Law—Questions and Answers." *Philosophical Foundations of Tort Law*, ed. David G. Owen. Oxford: Clarendon Press, 1995.

Hornstein, Donald T. "Lessons from Federal Pesticide Regulation on the Paradigms and Politics of Environmental Law Reform." *Yale Journal on Regulation* 10 (1993): 369–446.

House Committee on Government Reform, Minority Staff Special Investigations Division. *Flash Report: Key Impacts of the Energy Bill—H.R. 6*, Washington, D.C.: GPO, July 2005, http://oversight.house.gov/documents/20050726164801-76366.pdf.

House Committee on Oversight and Government Reform. *Political Interference with Climate Change Science Under the Bush Administration.* 110th Cong., 1st Sess., 2007.

Howard, Phillip K. *The Death of Common Sense: How Law Is Suffocating America.* New York: Warner Books, 1994.

Hymel, Mona. "The United States' Experience with Energy-Based Tax Incentives: The Evidence Supporting Tax Incentives for Renewable Energy." *Loyola University Chicago Law Journal* 38 (2006): 43–80.

Intergovernmental Panel on Climate Change (IPCC). *IPCC Second Assessment: Climate Change 1995.* 1995. http://www.ipcc.ch/pdf/climate-changes-1995/ipcc-2nd-assessment/2nd-assessment-en.pdf.

Intergovernmental Panel on Climate Change (IPCC). *Climate Change 2001: Mitigation.* Edited by B. Metz, O. R. Davidson, R. Swart, and J. Pan. New York: Cambridge University Press, 2001.

Intergovernmental Panel on Climate Change (IPCC). *Climate Change 2005: The Science of Climate Change.* New York: Cambridge University Press, 2006.

Intergovernmental Panel on Climate Change (IPCC). *Climate Change 2007: Impacts, Adaptation, and Vulnerability.* Contribution of Working Group II to the Intergovernmental Panel on Climate Change. Edited by Martin L. Parry and Osvaldo Canziani. New York: Cambridge University Press, 2007.

Intergovernmental Panel on Climate Change (IPCC). *Climate Change 2007: Mitigation of Climate Change.* Contribution of Working Group III to the Fourth Assessment Report of the Intergovernmental Panel on Climate Change. Edited by B. Metz, O. R. Davidson, P. R. Bosch, R. Dave, and L. A. Meyer. New York: Cambridge University Press, 2007.

Intergovernmental Panel on Climate Change (IPCC). *Climate Change 2007: Synthesis Report.* Contribution of Working Groups I, II, and III to the Fourth Assessment Report of the Intergovernmental Panel on Climate Change. Geneva: IPCC, 2007.

Intergovernmental Panel on Climate Change (IPCC). *Climate Change 2007: The Physical Science Basis.* Contribution of Working Group I to the Fourth Assessment Report of the Intergovernmental Panel on Climate Change. Edited by Susan Solomon, Dahe Qin, Martin Manning, Melinda Marquis, Kristen Averyt, Melinda M. B. Tignor, Henry LeRoy Miller, Jr., and Zhenlin Chen. New York: Cambridge University Press, 2007.

International Harvester v. Ruckelshaus. 478 F.2d 615 (D.C. Cir. 1973).

"The Isolation of America." *Spiegel Online* (Aug. 31, 2007).http://www.spiegel.de/international/germany/0,1518,503176,00.html.

Izzo, Ralph. Testimony of Ralph Izzo, Chairman and Chief Executive Officer-Elect, Public Service Enterprise Group Inc., before the Subcommittee on Energy and Air Quality of the House Committee on Energy and Commerce, 110th Cong., 1st Sess., March 29, 2007.

Jackson, Tim, Katie Begg, and Stuart Parkinson, eds. *Flexibility in Climate Policy: Making the Kyoto Mechanisms Work.* London: Earthscan, 2001.

Jaenicke, Markin, and Claus Jacob. "Ecological Modernization and the Creation of Lead Markets." *In Towards Environmental Innovation Systems,* ed. Matthias Weber and Jens Hemmelskamp, 175–194. Berlin-Heidelberg: Springer, 2005.

Jaffe, Adam B., Richard G. Newell, and Robert N. Stavins. "Environmental Policy and Technological Change." *Environmental and Resource Economics* 22 (2002): 41–69.

Jaffe, Adam B., Richard G. Newell, and Robert N. Stavins. "Technological Change and the Environment." In *Handbook of Environmental Economics*, ed. Karl-Goran Maler and Jeffrey Vincent, 464–467. Amsterdam: Elsevier, 2003.

Jehl, Douglas, with Andrew C. Revkin. "Bush in Reversal Won't Seek Cut in Emissions of Carbon Dioxide." *New York Times*, Mar. 14, 2001: A1.

Johnston, David Cay. "Competitive Era Fails to Shrink Electric Bills." *New York Times*, Oct. 15, 2006.

Justus, John R., and Susan R. Fletcher. *Global Climate Change: Major Scientific and Policy Issues.* CRS Report RL33602, August 11, 2006.

Kahn, Matthew E. "The Death Toll from Natural Disasters: The Role of Income, Geography, and Institutions." *Review of Economics and Statistics* 87, no. 2 (2005): 271–284.

Kaldor, Nicholas. "Welfare Propositions of Economics and Interpersonal Comparisons of Utility." *Economics Journal* 49 (1939): 549–550.

Kamieniecki, Sheldon. *Corporate America and Environmental Policy: How Often Does Business Get Its Way?* Stanford: Stanford University Press, 2006.

Kant, Immanuel. *The Critique of Practical Reason.* Translated and edited with an introduction by Lewis White Beck. Chicago: University of Chicago Press, 1947.

Keith, Stuart N. "Note: The EPA's Discretion to Regulate Acid Rain: A Discussion of the Requirements for Triggering Section 115 of the Clean Air Act." *Cleveland State Law Review* 36 (1987–1988): 133–155.

Kelman, Mark. "On Democracy-Bashing: A Skeptical Look at the Theoretical and 'Empirical' Practice of the Public Choice Movement." *Virginia Law Review* 74 (1988): 199–273.

Kennedy, Duncan. "Cost-Benefit Analysis of Entitlement Problems: A Critique." *Stanford Law Review* 33 (Feb. 1981): 387–445.

Kennedy, John F. Special Message to the Congress on Urgent National Needs, May 25, 1961. http://www.jfklibrary.org/Historical+Resources/Archives/Reference+Desk/Speeches/.

Keohane, Nathaniel O., Richard L. Revesz, and Robert N. Stavins. "The Choice of Regulatory Instruments in Environmental Policy." *Harvard Environmental Law Review* 22 (1998): 313–367.

Kleypas, J. A., Richard A. Feely, Victoria J. Fabry, Chris Langdon, Christopher L. Sabine, and Lisa L. Robbins. *Impacts of Ocean Acidification on Coral Reefs and Other Marine Calcifiers: A Guide for Future Research.* June 2006. http://www.ucar.edu/news/releases/2006/report.shtml.

Kolbert, Elizabeth. *Field Notes from a Catastrophe: Man, Nature, and Climate Change.* New York: Bloomsbury Publishing, 2006.

Koplow, Douglas, and Aaron Martin. *Fueling Global Warming: Federal Subsidies to Oil in the United States.* Cambridge, MA: Greenpeace, 1998, http://archive .greenpeace.org/climate/oil/fdsuboil.pdf.

Kriz, Margaret. "Hot Opportunities." National Journal (Wash.), July 7, 2007. http://news.nationaljournal.com/articles/climate/intro.htm.

Krupp, Fred. Testimony of Fred Krupp, Environmental Defense, before the Subcommittee on Energy and Power, of the House Committee on Energy and Commerce, 110th Cong., 1st Sess., February 13, 2007.

Kuik, Onno, Paul Peters, and Nico Schrijver, eds. *Joint Implementation to Curb Climate Change: Legal and Economic Aspects.* Vol. 2 of *Environment and Policy.* Dordrecht: Kluwer Academic Publishers, 1994.

Kuttner, Robert. *Everything for Sale: The Virtues and Limits of Markets.* New York: Knopf, 1997.

Kyoto Protocol to the United Nations Framework Convention on Climate Change. Dec. 10, 1997. U.N. Doc. FCCC/CP/197/L.7/Add. 1.

Kysar, Douglas A. "Climate Change, Cultural Transformation, and Comprehensive Rationality." *Boston College Environmental Affairs Law Review* 31 (2004): 555–590.

Kysar, Douglas A. "It Might Have Been: Risk, Precaution, and Opportunity Costs." *Land Use and Environmental Law* 22 (2006): 1–57.

Kysar, Douglas A. "Sustainable Development and Private Global Governance." *Texas Law Review* 83 (2005): 2109–2166.

Laitos, Jan, Sandi B. Zellmer, Mary C. Wood, and Daniel H. Cole. *Natural Resources Law.* St. Paul, MN: Thompson West, 2006.

Lange, Oscar. "The Foundations of Welfare Economics." *Econometrica* 10 (1942): 215–228.

Lashof, Daniel A., and Dilip R. Ahuja. "Relative Contributions of Greenhouse Gas Emissions to Global Warming." *Nature* 344, no. 6266 (Apr. 5, 1990): 529–531.

Latin, Howard. "Good Science, Bad Regulation, and Toxic Risk Assessment." *Yale Journal on Regulation* 5 (1988): 89–148.

Latin, Howard. "Real Regulatory Efficiency: Implementation of Uniform Standards and 'Fine-Tuning' Regulatory Reforms." *Stanford Law Review* 37 (1985): 1267–1332.

Layzer, Judith. "Deep Freeze: How Business Has Shaped the Global Warming Debate in Congress." In *Business and Environmental Policy: Corporate Interests in the American Political System,* ed. Michael Kraft and Sheldon Kamienicki. Cambridge, MA: MIT Press, 2007.

Lazarus, Richard J. *The Making of Environmental Law.* Chicago: University of Chicago Press, 2004.

Lazzari, Salvatore. *Issue Brief for Congress: Energy Tax Policy.* Congressional Research Service Report, No. IB10054, April 22, 2005, https://www.policyarchive .org/bitstream/handle/10207/753/IB10054_20050422.pdf?sequence=21.

Lazzari, Salvatore. *Issue Brief for Congress: Energy Tax Policy: An Economic Analysis.* Congressional Research Service Report, No. RL30406, June 28, 2005, http://cnie.org/NLE/CRSreports/05jun/RL30406.pdf.

Lead Industries Ass'n, Inc. v. Environmental Prot. Agency. 647 F.2d 1130, D.C. Cir. 1979.

Lee, Jennifer 8. "Exxon Backs Groups That Question Global Warming." *New York Times*, May 28, 2003: C5.

Leggett, Jeremy. "The Ill Winds of Change: As Hurricane Follows Hurricane, the Trillion-Dollar Insurance Industry Is Now Waking Up to Global Warming." Guardian, Oct. 2, 1992: 29.

Levkin, Andrew C. "Bush vs. the Laureates: How Science Became a Partisan Issue." *New York Times*, October 19, 2004.

Liang, Stephen Y., K. J. Linthicum, and J. C. Gaydos. "Climate Change and the Monitoring of Vector-borne Disease." *Journal of the American Medical Association* 287, no. 17 (May 2002): 2286.

Libby, Ronald. *Eco-Wars: Political Campaigns and Social Movements.* New York: Columbia University Press, 1998.

Lin, Albert C. "Size Matters: Regulating Nanotechnology." *Harvard Environmental Law Review* 31 (2007): 349–361.

Lips, Karen R., Jay Diffendorfer, Joseph R. Mendelson III, and Michael W. Sears. "Riding the Wave: Reconciling the Roles of Disease and Climate Change in Amphibian Declines." *PLoS Biology* 6, no. 3 (March 2008). http://biology .plosjournals.org/perlserv?request=get-document&doi=10.1371%2Fjournal .pbio.0060072#special.

Liroff, Richard A. *Air Pollution Offsets: Trading, Selling, and Banking.* Washington, D.C.: Conservation Foundation, 1980.

Liroff, Richard A. *Reforming Air Pollution Regulation: The Toil and Trouble of EPA's Bubble.* Washington, D.C.: Conservation Foundation, 1986.

Lobell, David B. and Christopher B. Field. "Global Scale Climate-Crop Yield Relationships and the Impacts of Recent Warming." *Environmental Research Letters* 2, no. 1 (March 2007).

Logan, John R. "The Impact of Katrina: Race and class in Storm Damaged Neighborhoods." Brown University Research Paper. http://www.s4.brown.edu/ Katrina/report.pdf.

Lohman, Larry. *Carbon Trading: A Critical Conversation on Climate Change, Privatisation, and Power.* Uppsala, Sweden: Dag Hammarkjöld Foundation, 2006.

Lohr, Steve. "A Coal Executive with a Clean-up Mission." *New York Times*, Mar. 7, 2007: H2.

Lomborg, Bjørn. *Cool It: The Skeptical Environmentalist's Guide to Global Warming.* New York: Alfred A. Knopf, 2007.

Lomborg, Bjørn, ed. *How to Spend $50 Billion to Make the World a Better Place.* Cambridge: Cambridge University Press, 2006.

Lovins, Amory B. *Soft Energy Paths: Toward a Durable Peace.* Cambridge, MA: Ballinger Publishing, 1977.

Luntz, Frank. "The Environment: A Cleaner, Safer, Healthier America." Luntz Research Corporation, *Straight Talk.* 2002. http://www.ewg.org/files/LuntzResearch_environment.pdf

Lyman, Rick. "Reports Reveal Hurricanes' Impact on Human Landscape." *New York Times,* June 7, 2006: A16.

Lyndon, Mary L. "Information Economics and Chemical Toxicity: Designing Laws to Produce and Use Data." *Michigan Law Review* 87, no. 7 (1989): 1795–1861.

Malcolm, Jay R., C. Liu, R. P. Neilson, L. Hansen, and L. Hannah. "Global Warming and Extinctions of Endemic Species from Biodiversity Hotspots." *Conservation Biology* 20, no. 2 (April 2006): 538–548.

Malloy, Robin Paul. *Law and Market Economy: Reinterpreting the Values of Law and Economics.* Cambridge: Cambridge University Press, 2000.

Malueg, David A.. "Emissions Credit Trading and the Incentive to Adopt New Pollution Abatement Technology." *Journal of Environmental Economics and Management* 16 (1989): 52–57.

Mandel, Gregory N. "Promoting Environmental Innovation and Intellectual Property Innovation: A New Basis for Patent Rewards." *Temple Journal of Science, Technology, and Environmental Law* 24 (2005): 51–69.

Mandel, Gregory N., and James Thuo Gathii. "Cost Benefit Analysis versus the Precautionary Principle: Beyond Cass Sustein's *Laws of Fear.*" *University of Illinois Law Review* (2006): 1037–1080.

Matschoss, Patrick, and Heinz Welsch. "International Emissions Trading and Induced Carbon-Saving Technological Change: Effects of Restricting the Trade in Carbon Rights." *Environmental and Resource Economics* 33 (2006): 169–198.

Matthews, H. Damon, and Ken Caldeira. "Stabilizing Climate Requires Near Zero Emissions." *Geophysical Research Letters* 35, L04705 (2008): 1–5.

Mayhew, David R. *Congress: The Electoral Connection.* New Haven, CT: Yale University Press, 1974.

McCluskey, Martha T. "Efficiency and Social Citizenship: Challenging the Neoliberal Attack on the Welfare State." *Indiana Law Journal* 78 (2003): 783–876.

McCluskey, Martha T. "Thinking with Wolves: Left Legal Theory After the Right's Rise." *Buffalo Law Review* 54 (2007): 1191–1297.

McGarity, Thomas O. "On the Prospect of 'Daubertizing' Judicial Review of Risk Assessment." *Law and Contemporary Problems* 66 (autumn 2003): 155–225.

McGarity, Thomas O. "Our Science Is Sound Science and Their Science Is Junk Science: Science-Based Strategies for Avoiding Accountability and Responsibility for Risk-Producing Products and Activities." *University of Kansas Law Review* 52 (2004): 897–937.

McGarity, Thomas O. "Proposal for Linking Culpability and Causation to Ensure Corporate Accountability for Toxic Risks." *William & Mary Environmental Law and Policy Review* 26 (2001): 1–65.

McGarity, Thomas O. "Regulating Commuters to Clear the Air: Some Difficulties in Implementing a National Program at the Local Level." *Pacific Law Journal* 27 (1996): 1521–1627.

McGarity, Thomas O. "Some Thoughts on 'Deossifying' the Rule-Making Process." *Duke Law Journal* 41 (1992): 1385–1462.

McGarity, Thomas O., and Ruth Ruttenberg. "Counting the Cost of Health, Safety and Environmental Regulation." *Texas Law Review* 80 (2002): 1997–2058.

McGarity, Tom, and Wendy Wagner. *Bending Science: How Special Interests Corrupt Public Health Research*. Cambridge, MA: Harvard University Press, 2008.

McIntyre, Kevin J., Martin V. Kirkwood, and Jason F. Leif, eds. *Energy Policy Act of 2005: Summary and Analysis of the Act's Major Provisions*. Newark, NJ: Matthew Bender, 2006.

McKibbin, Warwick J., and Peter Wilcoxen. "A Better Way to Slow Climate Change." Brookings Policy Brief no. 17, 1997.

McKibben, Warwick J., and Peter J. Wilcoxen. *Climate Change Policy after Kyoto: Blueprint for a Realistic Approach*. Washington, D.C.: Brookings Institution Press, 2002.

McLean, Brian. Testimony of Brian McLean, Director, Office of Atmospheric Programs, Office of Air and Radiation, Environmental Protection Agency, before the Subcommittee on Energy and Air Quality of the House Committee on Energy and Commerce, 110th Cong., 1st Sess., March 29, 2007.

McMichael, A. J., D. J. Campbell-Lendrum, C. F. Corvalan, K. L. Ebi, J. D. Scherega, and A. Woodward, eds. *Climate Change and Human Health: Risks and Responses*. Geneva: World Health Organization, 2003.

McNeill, Judith M., and Jeremy B. Williams. "The Economics of Climate Change: An Examination of the McKibbin-Wilcoxen Hybrid Proposal for a Carbon Price for Australia." U21Global Working Paper No. 005/2007, 2007.

Mendelsohn, Robert, and James E. Neumann, eds. 1999. *The Impact of Climate Change on the United States Economy*. Cambridge: Cambridge University Press.

Mendelson, Joseph R. III, Karen R. Lips, Ronald W. Gagliardo, George B. Rabb, James P. Collins, et al. "Confronting Amphibian Declines and Extinctions." *Science* 313, no. 5783 (July 7, 2006): 48.

Metz, Bert, and Detlef van Vuuren. "How, and at What Costs, Can Low-Level Stabilization be Achieved?—An Overview." In *Avoiding Dangerous Climate*

Change, ed. Hans Joachim Schellnhuber, 337–345. Cambridge: Cambridge University Press, 2006.

Meyer, Aubrey. *Contraction and Convergence: The Global Solution to Climate Change*. Totnes, Devon: Green Books, 2000.

Meyer, Ryan. "Intractable Debate: Why Congressional Hearings on Climate Fail to Advance Policy." *Perspectives in Public Affairs* 3 (2006): 85–99.

Michaelowa, Axel, and Sonja Butzengeiger. "EU Emissions Trading: Navigating Between Scylla and Charybdis." *Climate Policy* 5, no. 1 (2005): 1–5.

Miles, Jonathan. "Tobacco Road." New York Times, May 6, 2007, Book Review Section, 6 (reviewing Allan M. Brandt, *The Cigarette Century: The Rise, Fall, and Deadly Persistence of the Product That Defined America*, New York: Basic Books, 2007).

Miller, Frank, and Rolf Sartorius. "Public Goods and Population Policy." *Philosophy and Public Affairs* 8 (1979): 148–174.

Mineral Lands Leasing Act of 1920. 30 U.S.C. §1331 *et seq.*

Mineral Leasing Act of Acquired Lands. 30 U.S.C. §351 *et seq.*

Mintzer, Irving M., Art Kleiner, and Amber Leondard, eds. *Confronting Climate Change: Risks, Implications, and Responses*. Cambridge: Cambridge University Press, 1993.

Mishan, Edward J. *Cost-Benefit Analysis: An Introduction*. New York: Praeger, 1971.

Montenegro, A., Victor Brovkin, Michael Eby, David Archer, and Andrew J. Weaver. "Long Term Fate of Anthropogenic Carbon." *Geophysical Research Letters* 34, L19707 (2007): 1–5.

Montreal Protocol on Substances That Deplete the Ozone Layer, Jan. 1, 1989. Reprinted (prior to date of enactment) in *International Legal Materials* 26 (1987).

Mooney, Chris. "Some Like It Hot." *Mother Jones* 30, no. 3 (May–June 2005): 36.

Mooney, Chris. *The Republican War on Science*. New York: Basic Books, 2005.

Moore, Thomas G. *Climate of Fear: Why We Shouldn't Worry about Global Warming*. Washington, D.C.: Cato Institute, 1998.

Morlot, Jan Corfee, ed. *Climate Change: Mobilising Global Effort*. Paris: Organisation for Economic Co-operation and Development, 1997.

Morlot, Jan Corfee, and Shardul Agrawala, eds. *The Benefits of Climate Change Policies: Analytical and Framework Issues*. Paris: Organisation for Economic Co-operation and Development, 2004.

Morris, Michael G. Testimony of Michael G. Morris, Chairman, President and Chief Executive Officer, American Electric Power, before the Subcommittee on Energy and Air Quality of the House Committee on Energy and Commerce, 110th Cong., 1st. Sess., March 20, 2007.

Mortimer, Lucy. "An Uncertain Path." *Carbon Finance* 3, no. 20 (April 2006). http://www.carbon-financeonline.com.

Mueller, Dennis G. *Public Choice against Populism: A Confrontation between the Theory of Democracy and the Theory of Social Choice*. San Francisco: Freeman, 1982.

Mufson, Steven. "Climate Change Debate Hinges on Economics." *Washington Post*, July 15, 2007: A1.

Myers, Norman, and Jennifer Kent. *Perverse Subsidies: How Tax Dollars Can Undercut the Environment and the Economy*. Washington, D.C.: Island Press, 2001.

"NASA Leader: Who Says Warming Is a Problem?" *New York Times*, June 1, 2007. http://www.nytimes/com/2007/06/01/science/earth/01griffin.html.

National Commission on Energy Policy. *Ending the Energy Stalemate: A Bipartisan Strategy to Meet America's Energy Challenges*. Washington, D.C.: National Commission on Energy Policy, 2004. http://www.energycommission.org/ht/a/GetDocumentAction/i/1088.

National Development and Reform Commission, People's Republic of China. "China's National Climate Change Programme." June 2007, http://en.ndrc.gov.cn/newsrelease/P020070604561191006823.pdf.

National Energy Act. Pub. L. No. 95-618, 1978.

National Energy Policy Development Group. *National Energy Policy*. Washington, D.C.: The White House, May 2001.

Near v. Minnesota, 283 U.S. 697 (1931).

Nesmith, Jeff. "Climate Debate Sizzles as Democrats Take Over: ExxonMobil Is Accused of Paying Skeptics." *Atlanta Journal-Constitution*, Jan. 4, 2007: 6A.

Newell, Richard G., Adam B. Jaffe, and Robert N. Stavins. "The Induced Innovation Hypothesis and Energy Saving Technological Change." *Quarterly Journal of Economics* 114 (1999): 941–975.

Newsweek Poll. Conducted by Princeton Survey Research, August 1–2, 2007. http://www.pollingreport.com/enviro.htm.

New York Times Co. v. U.S., 403 U.S. 713 (1971) (Pentagon Papers Case).

Nocera, Joe. "Exxon Mobil Just Wants to Be Loved." *New York Times*, Feb. 10, 2007: C1.

Nordhaus, Robert R., and Kyle W. Danish. "Assessing the Options for Designing a Mandatory U.S. Greenhouse Gas Reduction Program." *Boston College Environmental Affairs Law Review* 32 (2005): 97–163.

Nordhaus, William D. "Accompanying Notes and Documentation of DICE-2007 Model: Notes on DICE-2007.delta.v8 as of September 21, 2007." October 2007. http://nordhaus.econ.yale.edu/Accom_Notes_100507.pdf. Accessed February 2008.

Nordhaus, William D. "A Review of the *Stern Review* on the Economics of Climate Change." *Journal of Economic Literature* 45 (Sept. 2007): 686–702.

Nordhaus, William D., ed. *Economics and Policy Issues in Climate Change.* Washington, D.C.: Resources for the Future, 1998.

Nordhaus, William D. *Managing the Global Commons: The Economics of Climate Change.* Cambridge, Mass.: MIT Press, 1994.

Nordhaus, William D. *The Challenge of Global Warming: Economic Models and Environmental Policy.* September 2007. http://nordhaus.econ.yale.edu/dice_mss_091107_public.pdf. Accessed February 2008.

Nordhaus, William D. "The *Stern Review* on the Economics of Climate Change." May 3, 2007. http://nordhaus.econ.yale.edu/stern_050307.pdf. Accessed February 12, 2008.

North, Douglass C. *Institutions, Institutional Change, and Economic Performance.* Cambridge: Cambridge University Press, 1990.

Nozick, Robert. *Anarchy, State, and Utopia.* New York: Basic Books, 1974.

O'Driscoll, Patrick. "Animals Scramble as Climate Warms." *USA Today*, June 5, 2006.

Office of Management and Budget. *Economic Analysis of Federal Regulations Under Executive Order 12866.* 1996. http://www.whitehouse.gov/omb/inforeg_riaguide/.

Office of the Auditor General of Canada. *2006 Report of the Commissioner of the Environment and Sustainable Development to the House of Commons.* http://www.oag-bvg.gc.ca/domino/reports.nsf/html/c20060900se01.html.

Office of the Inspector General, Department of the Interior. *Investigative Report, Minerals Management Service: False Claims Allegations.* September 7, 2007. http://www.doioig.gov/upload/Qui%20tam.pdf.

Okonski, Kendra, ed. *Adapt or Die: The Science, Politics, and Economics of Climate Change.* London: Profile Books, 2003.

Olmstead, Sheila, and Robert Stavins. "An International Policy Architecture for the Post-Kyoto Era." *American Economic Review* 96, no. 2 (May 2006): 35–38.

Olson, Mancur. *The Logic of Collective Action.* Cambridge, MA: Harvard University Press, 1971.

Olson, Mancur. *The Logic of Collective Action: Public Goods and the Theory of Groups.* New York: Schocken Books, 1965.

Organisation for Economic Co-operation and Development. *Climate Change: Evaluating the Socio-economic Impacts.* Paris: OECD, 1991.

Organisation for Economic Co-operation and Development. *Responding to Climate Change: Selected Economic Issues.* Paris: OECD, 1991.

Organisation for Economic Co-operation and Development and International Energy Agency. *Climate Policy Uncertainty and Investment Risk.* Paris, France: OECD, 2007.

Ott, Hermann E., Bernd Brouns, Wolfgang Sterk, and Bettina Wittneben. "It Takes Two to Tango—Climate Policy at COP 10 in Buenos Aires and Beyond." *Journal for European Environmental and Planning Law* 2 (2005): 84–91.

Outer Continental Shelf Lands Act. 43 U.S.C. §1331 *et seq.*

Oxfam International. *Financing Adaptation: Why the U.N.'s Bali Climate Conference Must Mandate the Search for New Funds.* Dec. 4, 2007. http://www.oxfam.ca/news-and-publications/publications-and-reports/financing-adaptation-why-the-un2019s-bali-climate-conference-must-mandate-the-search-for-new-funds/file.

Pacala, Stephen, and Robert Socolow. "Stabilization Wedges: Solving the Climate Problem for the Next 50 Years with Current Technologies." *Science* 305, no. 5686 (2004): 968–972.

Page, Edward A. *Climate Change, Justice, and Future Generations.* Northhampton, MA: Edward Elgar, 2006.

Parfit, Derek. *Reasons and Persons.* Oxford: Clarendon Press, 1984.

Parikh, K., J. Parikh, T. Muralidharan, and N. Hadker. *Valuing Air Pollution in Bombay.* Bombay: Indira Gandhi Institute of Development, 1994.

Parson, Edward A. *Protecting the Ozone Layer: Science and Strategy.* Oxford: Oxford University Press, 2003.

Patz, Jonathan A., Diarmid Campbell-Lendrum, Tracey Holloway, and Jonathan A. Foley. "Impact of Regional Climate Change on Human Health." *Nature* 438 (2005): 310–317.

Pawa, Matthew F., and Benjamin A. Krass. "Behind the Curve: The National Media's Reporting on Global Warming." *Boston College Environmental Affairs Law Review* 33 (2006): 485–509.

Pearce, David W., W. R. Cline, A. N. Achanta, Samuel Fankhauser, R. K. Pachauri, Richard S. J. Tol, and P. Vellinga. "The Social Costs of Climate Change: Greenhouse Damage and the Benefits of Control." In *Climate Change 1995: Economic and Social Dimensions of Climate Change*, ed. J. P. Bruce, H. Lee, and E. F. Haites. Cambridge: Cambridge University Press, 1995.

Pearson, Ben. "Market Failure: Why the Clean Development Mechanism Won't Promote Clean Development." *Journal of Cleaner Production* 15, no. 2 (2007): 247–252.

Percival, Robert V. "Checks without Balance: Executive Office Oversight of the Environmental Protection Agency." *Law and Contemporary Problems* 54 (Aug. 1991): 127–204.

Percival, Robert V. "Who's Afraid of the Precautionary Principle?" *Pace Environmental Law Review* 23 (2005): 21–81.

Peters, Eric. "Seppuku for the U.S. Auto Industry." *American Spectator* (July 6, 2007). http://www.spectator.org/dsp_article.asp?art_id=11687.

Popp, David. "Pollution Control Innovations and the Clean Air Act of 1990." *Journal of Policy Analysis and Management* 22, no. 4 (2003): 641.

Porter, Theodore. *Trust in Numbers: The Pursuit of Objectivity in Science and Public Life.* Princeton: Princeton University Press, 1995.

Posner, Richard A. *Catastrophe: Risk and Response*. New York: Oxford University Press, 2004.

Posner, Richard A. "Utilitarianism, Economics, and Legal Theory." *Journal of Legal Studies* 8 (1979): 103–140.

Posner, Eric A., and Cass R. Sunstein. "Climate Change Justice." John M. Olin Law and Economics Working Paper No. 354 (Aug. 2007). http://papers.ssrn.com/sol3/papers.cfm?abstract_id=1008958

Pounds, J. Alan, Martín R. Bustamante, Luis A. Coloma, Jamie A. Consuegra, Michael P. L. Fogden, Pru N. Foster, Enrique La Marca, Karen L. Masters, Andrés Merino-Viteri, Robert Puschendorf, Santiago R. Ron, G. Arturo Sánchez-Azofeifa, Christopher J. Still, and Bruce E. Young. "Widespread Amphibian Extinctions from Epidemic Disease Driven by Global Warming." *Nature* 439, no. 7073 (Jan. 12, 2006): 161–167.

Pring, George. "The United States Perspective." In *Kyoto: From Principles to Practice*, ed. Peter Cameron and Donald Zillman. London: Kluwer Law International, 2001.

Rabin, Robert L. "Federal Regulation in Historical Perspective." *Stanford Law Review* 38 (1986): 1189–1326.

Raffensperger, Carolyn, and Joel Tickner, eds. *Protecting Public Health*. Washington, D.C.: Island Press, 1999.

Rawls, John. *A Theory of Justice*. Cambridge, MA: Harvard University Press, 1971.

Rawls, John. *The Law of Peoples*. Cambridge, MA: Harvard University Press, 1999.

Regens, James L., and Robert W. Rycroft. *The Acid Rain Controversy*. Pittsburgh: University of Pittsburgh Press, 1988.

Repetto, Robert, and Duncan Austin. *The Costs of Climate Protection: A Guide for the Perplexed*. Washington, D.C.: World Resources Institute, 1997.

Revelle, Roger, and Hans E. Suess. "Carbon Dioxide Exchange between Atmosphere and Ocean and the Question of an Increase of Atmospheric CO2 During the Past Decades." *Tellus* 9 (1957): 18.

Revesz, Richard L. "Environmental Regulation, Cost-Benefit Analysis, and the Discounting of Human Lives." *Columbia Law Review* 99 (May 1999): 941–1017.

Revesz, Richard L. "Federalism and Environmental Regulation: A Public Choice Analysis." *Harvard Law Review* 115 (2001): 553–641.

Revkin, Andrew C. "Climate Expert Says NASA Tried to Silence Him." *New York Times*, January 29, 2006.

Revkin, Andrew C. "Link to Global Warming in Frogs' Disappearance Is Challenged." *New York Times*, Mar. 25, 2008.

Revkin, Andrew C., and Matthew C. Wald. "Solar Power Captures Imagination, Not Money." *New York Times*, July 16, 2007: A1.

Ricci, Francesco. "Environmental Policy and Growth When Inputs Are Differentiated in Pollution Intensity." *Environmental and Resource Economics* 38 (2007): 285–310.

Rice, John G. Testimony of John G. Rice, Vice Chairman, General Electric Company, before the Subcommittee on Energy and Power, of the House Committee on Energy and Commerce, 110th Cong., 1st Sess., February 13, 2007.

Rich, Robert F., and Kelly R. Merrick. "Use and Misuse of Science: Global Climate Change and the Bush Administration." *Virginia Journal of Social Policy and the Law* 14 (2007): 223–252.

Riker, William H. *Liberalism against Populism: A Confrontation between the Theory of Democracy and the Theory of Social Choice*. San Francisco: W. H. Freeman, 1982.

Rio Declaration of the United Nations Conference on Environment and Development (UNCED). June 14, 1992.

Rio Declaration on Environment and Development, U.N. Doc. A/CONF.151/5/ Rev. 1, 1992. Reprinted in *International Legal Materials* 31 (1992): 874.

Roberts, J. Timmons, and Bradley C. Parks. *A Climate of Injustice: Global Inequality, North-South Politics, and Climate Policy*. Cambridge, MA: MIT Press, 2007.

Rogers, James E. Testimony of James E. Rogers, Chairman, President and CEO, Duke Energy Company, before the Subcommittee on Energy and Air Quality of the House Committee on Energy and Commerce, 110th Cong., 1st. Sess., March 20, 2007.

Rogner, H.-Holger, D. Zhou, R. Bradley, P. Crabbé, O. Edenhofer, B. Hare, L. Kuijpers, and M. Yamaguchi. "Introduction." In *Climate Change 2007: Mitigation*, 102–103. Cambridge: Cambridge University Press, 2007.

Rosenberg, Norman J., W. E. Easterling III, P. R. Crosson, and J. Darmstadter, eds. *Greenhouse Warming: Abatement and Adaptation*. Washington, D.C.: Resources for the Future, 1989.

Rosenthal, Elisabeth. "As Earth Warms Up, Virus from Tropics Moves to Italy." *New York Times*, Dec. 23, 2007: 21.

Roughgarden, Tim, and Stephen H. Schneider. "Climate Change Policy: Quantifying Uncertainties for Damages and Optimal Carbon Taxes." *Energy Policy* 27 (1999): 415–429.

Salant, Jonathan D. "U.S. Energy Industry's Lobbying Pays Off with $11.6 Bln in Aid." *Bloomberg News*, July 27, 2005. http://www.bloomberg.com/apps/news? pid=10000103&sid=agbeVimf04Ec&refer=us.

Sandalow, David B. "President Bush and Oil Addiction." Feb. 3, 2006, http:// brookings.edu/views/op-ed/fellows/sandalow_20060203.htm.

Sarewitz, Daniel and Roger Pielke, Jr. "Breaking the Global-Warming Gridlock." *Atlantic Monthly*, July 2000.

Schelling, Thomas C. "What Makes Greenhouse Sense?" *Foreign Affairs* 81 (May–June 2002): 2–9.

Schneider, Keith. "New View Calls Environmental Policy Misguided." *New York Times,* March 21, 1993.

Schneider, Lambert. *Is the CDM Fulfilling Its Environmental and Sustainable Development Objectives? An Evaluation of the CDM and Options for Improvement.* Berlin: Oko-Institut, 2007. http://www.panda.org/aboutwwf/where_we_work/Europe/news/index.cfm?uNewsID=118260.

Schneider, Stephen H., Armin Rosencranz, and John O. Niles, eds. *Climate Change Policy: A Survey.* Washington, D.C.: Island Press, 2002.

Schrag, Daniel P. "Confronting the Climate-Energy Challenge." *Elements* 3 (June 2007): 171–178.

Schultze, Charles. *The Public Use of the Private Interest.* Washington, D.C.: Brookings Institution, 1977.

Schwartz, Peter, and Doug Randall. *An Abrupt Climate Change Scenario and Its Implications for United States National Security.* San Francisco, CA: GBN Global Business Network, 2003.

Scott, Dean. "Business Roundtable Urges Emissions Curbs, Calls for Expanded Greenhouse Gas Registry." *Environment Reporter (Bureau of National Affairs)* 38 (July 20, 2007): 151.

Scott, Dean. "Costs Imposed by U.S. Greenhouse Gas Cap May Be Offset by Projected Economic Growth." *Environment Reporter (Bureau of National Affairs)* 38 (March 2, 2007): 481.

Secretariat of the Convention on Biological Diversity. Cartagena Protocol on Biosafety to the Convention on Biological Diversity. Jan. 29, 2000. Montreal: Secretariat of the Convention on Biological Diversity. http://www.cbd.int/doc/legal/cartagena-protocol-en.pdf.

Seelye, Katherine Q. "President Distances Himself From Global Warming Report." *New York Times,* June 5, 2002.

Sen, Armartya K. *Collective Choice and Social Welfare.* San Francisco: Holden-Day, 1970.

Sen, Amartya K. "Isolation, Assurance, and the Social Rate of Discount." *Quarterly Journal of Economics* 81 (1967): 112–124.

Sen, Amartya. "The Possibility of Social Choice." *American Economic Review* 89, no. 3 (June 1999): 349–378.

"Set America Free": A Blueprint for U.S. Energy Security. http://www.setamericafree.org/blueprint.pdf.

Shabecoff, Philip. "Global Warming Has Begun, Expert Tells Senate." *New York Times,* June 23, 1988.

Shapiro, Sidney A. "Administrative Law After the Counter-Reformation: Restoring Faith in Pragmatic Government." *University of Kansas Law Review* 48 (2000): 689–750.

Shapiro, Sidney A., and Robert L. Glicksman. *Risk Regulation at Risk: Restoring A Pragmatic Approach.* Stanford, CA: Stanford University Press, 2003.

Shapiro, Sidney A., and Christopher H. Schroeder. "Beyond Cost-Benefit Analysis: A Pragmatic Reorientation." *Harvard Environmental Law Review* 32 (2008): 433–501.

Shapiro, Sidney A., and Joseph P. Tomain. "Rethinking Reform of Electricity Markets." *Wake Forest Law Review* 40 (2005): 497–543.

Sharma, Subodh, Sumana Bhattacharya, and Amit Garg. "Greenhouse Gas Emissions from India: A Perspective." *Current Science* 90, no. 3 (2006): 326–334.

Sheeran, Kristen. "Beyond Kyoto: North-South Implications of Emissions Trading and Taxes." *Seattle Journal of Social Justice* 5 (spring–summer 2007): 697–715.

Sherer, F. M. "Schumpeter and Plausible Capitalism." In *Economics of Technical Change*, ed. Edwin Mansfield and Elizabeth Mansfield. Brookfield, VT: Edward Elgar, 1993.

Shue, Henry. "Avoidable Necessity: Global Warming, International Fairness, and Alternative Energy." In *NOMOS XXXVII: Theory and Practice*, ed. Ian Shapiro and Judith Wagner DeCew. New York: New York University Press, 1995.

Shue, Henry. "Climate." In *A Companion to Environmental Philosophy*, ed. Dale Jamieson. Malden, MA: Blackwell Publishers, 2001.

Shue, Henry. "Global Environment and International Inequality." *International Affairs* 75 (1999): 531.

Shui, B., and R. C. Harriss. "The Role of CO_2 Embodiment in U.S.–China Trade." *Energy Policy* 34 (2006): 4063–4068.

Siegel, Joseph A. "Terrorism and Environmental Law: Chemical Facility Site Security vs. Right-to-Know?" *Widener Law Symposium Journal* 9 (2003): 339–385.

Sinden, Amy. "In Defense of Absolutes: Combating the Politics of Power in Environmental Law." *Iowa Law Review* 90 (2005): 1405–1511.

Singer, Peter. *One World: The Ethics of Globalization*. New Haven, CT: Yale University Press, 2002.

Sinnott-Armstrong, Walter, and Richard B. Howarth, eds. *Perspectives on Climate Change: Science, Economics, Politics, Ethics*. Vol. 5 of *Advances in the Economics of Environmental Resources*. Amsterdam: Elsevier, 2005.

Smith, Anne E. Testimony of Anne E. Smith, Vice-President, CRA International, before the Subcommittee on Energy and Air Quality of the House Committee on Energy and Commerce, 110th Cong., 1st Sess., March 29, 2007.

Smith, Frances B. "The Human Costs of Global Warming Policy." In *The Costs of Kyoto*, ed. Jonathan Adler, 39–48. Washington, D.C.: Competitive Enterprise Institute, 1997.

Smith, Rebecca. "Inside Messy Reality of Cutting CO2 Output." *Wall Street Journal*, July 12, 2007: A1.

Sokol, David L. Testimony of David L. Sokol, Chairman and CEO, Mid-American Energy Holdings Company, before the Subcommittee on Energy and Air Quality of the House Committee on Energy and Commerce, 110th Cong., 1st. Sess., March 20, 2007.

Speth, James Gustave. "Development Assistance and Poverty." Chap. 7 in *Stumbling toward Sustainability*, ed. John C. Dernbach, 163–172. Washington, D.C.: Environmental Law Institute, 2002.

Stanton, Elizabeth A., and Frank Ackerman. *Florida and Climate Change: The Costs of Inaction*. Nov. 2007. http://www.ase.tufts.edu/gdae/Pubs/rp/FloridaClimate.html.

Stavins, Robert N. *A U.S. Cap-and-Trade System to Address Global Climate Change*. Brookings Institution, 2007. http://www.brookings.edu/projects/hamiltonproject/Research-Commentary.aspx.

Stavins, Robert N. *Policy Instruments for Climate Change: How Can National Governments Address a Global Problem?* Washington, D.C.: Resources for the Future, 1997.

Stavins, Robert N., Judson Jaffe, and Todd Schatzki. "Too Good to Be True? An Examination of Three Economic Assessments of California Climate Change Policy." http://ssrn.com/abstract-973836.

Stavros, Richard. "Merger Frenzy." *Public Utilities Fortnightly* (Apr. 2007): 22.

Stern, Nicholas. *The Economics of Climate Change: The Stern Review*. Cambridge: Cambridge University Press, 2007.

Stewart, Richard. "Regulation, Innovation, and Administrative Law: A Conceptual Framework." *California Law Review* 69, no. 5 (1981): 1256–1377.

Stewart, Richard B. "Controlling Environmental Risks Through Economic Incentives." *Columbia Journal of Environmental Law* 13, no. 2 (1988): 153–169.

Stockholm Convention on Persistent Organic Pollutants. May 17, 2004. Reprinted in *International Legal Materials* 40 (2001): 532.

Stolberg, Sheryl Gay. "Bush Proposes Goal to Reduce Greenhouse Gases." *New York Times*, June 1, 2007.

Stone, Christopher D. "Is There a Precautionary Principle?" *Environmental Law Reporter* 31 (2001): 10790–10799.

Stone, Deborah A. *Policy Paradox: The Art of Political Decision Making*. New York: Norton, 1997.

Stone, Peter H. "Feeling Storm-Tossed." *National Journal (Wash.)* (July 7, 2007): 28.

Stott, Peter A., D. A. Stone, and M. R. Allen. "Human Contribution to the European Heatwave of 2003." *Nature* 432, no. 7017 (Dec. 2004): 610.

Strasser, Kurt. "Cleaner Technology, Pollution Prevention, and Environmental Regulation." *Fordham Environmental Law Journal* 9 (1997): 1–106.

"Sunlit Uplands: Wind and Solar Power Are Flourishing, Thanks to Subsidies." *Economist* (June 2007): 2.

Sunstein, Cass R. *After the Rights Revolution: Reconceiving the Regulatory State.* Cambridge, MA: Harvard University Press, 1990.

Sunstein, Cass R. "Beyond the Precautionary Principle." *University of Pennsylvania Law Review* 151 (2003): 1003–1058.

Sunstein, Cass R. "Irreversible and Catastrophic." *Cornell Law Review* 91 (2006): 841–897.

Sunstein, Cass R.. *Laws of Fear: Beyond the Precautionary Principle.* Cambridge: Cambridge University Press, 2005.

Sunstein, Cass R. "Of Montreal and Kyoto: A Tale of Two Protocols." *Harvard Environmental Law Review* 31 (2007): 1–66.

Sutherland, Ronald J. "'Big Oil' at the Public Trough? An Examination of Petroleum Subsidies." *Cato Policy Analysis* (February 1, 2001): http://www.cato.org/pubs/pas/pa-390es.html.

Swift, Byron. "Command without Control: Why Cap-and-Trade Should Replace Rate Standards for Regional Pollutants." *Environmental Law Reporter* 31 (March 2001): 10330–10341.

Taylor, Margaret R., Edward L. Rubin, and David A. Hounshell. "Regulation as the Mother of Invention: The Case of SO_2 Control." *Law and Policy* 27 (2005): 348–378.

Tennessee Valley Authority v. Hill. 437 U.S. 153 (1978).

Thorson, Dag Einar, and Amund Lie. "What Is Neoliberalism?" Department of Political Science, University of Oslo (2006). http://folk.uio.no/daget/What%-20is%20Neo-Liberalism%20FINAL.pdf.

Tol, Richard S.J., Thomas E. Downing, Onno J. Kuik, and Joel B. Smith. "Distributional Aspects of Climate Change Impacts." *Global Environmental Change* 14 (2004): 259–272.

Toman, Michael A., ed. *Climate Change Economics and Policy: An RFF Anthology.* Washington, D.C.: Resources for the Future, 2001.

Toman, Michael A., Richard D. Morgenstern, and John Anderson. "The Economics of 'When' Flexibility in the Design of GHG Abatement Policies." *Annual Review of Energy and the Environment* 24 (1999): 431–460.

Tornatzky, Louis, Mitchell Fleischer, and Alok K. Chakrabarti. *The Processes of Technological Innovation.* Lexington, MA: Lexington Books, 1990.

Toth, F. L., ed. *Cost-Benefit Analyses of Climate Change: The Broader Perspectives.* Basel: Birkhäuser, 1997.

Tóth, Ferenc L., ed. *Fair Weather? Equity Concerns in Climate Change.* London: Earthscan, 1999.

Trask, Jeff. "Note: Montreal Protocol Noncompliance Procedure: The Best Approach to Resolving International Environmental Disputes?" *Georgetown Law Journal* 80 (1992): 1973–2001.

Treaty on European Union, April 16, 2003, 2002 O.J. C325.

Trouwborst, Arie. *Evolution and Status of the Precautionary Principle in International Law*. The Hague: Kluwer Law International, 2002.

"Truth in Global Warming." *Wall Street Journal*, Editorial, July 10, 2007: A15.

Ullman-Margalit, Edna. *The Emergence of Norms*. Oxford: Oxford University Press, 1977.

Ullman-Margalit, Edna. "The Generalization Argument: Where Does the Obligation Lie?" *Journal of Philosophy* 73, no. 15 (Sept. 2, 1976): 511–522.

U.N. Development Programme. UNDP's Adaptation Portfolio. http://sdnhq.undp.org/gef-adaptation/projects.

U.N. General Assembly. Fifty-fifth Session, Official Records, Agenda item 101, *High-Level International Intergovernmental Consideration of Financing for Development: Final Report*. Prepared by the United Nations Secretary-General, A/55/1000, 2001. www.un.org/esa/ffd/a55-1000.pdf.

U.N. Security Council, Department of Public Information. "Security Council Holds First-Ever Debate of Impact of Climate Change on Peace, Security, Hearing Over 50 Speakers." News release, April 17, 2007. http://www.un.org/News/Press/docs/2007/sc9000.doc.htm/.

Union of Concerned Scientists. *How to Avoid Dangerous Climate Change: A Target for U.S. Emission Reductions*. Sept. 2007. http://www.ucsusa.org/global_warming/science/emissionstarget.html.

Union of Concerned Scientists. *Scientific Integrity in Policymaking: An Investigation into the Bush Administration's Misuse of Science*. March 2004. http://www.ucsusa.org/assets/documents/scientific_integrity/rsi_final_fullreport_1.pdf.

Union of Concerned Scientists. *Smoke, Mirrors, and Hot Air: How ExxonMobil uses Big Tobacco's Tactics to Manufacture Uncertainty on Climate Science*. Jan. 2007. http://www.ucsusa.org/news/press_release/ExxonMobil-GlobalWarming-tobacco.html.

United Nations Foundation, Sigma Chi, The Scientific Research Society. *Confronting Climate Change: Avoiding the Unmanageable and Managing the Avoidable*. Feb. 3, 2007. http://www.unfoundation.org/files/pdf/2007/SEG_ExecSumm.pdf.

United Nations Framework Convention on Climate Change. Opened for signature May 29, 1992, S. Treaty Doc. No. 102-38 (1992), 1771 U.N.T.S. 107.

United Nations Statistics Division. Millennium Development Goals Indicators, Carbon Dioxide Emissions (CO_2), metric tons of CO_2 per capita (last updated 1 Aug. 2007).http://mdgs.un.org/unsd/mdg/SeriesDetail.aspx?srid=751&crid=.

United States ex rel. Johnson v. Shell Oil Co. 33 F.Supp.2d 528 (E.D. Tex. 1999).

United States v. Am. Elec. Power Serv. Corp. No. C2-99-1250 (S.D. Ohio, Oct. 9, 2007).

United States v. Philip Morris USA, Inc., 449 F. Supp. 2d 1 (D.D.C. 2006).

U.S. Congress, Office of Technology Assessment. *Gauging Control Technology and Regulatory Impacts in Occupational Safety and Health-An Appraisal of*

OSHA's Analytical Approach. OTA-ENV-635. Washington, D.C.: U.S. Government Printing Office, 1995.

U.S. Environmental Protection Agency. *A Review of the Impact of Climate Variability and Change on Aeroallergens and Their Associated Effects*. Dec. 29, 2006, 71 Fed. Reg. 78,432.

U.S. General Accounting Office. *Global Warming: Emission Reductions Are Possible as Scientific Uncertainties Are Resolved. GAO/RCED 90-58*. Washington, D.C.: General Accounting Office, 1990.

U.S. PIRG and Friends of the Earth. *Final Energy Tax Package Overwhelmingly Favors Polluting Industries*. Washington, D.C., July 27, 2005.

van Ireland, Ekko, C. Joyeeta Gupta, and Marcel Kok, eds. *Issues in Climate Change Policy: Theory and Policy*. Cheltenham: Edward Elgar, 2003.

Vanderzwaag, David. "The Precautionary Principle in Environmental Law and Policy: Elusive Rhetoric and First Embraces." *Journal of Environmental Law and Practice* 8 (1999): 355, 358.

Vanderzwaag, David. "The Precautionary Principle and Marine Environmental Protection: Slippery Shores, Rough Seas, and Rising Normative Tides." *Ocean Development and International Law* 33 (2002): 165, 170–173.

Verchick, Robert R.M. "Risk, Fairness, and the Geography of Disaster." *Issues in Legal Scholarship*. Symposium on Catastrophic Risks: Prevention, Compensation, and Recovery (2007): article 6. http://www.bepress.com/ils/iss10/art6.

Viscusi, W. Kip. "The Value of Life." In *The New Palgrave Dictionary of Economics and the Law*, ed. Peter Newman. New York: Palgrave MacMillan, 2008.

Vladeck, David C. "Preemption and Regulatory Failure." *Pepperdine Law Review* 33, no. 1 (2005): 105–110.

Vogel, David. "A Case Study of Clean Air Legislation 1967–1981." In *The Impact of the Modern Corporation*, ed. Betty Bock et al. New York: Columbia University Press, 1980.

Vogel, David. *Fluctuating Fortunes: The Political Power of Business in America*. New York: Basic Books, 1989.

Vogel, David. *National Styles of Regulation: Environmental Policy in Great Britain and the United States*. Ithaca, NY: Cornell University Press, 1986.

Wagner, Wendy E. "Choosing Ignorance in the Manufacture of Toxic Products." *Cornell Law Review* 82 (1997): 773–855.

Wallace, David. *Environmental Policy and Industrial Innovation: Strategies in Europe, the USA, and Japan*. London: Royal Institute of International Affairs, Energy and Environmental Programme, 1995.

Wara, Michael W. "Is the Global Carbon Market Working?" *Nature* 445 (February 2007): 595–596.

Wara, Michael W. "Measuring the Clean Development Mechanism's Performance and Potential." *UCLA Law Review* 55 (2008): 1759–1803.

Weart, Spencer R. *The Discovery of Global Warming*. Cambridge, MA: Harvard University Press, 2003.

WEFA, Inc. *Global Warming: The High Cost of the Kyoto Protocol*. 1998. http://www.heartland.org/policybot/results/11399/Global_Warming_The_High_Cost_of_The_Kyoto_Protocol.html.

Weidenbaum, Murray L. and Robert DeFina. *The Cost of Federal Regulation of Economic Activity*. Washington, D.C.: American Enterprise Institute, May 1978, Reprint 88.

Weitzman, M. "Gamma Discounting for Global Warming." Discussion paper, Cambridge, MA: Harvard University, 1998.

Weitzman, Martin. "On Modeling and Interpreting the Economics of Catastrophic Climate Change." January 2008. http://www.economics.harvard.edu/faculty/weitzman/files/modeling.pdf.

Weitzman, Martin. "Structural Uncertainty and the Value of Statistical Life in the Economics of Catastrophic Climate Change." Working Paper 07-11, AEI Brookings Joint Center, 2007. http://aei-brookings.org/admin/authorpdfs/redirect-safely.php?fname=../pdffiles/WP07-11_topost110607.pdf.

Weitzman, Martin. "The *Stern Review* of the Economics of Climate Change." February 2007. http://www.economics.harvard.edu/faculty/weitzman/files/JELSternReport.pdf.

Weyant, John P. *An Introduction to the Economics of Climate Change Policy*. Arlington, VA.: Pew Center on Global Climate Change, 2000.

White House. "President Signs Energy Policy Act." Press release, Oct. 8, 2005. http://www.whitehouse.gov/news/releases/2005/08/20050808-6.html.

White House. "State of the Union 2006." Jan. 31, 2006. http://www.whitehouse.gov/stateoftheunion/2006.

White House. "State of the Union 2007." Jan. 23, 2007. http://www.whitehouse.gov/stateoftheunion/2007/.

Whites, James C., William Wagner, and Carole N. Beal, eds. *Global Climate Change: The Economic Costs of Mitigation and Adaptation*. New York: Elsevier, 1991.

Whitman v. American Trucking Associations, 531 U.S. 457 (2001).

Wiener, Jonathan Baert. "Global Environmental Regulation: Instrument Choice in Legal Context." *Yale Law Journal* 108 (1999): 677–800.

Wiener, Jonathan B. "Precaution in a Multi-Risk World." In *Human and Ecological Risk Assessment: Theory and Practice*, ed. Dennis J. Paustenbach. New York: Wiley, 2002.

William J. Clinton Presidential Foundation, Energy Forum. *New Thinking on Energy Policy*. http://www.clintonfoundation.org/.

"Wingspread Statement on the Precautionary Principle." In *Protecting Public Health and the Environment: Implementing the Precautionary Principle*, 353–354. Washington, D.C.: Island Press, 1999.

Wollstonecraft, Mary. *A Vindication of the Rights of Women*. Ed. Carol H. Poston. New York: Norton, 1975.

World Bank. *Clean Energy and Development: Toward an Investment Framework*. Washington, D.C.: World Bank, 2006.

World Health Organization. *The World Health Report 2002*. Geneva: WHO, 2002. http://www.who.int/whr/2002/en/.

Worldwatch Institute. *2008 State of the World: Innovations for a Sustainable Economy*. New York: W. W. Norton, 2008.

Yohe, Gary, and Richard S. J. Tol. "Indicators For Social and Economic Coping Capacity: Moving Toward a Working Definition of Adaptive Capacity." *Global Environmental Change* 12 (2002): 25–40.

Young, H. Peyton. *Equity in Theory and Practice*. Princeton, N.J.: Princeton University Press, 1994.

Zoli, Elise, and Aladdine Joroff. "Making Silver Linings." *Environmental Forum* 24, no. 3 (May–June 2007): 22–26.

Index

American and Comparative Environmental Policy
Sheldon Kamieniecki and Michael E. Kraft, series editors

Russell J. Dalton, Paula Garb, Nicholas P. Lovrich, John C. Pierce, and John M. Whiteley, *Critical Masses: Citizens, Nuclear Weapons Production, and Environmental Destruction in the United States and Russia*

Daniel A. Mazmanian and Michael E. Kraft, editors, *Toward Sustainable Communities: Transition and Transformations in Environmental Policy*

Elizabeth R. DeSombre, *Domestic Sources of International Environmental Policy: Industry, Environmentalists, and U.S. Power*

Kate O'Neil, *Waste Trading among Rich Nations: Building a New Theory of Environmental Regulation*

Joachim Blatter and Helen Ingram, editors, *Reflections on Water: New Approaches to Transboundary Conflicts and Cooperation*

Paul F. Steinberg, *Environmental Leadership in Developing Countries: Transnational Relations and Biodiversity Policy in Costa Rica and Bolivia*

Uday Desai, editor, *Environmental Politics and Policy in Industrialized Countries*

Kent Portney, *Taking Sustainable Cities Seriously: Economic Development, the Environment, and Quality of Life in American Cities*

Edward P. Weber, *Bringing Society Back In: Grassroots Ecosystem Management, Accountability, and Sustainable Communities*

Norman J. Vig and Michael G. Faure, editors, *Green Giants? Environmental Policies of the United States and the European Union*

Robert F. Durant, Daniel J. Fiorino, and Rosemary O'Leary, editors, *Environmental Governance Reconsidered: Challenges, Choices, and Opportunities*

Paul A. Sabatier, Will Focht, Mark Lubell, Zev Trachtenberg, Arnold Vedlitz, and Marty Matlock, editors, *Swimming Upstream: Collaborative Approaches to Watershed Management*

Sally K. Fairfax, Lauren Gwin, Mary Ann King, Leigh S. Raymond, and Laura Watt, *Buying Nature: The Limits of Land Acquisition as a Conservation Strategy, 1780–2004*

Steven Cohen, Sheldon Kamieniecki, and Matthew A. Cahn, *Strategic Planning in Environmental Regulation: A Policy Approach That Works*

Michael E. Kraft and Sheldon Kamieniecki, editors, *Business and Environmental Policy: Corporate Interests in the American Political System*

Joseph F. C. DiMento and Pamela Doughman, editors, *Climate Change: What It Means for Us, Our Children, and Our Grandchildren*

Christopher McGrory Klyza and David J. Sousa, *American Environmental Policy, 1990–2006: Beyond Gridlock*

John M. Whiteley, Helen Ingram, and Richard Perry, editors, *Water, Place, and Equity*

Judith A. Layzer, *Natural Experiments: Ecosystem-Based Management and the Environment*

Daniel A. Mazmanian and Michael E. Kraft, editors, *Toward Sustainable Communities: Transition and Transformations in Environmental Policy*, second edition

Henrik Selin and Stacy D. VanDeveer, editors, *Changing Climates in North American Politics: Institutions, Policy Making, and Multilevel Governance*

Megan Mullin, *Governing the Tap: Special District Governance and the New Local Politics of Water*

David M. Driesen, editor, *Economic Thought and U.S. Climate Change Policy*